alone

BY THE SAME AUTHOR

The Ghost Runner:
The Tragedy of the Man
They Couldn't Stop

alone

THE TRIUMPH AND TRAGEDY OF
JOHN CURRY

BILL JONES

B L O O M S B U R Y

LONDON · NEW DELHI · NEW YORK · SYDNEY

First published in Great Britain 2014

Copyright © 2014 by Bill Jones

The moral right of the author has been asserted.

Bloomsbury Publishing Plc
50 Bedford Square
London
WC1B 3DP

www.bloomsbury.com

Bloomsbury is a trademark of Bloomsbury Publishing Plc

Bloomsbury Publishing, London, New Delhi, New York and Sydney

A CIP catalogue record for this book is available from the British Library

Hardback ISBN 978 1 4088 5342 9
Export Trade Paperback ISBN 978 1 4088 5343 6

10 9 8 7 6 5 4 3 2

Typeset by Saxon Graphics Ltd, Derby
Printed and bound in Great Britain by
CPI Group (UK) Ltd, Croydon CR0 4YY

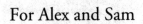

For Alex and Sam

'Everyone wants to fly too close to the sun'

John Curry

Contents

Introduction

On a cold winter's evening in February 1976, 20 million Britons turned on their television sets to watch the ice skating. It didn't matter that most of them, myself included, knew nothing about the sport. All of us were in the grip of something mystical, something transcendental, something far beyond the delirium of a Briton in pole position for Olympic glory. On paper, it made no sense. With its salchows and spins, its loops and lutzes, figure skating spoke an alien language. But this man; this beautiful man. He made absolute sense, and all of us – from Bridlington to Bournemouth – were glued. John Curry. That was his name. At times, he had seemed like an alien, too.

He had won, of course. In 50 glorious days he had won everything. The European, the Olympic, and World titles were all his. Even to mere mortals, able only to shuffle in their shoes, it was clear that we had all witnessed some kind of sporting epiphany. Curry had not been merely on the ice. He had been *of* the ice, his energy seemingly drawn from deep within the earth. Where muscled men normally preened like mating cocks, Curry had flown and swooped, his back peerlessly arched, the pencil-thin blade of his skates slicing a soundless masterpiece into the ice.

In that brief moment, through the restrained mastery of Curry's triumph, sport had, for a moment, stood high above itself. All of us, in our ignorance, had felt the plates shift. Out of the intricate absurdities of rules and competition and Cold War politics, this permed Adonis had created something life-affirming. Driven by John Curry's feet, sport had transfigured itself into art. Masculinity, for its own sake, had been trounced by beauty. And therein lay another reason why so many millions had watched, and why Curry intrigued every one of them.

For decades, sportsmen had worn their testosterone like a badge of honour. Curry's skating was mesmeric and sensual – erotic, too – but stereotypically masculine? No. Women adored him. And men, or lots of them, bereft of anything better, resorted to the lexicon of the barracks. Curry skated like a gay – like a woman – they whispered, and in the hours which followed his Olympic gold, his 'secret' had bled out; inadvisably shared with a reporter who had promptly passed on his scoop to the world.

In mid-1970s Britain, few people openly admitted to being gay and celebrity disclosure was virtually unknown. After the Olympics, Curry would have been famous anyway. In the light of his 'coming out', however, the skater's overnight fame acquired a sinister edge. Suddenly, everyone wanted a piece of him. Chat shows, newspapers, magazines, advertisers, impresarios and even would-be wives beat a path to his door. Parkinson wanted him. The Queen wanted him. The BBC Sports Personality of the Year wanted him. In 1976, few faces were better known and, to all who wooed him, Curry was charming, polite, well-spoken and happy to flesh out the bones of his life story so far.

Born into a prosperous self-made West Midlands family, he had wanted to be a dancer from the age of seven. Unable to secure his father's blessing for ballet lessons, he'd turned to skating to find release for his musically expressive urges. To reach the pinnacle of figure skating he'd fought the sport's resistance to his style for 20 years. Now he was there, and his intention was to create a 'theatre of skating'; a glorious new art form that would conquer the world. At which point – for most of the millions who had watched him weeping on a podium in Innsbruck – Curry's story abruptly ends. Ask around today, and no one seems sure what happened to him. Is he alive? Is he dead? Wasn't he the 'fairy' who won the skating?

The reality – as I have spent over two years finding out – is one of the most moving lives of any post-war British public figure. From his father's suicide to Curry's AIDS-related death – at the age of 44 in 1994 – it is a story parenthesised by tragedy but filled out with courage and achievement at the highest level. True to his promise, Curry played at the Royal Albert Hall, the New York Metropolitan Opera House, the London Palladium and the John F. Kennedy Center in Washington, DC. Wherever he performed, his bold, new work was fêted. In Manhattan, where he lived for many years, he could do no wrong. In Britain, where homophobia had blighted his early years, he was cruelly forgotten.

For a biographer, Curry's performing life was relatively easy to unravel. Curry the man, on the other hand, was (and to some extent remains) a much harder proposition. 'How do you write a book about a black hole?' pondered one of his friends. It was a good question. From an early age, the skater had been predisposed towards secrecy. Little he saw in his life gave him reason to amend that stance. As a teenager, he knew that his homosexuality might have led him to prison. As an AIDS victim, he was consumed by fear, shame and self-loathing. Along the 25-year journey between those two points, Curry rarely shifted from 'obsessively private'.

Out on the ice, Curry was never short of miraculous. Away from it, he was possessed by such morbid darkness it robbed him of joy. Despite a string of lovers he usually failed to establish lasting relationships and lived mostly alone. His sexual tastes were violent, and his moods could swerve dangerously from near-suicidal to diva-like bullying. Nothing he did seemed to please him. No pleasure ever seemed to last. He mercilessly sacked coaches, producers, managers and skaters with selfish abandon. And yet he could bring tears to the eyes of anyone who watched him skate. To say he was conflicted is an understatement. To describe him as a 'black hole' is not far short of the mark.

Thankfully, a number of small miracles have helped me throw light into that darkness. From two sources, around 200 of Curry's letters have informed this long process; some to his first lover, Heinz Wirz, the rest to the remarkable woman in New York who 'adopted' him. To read them is to hear Curry's true voice. At times, cruel. At times, wildly funny and sexually explicit. At times, bursting with expectation. In many of them, no details are spared – especially to Wirz. In almost all of them, you can hear the pleading voice of a lonely child, wrestling with the torment of his genius and hungry for approval. In one of the letters there sits a forlorn lock of his hair. Even the countless addresses are revealing. Peripatetic, rootless, constantly on the move, Curry never stayed anywhere long and the inside pages of his three battered passports are a blizzard of red ink.

Alongside the correspondence I have also drawn on conversations with around a hundred people who knew him well – or thought they did. Skaters, musicians, lovers, actors, ice engineers, directors, producers, coaches, childhood friends, adult friends and close family. Each was familiar with one side of him. Very few got the whole picture. And many of his male friends are already dead.

Curry's story is not just a life. From his first clandestine gropings, through the release of 'liberation' to the curse of AIDS, his 44 years trace a heartbreaking path that was followed by an entire generation of men. More Americans died of AIDS, it is said, than fell in Vietnam. In the blighted company of John Curry that nightmare passage takes human flesh. In New York, one by one, his friends and ex-lovers were consumed. As solitude crowded in, he fled home where, in the final years of his life, he allowed the world to see what disease had done to his magnificent body.

Today, those photographs are still shocking but they were not entirely altruistic. Curry had never pursued material wealth, was never rich and left just £6,000 when he died. Long before that, he had tried acting to redirect his career. Panto in Liverpool. Shakespeare in Nottingham. Musicals on Broadway. None of it filled his bank account. None of it remotely compared with the nascent ice ballet he had walked away from, crushed and disillusioned by power politics and commercialism. By 1992, exploiting his own decline was all he had left, and if it helped his mother he would do it.

Soon after that February night in 1976, after Alan Weeks had exploded with patriotic delight, most of us quickly forgot about John Curry. That was the way he wanted it. He didn't crave celebrity. He didn't want to be Torvill and Dean. Hopefully, *Alone* will finally show people what a remarkable figure he was. Tortured, brilliant, pioneering and brave, he was both intriguing as a man and extraordinary as an artist. In the opinion of one of his closest companions: 'His death was a tragedy. But his life was not. His life was never a tragedy.' Now you decide.

Bill Jones

Prologue

There is absolute blackness; there is cold; there is the smell of the ice. Deep within the inky gloom, someone coughs. There are people in there, furiously concentrating on an empty smear of light. Suddenly, within it, a figure appears. His shoulders are hunched, and his hands are pushed deep into his pockets. Clad in white, he seems illuminated from within – a dazzling statue – until a solitary piano stirs him into life.

Now there is a new sound: a metallic rasp; cold steel on colder ice. Frozen dust sparks from his heels. Friction and weight, not muscle, yield movement and direction. No other impulse is required. Invisible strings pull him forwards, then backwards. The man's power, like the light, seems to come from some deep, brooding well. Shapes flow and his body unfurls. He pleads and he beckons. Nothing is forced and everything has a purpose. He is telling us a story; his story: I am a man trapped in a strange place; a lost and lonely man. I am a man on the moon.

As the music builds, so does his urgency. Gesturing skywards, his arms plead for rescue. None comes. Every night he beckons to the mute stars until tears stain his face. No one is coughing now. Thousands are frozen in reverential silence. Lost within the darkness, even stagehands and fellow skaters stand transfixed in the wings; just as they always do. No one has ever seen anything like it. Sometimes it is so intense, so raw, they turn away. Many of them are crying.

Out on the ice, as the moon leaves the sun, the chill has returned. Darkness has fallen. In the fading light, not even the thunderous applause can liberate the lunar castaway. Tomorrow night, he will try again. And the night after that. But he will never escape. He is trapped in his own solitary miracle. He is alone.

One

'I am a dancer'

John Curry had always travelled light. He never owned a house. He never possessed a car. His luggage would always be a single case, two at worst. Even before his death, the very few things he owned had been sold, abandoned, lost or simply given away. To close friends had gone the prized skating boots he'd once boiled to soften the leather. To an auction house, his medals and the picture from Andy Warhol. To others, the meticulous needlepoint artwork he'd crafted as his life ebbed away under the watery skies of a Warwickshire spring.

After his death, he left virtually no money and precious little else. His clothes were dispatched to a charity shop, and what remained was stored in a handful of cardboard boxes, taped and secreted in his mother's loft. Inside them was the knotted residue of his days. Unopened letters. Thick bundles of telegrams. Piles of faded newspaper cuttings. And amidst the dog-eared detritus, the real clues; the precious handholds on the intriguing 'black hole' of his life.

A tarnished silver trophy ('1958 – John Curry – 3rd'); his National Insurance card; three battered passports; a telegram from Elton John; carefully kept air mail from a woman in New York; a photograph of Lord Mountbatten and another of a well-known BBC reporter, ruggedly handsome in battle fatigues. Plastic folders stuffed with photographs and coded memories. Unsigned Valentine's cards; a photograph of a man holding a riding crop; Curry in bathing trunks on a Long Island beach; doodles and drawings and the fitting details for a biker's black leather jacket.

Taken individually, the random content of the boxes is revealing. What is missing from them, however, is even more so. No love letters. No childhood souvenirs. No school reports. No family snaps. Not until he is 16 – posing nervously on a first trip to London

– does Curry himself appear in a photograph. Upend them, and apart from a few images of his mother there is little evidence of his family, and not a trace of his father.

It is as if his life had started only long after his childhood ended; which, in one sense, is precisely what he always felt had happened.

———

For a man so indifferent to material trappings, John Anthony Curry's childhood had been awash with them. Not for him the irritating shortfalls of post-war Britain. When he was born on 9 September 1949, petrol and soap were still being rationed, but the fortunes of the Curry household appeared to be rising fast. The family home was an imposing Edwardian villa on the southern edge of Birmingham in the black heart of the Midlands. Outside in its rambling gardens, apples grew fat on the trees and John played around them, a melodious infant born with a skip in his step. Indoors, his mother baked cakes. Somewhere out on the road his father wheeler-dealed, worried and drank.

In time, the future Olympic champion would share many things with Joseph Henry Curry. Both would die young; both were afflicted by darkly suicidal thoughts; and both had a compulsion for secrecy. Unlike his father, however, John would rarely drink. He had seen what it could do in his childhood house of secrets. He had watched the sad nightmare building to the bleak tragedy of his father's death. He had wondered about the other curious voids in his father's story, too. Joseph's war record had earned him a Military Medal, and yet no one seemed entirely sure why. Nor, for obvious reasons, was his family's business ever a matter for open discussion. Since as far back as anyone could remember, the Curry dynasty had traded in guns, and – as a steadfast dynastic aside – the first-born Curry men had all been given the same first name.

John's father had been born in 1915 and christened Joseph just like his own father and grandfather before him. And, just like them, he'd been groomed for a working life in the murky world of small arms and munitions. For a young man living in Birmingham between two world wars, it was neither a bad nor a strange place to be.

Ever since the English Civil War, the city's gun-makers had flourished. For centuries, the redbrick 'gun quarter', around

Steelhouse Lane and Shadwell Street, had grown plump on man's inability to keep the peace. It was rifles from Birmingham that had won the Battle of Waterloo. It was pistols from Steelhouse Lane – where the Curry family had their workshop – that had echoed across the bloodied fields of the Crimea and the American Civil War. Even the city's most famous motorcycle, the BSA, had its roots in the gun trade. In the mid-nineteenth century, trading as the Birmingham Small Arms Company, BSA had even supplied 20,000 rifles to the Turkish infantry.

Whoever they were bad for, guns had been good for the Currys. In the only photograph of her husband which John's mother ever kept, prosperity oozes from every corner of the frame. To the right sits John's great-grandfather Joseph, eyes asparkle above a thick handlebar moustache and goatee beard. To the left, John's balding grandfather smiles kindly behind frameless spectacles, and at the rear stands the youngest Joseph – John's father – dark-eyed, high-browed, his lips slightly apart as if uncertain how, or when, to form a smile for the camera. The picture is a study in self-made urban respectability. Each man is immaculately tailored and a patterned silk handkerchief peeps ostentatiously from each jacket pocket. But the world of arms was a secret and insalubrious one – and, however great the rewards, John Curry's father wanted no part in it.

By the time the three Josephs posed for their family photograph, Joseph Curry junior had gone his own way. Although stuck with the family forename, he opted not to follow his forebears into the family business. Today, no one seems entirely sure why. Quite possibly, Joseph had seen a collapse coming and opted to venture out alone. By the mid-1930s, despite the twentieth century's periodic infatuation with mass slaughter, Birmingham's gun-makers had gone into steep decline. The price of their craftsmanship was too high, and the cost of mass-produced American alternatives had become attractively low. But there were other, more persuasive, reasons.

As an ice skater – and an artist – John Curry would never be content to let prevailing norms dictate his choices. He was also wildly inventive and utterly unafraid of risk. As Europe drifted towards yet another war, these self-same qualities now began to surface in John's father. Over one million people lived in Birmingham; its workforce was highly skilled and the city was awash with engineering brilliance. Businesses bloomed overnight and every one of them had accounts to do. Sooner or later, Joseph Curry, now promoting himself as the purveyor of high-quality accounting machines, would find his way to their gates. No more inky ledgers. No more columns of calculations and crossings out. By simply acquiring one of Mr Curry's calculators, hours of tedium could be liberated.

It was a stroke of entrepreneurial cunning, but bigger forces would soon twist Joseph Curry's life in quite different directions. When war broke out in 1939, he joined the Royal Army Ordnance Corps, that section of the army devoted to the supply and maintenance of weaponry and ammunition. It was a perfect fit, promised a quiet war and his entry report described a 'reliable, hardworking, ambitious and well-spoken' man who scored ninety-nine out of a hundred for his verbal skills. But Joseph's war – as a storeman – was set to be a desperate and unhappy one. When he resurfaced sometime in early 1944, he was nursing the invisible scars of experiences that had changed him for ever; and of which he would never properly speak before he died.

———

There were gaps in Rita Richards' story, too, but for very different reasons. In her life she would have four surnames, but only two husbands. And while Joseph's experiences ultimately steered him towards alcohol, his future wife always wrapped her own inside a toughly unsentimental pragmatism that required the past to be kept firmly in its place. 'I don't believe in keeping the past. Not any of it,' she says. It was a credo well evidenced by her son's cardboard boxes.

It was no accident, in later years, that Rita retained just a single picture of John's father. Nor was it a form of rearguard punishment for the darkness his disease had inflicted on his family. She would keep none of John's letters, school reports or early photographs, either. Nor those of her other two sons. Even if John had wanted them, Rita had already thrown them all away. 'She makes no sentimental investment in items,' says John's brother Andrew. 'She lives in the now.' There are worse ways of compensating for dislocation and abandonment.

Rita had been born in Worcester shortly after Christmas 1913. Ten days later, her mother was dead. Shortly after that, her father decided that he was unsuited to child rearing, and passed the infant Rita on to the family of his wife's brother. She would have no further contact with her father. Having been born a Richards, she now – informally – took the name Pritchard. She also turned her back on the family she had once, albeit briefly, been part of. 'I had several sisters, I think, who I didn't know,' she says. 'I don't know why. Not interested really.'

Home now was in the Yardley district on the eastern fringes of Birmingham. Uncle Jack Pritchard worked in the stables of a thriving undertaker. His wife Virginia – or Ginnie – looked after Rita. The couple had no other children, and, although not rich, Rita remembers growing up 'without ever going short'. 'They could never throw their money around,' she remembers. 'But there was only me.'

By the time the Second World War broke out, Rita had matured into an impulsive, single-minded woman with a ready laugh and a refined sense of fun. In later years this evolved into a compulsion for fine cars, which she would drive very quickly. While she was working behind the counter at a Birmingham drapers, these were luxuries she couldn't yet contemplate. But Rita's grey-blue eyes and short-cut brown hair drew the gaze of those men whose minds were not distracted by Hitler's troop movements. And in 1939 – just as the world was plunged into darkness – she suddenly found herself with a husband, Neville James Hancock. Four years later, however, she was divorced and single again.

They had met while they were both working at the Rover car factory in Solihull. Much more than that she would never really say. Living in the present made the task of interring the past that much easier. 'I don't talk about it. It was my fault. I made a mistake and thought it better to finish.' Only those who needed to know would be let in on her 'mistake', and in any event, Rita would not be alone for long.

On 11 August 1945, three months after VE Day, she was married for the second time. On the wedding certificate she was named as Rita Agnes Hancock, formerly Richards. Her husband's name was given as Joseph Henry Curry, a dealer in accounting machines, son of Joseph Henry Curry, 'gun maker'. Rita had her fourth surname, and Joseph was home from the war.

Just as she could be economical with her disclosures, so now would be her new 30-year-old husband. Joseph had left the army as a corporal with a Military Medal, awarded to servicemen below officer rank who had demonstrated 'acts of gallantry and devotion to duty under fire'. For a man who had never held, let alone fired a weapon, it was a curious accolade which, according to the citation, had been 'gazetted' in February 1944. Beyond that there was no official account and Joseph's reluctant, unofficial version was hampered by his own reticence.

According to army records, Joseph had been taken prisoner near St Omer in the first hours of the British Army's shambolic flight to Dunkirk in May 1940. For the next three-and-a-half years he was incarcerated at Stalag XXA, a vast POW camp in central Poland housing up to 20,000 emaciated squaddies in and around a cluster of nineteenth-century forts. When the war was over, some 14,000 soldiers would be left behind, buried in the camp's makeshift graveyards. Only a handful ever successfully escaped. John Curry's father had been one of them.

As the war intensified, so did Joseph's determination to get home. He joined an escape committee. He plotted. He watched. And in late October 1943, desperate to avoid a fourth winter of captivity, Joseph somehow broke free and made his way to Poland's Baltic coast. There he boarded a coal ship, concealed himself in its hold and kept his nerve until it entered the neutral waters of Sweden. His reward was a medal he chose never to celebrate, and a face temporarily blackened by coal dust.

Joseph was back in Birmingham, but his years living on boiled cabbage and potatoes in a German POW camp had ravaged him. Pencil-thin, and prone to terrifying night sweats, he was diagnosed by the army as having lymphadenitis and released back into civilian life. No one seemed entirely sure what was wrong with him but Joseph's symptoms were real enough. More likely he was displaying the incipient tuberculosis that would strike him down ten years later. He may also have started to drink.

Either way, he was free and back in a city where there was money to be made, and girls to help him spend it. In the accounts department at Swallow Raincoats, on Great Hampton Street, he'd spotted one: Rita Hancock; petite, shiny brown hair, with a hint of devil about her. He'd sold the company one of his adding machines and taught her how to operate it. They'd grown close. 'He came across as a thoughtful man in lots of ways. Quite a caring man. Or he appeared to be,' remembers Rita.

It was a time for mistakes and impulsive decisions. In Berlin, the Third Reich was in ruins. In Birmingham, Joseph and Rita were in the throes of a highly charged post-war love affair. Although they barely knew each other, the couple convened one August Saturday and were married without fanfare at the city's Register Office in Broad Street. There had been no question of a grand church ceremony. Joseph's family were Roman Catholic and Rita's first marriage would have had to be annulled. 'I suppose I was the scarlet woman,' chuckles Rita. The following March she gave birth to her first son.

According to family tradition, the naming of this latest Curry male should have been simple. In living memory, Joseph had always begat Joseph and Rita's husband saw no reason why that should change. Rita, however, was having none of it. Although she had warmed to her new father-in-law – 'a nice little neat man' – she was not about to be dictated to by strangers, especially not strangers with domestic tribulations of their own. Rita's 'nice little neat' father-in-law was living with a younger woman and her husband's mother, thought Rita, was 'a horrible, horrible lady'. No, she would not swallow a word of Curry cant over the naming of her firstborn. Yes, he could be called Joseph. But his first name would be Michael.

As a concession, Rita would allow the infant Michael Joseph Curry to be christened at a Roman Catholic church, but her victory came at a worrying cost. 'For a couple of months afterwards he [Rita's husband] wouldn't speak to me,' she reveals. Barely a year after their wedding, an icy fog had blown across their relationship, which in due course would become a semi-permanent storm. For the time being there were abundant distractions. Joseph's industriousness was seeing him make headway and by 1948 they had a second son. No arguments this time. Michael's younger brother was called Andrew. And his middle name was Paul. Not Joseph.

———

Although not directly, the Luftwaffe had been gunning for the Curry family. Between 1940 and 1943, over 2,000 tons of high explosive had been dumped on the city. Some 300 factories had been destroyed, among them the premises of BSA, the Birmingham Small Arms company. It was yet another reason for Rita's husband to stay well clear of the fading family business. As a child, Andrew would remember seeing a pile of handguns in his grandfather's workshops on Steelhouse Lane, with labels suggesting they were destined for the Middle East. New languages. New quarrels. New clients. Joseph was having none of it.

No longer content with merely selling accounting machines, he'd borrowed money and set up a factory to make them himself. Soon Joseph Curry Limited, at Hay Mills, on Arthur Road, would be employing a 30-strong workforce of its own, from skilled lathe operators to sales teams and secretaries. Whatever illness was eating away at him, Rita's husband seemed stimulated by risk. It would be a trait he passed on to his son John. But Joseph was also a grafter and a formidable networker, and the fledgling business swiftly made progress. Clients included Singer Sewing Machines and National Cash Registers, and the expanding Curry clan began to enjoy the rewards in a fast-ascending lifestyle.

By the late 1940s they were living in a rented house on Moorpark Road in Northfield, a looping crescent of pre-war mock-Tudor semis, boasting stained-glass rural motifs and leaded windows. For their time, the houses oozed suburban distinction. These were residences for the new men of post-war Britain; homes for the young professionals and budding entrepreneurs putting bomb sites like Birmingham back on its feet. There was a garden front and back for the two boys, and, across the road, a thick barrier of woodland held the city at bay.

By early 1949, Rita and Joseph were ready to move on. Northfield would soon be neither big enough – nor grand enough – for their requirements. On 9 September that year – in the brightly named Sorrento Maternity Hospital – the couple welcomed a third child into the family. At 8lb 12oz, this one would be the heaviest Rita bore, and he too would be spared the traditional forename. Alongside Michael and Andrew, they now had John Anthony. As a further concession to Rita's influence, he was even christened in an Anglican church. Three sons and an enormous new house. The 1950s had arrived and so, it seemed, had the Curry family.

Decades later John would insist that he was 'a working-class boy from an ordinary home'. He was nothing of the kind. Working-class children didn't go to fee-paying schools and the family's new address – John's home for the next 16 years – was anything but ordinary. Bristling with Edwardian self-importance, No. 946 Warwick Road, Acocks Green – on the traffic-heavy southern fringes of Birmingham – was Joseph Curry's ambition realised in three dimensions.

From cellar to attic, everything about it was grand. A large garden – with brick sheds and a swing for the children – stretched out to the side and rear. Visitors ascended two broad stone steps, rang the bell and entered a dark wood-panelled hall into which multi-coloured light fell through leaded glass panels. Leading off from the hall were a kitchen, drawing room, dining room and living room. Stairs rising out of the hall led to two upper floors, six bedrooms and the furniture-stuffed attic beyond. The ambience was comfortable rather than cosy; one in which austerity and affluence seemed suitably commingled.

Within a year or two of their arrival at No. 946 – now an old people's home – the lives of the five-strong Curry family had settled into a pattern, albeit one with ominous hints of what was to come. Rita didn't work, and stayed at home with the children. Joseph, on the other hand, worked extraordinarily hard, was insatiably 'hands on' and often returned late in a mood of bubbling truculence that wasn't easy for his children to understand.

To help run the place, a gardener and a cleaner would pop in every week, and an au pair was employed to look after the three boys. One of them, Jane Eenhorn, a 21-year-old Dutch girl, had been looking to improve her English when she first came to Warwick Road in the summer of 1953. Michael had a room of his own. Andrew and John were sharing a bedroom. There was a family boxer dog, too, called Ricky, which adored John and which growled proprietorially whenever anyone went near his friend. That September, shortly after his fourth birthday – at which Ricky had eaten John's birthday cake – Jane had even escorted Rita's youngest to his first day at school. She remembered a little boy with a big satchel. 'I liked him very, very, very much,' she says, 'He was very sweet, very intelligent and friendly.'

Everywhere she looked Jane saw the material fruits of Joseph's success. The year she arrived, a first television set had been installed, and the family clustered around it to enjoy the Queen's Coronation. Out on the drive was the latest in a long sequence of ostentatious motor cars. Determined to uphold her independence, Rita had taken driving lessons, which her husband confidently expected to end in disappointment. On the day of her test he'd even bought her flowers as consolation for the failure he felt sure would come. But Rita had passed, and – very reluctantly – would stop driving only at the age of 97, when the insurance company discovered she'd been telling them she was 12 years younger than she actually was.

It was the end of a lifetime of near misses. On one occasion, in a beloved red Hillman Minx, Rita had parked outside a newsagent's while she popped in with her sons to buy some sweets. While they were inside, the Hillman was written off by a passing vehicle. From that day on, Rita never got into a red car again. Another time, she'd borrowed her husband's Alvis and crumped it against their right-hand gatepost. A week or so later she'd repeated the trick, this time against the left-hand gatepost. Never mind, the garage told Joseph, we've still got some paint left from the last time.

All through her life, Rita's driving – and her love of Jaguars – had the power to terrify her children. After one skating event in London, over a hundred miles away, she'd driven an ashen-faced John back to Acocks Green in around 80 minutes. 'There wasn't so much traffic on the road then,' she chuckles. 'That's true,' says Andrew. 'But there weren't any motorways either.' Thirty years later, when John was dying, and required regular specialist treatment, the same helter-skelter journey to and from London with Rita could still reduce him to a furious quiver. 'I've had to have words with mother,' he once told his brother to explain a fraught post-hospital atmosphere. 'I'm never taking *him* to London again,' she countered. But of course she did.

The rewards for Joseph's industry were self-evident. However, the rapid accumulation of luxury goods couldn't conceal the hole at the heart of his family. Even the young Dutch au pair could see that. 'We saw very little of Mr Curry,' she recalls. 'He did not join the rest of the family at mealtimes. Or rarely did. He came in late and had his supper alone.' It was not always so. Rita was an exemplary cook, whose desserts and cakes left John with a lifelong weakness for puddings and sugar. For most Sunday lunchtimes, Joseph would join the family group for a traditional roast. 'I remember one time John said, "I'll have another dollop of that",' says Rita. 'His father said "You'll have a dollop of this" and tapped him across the face and John went mad. I think that was about the only time he was hit.'

Even in an era when fathers rarely attempted to bond with their children, Joseph's reserve and limited emotional vocabulary were extreme. On the few occasions he assumed direct control, his contribution appears to have been witheringly unsympathetic. He was also guilty – according to remarks later attributed to John – of far more than a periodic 'dollop'. In one story Curry apparently claimed he was repeatedly slapped without ever really knowing why. 'To discuss my father's behaviour with strangers was tantamount to treason,' he told a friend. Joseph was ill; that was all anyone else needed to know. 'Being a father was not easy for him,' admits Rita. 'I don't know why. He was always there for them, but he was not a touchy-feely dad. He was a distant dad. The only one he ever showed any affection for was Andrew.'

In the summer before she returned to Holland, Jane Eenhorn spent four weeks in the Channel Islands with Rita and the three boys. Under the Jersey sun, John's hair, which was naturally dark, bleached near-white. Every day was spent on the beach, where Rita stretched out on a deckchair in her white bathing costume and headband. Every evening was spent at a hotel with a dining terrace afire with geraniums. Throughout that hot summer, Joseph stayed at home, drumming up business. Holidays had never been his style. No one was remotely surprised that he'd kept away.

In the childhood years that followed, Rita would regularly drive the children down to Cornwall, spending five or six weeks at Sennen Cove or Praa Sands, where John especially came to love the rugged shoreline and the thudding breakers. Occasionally, Joseph would join them at weekends, but his presence seems to have been neither expected nor required. The youngest boy's emotional compass had now swung firmly towards his mother. Given the storm clouds that were massing, it was perhaps as well.

––––––

Unsurprisingly, John's first childhood memory revolved around Rita. She'd been putting him to bed and 'was wearing a yellow, light woollen dress with a very full skirt'. As she spun to leave, the drowsy child saw the fabric lit magically from behind. From then on, he would always insist on a repeat performance whenever his smartly dressed parents headed out to one of the evening functions Joseph's status as a local businessman required of them. It was the recollection of a child with an innate penchant for fantasy.

At school they called him a 'cissy', but he really didn't seem to care. Out in the garden, his older brother Michael posed with a toy rifle for the au pair's camera. Back in the house, John played with his favourite Christmas present, a cardboard theatre set; drawing the cord that raised the curtain, and sliding forward the tiny figures under home-made spotlights to act out stories like *Gulliver's Travels*, wearing the tiny costumes John had made. Few people were invited into this world. 'It was a solitary pursuit,' he confessed later.

John's musically restless feet, however, were witnessed by everybody. 'I am a dancer,' he would tell Jane Eenhorn, as he skipped from room to room, or waltzed silently through the house. 'I never knew why I did it. I just could not stop myself.' Even a trip upstairs could develop into a piece of intricate private choreography. 'Two up, one down, then three up and a skip and a hop ... Sometimes I still catch myself doing it,' he confessed in 1978, as he found fame and the world demanded his back story.

Neither of his two brothers joined in. Michael was a taller, more physical child – 'harem-scarem,' says Rita – and John was far happier in the quiet company of Andrew. John's fledgling theatricality, however, did yield one unexpected companion. If he wasn't working late, Joseph Curry liked nothing better than a night at the theatre, watching a light opera or a musical. 'I must have seen more versions of *The Desert Song* than anyone else of my generation,' boasted John. And since neither Rita, Michael nor Andrew appeared remotely interested, it was the youngest son who became his father's willing conspirator in the quest for low-brow musical entertainment. *Bless the Bride, Annie Get Your Gun, The Student Prince.* 'I saw them all. I loved them,' he said.

Such moments of togetherness were rare. Joseph's health was fragile, and his lifestyle was doing little to heal whatever hidden damage had been done in a POW camp. Around 1953 he was diagnosed with tuberculosis. A short time later, just one week after starting school, five-year-old Andrew was also found to have contracted the disease. Whatever tenuous family rhythms had been established behind the gothic façade of 946 Warwick Road were permanently disrupted.

Andrew would spend the next three years in bed, and see no other children until his recovery was complete. His schooling would be irrecoverably devastated, and he would spend a lifetime battling to catch up. 'I remember very little about my childhood,' he says ruefully today. Some bits he forgot. Others he chose never to remember in the first place.

Although no longer a Victorian sentence of death, tuberculosis was still highly contagious and required scrupulously observed periods of quarantine. Fortunately, in Warwick Road there was sufficient room to keep the two patients properly isolated. Separated by a corridor, and communicating occasionally by reflecting mirrors, father and son were confined to their rooms and put on a course of streptomycin. Each had his own plates and cutlery. Meanwhile the rest of the household, including John, were immunised and subject to regular check-ups. It was an awkward regimen, designed to protect other people, but Joseph Henry Curry had spent his war locked in a stalag. However necessary, convalescence clearly felt like another prison sentence.

Nobody really knew why Joseph had descended into heavy drinking. Or precisely when heavy drinking had become alcoholism. Everyone just knew what it did to him. In his cups, Joseph could be abusive, cruel, irrational and viciously argumentative but – according to Rita and Andrew – never violent. His favourite drink was brandy. His favourite haunts were the Oddfellows Arms and the snooker clubs of Birmingham, where he'd play badly and return in a loser's fury. 'It was very easy to start arguments. Not discussions, arguments. Any time of day. More with Mum than me,' remembers Andrew. 'But she could stand up to it. Or she'd hide or go and do the ironing or something.'

The prospect of a protracted recovery in bed was an insufferable one for a man with a drink problem and a business to run. He would take the medicine, but he would absolutely not abide by the house arrest. 'If he felt he could do it his way, he would do it his way,' explains Andrew. In defiance of the doctors, Joseph went back to selling adding machines. To the open-ended loss of his favourite brother, John could now add the increasingly unstable behaviour of his father. It was an unfortunate piece of timing. For some time he'd been building up to a difficult question.

———

It would have dismayed John's father to discover that many regarded his beloved musicals as hilariously camp. In the world view of an ex-soldier, things like ballet were sexually suspect. Musical theatre, on the other hand, was nonsense; but nonsense utterly free of connotations. It was a distinction John was far too young to understand, and a line he had subconsciously already crossed. Flush with some recent birthday cash he'd returned from a record shop in Acocks Green with *Swan Lake* and *The Nutcracker Suite* ('none of which I'd heard before') and proudly laid them before his father. 'He was very disappointed. "Oh dear," he said, "I thought you might buy something you'd keep."' Undeterred, John ploughed on with his question.

Choosing a moment when his father was sober, he'd entered the family sitting room behind his mother, and listened quietly while she asked Joseph whether John could take ballet lessons. The answer was an unqualified no. 'I remember … my father getting quite cross and saying, "No, he absolutely could not" and that was the end of that. It was never brought up again.' Mystified, John retreated upstairs to his wooden theatre.

Years later he would conclude that 'at the time … dancing was rather precious and refined and not really the thing that a factory owner's son would do.' He would also claim, in one baffling aside, that his father 'had me mapped out to become a priest.' Beyond that, John never proffered any deeper public analysis of his father's hostility. Even at seven, it seems probable that John's nascent sensibilities had stirred confusion in a father raised a Catholic (albeit an indifferent one) and shackled in a POW camp with thousands of men. If his son was going to be 'a bloody queer', it would not be with his assistance. Whatever his reasoning, Joseph had seriously underestimated his youngest son. A few weeks later, John sent his mother back into the sitting room with a second question. And this time he got the answer he wanted.

Along with 27 million others, the Coronation had enthralled the Curry family. But John, ever an enthusiastic monarchist, had drawn his own inspiration from the contents of their new television. On his travels with Rita, John had already seen Margot Fonteyn dance on stage and been hypnotised. Now, during a televised version of *Aladdin on Ice*, he'd been moved once again. Sweeping around a rink – surrounded by exploding cars and pantomime villains – were skaters who moved with such flow and precision he 'got goose bumps'. 'I had a new passion,' he said, and a subsequent trip to the Birmingham Hippodrome to see *Humpty Dumpty on Ice* had confirmed it. As he skipped home that night he told his au pair, 'This is what I am going to be.'

Whatever dark prejudices Joseph held against ballet lessons no longer applied. 'Skating, being a sport, was approved of,' recalled John, 'whereas the dancing idea had been treated with grave mistrust.' In the summer of 1957, Joseph nodded his assent to this new, properly masculine, pursuit. By September of that year, around the time of his seventh birthday, John was frantic to start. For months, 946 Warwick Road had been silenced by illness. Escape, in whatever form, had become a necessity.

———

Ice rinks are strange places to grow up in. Bodily warmth is maintained only by a sharklike constancy of movement and, inside most of them, daylight is a stranger. From the moment he stepped inside Birmingham's now-demolished Summerhill Ice Rink, John was captivated by all of it. 'The first thing that hit me was the smell … of damp wood, damp cold air, coconut matting and some sort of ammonia.' He would later call it the smell of home, and, before anyone had really heard his name, he would spend almost 20 years inhaling it. 'He was at his happiest on the ice,' says Andrew. Secretly, this was where he would begin to dance.

On this first morning, uncertain whether John would persevere, Rita had booked a single three-shilling lesson. She'd bought him new boots, and John had clonked down on to the ice where his first teacher was waiting to take his hand. Bend your knees and keep your back straight, he was told. Until his death, Curry would never fail to pay homage to this man. With his 'back like a ramrod', Ken

Vickers was a skater who understood the power of style over mere technique. In the shape of this strangely confident seven-year-old stumbling towards him, Vickers had found his perfect pupil.

Everywhere John looked, beginners were galumphing around the rink. Some clung to the barrier. Others fell back helplessly as their blades sped ahead and away from them. For a moment, the magical insanity of it all might have struck him. More likely, he grasped its possibilities in an instant; two edges of polished steel, each one barely 4mm across, on an oval of artificially frozen water; a combination of metal and ice liberating movement through the almost complete elimination of friction. After a handful of steps holding Vickers' hand, he let go. I can do it myself, he told him. 'And I could. I went off skating around quite naturally.'

The newly engineered pieces of John's life now fell quickly into place. Being an expressive – and emotionally self-sufficient – child, he thrived on the freedom he found on the ice. He also seemed to relish the discipline it required of its students. Every Wednesday afternoon, Rita would drive him to Summerhill for his 15-minute weekly lesson with 'Mr Vickers'. 'It was a bit of a dump, I suppose but I loved it,' he said. While her son practised, Rita, ever practical, bobbed off shopping. 'I'd drop him at the door and say I'll be back in an hour. I couldn't sit around like some of the mothers did.' But for John nothing else in his week mattered. He thrived on Ken's uplifting mantra: that the ice should be more than a mere tool, and that he and it should somehow become one, and be of each other.

It would have mystified Joseph. But Joseph wasn't paying much attention. One Christmas the family had gone to Aldeburgh in Suffolk, where the famous mere had frozen hard-deep like iron plate. John had never seen so much ice and one bitter morning – wearing his school blazer and cap – he'd performed under luminous winter skies; spins and arabesques for onlookers who'd come merely to step gingerly on to the lake in their balaclavas and duffel coats. A passer-by took some photographs, and the pictures passed into legend. Whether Joseph was impressed is not recorded. All John could recall were the terrifying stories his father had told him about pond ice; about holes that opened and snapped shut and locked you underneath, looking up but never able to break free.

At Summerhill, the boy's promise had already been noted. One morning, Rita had been taken politely to one side and told that – provided he put in the effort – her son might have a future. Neither of them had needed it to be said. Not only was John displaying genuine artistic flair, he was also fiercely competitive. Winning, he'd soon discovered – quite by accident – was like getting your own way. It put you in control. For one of his early skating sessions, he'd arrived wearing his usual short trousers – plus a new sweater given him by Rita – and been told to ignore the strangers watching him from rink-side.

In sequence, he was asked to perform a spiral turn, a waltz jump and an upright spin. In between each move, other children had done the same and at the end John was told he'd won a prize. 'I didn't even know I'd been in a competition,' he said, but he'd enjoyed beating the girl 'in the new frilly frock' who'd wept when she managed only second place. Ruthlessness wouldn't yet be a defining quality of Curry's, but seeing other children who were more proficient drove him on. Losing drove him even harder. 'He was wanting to prove something to himself,' insists Rita, 'but not to his father.'

Blooded by his first childhood victory, John found himself sucked ever deeper into competition skating. As he got older, and the standard climbed, John's presence on the makeshift podiums grew increasingly familiar. In 1958, he picked up his first tiny silver eggcup for a third-place finish in the Walker Trophy. Other eggcups quickly followed, and after every tournament so did the official photograph. In the earliest one, John forces a gap-toothed smile; his hair is plastered to his forehead and a crisp white shirt is tucked into plain dark trousers. The black skates on his feet look enormous, and of the three boys clutching silverware only John's bow tie is straight.

A few years later and the bow tie is still there, but the self-consciousness has gone. Now there are tailored grey suits, with double-breasted matador jackets and a razor-sharp crease down each trouser leg. At around ten years old, John's body had started to develop its beautiful proportions. Long legs, which were powerful but never more than lean. A narrow waist with almost imperceptible buttocks bending into Curry's famously straight back, topped off by pleasingly broad shoulders. Though he had a lifelong fixation with his weight – and sometimes other people's – there was never any fat on John Curry. Nor any conspicuous muscle, either.

As a grown man, John was so good-looking it was not unusual for men and women, gay or straight, to find themselves ogling him. As a child moving towards his teens, a girlish delicacy hovers across his features, but already he is classically handsome. His eyebrows are dark, his chin is strong and his nose and lips appear as if sculpted. There is also a tenderness – a vulnerability – which his face would never quite lose, and which his skating so evidently expressed.

'In Birmingham he skated because he loved to skate,' says childhood friend Maggie McKone.

> I think he'd have been happy not doing competitions but that was what you had to do. In those days you used to be able to put your own music on [in the rinks] and he was always ahead of the game. While everyone else was prancing around to the music from *Dambusters* or something, John discovered Wagner. Then he came with Stravinsky's *Rite of Spring*, and one of the coaches said, 'I wish someone would murder that kid'. People would say, how on earth can you skate to that?

By the early 1960s, John's skating had become all-consuming. To get more time on the ice, he'd started going to the Solihull rink, barely five minutes from the family home on Warwick Road. He'd also parted company with Ken Vickers, and was struggling to find a coach sympathetic to his own powerful instincts. Being ahead of the game was proving troublesome. As a child he'd skipped to the songs inside his head. On the ice, he was compelled by the same urge to marry movement to music, the same craving for dance that had so appalled his father. It wasn't a choice. It was a blind spot. He simply couldn't see things any other way. But it was a compulsion that mystified his elders and which would eventually plunge John Curry into battle with the conservative godfathers of British skating.

As a properly regulated sport, figure skating – no less than football or cricket – was bound by rules that had evolved over decades. Many of them required mathematical precision, and the mandatory musical programmes were usually seen as little more than a showcase for athleticism; decorous aural backgrounds against which muscled

Eastern Europeans could strut through the required pyrotechnics before someone handed over the medals.

Even in his early teens, this was not how John Curry saw it at all. When he'd first assembled a routine to Josef Strauss's 'Village Swallows' his arms had instinctively reached up and his fingers had fluttered like wings. There was no conscious thought process to this. In his own words, whenever he heard music 'it just happened'. Triple jumps and toe loops would never come as naturally as the expressive use of his arms, and he'd no time for the coaches who told him it was unmanly, and who wanted to convert him into a 'jumping robot'.

'I used my hands. I never could see why they shouldn't pass waist level. It just didn't seem to make sense ... so I did it. One teacher I had when I was quite young would say, "Well no no John. You mustn't do that. It's not a movement for a man" and I couldn't see why. They'd been used to seeing only girls use their arms and I suppose they thought it strange from a boy.' Unwilling to compromise, Curry earned an early reputation as someone who was difficult – unwisely stubborn – and there was talk of sending him to a psychiatrist. They were worried about him at school as well. And not without reason.

———

What had started as a short Wednesday afternoon diversion was now becoming an addiction. While her husband slept on brandy, Rita would rise early – often at 5.30 a.m. – and drive John to his lesson. A couple of hours later she'd be back to taxi him to school for lessons until 4 p.m., when she'd once again chauffeur him across town for two more hours on the ice. 'We never missed,' he boasted later. 'It was really the highpoint of my day. That rather than school.'

One of Curry's later intimates would describe him as 'rather undereducated', suggesting that behind John's regal accent and cultivated disdain was a knowledge vacuum that he fought desperately to conceal; something more than his atrocious spelling or his chronic myopia for numbers. It was quite probably true. The school years of all three Curry boys, it seems, were an ungovernable mess, disturbed by Joseph's increasingly erratic behaviour, by illness and by their own confused indifference to the entire process. Today it is almost impossible to ascertain who went where for school. Or when.

Some things, however, seem reasonably certain. Racked by tuberculosis – but attended by a bedside private tutor – Andrew didn't start 'normal' education until he was almost nine. When he was well enough, the three brothers were parcelled off to an obscure private boarding school in the depths of Somerset. It was a puzzling choice. Barely thirty children attended St Andrew's, and although the pinnacled gables of Knowle Hall promised nobility, the effect was rather more 'youth hostel' than dormitory for the nation's elite. Nobody dared question why Joseph had chosen it. According to Andrew, their father 'had this view that the children should be a unit altogether'. All in or all out. 'They never complained,' says Rita. 'It seemed quite a nice place at the time.'

Unexpectedly, the youngest Curry brother had settled well, missing neither his skates nor his father. In the period before enthusiasm mutated into obsession, John seemed happy merely not to be at home. 'The skating was an escape which … I found I could dispense with; I did not miss it at all.' Instead, it seems, John floated back into his 'fantasy games', for ever skipping and humming, and (so he later insisted) never far away from a poem by Lord Byron or a Thomas Hardy novel. 'I had no desire for the holidays to hasten along,' he said.

After 18 months, Joseph suddenly recalled his sons from Somerset. No formal explanation was ever given for this decision. 'I think he just wanted them back,' proffers Rita. Returned to Acocks Green, as the domestic darkness closed in, John fled back to the ice. 'When I did find myself at home, skating suddenly seemed very important again.' The dreary rinks of Summerhill and Solihull, with their canned music and stumbling weekenders, had become a refuge. Regardless of the financial burden on his father, schoolwork had become little more than a necessary chore.

Undeterred, Joseph Henry dug deeper into his pockets. After far-flung St Andrew's, John found himself at the nearby Cedarhurst Preparatory School. In a grand old house, enveloped by mature woodland, the headmaster, Mr H. B. Callaghan, governed his establishment like a barracks. The BBC reporter Michael Buerk, a pupil around the same time as Curry, remembered him as a 'splendid old buffer'. Others recall a scarcely loveable eccentric with an enormous moustache and orange suede shoes whose catchphrase was 'you blithering idiot', and who once pinned a passing pupil to the banister with the words, 'I've got you now'. The 13-year-old John Curry must have loathed it. Within a few years he would encounter, and revolt against, another purveyor of irksome military tutelage. Bullies like H. B. Callaghan were far too close to home.

To compensate for his aversion to education, Curry stepped up his training. With Rita as his indefatigable getaway driver, every shred of his daily energy was left on the ice. Eggcups had now become freshly engraved jug-handled trophies. After winning the national Novice Cup in London, he'd even been dangled a role in a professional touring ice show. But that was never going to happen. In September 1963, John had started lessons at the renowned Solihull School, for which his father was paying fees of around £150 a term. The equivalent, 50 years later, would have been £10,000. It was an expense for which Joseph felt entitled to expect more from his son than a bit part in a touring Christmas gala on ice. But John's father would see no return on his investment.

Set in grounds peppered with spreading trees, Solihull School has the look of an establishment that means business: geometrically precise striped lawns; hanging baskets bursting with flowers; a tuck shop presiding over the baize-like cricket square. There's even a hint of Ivy League about the venerable assembly hall, with its white wooden bell-tower and wind-battered flag. The school's Latin motto, a single word, oozes class: *perseverantia*. Persistence. Perseverance.

Sometime in the spring of 1963, John would have gathered in that sunlit hall to sit his 13+ entrance examination which, to everyone's surprise, he passed. By September, he'd been kitted out with the school's regulation uniforms and was ready to start. A tweed woollen suit for the winter; blazer and flannels for the summer. Rugby colours and cricket whites were obligatory. Boaters were not. 'It was a rugby playing, cricket playing ethos,' recollects one contemporary. 'I'm not really sure what he was doing there. He was in a different world. A square peg in a round hole.'

Before the academic year was out, John's will had asserted itself. Playing rugby, he'd insisted, would damage his ankles and he was allowed to play table tennis instead. His attempts to evade the school's Combined Cadet Force, however, were less successful. A dose of military discipline was seen as a vital bulwark in the nation's future defences, and no one was considered exempt. Truculently John slouched to parades with filthy gaiters and was promptly handed Wednesday afternoon detention for his mutinous attitude. 'I wish I'd joined the navy,' he told his mother. Precious ice time had been the casualty of this private war.

No less than in later life, Curry's contemporaries found him an elusive bundle to understand. 'It was a mystery where he came from and where he went to,' says Andrew Levens, a friend and fellow student of John's at Solihull. 'He was quite secretive about some things. Secretive about his family and what he'd been doing before. He was an odd mixture of the totally focused and idiosyncratic.'

On a CCF adventure camp in the Brecon Beacons, Levens and Curry had shivered around a campfire, and shared a tent, but there would be few late-night disclosures. Only once did John's home life break cover. Upon joining the cadets, he'd been given a uniform that had formerly belonged to a pupil of the rank of sergeant. The three stripes had been removed, but when Joseph saw the leftover stitching on the sleeves he had flown into a rage. 'John wouldn't tell me why. It was clear he didn't want to tell me any more. He'd volunteered the story about the stripes, but he did not want to talk about the darker side of his father.'

At home, Joseph fumed powerlessly about John's incomprehensible priorities. It was like the *Swan Lake* record all over again. After buying a pair of winkle-picker birthday shoes, he'd insisted John 'go back, change them and get a proper present.' At school, apart from modest grades for art, there was little evidence that Joseph's money was being well spent. At the end of his first term, John's form position was 20th in a class of 25. The following spring it had struggled up to ninth, only to slump back down to 19th when term ended for Christmas in 1964.

John's parents had seen enough. After conversations with the headmaster, they decided that their son should be allowed to pursue his skating on a full-time basis. If the head was right, he'd quickly fall out of love with it and come slouching back to sit his O-level examinations within a year. On 1 April 1965, John left Solihull

School, with no qualifications, and absolutely no intention of getting any.

He was just 15.

———

Although battle had never been formally joined, the teenager had outflanked his father and the outcome was a mortal blow to Joseph's hopes for his son. In six years he had seen his son skate just twice. By the summer of 1965, there seemed little prospect of him seeing John skate again. When he was sober, which wasn't very often, there was a business to run. He'd show Andrew the ropes while he could. His youngest son could take care of himself.

At 946 Warwick Road, the walls closed in. According to John, his father always 'seemed to be preparing for a drinking bout or recovering from one … there wasn't very much in between.' By day Joseph tried desperately to find mental salvation in a business upon which 40 people now depended for a living. By night he wrestled with prolonged bouts of sleeplessness. 'There were some awful things but they're shut away,' says Rita. 'I choose not to articulate them.' At home his habits became more reclusive. Melancholy bouts of sadness alternated with bleak and drunken paranoia. 'Being ill, being an alcoholic, having responsibilities. Which is worst?' wonders Andrew.

Periodically there would be abstinence and lucidity. At one point during his decline he'd agreed with Rita that he should try rehab. 'When he came back he seemed all right, but he really wasn't. I don't know what they did to him, but it seemed to weaken him in mind and body. He wouldn't talk about it much. Inwardly I think he was ashamed. I think he was angry with himself.' During the same lull, he took John out to the United States, where he had business with a client, the Minnesota Mining and Machining Company. When they got back, Andrew's first question to John was: Did Dad get drunk all the time?

Just occasionally, when the clouds parted, Joseph's energy returned. He travelled to Ireland and bought a large house and land in Tipperary, hoping to take advantage of tax breaks for entrepreneurs. He'd been in the crowd at Wembley when his son won the Novice Cup and John was certain he'd detected a glimmer of approval. But as Christmas approached in 1965, the dwindling spark inside Joseph Henry Curry flickered weakly and then expired. Or as John would later summarise bleakly: 'After four difficult years, when I was 16 my father died.'

It was an understatement of revealing coldness. On the morning of 30 December – just two days after his wife Rita's fifty-second birthday – Joseph's fully clothed body had been found by a chambermaid in a bedroom at the Great Western Royal Hotel, near Paddington Station in London. He left no note and appears to have died alone. At the inquest two weeks later, it was determined that Joseph Curry – '50 years – an engineer' – had taken his own life by 'acute chloral poisoning, self-administered'.

According to the coroner, Gavin Thurston, the dose was too large to have been anything but deliberate, so to Rita's confused pain and loss was added the public shame of suicide. Except to Rita, this would never be anything but a tragic accident. She'd been perfectly aware of Joseph's intake of chloral hydrate. Joseph's own doctor had prescribed it, to be self-administered in liquid form. Taken with alcohol, it was known as a 'Mickey Finn' – a knockout drug with hypnotic side effects – and it was widely used by chronic insomniacs.

Few people fully understood its addictive qualities, or the side effects, especially for a heavy drinker. If Joseph had been stupefied and feeling wretched in a soulless London hotel, it was not impossible that a terrible accident had happened. And that was how Rita would always see it; as a terrible accident, emotionally complicated by the guilt of relief. 'It felt like a cloud had lifted when I was alone,' she admitted almost half a century later.

Whatever had happened, the Curry family now wrapped Joseph's death in a cloak of perpetual silence. Few people were told. Theories and speculation were discouraged. It helped that the local paper ('Man's Overdose Of Drug') got Joseph's age wrong by 23 years, and that the death of a local war hero merited no more than a single paragraph on an inside page.

Within No. 946 Warwick Road, the box was closed tight. Outside it, the secrets were kept. A less constrained life got swiftly underway. As the New Year began, and the family gathered for a memorial Mass at the Sacred Heart Church in Acocks Green, John was clearly not anticipating an extended period of mourning. As he subsequently told a close friend in New York: 'We were delighted. We were happy. We were free of him.'

In later years, even John's closest friends knew nothing of the truth. There was lurid speculation, and there were muddied versions of Joseph's death – involving guns, gas ovens and railway lines – which John himself sometimes peddled, but which made no mention of chloral hydrate; or the unhappy man sprawled on a bed in his lonely hotel room.

Ironically, Joseph's blinkered intransigence had helped inspire the outcome he'd most wanted to thwart. One way or another, his son would now unlock his urge to dance, fuelled by an enduring sense of injustice. Indeed, Curry's entire life quickly begins to resemble a magnificent never-ending act of revenge; a thing of mythic beauty constructed for a father who was no longer there to see it.

Two

'Forbidden fruit'

If Joseph Curry had harboured any secret fear about his son's sexuality, it was neither misplaced nor unusual. To be gay in 1950s and early 1960s Britain was a terrifying, and lonely, thing. Homosexual acts, even in private, were a criminal offence. Queer-bashing – especially in London – had almost attained the status of a routine weekend sport. In public life, a furious witch-hunt seemed hell-bent on ruining homosexual men holding high public office. And in public toilets, policemen skulked in cubicles hoping to add to the hundreds of men locked behind bars every year merely for acquiescing to their apparently incomprehensible desires.

It was a father's job, surely, to protect his son against this curse. By sending him to exclusive fee-paying schools, however, Joseph had sequestered him in places where illicit sexual experimentation was rife. At his school in Somerset, John had found a special male friend 'who was on [his] wavelength'. He'd even bought him a copy of Byron's *The Prisoner of Chillon* and inscribed it 'to my eternal spirit of the chainless mind'. 'I think it must have frightened him because when I went back after Christmas he had left,' John later confided.

Even Solihull School had been touched by this post-war mood of revulsion. In 1947, Brigadier Harry Butler Hitchens had been appointed headmaster; a 6' 6" tower of military bristle, his references for the job included Field Marshal Montgomery and Dwight D. Eisenhower. In 1963, just four weeks before John started at Solihull, Hitchens had killed himself as black rumours closed in around his good name. There was talk of a sordid moment in a Rugby toilet. Stories of jilted schoolboy lovers – and blackmail threats – were muttered and then silenced as the school moved swiftly to bury speculation. In its official history today it speaks only of the

Brigadier's 'sad death'. These would be the whispered shadows of John's adolescence.

———

Whatever had happened in Paddington, Joseph's agony was over, and his secrets had now been transferred to his shell-shocked survivors. Inside No. 946 the dead businessman's dealings were unravelling fast. To fund new building work, Joseph had borrowed heavily and the rudderless company was struggling to meet the debt. 'Before his death I don't think things [at his business] were easy, but Dad was still good enough to cope with it. Afterwards it went downhill fast,' says Andrew.

There was worse. Joseph's troublesome loan had been partly secured against the family home on Warwick Road. By pronouncing death by suicide, the coroner had invalidated Joseph's life insurance and not a penny would ever be paid out. Rita steadied herself and took control. Pressure had crushed Joseph Curry, but it would not crush his widow. For as long as they could, she would keep the business ticking over, and she would cling on to the family home. The Currys would not go under or starve, and there would always be a gleaming car on the drive.

Since his abrupt departure from Solihull School, John's education had continued fitfully under a private tutor. 'Mutual loathing', Curry called it, and neither party was sorry when Rita's enforced review of household expenditure brought it to an end. 'My tutor hated the arrangement as much as I did,' John recounted later. 'I think he was very glad to see the end of me and my grubby exercise books when the situation was finally terminated.' For what it was worth – and it had not come cheap – John's formal education was concluded. Rita could no longer afford it, and her son now wanted only one thing. If he was to progress his self-confessed 'perverse ambition' as a skater, he had to be in London.

Rita's blessing, when it came, was not surrendered easily. Ice skating – as a viable career – mystified her no less than it had infuriated her dead husband. With Joseph alive, rational debate had been impossible. Alone, she could still make no impression on the stubborn granite of John's conviction. 'I had failed to make my parents accept skating as a tolerable way of earning a living,' he explained later. 'They had both remained unconvinced either about its possible financial rewards from performing … or indeed about its social "suitability".'

It may have been a deficiency of parental conviction, but it would prove chillingly accurate.

———

In the summer of 1966, having worn down Rita's resistance, John packed his skates and headed for the Streatham Ice Rink in south London. It was the first journey in a lifetime of rootless wanderings. It was also one of his shortest. By prior arrangement he'd met up with the Swiss-born coach Armand Perren in London, only to discover that Perren himself was switching to a new job at the Solihull rink, barely a mile from Curry's family home. Ignominiously, the 16-year-old's 'symbol of independence' had been cut short, and he was back in his old bedroom.

It had not been an entirely wasted trip. Staying in London digs had given John his first bitter taste of big city loneliness. He'd also made his first pivotal friend. On the ice at Streatham, hungry for companionship, he'd been fascinated by another one of Perren's students, a vivacious teenage skater, with an appealing round face and large blue eyes. 'I'd see John standing in the corner watching me skate and then he'd follow me around the ice … he'd stare at me a lot. Every time I turned around John would be there.'

In many ways, Lorna Brown was everything John was not. Gregarious, extrovert and with a melodic Tynemouth accent, she bubbled where John brooded. 'We instantly became like brother and sister,' she says. If either of them – John especially – was hoping for a physical connection, it did not materialise. In due course, Lorna and John would share a bed together, but they would never be lovers.

Lorna was heterosexual. John, on the other hand, was very slowly discovering that he was something else. 'He always said he loved me, but we were just beautiful friends without any sexual undertones.' When Perren moved north to Solihull, Lorna moved, too. It was fortunate for John's sanity that she did. Curry would make a habit of dumping his coaches, and, before long, Perren would be the first.

On paper, he'd seemed the perfect choice as John's first serious mentor. During the 1930s he'd skated in the United States as one half of a world-famous ice-dancing team. After the war he'd choreographed and skated at Blackpool's Pleasure Beach, going on to become both a sought-after teacher and skilled choreographer. In the flesh, however, Perren was old school, dogmatic, and ominously ill equipped to deal with hormonal teenagers, let alone one with such a non-negotiable sense of destiny as John.

By the mid-1960s Perren's once-sparkling career was in reverse, and his behaviour was becoming eccentric. For lessons he wore a dark double-breasted suit and tie, and if a pupil arrived two minutes late he would walk from the rink and not return. As one contemporary described him: 'He always had snots out of his nose. He sometimes didn't come in [to the rink] because he was drunk and he went to the races all the time and lost his money.' It was a match with no future.

For around six months, teacher and pupil skirmished on the ice at the Solihull rink. Curry was industrious, energetic – bursting with ideas – but technically raw. He fully understood the need to master figure skating's basic building blocks; its axels, toe loops and spins. But he also baulked at its rulebook rigidity. To the teenager, skating's magic lay in glide and flow – dance – not circus trickery. Broke, and barely 17, these were not yet thoughts he could either action or articulate. Through gritted teeth he persevered with the man he called 'Mr Perren' to his face and 'fatso' when safely back home.

No. 946 Warwick Road had changed. If it had been gloomy before, a new light was shining and to Lorna Brown it was always a happy place. After moving to Solihull, she'd been given a room there and would join the family around a long kitchen table for supper. 'We'd laugh a lot. An enormous amount. It was crazy and when John laughed his really strange laugh his shoulders would go up and down and that would set me off.' At midnight, when the rink could be hired cheaply, Lorna and John made their way through the deserted streets of Acocks Green to find Armand Perren standing woozily on the ice in his camel-hair coat. 'We were exhausted and he'd put Swiss music on and start dancing ... He was strange. A nightmare really.'

But Perren was no fool and understood competition skating. Under his guidance, Curry found that his audience was growing. After victory in the 1966 Northern figure skating championships,

John was chosen to skate in a senior competition in Prague. The two men travelled together and John skated to Liszt's Hungarian Rhapsody No. 2. From the stands, another teenage skater watched in admiration. 'It was the best thing I had ever seen on ice. He was just brilliant. He might have missed one or two of the jumps. But he always did back then.' The spectator's name was Heinz Wirz. He was 18 years old, and he would shortly become John Curry's first lover, and one of his very few lifelong friends.

Wirz had known immediately he was looking at raw genius. A gifted skater himself, he would be a Swiss pair's champion, and a two-time professional world champion, before switching to the sequins and gloss of touring ice shows. In Prague, John's mysteriously effortless programme had mesmerised him. Away from the ice – when the two were introduced – Heinz had been equally dazzled by the teenager's matinee looks and his carefully crafted public school charm.

If nothing else, his father's money had bought John the haughty syntax of a minor royal. It was never 'I have to', but 'one has to', and John's lofty elocution would always be the first barrier strangers had to overcome. It was also an accent that partnered nicely with expressions of contempt, and, even at 16, Curry was the master of theatrically snorted disgust. 'I remember one day we sat at dinner and John said to me, "Heinz, you don't put your face to the food, you put the food to your face."'

Curry's withering humour proved seductive, and the two young men established an immediate rapport. When John told Wirz where he lived and trained, the Swiss skater asked Perren if he could accommodate an extra pupil. It was summer, he was on college vacation and there'd been a look in the English boy's eye. Shortly afterwards, he too was installed under the roof of No. 946 Warwick Road. 'The house was beautiful, I had my own room, and Rita brought me tea in the morning, then John and I would go to the rink together.' He remembered Rita's shortcake, and her beautiful metallic-blue car. But he also noticed that money was tight and that their 'family finances were diminishing'. 'There was always enough food but I know that he wasn't allowed to go to the theatre. Cinemas also we didn't go, but it wasn't really necessary because John read his skating and ballet books. We got on well. Nothing sexual. We skated every day.'

Curry had never had a friend like Heinz; not a male one. There had been girls who flitted around the garden with him wearing imaginary skates, and there had been flickering kindred spirits at school, but nothing like this. Until he met Heinz, solitude had seemed the best option. As he later explained it: 'Skating didn't put me into an isolated position, I did.'

Down at the Solihull rink, meanwhile, Curry's relationship with Perren had continued to fester. For a time, the Swiss teacher had even joined the menagerie at No. 946, but, distanced by age, language and attitude, he and John could not see eye to eye. 'One night John had had his blade adjusted because it was loose. The next day it came off completely and there was a huge argument between the two of them. It was frightening,' remembers Lorna. 'Perren called John a liar. John said he wasn't a liar and threw his blade into the middle of the ice. He then hobbled to the side of his rink, and rang his mum to tell her it was over.' After six months of dog-fighting, the partnership was dissolved.

Perren's sacking, however, was no random spat. Rather, it was Curry's first known act of premeditated ruthlessness. Quietly, John had been plotting a return to London. He'd already identified a new coach and a new rink and had some foggy notion of how he'd survive financially. Living with his mother – and skating at his local rink – was stifling him, and soon Heinz would be back in Switzerland. Shortly after his seventeenth birthday, he repacked his suitcase and headed south for the second time in a year.

On a bend of the Thames where the river sweeps lazily by, a five-storey block of luxury flats gazes back towards Richmond Park. The borough's older residents remember this spot – next to the tennis courts and down from the resplendent Richmond Bridge – as the former site of a world-famous ice rink, once as majestically arched and cavernous as a Victorian railway station. For almost ten years this hangar would be the fulcrum around which John Curry constructed his life. Today, not a trace of it remains.

Richmond rink would lead him to his friends. It would determine when, or whether, he could work; also the kind of work he could do. Its opening times would govern the time he went to bed, and the time he set his alarm. Living and training alone like this would place restraints on his normal social and emotional development similar to those imposed of an inmate at an institution. When he was eventually set free by Olympic glory he would enter a real world for which he was woefully underprepared.

He had guessed it might be tough. His earlier stay in London had left him homesick, and he was under no illusions about bedsit-land. It was the 1960s and London was full of young singles shivering in overpriced digs. In nine years, he would move around ten times. Alwater Close. Richmond Road. Clevedon Road. Roland Gardens. Denton Road. Collingham Road and others. Nowhere matched the grandeur of Warwick Road. Nothing compared with the smell of Rita's baking.

At best, his lodgings had a one-ring cooker wedged into a box room with a dodgy single bed, and random pieces of decrepit furniture. At worst, he had just a bed. Good or bad, he was always cold and almost always famished; unsatisfied by a diet of tuna and baked beans, or tins of fruit cocktail washed down with lashings of cream. In letters to Heinz in Switzerland, he chronicled his existence in prose worthy of Joe Orton:

> I am sitting in the lounge and Mr and Mrs Walker are in the kitchen. They don't know I'm here and they are talking about me. They say they are angry with me and I waste the electricity. Well I don't care ... as they are rather poor people and don't really count ... Mr and Mrs Walker have gone out – the house is empty – just me and their two GAY dogs.

Out of absolute necessity, Curry had found himself a job. There were no grants, and there could be no sponsorship for an amateur sportsman in the late 1960s. Rita's contributions were now limited to the odd £10 postal order for a sensible coat. If he was to make it, he would be paying his own way. Just over the bridge from Richmond Ice Rink – in a small family supermarket – he stacked shelves and shuffled coleslaw on the refrigerated counter, where his artistic talents earned him a promotion to cold meats. 'I did it very nicely but took far too long and they said, you've got to sell it not just arrange it.'

When the owners wearied of his impeccably serried sausages, John took his suspect work ethic to National Cash Registers on

Marylebone Road, a company with ties to the Curry family business. Once again, as a receptionist, he revealed his unsuitability for conventional working norms. Showing clients to meetings, and drawing up rosters, would have been soporific to a non-athlete, but Curry was already permanently exhausted. In his own words, 'I was the sleepiest receptionist in London. Trying to look as if I was awake … was the most difficult aspect of the job.'

Even John's teenage energy levels were struggling to cope with his schedule. To enjoy the ice before public sessions began required him to be at the rink by 6 a.m. sharp. Depending on his current digs, this would necessitate either a five o'clock alarm followed by a long walk, or an early Tube train. After six hours' practice, he'd dash into London to commence his shift at NCR, after which he would invariably retreat to his digs alone. Solitude was both a necessity, and a choice. Out of his £13 weekly wages, only £1 was left for 'entertainment' once lessons and lodgings had been paid for.

'I always feel very lonely on Friday nights and Saturday,' he told Heinz.

> In the week there is skating and work, but at the weekend I have time to think. Thinking is the worst thing a person can do! No, I really mean it. When one thinks one starts to think of nice things that have happened in the past and that makes one sad … otherwise one thinks of sad things and that just depresses me. You cannot win!

Penny Malec could see that he was lonely. Like John, she worked shifts – as a producer at the BBC World Service – and, like John, she adored the seedy splendour of the Richmond rink, 'smelling of ice and dry ice and chemicals and rubber and sweat … not posh … not glamorous … where all you hear is the tzt tzt of the skates on the ice'. In the mornings, as she scuttled around its perimeter, she gaped at John's elegance. During the lunchtime break, before they both sped off to work, they began to talk. 'I was magicked by him,' she says. 'He was lost, hungry and poor. Here was someone – me – who took him home, gave him company and a meal.'

But Penny was far more than a decent supper. Highly intelligent – and eight years older than John – Penny was like no one he had ever met. She had a degree in drama and philosophy and she loved ballet and music. Alongside her, the vacuum left by Curry's fragmentary schooling began to be filled. She also seemed utterly uncowed by John's caustic debunking wit. 'I was 24 and very badly coordinated. I can't catch a ball. I'm not terribly well put together. So we liked each other at an intellectual level and he had very little outlet for his intellectual appetites. He and I were alike,' she adds.

> We would become obsessed with one thing and then move on. Shakespeare ... Dickens ... I think he went to his first Shakespeare with me. Much later on we'd do long car journeys together and sing songs from the shows and we both knew all the words from the musicals ... We joked about releasing an album called 'John and Pen Do Songs from the Shows'.

At weekends, the pair would go for afternoon tea in Hampstead, followed by a stroll on the nearby Heath, when nothing would be off limits. 'He told me, "They said my father committed suicide." That was how he always put it. He couldn't quite bear the fact that he probably did.

Together they would listen to music or go to the cinema. Penny even stood patiently by while John spent 90 minutes choosing a new shirt ('which I probably subbed him for'), but despite their proximity, they were never sexually attracted to each other. 'I think John was wondering if he was gay but wasn't sure that he was. On Richmond Hill he'd talked about having a family and children and I'd said, "Do you really think you will"?'

Penny wasn't the only female witness to John's state of confusion. There were many others. Linda Davis had been a pupil of Armand Perren's, when Curry first turned up nervously in Streatham. 'He was already amazing then,' she says. 'He had a strength and a grace. It wasn't effeminate. It was beautiful.' Like John, she was living in lacklustre digs and working all hours to pay for her lessons. At 17 she was also strikingly beautiful, and had fallen ever so slightly in love with the stranger from Solihull.

One Saturday afternoon he'd turned up outside the Bayswater boutique where she worked. They'd gone for pancakes together; talked about their futures; and later – bizarrely – he'd taken her to Paddington and shown her the hotel where his father had died. The following Saturday, John was back and the couple held hands as they walked for their pancakes. 'He was very warm but he was not interested in that way.' For two years running, they went as a couple to the skaters' ball at the Kensington Palace Hotel, where they danced all night but went home alone with no goodnight kiss. 'People thought – oh look, they're dancing – John likes Linda. But of course he never did. Not that way.'

It was almost as if John was willing himself to be what he dubbed 'a normal'. After Lorna Brown had returned to London from Solihull, he'd boasted about his 'crush' on Linda's 'beautiful soul'. Reunited, he and Lorna play-acted *Romeo and Juliet* before hopping into bed – for comfort and warmth – and when Birmingham friend Maggie McKone travelled down from the Midlands to see him, they too crept under the sheets. 'We sleep together in a tiny bed and she thinks it is strange that anyone does not have sex,' John told Heinz. 'The thought of a woman makes me feel ill – not like the real thing. The first night we were in bed – I was nearly asleep and Maggie said, "Don't you ever fancy anyone?" I answered "very seldom". AND THAT WAS THAT! HA HA.'

Patricia Dodd was another stunning young woman to be 'magicked' by Curry's budding charisma. She was born in Toronto, but her father's work with BOAC had brought the family to London and a fine riverside apartment near the Richmond Ice Rink. Poised, balletic – and intense – at 19 Patricia was a world-class skater with a musically fluent style John adored. 'I loved John and I know he loved me. I found him very attractive. I don't know any woman who wouldn't have. He charmed. But he couldn't respond as a heterosexual.'

After Patricia's father took a job in South Africa, John stayed with her for a while in a spare room. 'I also shared a bed with John – no sex. When I got into bed the language was, you don't go anywhere. You can share the bed but you don't go anywhere.'

If there had truly been a battle inside John, it was lost some time in 1968. It cannot have been easy. Barely 12 months before, the Sexual Offences Act had decriminalised homosexuality between consenting males, providing they were 21 and not in the Armed Forces. Social attitudes, however, move more slowly than law-makers, and an 18-year-old practising homosexual – who by this time was also taking ballet lessons – could scarcely have been more exposed. Secrecy had always come easily in John's family. From now on, it would be his default way of life.

Precisely how – and with whom – Curry had lost his virginity is unknown. Penny Malec believed it to be a skater at Richmond rink – 'someone older and unpleasant' – but she couldn't be sure. 'He was terrified of dealing with his sexuality … I know he was dreading it … but afterwards he told us it had been easy. "Like falling off a log," he said.' The man's identity was immaterial. However it had happened, the experience ended Curry's uncertainty and by the end of 1968 he had also resolved the unspoken connection made in Prague two summers earlier with a blond Swiss teenager.

His love affair with Heinz Wirz was underway and a wonderful tumult of angst-saturated love letters had begun.

———

According to Wirz, it was John who initiated the romance. 'He told me that he fancied me and that was it.' Undaunted by geography, the pair excitedly re-engineered their lives. From Switzerland, Wirz found a place at a London college and a room near Gloucester Road Tube station. 'I could tell my mum I was studying, and I did it for three months while we had our love affair and that was it. I was there for John.'

Whenever Wirz was out of town, John picked up his fountain pen. At the affair's peak – in the spring of 1969 – he was writing once, sometimes twice a day; letters that spared Heinz no details; letters that swung from exuberance to black self-loathing, written in a hand which varied as wildly as his moods. Sometimes tight and compact like a school exercise; sometimes scratchy and littered with winsome drawings of harlequins' faces or tear-shedding self-portraits; sometimes clumsily typed with one finger at his desk at NCR. The tone is often puerile and bitter; the spelling throughout is abominable; and every one of them is signed 'Bunny' – the nickname given to him by his dead father.

> When you come back to England, I want to marry you. Some boys do get married you know. I want you to drink my blood, and I your's [sic]. Please don't think I'm crazy but they say a man in love is a madman …

I do so love to have your letters; it is smashing to know that someone cares about me – that one is not alone in the world, no matter what …

At the rink, on the train, after work; everything seems rather strange and lonely. I have got used to having you with me most of the time and now it seems strange to be one. Work was quite interesting today as I had something to do. I fell asleep on the train.

In letter after letter, the daily minutiae of Curry's desolate London life were laid bare.

At the weekends he tans himself by Richmond open-air swimming baths, offering detailed reports on his weight, the colour of his skin and hair and the boys he has observed pool-side. 'I am going to do some body building; I hate my skinny arms maybe I could loose [sic] a bit of [sic] my waist and bottom as well.' He reads *The Catcher in the Rye* ('I have not laughed so much for weeks'); he has regular dreams about the Queen; he goes to the cinema, preferring musicals and often seeing the same film again and again; or he stays in his bedsit 'and plays the fool to my old records'. 'The Nun's Chorus was the best. I wore the cover from the bed and a black pullover so that my face showed through the hole in the neck. At 830 I went to bed. Oh I do so miss you. All my love Bunny.'

During the hot summer of 1969 – at a time when Heinz was back home – Curry's sense of abandonment intensified. Previously playful introspection slid worryingly towards existential self-pity. In one vivid description of a horribly listless Sunday in July, Curry mapped out his boredom. Much bleaker reflections would follow:

Today has been one of those awful days. Everything is up the shoot. First I went to swim and sunbathe but it was so cold I left quickly … then I walked down King's Road – that was boring. After I had an awful lunch … so I walked to Westminster and looked around the Abbey – that is always lovely. And now I'm at the Tate but I'm very lonely (Oh! A nice lady just gave me a sweet!) … I would go to a bar but I don't know where any are. If I had been you I think 20 men would have spoken to me by now, but because it's me not one has.

Do you think it is because I am so ugly or something? Lots of people watch me, and stare at me, but no-one talks to me … I thought I'd go to the Festival Ballet but they are doing *Coppelia* and I don't like that ... So now I'm sitting in Leicester Square. There's a bunch of stupid Swiss or German young boys about 14–15 years. I hate them.

There were some places in London which homosexuals could visit safely for 'company'. The teenage Curry had very quickly found most of them. The Sombrero on Kensington High Street (also known as 'Yours Or Mine') had a raised, underlit dance floor and a 10/- entrance charge. In Earl's Court, the Coleherne pub had segregated bars – one for gays, one for straights – and a thriving leather scene flourished behind its blacked-out windows. Almost inevitably, Curry had succumbed to temptation. 'I enjoy to be liked and watched,' he teased Heinz.

Shortly after his miserable West End Sunday, John met – and apparently slept with – a French boy called 'Gilles' he had smooched with in the Sombrero. By early August, he had made his confession, and the romance with Heinz was over. Monogamy would always be problematic for John Curry. Nothing permanent ever seemed to happen. Friendship was different. When he could, Heinz would still travel to London by boat and train on Fridays, returning to Switzerland on Sunday evenings. And for the time being, Curry would still pour out his letters. 'We stayed great friends. Always. Even after he went to other people.'

However cruelly Curry neglected him, Wirz would always love him; never let him down. Even when John's peccadilloes caused him pain, he would endure them for his friend's sake. Both men had lost their fathers young and, intuitively, Heinz probably knew Curry had nowhere else to turn. For his part, Curry knew no other man who would listen.

> Do you think I shall ever be happy Hene [John's nickname for Heinz]? Because everywhere I go I get miserable very quickly and I don't think anyone will ever love me. I know that I'm pretty difficult but that is because I have never met anyone who can tame this shrew. But I'm not as horrible as all that am I? I hope you ... are not angry with silly little me because one should not be angry with sick people in the head or children, and I'm like a sick-headed child.

Curry had not forgotten what he was doing in London. In spite of his moods, he never once loosened his grip on the skating. Every weekday for almost eight years, he would shake off his wretched dreams, and make his way to the rink. Nowhere was he happier. It was such an easy place to get lost.

Few sports demand more concentration, or set standards of such improbable complexity. Merely to move forwards and backwards with Olympian grace requires years of practice. To spin and fly without falling requires many years more. For even a natural, it requires a journey measured in tiny increments. It is also – or was – a sport judged against a rulebook worthy of Euclid.

John's feet wanted to dance. But if he was to win tournaments they would be required to understand geometry. Until the 1990s competitive figure skating was broken down into three scoring sections: a long free programme and a shorter technical programme – both performed to music – preceded by the so-called compulsory figures themselves; fastidiously carved shapes and patterns skated on clean 'patches' of ice in front of owl-like judges watching every tracing for wobbles and discrepancies.

It was an artless discipline; a leftover of the pre-television age, which most skaters resented, and which very few spectators ever bothered with. In a closed rink, each skater in turn would draw circles on the ice defined by a glossary and pattern book all of its own. Brackets. Rockers. Counters. Loops. Circle Eights and Serpentines. Just like musical scales to a pianist, these were the arcane hieroglyphics of Curry's sport. Different feet and edges; different shapes; different directions. 'Very calm, very still, very precise,' said Curry. 'It's a beautiful form, a very pure idea.'

In the sport's infancy, these so-called school figures had been the key measure of a skater's mastery, not his or her ability to move an audience to tears. Up until the 1960s, they still counted for up to 60 per cent of a skater's final score. Only very slowly was their importance starting to wane. Artistry was increasingly what audiences wanted. It made no sense when a brilliant free skater could be beaten by someone with a perfect set of figures that no one had seen. Just as it was unthinkable that a television channel would ever free up its schedule for such mundane fare.

In time, the proportion of marks would shift decisively in favour of creative skating, before the 'compulsories' withered away completely. But not in Curry's day. As a competitor he would never be a winner until he had mastered them. They were also fiendishly difficult. And if there was one depressing thought on his mind, as he made his way to Richmond, it was the prospect of yet more practice 'patches'. And yet more rollockings from the latest Swiss autocrat he had chosen as his teacher.

Everyone in skating knew Arnold Gerschwiler. He had the ice in his bones. His nephew had been an Olympic silver medallist in 1948. He'd discovered 42 champions, and since 1938 he'd run a team of coaches at Richmond looking after skaters from all over the world. John's new Canadian friend Patricia Dodd was one of them; 'the big guy' she called him, a 55-year-old rod of iron forged in the same Alpine metal as the man Curry had already ruthlessly abandoned.

Eventually this, too, would end catastrophically. The Swiss coach had never encountered a more arrogant and wilful human being and his pupil came to despise Gerschwiler as a homophobic bigot, a philistine and a violent bully. No one in the world, however, taught the soul-sapping school figures quite so brilliantly. It was for this that John met him at Richmond every morning at six o'clock. It was for this that he put up with their spats. 'My figures have turned to ashes,' he confessed in his daily written commentary to Heinz Wirz. 'Yesterday Mr Gerschwiler sent me off the ice. He has not done that to anyone for years.'

Three days later the same:

> Yesterday Gersch was furious and made me read a newspaper instead of finishing a figure. After I had read it I said to him it was very boring and he was even more angry … I don't know what to do about my hair – I thought maybe I would make it all darker but I like blonde better … After a lot of thought I have decided to live the life of a 'saint' – that is difficult for me. HA HA. I am so lonely, Heinz. While you lived in England I told you I was usually lonely … I have been to bed 7 or 8 every night (You see I am being good) …
>
> This morning I skated diabolical figures. Mr Gerschwiler shouted at me and I thought he was going to slap my face (he is a very butch number! HA). He did not hit me in fact …

Gerschwiler was worried. Curry's salacious correspondence may have been private, but John's fey manner – which always teetered on camp – was not. The boy was just 18 and playing with fire. Rumours were circulating, and the delicacy that distinguished his free skating was unpopular with the sport's establishment. Homosexuality was no stranger to ice skating – Arnold wasn't a fool – but he didn't like it, and thought some adult advice might help.

> He started to talk about the 'people with whom I mix'. I said to him that I got very lonely. Then I said that if he thought I was gay ... I had hardly said the word and he said 'No, no, I don't think that about you'. Then he said everyone goes through phases when they are not sure what they like and want. So. It's alright!! Oh he always gives me such confidence. I think he is great ... PS My hair ... is now a sort of light brown with a tinsy winsy bit of ash.

The subject was closed. For the moment, where it mattered, 'Gersch' had no cause for complaints. John's work rate remained impressive despite his joyless state of impecunious exhaustion. In competition – steered by Arnold Gerschwiler – Curry was also enjoying a succession of important triumphs. In 1967 he'd been crowned British Junior Champion. The following year he'd won free skating's Jennings Trophy, and come second in the British Men's Figure Skating Championships. Only two things seemed to stand in his way. His chattering nerves and an athletic teenager dubbed 'the George Best of the ice rink'.

———

Haig Oundjian appeared to have everything that John Curry did not. He was sleek, extrovert and prodigiously sporty. He oozed the playboy confidence of the well-born, drove a car and wore his clothes like a model. Both men were good-looking and turned heads, but Oundjian flowered in company and women melted at his boots.

Like John's, Haig's family – with its Armenian roots – represented a fiercely proud, self-made success story. But there the similarity ended. Oundjian's grandfather had fled the genocide; his grandmother was a Gulbenkian, and his father had played at junior Wimbledon before importing the carpets from Iran which would establish the dynastic fortune. Haig was comfortable, rich and heterosexual and John Curry loathed every inch of him. 'But he jumps so well,' a judge once said to Curry of Haig. 'Yes,' sniffed John, 'but then so does a horse.'

Everything seemed to come so easily to Oundjian, even his skating. During the early 1950s, his family had moved to Toronto, where he'd spent his winters perambulating the deep-frozen lakes and rinks of Ontario. Instinctively gung-ho, Oundjian embraced the sport's high-flying possibilities and became known for his vaulting athleticism – and he returned to Britain ready to take on the world.

By the mid-1960s, Haig had become aware that he had competition. Before their rivalry took off there had even been a moment of acute embarrassment when, according to Oundjian, Curry made an ill-judged advance. 'We were both about 17; he'd had a rough time at school because of his sexual orientation … and maybe he was a bit touchy-feely,' says Haig today. 'I said, "Look, John, I think you look great and you've got a great body but I'm into girls." After that I think he labelled me as this playboy.'

Haig had been to boarding school, too. He knew what happened after lights out. It just wasn't his thing. Snubbed and humiliated, Curry retreated to alchemise rejection into jealousy. 'He projected this thing – I have a sad life, I'm different. No one loves me. I'm never going to be popular,' says Oundjian. What no one expected Curry to be – not at first glance – was such a ferocious competitor. 'I liked winning,' he explained, 'principally because I disliked losing.' It might have been the mission statement for his entire life.

In 1968, Oundjian had been the favourite for the 1968 Jennings Trophy but his 'touchy-feely' rival had outscored him on the day. 'It was such a shock. I was devastated,' admits Haig. Four weeks later, he took his revenge, winning the British Championships at Curry's expense. Oundjian and Curry. The scene was set. For the next three years, these two men – born within six months of each other – would be locked in a domestic duel for the sport's top honours.

It was a glorious rivalry rich in sub-plots and (from John) theatrically sniping asides. Oundjian's coach was Arnold

Gerschwiler's half-brother, Jacques. Jacques taught Haig at Streatham, and Arnold taught (and fought with) John at Richmond. 'Two rinks. Two totally different camps,' explains Haig today. 'This is like Birmingham and Aston Villa.'

True to the derby spirit, the Gerschwiler brothers also employed very different styles. Where Arnold favoured formulaic dogma, Jacques opted for spirit and elegance. The result was a battle between two men who didn't get on, groomed by two brothers to showcase diametrically opposite visions. Virtually the only common ground they shared was the ice; and on that, Oundjian had the edge.

In a sport which scored points for jumps, John Curry had a problem. He couldn't jump. Haig Oundjian, however, was a flier. 'John was not a good jumper. He was a tiny little jumper,' claims Haig:

> When you do a jump in skating – let's say a double jump – that's two revolutions and land backwards. But John would go up and do one-and-a-half revolutions, land forward on one foot, finish the turn on the ice and skate backwards. It was called cheating. You land with a cheat. Later, you'd have the Russians going three foot in the air and John only getting eight inches in the air.

All John wanted to do was to float and dance. All Haig wanted to do was fly. As the 1969 British Championships drew nearer, Curry shared his losing battle to overcome gravity with Heinz Wirz:

> I feel awful. I feel like screaming until I explode. This morning I had two violent lessons. One figures; one free. Poor Mr Gerschwiler nearly lost control of himself but he was nice in the end … my stamina is getting better … I landed every jump although the triple salchow was awful.

And then later, ruefully: 'There is no end to the work one must do, is there?'

The salchow, the axel and the lutz are the jumps no competitive skater can hide from. To the layman, when performed at speed they melt into one. To a judge they are the cornerstones of accomplishment. Each is defined by the direction of spin, or by the different foot required for take-off and landing; each can be performed as a single, double or triple spin. Since the age of eight, Curry had been quietly terrified of all of them.

In competition – or practice – you either land them or you fall in a tinselled heap. Margin for error simply doesn't exist. In 2011, when an American skater completed a quadruple lutz – fully rotating four times in the air – it was rightly deemed a sporting miracle. In December 1969, as the UK Championships began, Haig Oundjian was, according to John, struggling to stay upright on a single:

> Haig was thinking he was great and marvellous as usual. He started his wonderful programme and fell on his hooked nose on a single axel!! That was fun. He is so big-headed now. He said to someone the other day 'After seeing John skate, I have nothing to worry about'. Well we shall see.

Four days later, Wirz heard from his friend again; a telegram. 'Landed everything but still came second – Bunny'. Curry had lost. Once again, Oundjian had bested him and taken the British title. John's disappointment was fortified by real anger. 'I knew the judges sort of wanted Haig to win. I skated better than I have for ages … and I smiled as much as I could. The people loved it but the judges apparently did not. So that was that.'

It was exactly as Arnold Gerschwiler had predicted. Skating wasn't ready for his pupil's idiosyncratic style; for what he called 'John's arm-waving'. The judges didn't want artistic nuance, they wanted masculine dynamism. Not to provide it simply stirred the ingrained disgust that the Sexual Offences Act couldn't wash away. Call it effeminate; call it effete; call it what you like, but in Gerschwiler's book Curry would make progress only when he started skating like a man. Or when he tried to make everything look a bit harder.

No one ever expressed it like this; that Curry was a 'poof' and insufficiently virile to meet the sport's template of well-oiled manliness. Perception – and hence the judge's marking – proceeded on the basis of innuendo. 'If I live a lifetime I will not vote for Curry as the best skater in the world,' said one German skater. Everyone knew why. But until 1976, that was about as close as anyone got to saying it.

Ironically, Haig Oundjian would have understood. At boarding school they'd mocked his swarthy looks and Armenian roots, calling him 'Abdul' and 'nignog'. 'But I was a good athlete, a good sprinter, so it was "Abdul, we need you on the team."' At the 1968 Olympics he'd received his lowest score from a British adjudicator, and later that year, after winning the UK Championships, he'd heard one judge remark, 'Oh my God, we're going to have a foreigner as a British champion.'

John might have thought the British judges were on Oundjian's side, but his rival was convinced of the opposite. As a child he'd been constantly warned against the evils of British racial prejudice. During the war his father had been posted to the front, supposedly because his surname meant he'd never show up as a British casualty. 'The British will hurt you,' he warned his son. 'They can't help themselves.'

Ice skating – of which Haig's father strongly disapproved – merely validated his point. Its scoring was suspect, and deep prejudice was at play. Or so he insisted. Suddenly, it seemed, even a gay man was higher up the pecking order than an Armenian. 'Ninety per cent of our judges were women. John projected himself as this unloved, needy English guy, and I was this foreign guy with all the affluence; athletic; a big jumper. It's that John thing. "Look at me I'm poor and Haig drives a car."'

Today, not one of Oundjian's contemporaries accepts this analysis. Racial discrimination, they say – however finely he studies the scorecards – never held him back. Not only did he win the UK title three times, but he also represented Britain at two Winter Olympics. Nevertheless, Oundjian remains adamant. Few other sporting outcomes are determined by subjective whim, and skating's judges were not then so immune to the polluted air they breathed.

Licking his wounds as Christmas approached in 1969, Curry had a choice: either to change or to wait for the world to come to him. No one who knew him well thought the first option very likely. Nothing in his letters suggested he was mellowing. 'Tomorrow someone is going to photograph me at the rink. I think I'll ware [sic] a pink see through shirt and leather pants and naturally some glitter in my hair.' And two days later:

There was a nice looking boy at the rink this morning. I'm sure he fancied me but I would not bother to chase him. I think I'm going normal. I never seem to fancy anyone ... Mr Gerschwiler keeps saying to me 'Wait till I get you up in Davos'. I wonder what he means. Maybe he likes to have sex dressed all in leather lying in the snow. Oh I can't wait ...

A spell of winter training in Switzerland had been arranged, but not for the ludicrous reasons Curry surmised. Lately, Gerschwiler's concern for John's mental welfare had passed beyond the ice rink. At Arnold's behest, Curry had even been to see a psychiatrist. 'We talked for ages. He gave me hundreds of pills.' Back in his bedsit John showed no sign of any benefits. 'I really feel sorry for anyone who gets tangled up with me. I really do.' Maybe the altitude would clear his head.

———

At 1,560 metres, Davos in Switzerland is Europe's highest city. Since the late nineteenth century, wealthy British had made it their Alpine home from home. Robert Louis Stevenson had convalesced there. Sir Arthur Conan Doyle had written a paper lauding the quality of its skiing. For decades, the Davos clientele had been as rarefied as the mountain air, and, as the snow piled up in January 1970, their number included John Curry. He was not, however, sharing the excitement of his illustrious predecessors. 'I hated it' was his simple assessment a few years later. It was the reaction Gersch had probably expected.

Davos was his patch. Switzerland was his country. For several years he'd dragged his best skaters up into the mountains for a three-month 'boot camp' on the renowned open-air Davos Eisstadion. When the winds rasped and blizzards shut out the sky's watery light, there was no crueller place on earth to practise. If his pupils could survive Davos, and its open-air rink, they'd hack it anywhere.

In Davos, Gerschwiler felt certain he could tame his most complex pupil. But in their two years together so far, John had been kept away from his coach's infamous boot camp by his poverty. Finally, it had taken Haig's irksome domestic supremacy to get

Curry on a train bound for the Alps shortly after Christmas 1969. When he arrived 24 hours later – in the teeth of a snowstorm – it was the fourth anniversary of his father's suicide. And after barely a day on the frostbite-inducing rink, he was in despair:

> I am sitting alone in my room with nothing to do and nowhere to go on New Year's Eve. All this beauty is going to waste … I think the girls [Gerschwiler's other pupils] are going out but I don't want to pay 40 francs to dance with some stupid bitch of a girl. Oh last night I had the most awful dream. It is four years since my dad died. I dreamed my mother came into my room and said there had been a mistake about dad. She gave me a letter from him and a gift of gloves. Suddenly it was as if we had lots of money because of dad dying and I was so happy … not even a bit sad that he was dead. It was just horrifying to think that maybe I am like that.
>
> I would just love a man right now. As it is all I have is a half packet of biscuits and Radio Luxembourg and they won't do at all. I wish I had some sleeping drugs. I'd make myself a nice long sleep.

Curry had spoken to Heinz before about the black dreams of his father. In Davos, exhausted and bored, the nightmares returned. From one day to the next his mood could lurch between flirtatious elation and morbid self-hatred. If the sun shone, his impishness returned, but since it rarely did, Curry simmered and raged against the man who had designed such torture.

Before dawn's first light, Gerschwiler's skaters had to be ready on the ice. In the bitter air, Curry's nostrils sometimes 'sealed themselves together' and a damp handkerchief left in a pocket froze itself to the skater's leg. If a breeze blew off 'Bald Mountain' (as John called it) spindrift streamers spiralled around the ice, and whenever the sun softened its rutted surface the ice refroze again into treacherous, steely tracks. Even when blizzards shut down the rink, the agony continued. 'If it was snowing, he would make you run up the mountain,' remembers Patricia Dodd. 'John hated it, but you had to maintain condition.' Until the darkness fell again, this was Gersch's daily plan.

Curry was depressed and demoralised, and his skating began to fall apart. The previously infrequent spats with Gerschwiler became a daily, and very public, occurrence.

I have never been so miserable anywhere in my life. I hate Davos
… At lunchtime Mr Gerschwiler said 'what is the matter, don't
you like it here'. 'No,' I said. 'Well you know where the station
is,' he said … How can one train figures on ice like this? It is up
and down, hard as a rock. Mr Gerschwiler says … I am spoilt and
that skating in such bad conditions will make a man of me …

Nothing about Davos made any sense. Competitive skating no
longer took place outdoors, so why were they exposing themselves
to frostbite? To improve his figures, John needed pristine ice, not a
glorified frozen pond, and Gerschwiler's dislike of John's musical
free skating was now manifesting itself as unrestrained disgust. After
a warmly applauded exhibition skate for Davos residents, Curry
was ordered to desist from using the music of *La Bohème*. Demanding
a reason, Gerschwiler told him it was 'too soft'. Old, unspoken
prejudices were seeping out in the January cold. Curry's filthy mood
hardened.

You know it quite frightens me to realise all the horrible things I
think when I am in such moods. I would like to do something
really perverted or kill someone with a knife or something. It is
really awful but when I look at people I see in my mind the
terrible things I am doing to them and I know it is horrible but I
get pleasure from the pictures in my mind.
    I don't know what will happen to me … I am having the worst
dreams I have ever had.

Closeted in his room, Curry's soothed his crushed spirits listening
to Gounod's *Roméo et Juliette*. 'It is so beautiful I cannot tell you,'
he told Wirz in a letter dreamily outlining his plan to be a champion
by 1975: 'Even a silly thing like me can learn something in that
time … Tell me what you think because I cannot trust my own
mind any more.'

By early March, Curry was in open mutiny, and the Swiss coach's
Teutonic resolve crumbled in tearful despair. It was a pitiful
situation. No one had ever treated him like this. And yet rarely had
he seen a skater with such potential. Even giving John a German
phrasebook hadn't helped. Now Curry was refusing to jump during
practice unless Gersch lifted his ban on *La Bohème*. It was hopeless.

Gerschwiler was supposed to be the man in control – the man with experience – and yet Curry somehow undermined his every move.

As the winter ended, John's letters to Heinz show that he drew secret comfort from his triumph:

> Mr Gerschwiler has his problems in life and his big problem is John Curry. We had another tiff yesterday and he was so upset that his voice went and he had to turn away from me … it makes me feel bad to be naughty …
>
> I have said I will not skate like everyone else and he said 'You will skate like a <u>man</u>'. I said 'I don't want to skate like any man I have ever seen'. But one cannot tell him anything. He just does not like slow music. I think he is afraid of his own thoughts. Do you understand?

———

It all ended just in time. As the snow melted, Gerschwiler's winter camp disbanded and Curry joined his mother for a few days close to the seaside in Suffolk, the place where he'd skated in his school cap 15 years before. As always – from wherever he found himself – the letters still poured out to Heinz:

> I'm rather bored and lonely here at Aldeburgh. I think I'll always love London best. I hate to be away from it for very long … I really am a funny boy you know and I often wonder if I'll ever be happy in life. I'm OK while I'm skating but when I've got nothing to do I get so lonely … I just hope there will always be a 'Hene' nearby.

Now that he was restored to the city, Curry's days resumed the rhythms of the previous summer. In the afternoons he still worked at National Cash Registers – now newly promoted to the Accounting Machine Showroom, where he parroted demonstrations of contraptions that mystified him. He went to ballet class and modern dance lessons. He gorged on cakes and cream and then fretted about his weight. He drank sherry with his BBC friend Penny Malec, after which they 'giggled like mad children'. He joined a health club to build up his muscles. He became convinced his hair was falling out, and he chuntered constantly to Heinz about his general unworthiness. 'Normal people make me nervous,' he said.

> You know you are in love with a dream – not really me; it is a bit me and a bit Jean Brodie, a bit Katherine Hepburn and a bit Bette. With all those women in me, it is no wonder I'm queer.

Curry's lack of money hadn't changed, either. He owed Gersch for his lessons and his mother for a plane ticket to a one-off competition in the United States. To save money he repeatedly dodged his fare on the London Underground, and in a begging note to Heinz Wirz – asking for a £50 loan – he speculated openly about earning some extra cash as a rent boy.

By the spring, Curry and Gersch had suspended hostilities. The grisly prospect of a lifetime spent selling cash registers had filled him with dread. Skating was all he had, and he had no choice now but to excel at it. To vanquish Haig Oundjian, full training had resumed at Richmond Ice Rink. Six o'clock starts every morning. Monday to Friday. No money. No excuses.

Once he was away from the paralysing blizzards of Davos, however, something had been unlocked. For the first time in months, joy flowed through John's skating. And for the first time ever – possibly worn down by Curry's intransigence – Gerschwiler seemed willing to acknowledge his pupil's vision. 'I nearly died of shock,' he told Heinz, 'Gersch said that I was doing lovely movements in a manly way.'

> Today I had a flash of inspiration and made up a super new programme. Lots of jolly sailor hornpipe steps. It just fell into place. Clever little me ... really I'm a very lucky boy. I have lots of oppertunities [sic] ... so that I think it is a bit greedy and unreasonable of me to want to have 'love' as well. I also think I'm given skating to make up for the lonely life I shall have. Do you agree? It is better to give myself to something than to someone.

Curry's prediction was a little premature. Recently, a handsome stranger had been watching him practise; a tall man – about ten years older than John – with striking blond hair and a sun-weathered face which Curry had vaguely recognised. The two men had introduced themselves, become deep friends and by the autumn were sharing an address in South Kensington. It was a relationship which would have a profound impact on John Curry. Sadly for Heinz Wirz, it also marked a decline in the volume of letters from his old friend.

———

In the late 1960s, Julian Pettifer was the pin-up boy of BBC Television's cadre of onscreen journalists. Educated at Marlborough and Cambridge, Pettifer was brilliant, articulate and imbued with self-belief. He was also good looking and blessed with a steely hauteur. In 1968 the British Academy for Film and Television Arts had honoured him for his ground-breaking coverage of the Vietnam War. By 1970, as the face of programmes like *Tonight*, *24 Hours* and *Panorama*, he'd become a household name. He was also a homosexual with absolutely no intention of sharing that secret. 'Back then you didn't know the consequences,' he says. 'For God's sake, people could get fired for it in those days.'

Drawn to an ice rink by childhood memories of frozen ponds, Pettifer had been rendered mute by the vision of John Curry in full flight. 'I thought, God who's that, he's amazing.' The feeling was instantaneously mutual. Since Heinz and Penny, Curry had never met anyone quite so attuned to his passions. Both men adored the ballet. Both men loved the theatre, music and cinema. Both men were beautiful and both men were gay. In numerous other ways, however – and often literally – the two men were miles apart.

Pettifer was more streetwise and better educated than his new friend. He was also very well known. During their six-month friendship, Curry's hesitant awe would develop into full-blown infatuation, but Pettifer maintains that their relationship was never a physical one. 'If we'd had a wild affair I wouldn't be a bit ashamed of it, but we did not … I knew that he liked me … I knew that he sought my company … I think he did see me as something of a father figure who was reliable and was there for him.'

'He fell deeply in love with Julian Pettifer,' says Penny Malec, who had seen them together at Pettifer's basement flat in Roland Gardens and taken a strong dislike to John's new companion. 'I really, really didn't like him. He was very sophisticated. Older. Lived in a completely loathsome flat with fishes in the wall and everything painted black. A very masculine flat trying to make a statement.'

Today, in his late seventies, Julian insists this was no love affair. While he travelled the world for the BBC, Curry stayed in his home, principally to deter burglars. 'I knew he was always looking for a bed but most of the time I wasn't there … He also knew that I had someone else in my life, that I had loyalties elsewhere. John probably did have a crush on me but I was forbidden fruit if you like … Who knows? I certainly found him extremely attractive. He had a wonderful physique. But even gay men have non-sexual relationships.'

By early 1971, all Curry's letters were being addressed from Roland Gardens, where his news was laboriously tapped out on Pettifer's typewriter. 'Julian and I went to see *The Music Lovers*,' he told Heinz. 'Also we saw [the play] *After Haggerty* which was rather witty in parts' … 'I do miss Julian very much but I do not think he will be away too much longer. I live in his flat now and that makes me miss him even more.'

Whatever the precise nature of their relationship, Curry was changing under its influence. Pettifer was serious-minded and exuded a patrician air of class superiority. In his company, Curry's letters lost their schoolboy tone; 'Bunny' became simply 'John'. In place of gloom came a voice of positive-thinking maturity; a development he transferred to the ice with startling effect. In late August he won the St Gervais International in France, his first major skating honour.

'I stood up for the whole five minutes,' he gushed to Heinz:

> I missed triple loop – triple salchow – and the second double lutz … [but] it must have looked OK because a few people were moved to tears by my slow section. Tomorrow I shall skate my slow exhibition – the 'waving' one. The French are such artistic people they will understand it.

La Bohème was back and the momentum was with John. In December, at Richmond, he came up against Haig Oundjian for the third time in the British Championships. Every seat was taken. Julian Pettifer – who had given him the money for his skating outfit – was there to watch. His mother, Rita, had driven down from

Solihull. Penny Malec was looking on. So, too, was Linda Davis, the pancake girl from the Bayswater boutique. A few days before, John had told Heinz, 'I am working harder than I ever have done before and – touch wood – everything is going rather well.' After two days of competition, Oundjian was beaten. For the first time, John Curry was the British senior champion.

'Haig now is very gracious about John,' says Linda, 'but at the time he was furious … He stormed out of the rink. Normally we always chatted but he didn't say a word to me that day. He wasn't going to stay and discuss it. In the end, John had the edge and he couldn't accept that.'

Only three clouds studded Curry's horizon. Davos. Boot camp. And Arnold Gerschwiler.

———

It was very different this time. The previous year he'd vacillated between sexual despair and near-suicidal boredom. After Christmas in Solihull – 'Mum makes the best Xmas pud in the world' – he'd returned to Davos as a champion and with Gerschwiler's influence in retreat. By New Year's Eve he was hunkered in his room alone watching the snow fall, penning acid prose to Penny Malec:

> Haig [who was also in Davos] talks non stop about motorcars, places he has been to and girls. All very hearty. He got everyone down and most people think of him as a mouth … love your very own ice devil.

The winds howled and the ice was still pockmarked, but Curry's attitude had mellowed. After news reached him that Pettifer had survived a serious car accident in Scotland, he explained to Heinz why he felt so calm:

> It frightens me to think about him marrying a girl or not loving me any more, but then it is better not to think of such things. It is funny that this year I'm quite happy in Davos and I think that is because of Julian too. I'm not always looking for a lover as I was last year and I just think of hard work to make the time pass quickly.

There were other reasons for John's positivity. Throughout the summer Curry had pitched Davos to his friends as a winter idyll. Now, one by one, they were turning up to see him. Penny Malec had dropped by. Julian Pettifer, too. 'We'd gone along as the après ski,' recalls Penny. 'Drinks and fondues.' In the mornings, Curry gritted his teeth through his school figures. In the late afternoons – against the strict orders of Gersch – he hurtled down the mountains on a toboggan. Snowball fights and conversation had displaced morose self-doubt and nightmares about his father. Curry's relationship with Arnold Gerschwiler, however, was going downhill faster than his sledge.

Throughout early February, Davos had been blitzed by a snowstorm that seemed never-ending. At night, the shock waves of distant avalanches rattled the town's windows. By dawn, as the snowploughs carved open the streets, John trudged through fresh drifts for another bad-tempered session with Gerschwiler. 'Even if one completed a circle without being blown backwards at the halfway stage, one would sometimes look back only to see something like a mousetrail in the snow … feeling, all the while, as if we were freezing to death.'

Curry had seen enough. Earlier in the month he'd limped in four places behind Oundjian at the European Championships. As Gerschwiler and his pupil 'descended from the snowy wastes' for the World Championships in Lyons, the pair were no longer speaking. 'It was the cold that froze my rapport,' Curry explained. 'By the end of that winter we could not look at one another.'

Two months on an open-air rink had put his skating into reverse. On the 'untroubled perfection' of Lyons' indoor rink, John finished a lowly fourteenth, well behind his British rival. A few weeks later, Curry let Gerschwiler know that his Swiss precision was no longer required. 'John knew what he wanted, so he went,' says Heinz Wirz.

> One day John had come up to me and said; you know what 'Gersch' asked me today? He said jump in a way that people will know it's difficult and not so bloody easy. John had told him that things in ballet are difficult but still pretty and I want it to be like that. Gerschwiler was awful. Really really hard.

Humiliated and angry, the Swiss coach lashed out at his former pupil, telling him: 'You will never make it as a skater and you will never make it as a man.' By the time of his death in 2003, aged 89, Gerschwiler had grudgingly accepted that the first of his predictions might well have been wrong. The second one he was most certainly standing by. The 'ice devil', meanwhile, was alone again.

Three

'For the Morons'

On a dank day in Blackpool, barely a donkey ride from the Irish Sea, a few dozen holidaymakers are staring out across a patch of spot-lit ice. Suddenly, 30 skaters enter the auditorium at speed under thunderously amplified music. Sculpted men in pink bowler hats wearing tight red sparkling trousers. Slender girls – mostly – with peach-perfect posteriors and scarcely a square inch of flesh which doesn't shimmer or shine. It's fun, it's fast and its deliriously, athletically, good fun. But John Curry would have winced through every vulgar seaside second of it; and in 1971 this was the future that loomed.

These skaters spending their summers in Blackpool have come from, and have previously competed, all over the world. Each is a brilliant athlete but no longer interested in striving for amateur honours; this is what they do. Before the knees crumple, or the hip surgeons come calling, they're cashing in on their youth. It was a dilemma John Curry knew well. Three months with a travelling ice show, or a lifetime as a receptionist on Marylebone Road. He had faced it at 17, and in his twenty-second year he faced it again.

Every skater on the cusp knew the story. After another lacklustre tournament, there'd be a tap on the arm or a phone call, followed by an offer. For the very best, it would be Holiday On Ice, which came calling with its dollars. Since 1943, Holiday had been touring the United States and Europe, staging schmaltzy spectaculars stuffed with disillusioned amateurs who didn't gag at its skating dwarves or its cheesy themes. And if not Holiday On Ice, then maybe rival outfits like Ice Follies or Ice Capades, with Trixie the skating juggler warming up for the fabulous 16 dancing Ice-Capets, tonight performing 'Parade of the Wooden Soldiers'.

While his father was still alive, Holiday had offered the teenage Curry a three-year professional contract. When they refused to cede control over his choreography and costumes, John had turned his back. After his failure in Lyons, they came calling again, dangling £110 a week. Once again, they were rebuffed.

> To be told by the owner of the show that … I would never beat anyone in competitive skating and therefore I might as well accept his offer … was sufficient to make me more determined than ever. Back I would go to the chill of the bedsitter and the ice rink.

Or as he later put it: 'I would rather wash dishes.'

A radical new future was suggesting itself to John Curry, one in which he would set the parameters. Nothing would ever endear him to the gurning gloss of stadium ice shows. As with the prevailing machismo of competition, he was repulsed by it. From the beginning, he'd wanted to be a dancer and cherished skating as an art form in waiting, not merely a sub-species of gymnastics. Somehow, it had to be possible to imbue the glorious freedoms of the ice with the credibility, and repertoire, of ballet.

If he could somehow soften the calcified public perception of his sport; if he could somehow provide himself with a visible platform; maybe then he could take absolute control of a professional theatrical venture of his own; something bold; something to rattle even Holiday On Ice with its fists full of cash. 'It wasn't difficult to turn the money down. The reason I stuck it out was to win and [then] do what I really felt,' he explained.

Curry's single-minded ploy was land-mined with risk. By the early 1970s – like a fish in a torrent – he'd given himself only one way to go. The only way out, it seemed, was to prove Arnold Gerschwiler wrong and climb to the Olympic pinnacle of a sport he now longed to turn his back on. It was a forward orientation that suited his habitual separateness. 'I have a new exhibition to a Frank Sinatra song, "Ebb Tide",' he told Heinz. 'It is very slow and swirly and I do some very slow jumps at the start and then some very fast ones … just for the Morons.'

———

Curry's approach to the challenge was as brutally uncompromising as his view of his fellow human beings. Before leaving Lyons, and without the knowledge of the wounded Gerschwiler, John had introduced himself to a fashionable Canadian coach called Peter Dunfield. Twenty years before, Dunfield had competed with distinction in North America, but it was his 'modern attitude to teaching' that excited Curry and the two men quickly came to a private agreement. If John could pay his way, the Canadian would coach him for four months in New York between June and November. The 'if' amounted to a sum of around £700.

For a young man living out of a suitcase it was vast amount of cash. For a man with Curry's indifference to money, it was an obstacle of mountainous proportions. Back in London, however, reinstalled in Julian Pettifer's flat, Curry set about raising the funds. With Penny Malec's help he charmed a £400 overdraft out of his bank and with a further £300 loan (also courtesy of Malec) John was ready for what he called 'my exciting journey'. Favours and gifts from close acquaintances would always come easily to Curry. Repayment – although rarely demanded – would come a lot harder.

Throughout the spring of 1971, ahead of the trip John let his days drift. Since his split with Gerschwiler, he'd continued to practise at Richmond unfazed by the glowering proximity of his former coach. Revelling in his new-found freedom, Curry – to Gerschwiler's irritation – invited his ballet teacher to join him on the ice where unrestrained 'arm-waving' was now much in evidence. 'My new exhibition,' he wrote mischievously, 'is to music written specially for me by Chopin ... the encore (I am being very hopeful) is to the Russian dance from NUTCRACKER. Nice and short.'

The 'exhibition' Curry referred to was – to him – one of the irksome penalties of success. Major tournaments ran between December and March. Once they were over, the best skaters were dragooned on a short European tour – performing unrestricted programmes to paying audiences. As British champion, Curry's simmering presence was required. 'It is slave labour,' he spat, neglectful of the fact that his costs were borne by the National Skating Association, or that for once he could skate precisely as he wanted.

It was an obligation which once again accentuated John's growing isolation. 'He hated those tours,' remembers Heinz 'He had to share dressing rooms with farting, burping guys. There were very few people with the class that he had. They'd all come to do their tricks, and he didn't like that either.'

To ameliorate his distaste, Curry allowed himself contrasting distractions. In May, his mother had joined him during a short exhibition tour of France. 'We had a day in Paris … we walked for miles.' After dark, John promptly climbed into bed with a fellow skater from Britain. The exploratory inhibitions of Curry's first months in London had evaporated. 'John had sex not love,' explains David Barker. 'In the beginning it was all to do with sex.' It was also about breaking the law.

Startlingly blond, and with the looks to match, Barker had started ice dancing when he was 11. In May 1971 he was only 18. 'The law?' he says. 'I never concerned myself with those details. I just did it.' Although the career paths of the two men would cross again, their night together in France meant nothing to either. Barker found Curry 'boring and unspontaneous'. Curry, who was still proclaiming his love for Julian Pettifer, almost certainly felt the same about Barker. 'John had this grandness that made him unpopular with other skaters,' says Barker.

> We'd all flown out in a little plane to Lille and of course John wasn't there. He had to come a special way and arrive the day before or the day after … then we went to Paris and skated in the Grand Salon and instead of being with the group he went off somewhere special afterwards. It wasn't his gayness which caused him problems, it was his aloofness. If he'd been happy and smiling he'd have conquered that.

Nevertheless, by the end of June, Curry was in a state of high excitement. On the ice, his skating had acquired a confident new elegance, and the exhibitions – for all his grumbling – had satisfied an innate need to perform and to feel loved, if only by an audience of strangers. 'I love having people watch me,' he wrote. 'It inspires me to be better.'

> I have discovered I am very like – in my moods and home life – Marilyn Monroe. They say that she used to act in her bedroom by herself. Well you know, I do that … I must go and practise in front of the mirror. I must try and look very innocent and childlike. This is what Marilyn did … She had the <u>will</u> to be beautiful because she wanted everyone to love her.

More importantly, he felt certain that his balletic style was winning crucial admirers among even the 'morons'. Liberated from the steely governance of his two previous coaches, Curry confidently expected Peter Dunfield and America to embrace and complete him. Not for the first time (or the last) his optimism would prove catastrophically misjudged.

The forthcoming adventure, however, would inaugurate two of the most significant relationships in his life. One with a city. And the other with a woman.

————

Amid the sad knot of flotsam John left behind when he died, three items stand out: his British passports. From John Curry the fresh-faced 'student ice skater' to 'John Anthony Curry O.B.E', these battered documents chronicle a journey by way of the journeys they represent. Prague. Moscow. Geneva. Toronto. Amsterdam. Barcelona. Tokyo. Berlin. Stockholm. Madrid. Vancouver. Hono-lulu. Helsinki. Cairo. Oslo. And many more.

Faded visas. Scribbled signatures. Dates and departures. Baggage receipts. Airports and arrival halls. A mush of overlapping stamps in inks of every colour. Black, green, purple, pink and blue. Rectangles and circles. Squares and sticky labels. Only those marks that are beyond deciphering – the most blurred and blotted – keep their secrets. The rest, when carefully disentangled, trace out the gypsy arc of a lonely man's life. And one city above all dominates the list; the place where he would spend 15 years of his life; the city that first shocked, and then embraced him. New York.

> I am not very happy about New York. It is filthy dirty – smelly – overcrowded – dehumanised – and very very sordid. I have not been out yet because I feel quite sure that I shall be MUGGED – hit and robbed by thugs. So many awful things here. I'm quite frightened. Worst of all, most of the boys/men are fat!! I'm sure I shall be a virgin for the whole of the stay … PS. The other skaters are not very nice really but they are American so we must expect that.

With £100 in his pocket, John had touched down in New York on 20 June. The city, he said, 'was like a kettle about to blow its lid'.

Life there, he noted some years later in an ironic understatement, was 'full of extremes'. After six days he was penning pompous diatribes about Manhattan's squalor to Heinz Wirz. Barely a month later, he had fully integrated himself into a luxurious new nest and found himself a new 'mother' and lifelong benefactor in the process.

Throughout his life, Curry's knack for identifying besotted – mostly female – companions would cushion him from untold cold realities. In New York, as he reappraised the city's lascivious possibilities, he had been embraced by the most influential woman in the public storm that would become his life. And although it would eventually cause her both pain and joy, few people ever loved John Curry quite so long, or devotedly, as Nancy Streeter.

Born Nancy Angell in 1928, she had spent a lifetime living up to her surname. Her husband, Frank Streeter, was financial adviser to John Hay 'Jock' Whitney, then one of the world's wealthiest men. While Whitney mixed cocktails with Fred Astaire, or plotted presidential power with Dwight D. Eisenhower, Streeter adroitly juggled his employer's sprawling fortune. There was a lot to look after. Even at 22, Whitney was counting his millions in multiples, and Frank was well rewarded for his diligence.

By the 1970s success had taken the Streeters to East 72nd Street, New York, a stately apartment a few blocks out from Central Park. Rising from a low-ceilinged black and white tiled lobby, an elevator would open directly into sunlit quarters furnished in the manner of an English country retreat. Every horizontal surface sprouted forests of family photographs, and every wall bore the fruits of Frank's loyalty to 'Jock' Whitney. From his own father, Streeter had inherited a passion for collecting rare books and maps from the great age of exploration. On tome-heavy shelves, epic first editions – of pioneers like William Clark and Captain Cook – fought for space between fine oil paintings and antique plates.

Nancy Streeter had never needed to earn a living. In New York there were countless other outlets for her industry. Churches, hospitals, societies and schools; places run on goodwill and fuelled by philanthropy. Since she adored people – and was supremely well connected – Nancy's cultivated life was no less committed than her husband's. In her own words, 'When I get involved, I get involved pretty heartily.' If she was a housewife, then she was a gloriously well-endowed one, and for recreation she liked nothing better than the ice.

Now demolished, the New York Sky Rink was a city institution. It was perched on the sixteenth floor of an office block on West 33rd Street, its location alone making it unforgettable. The quality of its skaters made it more so. Everyone was welcome, but the Sky Rink – and the esteemed Skating Club of New York – had become a breeding ground for champions. 'There was no feeling of being cooped up,' remembers Dorothy Hamill, a future Olympic gold medal winner. 'It had huge windows that overlooked the New York skyline … It was almost a holy experience as the sunrise would fill the rink each day.'

Nancy Streeter worked on its management committee and was a capable skater herself. Her 14-year-old daughter Meg was training five hours a day there and flowering as an intermediate skater. Everyone knew Nancy, and – if they mattered – Nancy knew them, too. So when Peter Dunfield needed a billet for a promising English talent he'd found, his friends on East 72nd seemed the obvious choice. 'It was pure chance,' said Nancy, 'I had no idea six weeks would grow into so many years.'

The Streeters had three daughters, Meg, Ruth and Ellen. Overnight they had acquired a son (and 'brother') with such scrupulous charm that he slotted perfectly into their milieu of urbane good taste. Curry was upright, elegant and deported himself with the self-assurance of a young prince. He was also artistic and had a sharp sense of fun. Along with John's good looks and carefully crafted Englishness, the combination proved overpoweringly seductive. 'We all became close very quickly. It just fell into place,' explained Nancy, adding pointedly that 'it was clear he had not had a great deal of family life before'.

Indeed, John had never lived like this. Down on the tree-lined streets, ageing Hollywood stars popped into Neil's Coffee Shop for eggs over easy or into York Barbers (established 1828) for a wet shave. Stepping into the Streeter apartment from its private escalator, he crossed an entrance lobby festooned with curiosities, to enter a large twin-bedded room with its own en-suite facilities. For almost 20 years, this would be his – free of charge – whenever he needed it. All he had to do was pick up the phone.

East 72nd would become his New York comfort and his hiding place. It would be this apartment he rang within minutes of winning his Olympic gold. And it would be here that he told Nancy he was

HIV positive, many years before he breathed a word to his own mother. After his glorious triumphs, she dubbed his quarters 'the golden room' or 'the enchanted room' and, many years after his death, the memory of his presence there could still move her to tears.

John was to be no mere lodger. From the beginning, almost everything the Streeters now did included the bashful young skater. At the weekends there would be ballet, the theatre or the movies, and when summer baked the city they'd tumble into the family station wagon, tune the radio to a music station and head for their country retreat in Connecticut. 'We were a normal all-American family,' recalls Meg Streeter. 'There was a nice chemistry.'

On the Atlantic shoreline Curry would work tirelessly on his tan, often alone. In the evenings, they would gather for ping-pong or rumbustious meals on the patio. 'We would tease him. We would never allow him to take himself too seriously,' remembers Ellen Streeter, then 19. 'He was quite square. Everything with John seemed to be from the past, so he began to absorb that era through teenage eyes.'

In these early days, no one doubted his sexuality or questioned his motives. Frank Streeter was not threatened by his 43-year-old wife's new companion, and to his teenage daughters he was an alluring, if enigmatic, bundle of possibilities. 'I don't think I even knew there *were* people who were gay. I was just thinking this is nice. This guy's handsome. This guy's shy,' remembers Ellen. 'At first he was a little overwhelmed by us. Were all so New York chatty chatty chatty. Like a houseful of girls. Then gradually there was transition. From a shy boy into something a little more hip; into a force. In the company of lively New York girls ... and Nancy.'

In the early weeks, John had told Heinz the Streeters were 'very nice indeed – rather formal – but very nice'. Years later he deleted the qualification. 'One of the nicest homes I had ever been in,' he admitted, 'with the most tranquil home atmosphere I had experienced.' This was not Acocks Green. There were no ghosts and precious few secrets. At a very early stage, John felt sufficiently comfortable to tell Nancy about Julian and his feelings for men. In the afternoons they would discuss Nureyev together over a pot of Earl Grey tea. And when her husband came home from work Frank would reach for one of his beloved books, not a bottle of brandy.

'John and Nancy surprised all of us,' says Meg Streeter. 'I have a feeling that she was maybe the first person who really sat down and listened to what his vision was beyond competing. She was a History of Arts major and always had her finger on the arts world and I think initially they connected on that level.' After that it became much deeper. 'I think she was able to draw him out personally,' adds Ellen. 'Trust became the key. He realised that he could trust her. He needed a stable person in his life. A lot of people in his life didn't have that quality.'

It wouldn't be an easy journey for Nancy. In the coming years, she would travel alone to Europe to watch John skate. Her vibrant correspondence would prop him up when he was down. Her advice would steer him through the public hell of coming out in 1976. She'd see him garlanded onstage at the New York Met with the city at his feet. And she would be there as, one by one, his friends and ex-lovers began to die.

But much as John loved and periodically needed her, he could not sustain the role of a natural son. Dutifully, he would shower her with letters but later, as he tasted New York's 'extremes', Curry began to drift away. As Heinz Wirz already knew, and others would soon discover, John Curry was not overendowed with sentiment. As he moved forward, people – and possessions – very often got left behind.

———

The fear had gone. For six weeks, Curry soaked up everything New York could offer. 'He was just radiating this sense of wonder,' recalls Meg. Every afternoon, after six hours' training at Sky Rink, he'd wander alone, from block to block, popping into galleries or gazing winsomely into store windows. 'He was like an artistic sponge. Music. Books. Window displays. He'd suck it in. He was beaming with this sense of what people can do.' Only one familiar issue was casting its shadow. By mid-August, the relationship with his third coach was in tatters.

As always, it had started well. But after John had been in New York for just six weeks, construction work at the rink had required Dunfield to shift his classes to Toronto. Overnight, Curry's pampered sojourn with the Streeter family had been curtailed. 'A disaster ... a disaster for all of us,' he grumbled. After Manhattan, Toronto seemed dismal, and, shorn of his new 'family', Curry felt his Davos demons resurface. 'Feeling very lonely,' he told a friend. 'My skating seems to be getting worse by the minute.' And, as always, so was his mood. Peter Dunfield had never encountered anything like it. The boy's skating was – as he put it – 'strong and sensitive at the same time', but the Englishman's demeanour was a disgrace.

'In England he'd not been exposed to any opposition to what he did ... he didn't know how to cope with other big personalities around him,' says Dunfield. Back at the New York rink, the Canadian had already been required to arbitrate in spats triggered by Curry's 'rude actions and comments'. Relocated in Canada – and once again housed with a local family – John discovered that Dunfield's Toronto class was crammed with brilliant athletes. 'Every session was a competition and John just couldn't take it.'

As the ice shuddered with high-speed jumpers, Curry went into retreat. 'I didn't condemn his style,' insists Dunfield:

> It was his attitude. I never saw him sweat. He was more worried about the twist of a wrist than the triple jump. Also, in figure skating you might have to fall a few times and he didn't want to fall ... He was defeated. He had always been the best, but no one there was giving way. There was a glass mirror at one end so the skaters could check their positions and John just stood there and posed, so naturally people would hit him when they passed him because he didn't keep moving.

Curry was in turmoil. Not only did Dunfield's exhortations to 'get tough and be more manly' revolt him, but he also baulked at being told – repeatedly – that he was too old to win tournaments. 'Some of the harsh comments were not easily borne when I thought of the £400 that had purchased them,' he noted icily. Curry was 22 years old and the British champion. With Gerschwiler he'd been in control. He'd enjoyed his own music and his own space. In Toronto, the 'Morons' were closing in; and all of them skating like spinning tops. Only one man had caught his eye.

Two years before, Heinz Wirz had seen Toller Cranston skating and warned John that he might have a rival. Now for the first time they were on the ice together. Born in Hamilton, Ontario, the extravagantly named Toller Shalitoe Montague Cranston shared both John's age and his conviction that skating could elevate itself beyond the pedestrian bounds of sport. Over the next five years, their rivalry would generate one of the most curious sporting duels of all time. In the years beyond that, at different times, they would share and sack the same co-producer; endure separate but comparably disastrous experiences in business; and very publicly hate each other's guts.

In August 1971, however, they were strangers united by an experience that was crippling them both. 'Toronto that summer was the epicentre of skating in the world,' says Toller.

> There were no known skaters who were not on that ice. French champion. Austrian champion. American pairs champion. Haig Oundjian, I think. John Curry and me. I was nothing at that time. None of us could hack it in that environment. At the end of that summer I could not take it and I was ready to write a note saying I was quitting.

Subsequently, Curry never once mentioned seeing Cranston in Toronto. Perhaps the memory was too raw. But for Peter Dunfield, the fledgling rivalry between the two men had been the defining narrative of his summer. Session after session, he says, Cranston's bravado trumped Curry's posturing on the ice. 'When he trained, Toller didn't stop for 60 minutes. He was extrovert. Innovative. Athletic. Toller was never going to give and if he wanted an area of the rink, Toller got the rink. It blew John away. He lasted about a month and then he had to leave.'

Curry's sexuality, however – Dunfield insists – played no part. 'I knew all about that. It's not unusual in this sport but it wasn't offensive. Other skaters were entranced by their exposure to his [Curry's] movement on the ice but not by his attitude or his conduct. For me it was simple. Either he got with the programme or he left.' So Curry left.

His exit, when it came, was swift. In late August, after a dismal dawn session working on his school figures, Curry studied the shapes he'd left in the ice. 'Terrible, miserable figures,' he said. 'I looked at them and thought, "This is ridiculous … you are homesick … what are you doing here?"' Within two hours he was checking out flights back to London; by mid-afternoon he was airborne. The following morning, Julian Pettifer was at Gatwick airport to meet him. '[He] was obviously very nervous,' Curry wrote to Nancy:

> He could not even smile at me. Julian just had time to drive me to London and then he had to go straight to Heathrow and get a flight to Hong Kong on route to China. We had a chance to talk and he told me that he had been living with someone else while I was away and that he now felt very badly about it all and dishonest. To put you more in the picture, this other person has been visiting us and going out with us all the time I have known Julian – and he knew Julian before I did ... hardly the homecoming I have been thinking about for the past three months.

By lunchtime, Curry was sitting crestfallen on a train to Birmingham. It was unfortunate timing. Assuming her son to be in Canada, Rita had left just a few hours before for a short holiday in Scotland. 'The world has quite fallen from under my feet,' he told Nancy.

For the next three days, Curry lived alone in an empty family house full of complex memories. It was no place for an unhappy man with jetlag and a propensity for despair. 'I really wish that whatever controls me would leave me alone for some time,' he had once told Heinz. On the bed he'd slept in as a child, he curled up and wept, alone 'at the bottom of a deep pit [with] no interest in climbing out'.

By the time his mother returned, John was famished and frantic – 'at a very low ebb' – but it was almost certainly far worse than that. According to one account, Curry told Rita he'd be better off dead. Suddenly very little in his life seemed on track any more.

During his months in North America, his friendship with Julian Pettifer had begun to cool. Before Curry flew to New York, the two men had rarely seen each other. Now they were often living and working on different continents. 'Absence certainly does not make the heart grow fonder' was how Pettifer put it. 'Propinquity propinks.' Soon after his return, Curry had moved out of the journalist's flat, leaving Pettifer puzzled ever after by the skater's portrait of their time together. 'I am deeply saddened to discover John had such thoughts,' he says. 'He never spoke to me in those terms. I never spoke to him in those terms.'

However mutual their feelings had been – and for whatever reasons Curry might have exaggerated them – the experience left him nursing a sorrow that endured for many years. 'Quite by accident I turned on the TV and saw Julian the other day,' he wrote a few months later. 'Usually if this happens I turn off quickly but this time I did not. Now I feel so sad and full of emptiness. It is hard to live with a broken heart. Wonder if I'll ever feel differently?'

Since leaving home, Curry's relationship with his mother had been under periodic strain too. 'Mother has a habit of making me nervous and that makes me works badly,' he complained. Much as he adored her, he was abysmal at maintaining regular contact. During his New York summer, it had been Nancy who'd kept Rita informed. 'I used to know more or less where he was but he was a bit lax,' she says. Even Haig Oundjian had picked up on John's neglect. 'He was very rough, terribly rough, on Rita. But he was like that. He could suddenly switch off.'

Occasionally he would hitch-hike north from London to see her, but his letters and phone calls had become so infrequent that Rita shared her feelings of maternal dislocation with her Solihull friends. As a result, one of them had even contacted Curry directly, telling him he'd 'broken his mother's heart'.

> It [her letter] was so horrible I never even finished reading it; she said I was selfish and nasty and everything bad … Oh! I feel awful. I am going to write Mother a nice letter today … I'm going to tell how I feel about her and say it is not her I don't like, it is all the other things, like Michael.

John and his older brother Michael had never been close as children. Andrew, on the other hand, had remained a steady presence. Quiet and wisely measured, the middle brother had been left short of self-confidence by his years spent quarantined by tuberculosis. His was a softer, less accusing disposition than John's and the two always dovetailed well.

In Solihull, Andrew had fraternised harmoniously with John's skating friends. In London, he'd taken John to the theatre to see musicals. Occasionally, he'd even passed on his clothes to his impoverished younger brother. 'I'm sure he knows about me,' wrote John revealingly. 'But he would never speak about it. He is so kind.' Rita, on the other hand, appeared to know nothing about 'it', and Andrew would eventually be told only that he 'didn't really like girls'.

It was John's way to be oblique. Where possible he preferred hints to overt disclosure. Besides, in the early 1970s homosexuals rarely revealed their inclinations unless absolutely necessary. Gay men didn't formally come out. The risks were simply too high. If they were lucky, awareness dawned kindly on those around them. If they were not, they merely continued living the lie.

In the circumstances, Curry's 'low ebb' was understandable, but Acocks Green was no longer the place to turn it around. During his years in London, the family's financial health had worsened. The property in Ireland had been sold, and Warwick Road would shortly go the same way. Rita was moving a few miles north to a two-bedroom flat overlooking Sutton Park. 'I was sad to leave but it had never felt the same after Joseph's death,' she says. Whatever had gone wrong in Toronto wouldn't be put right at 'home'. After three weeks' contemplation, Curry caught the train to London where, once again, it would be a woman who reassembled the pieces and put him back on the ice.

———

No one had emerged with credit from the Toronto debacle, but not all the blame lay with John Curry. Like Perren and Gerschwiler before him, Peter Dunfield had utterly failed to penetrate the complex mindset of his troubled young student. Ordering him to 'man up' had merely emphasised the canyon that had always separated John from his contemporaries. It wasn't that he couldn't skate like a muscle-bound East European. He simply chose not to. And until he found a coach prepared to work with, and not against him, then Curry seemed destined to be seen as a brilliant, but peripheral, novelty act.

Behind the frustration, his strategy remained clear. In New York he had informed Nancy Streeter that he was going to win the Olympics and then launch his own ice dance company. Although that prospect looked distant – the 1972 Sapporo Winter Olympics were less than six months away – Curry now had someone at his side who might actually change his fortunes. Even as his relationship with Dunfield was imploding, he had been secretly wooing a successor. Once again, Curry's dramatic posturing had disguised a chilling ruthlessness.

Alison Smith was a dark-haired, no-nonsense skater who'd turned professional at eighteen. She lived by the Thames with her widower father, a nuclear physicist, in a grand Victorian apartment block. The young Canadian skater Patricia Dodd was a neighbour. Richmond and its ice rink were her second home. Arnold Gerschwiler had formerly been Alison's coach and, unlike John, she'd grown to respect the Swiss grandee. Those feelings were clearly mutual. By late 1970 he'd invited her to join his paid teaching staff under the Richmond rink's imposing arches.

When Arnold and John clashed, it was always Alison he turned to for help. 'He didn't want John to do any arm-waving as he called it and I saw the whole thing in a different light because I was an arm-waver myself.' A ray of light had broken through. Four years older than John, Alison also loved music and ballet. They also had mutual acquaintances – Heinz Wirz was a good friend to them both – and Alison's indifference to John's sexuality was authentic and persuasive.

'Arnold totally totally totally had a problem with John being gay. That's what the big problem was,' explains Alison. 'He was always trying to cover it up in John's skating and I was setting the bird free. That's basically all it was. Setting the bird free.'

Even before his final winter in Davos, John had been entranced by Alison. Four mornings a week, Gerschwiler had allowed Alison to work with his tiresome pupil. 'She makes me feel like working even when I don't want to. CLEVER GIRL,' gushed John. 'So cool and calm and helpful,' he told Nancy. After she'd successfully ironed out a long-standing technical problem with his backward jumps, Curry was sold. Arnold out; Alison in. Whatever the pain, he would have what he wanted. It was a hallmark John Curry putsch.

In the limbo weeks before his trip to North America, Curry and Smith had worked discreetly together. Once he was in New York, he bombarded her with letters. 'He was saying he couldn't stand it there and he wanted to come back. At first I said no and then I got the final letter that asked me straight out whether I would like to teach him, so I said yes … and when I showed Arnold the letter he was absolutely furious. He said, "Do you honestly think you can teach him?" But that year John moved up from fifteenth to twentieth in Europeans and Worlds and his success came as a huge shock for Arnold.'

Gerschwiler's wrath was unbounded. Richmond had been his fiefdom since 1937. His pupils included Princess Anne and the Hollywood actor James Mason. To have been dumped by John Curry was bad enough. To be usurped by one of his own junior coaches was a humiliation too far. 'From that time,' observed Curry, 'it seemed to Alison and me that normal levels of internal cooperation and goodwill at the rink had disappeared. It got to the point where both of us dreaded an impending training session.'

Curry and Smith had become, as he put it, 'untouchables'. And for once John had someone with whom to share his feelings of isolation. Frozen out by Arnold and his team, the pair withdrew into themselves, propelled by a smouldering sense of shared injustice. They grew tighter on the ice and closer off it. For the first time, Curry had a coach who completely understood and accepted him. It was only just in time.

Curry's year of trauma and plotting had finally caught up with his skating. In December 1971, Haig Oundjian had reclaimed the British title. Few sports demand such relentless attention to detail and Curry had become distracted. Under Alison Smith, that swiftly changed. He still baulked at the disciplines of school figures, and he still burned with impatience – 'I spent most of my time holding onto my temper' – but unlike Curry's previous coaches, Alison had a secret weapon: their mutual friend Heinz Wirz. When Curry was proving especially difficult, Smith would invite John's ex-lover over from Switzerland for the weekend. Appropriately briefed, Heinz would then find time alone on the rink with Curry. 'I'd suggest to him it would be a good idea if you took this line or that, and this was all because Alison had told me in advance. We both loved him, you see.'

Sheltered within this triumvirate, Curry flourished. Since Alison placed no boundaries on his free skating, John's jumping began to improve. 'I allowed him to be himself on the ice, and if he wanted more arm movements in a programme, then we put more in.'

Nobody had handled him like this before. No two people knew him so well or seemed so unwilling to judge.

It was a safety net that extended way beyond the rink. Although NCR had kept his job open, Curry had nowhere to live. In New York, Nancy Streeter had promised him an open door and a bed. In London, for the next five years, Alison Smith and her father would do the same. 'It was right on the rink; right on the river,' says Alison:

> We'd come out of the engine room door of the rink and it was literally like 20 steps into the apartment. He'd sometimes sleep in my room, and then – because he travelled a lot – I'd sleep in my father's room. Or he had a very beautiful leather sofa and John would sometimes fall asleep listening to music in there. If he brought a 'friend' back with him they'd be in the living room, so I just minded my own business. I didn't care …

Nor did Alison's bounty end there. If he had the money, Curry paid for his lessons. If he didn't, Smith worked for free. Her rewards, when they came, were more nebulous than cash. John Curry's fortunes were suddenly on the move, and his passport was filling up fast. In January 1972, her protégé had finished fifth in the European Championships at Gothenburg, Sweden, one place behind Haig Oundjian. For the first time, Nancy Streeter had travelled from New York to see him and John's appreciation was effusive.

> I did enjoy our meals together and seeing the skating with you made it nicer for me, but most of all I enjoyed our talks. I think it was really wonderful. Your being there was such a compliment to me and my skating.

The following month, Curry was in Japan for the Sapporo Olympics, where he finished a disappointing tenth, six places behind Haig Oundjian, and one behind the fast-rising Canadian Toller Cranston. The experience, however, had left an unexpected mark. At the opening ceremony, as helicopters showered pink roses over the national teams, Curry seethed at the 'blasé dilettantes' who mocked the Union Jack with 'ribald and facetious jokes'. 'I longed for someone to be standing near me who would share the same feelings, but those around me seemed to find yet another excuse for a snigger or a slice of cheap sarcasm.' 'The British team is the largest collection of snobs imaginable,' he complained to Nancy.

> Having very little snow in GB and no mountains at all, the bobsleigh skiers all train in St Moritz 'old chap' and as we have no sponsorship this means they are all rich 25–35 year olds. We must be the only team to have a Prince as a reserve bobsleigh man. TRUE. Prince Michael. Sometimes being a commoner is just gross.

Curry was nothing if not conflicted. To strangers, his lifelong streak of patriotic conservatism seemed at odds with the acrid asides and the unconventional private life. To intimates, it had always been this way. 'He was a bit of a prig, but he was not a cynic,' says Penny Malec. 'He thought being British was tremendously important.' Although he eschewed politics, Curry's instincts, like his accent, were old Tory and deeply unfashionable. After being detained by two police inspectors for fare dodging on the London Underground, he'd written indignantly: 'Me a criminal. Can you imagine? I told them my name was Bunny. They did not like that at all. You could tell they were strictly lower class. Ha ha.'

During the investiture of Prince Charles three years earlier, in 1969, John had wept in front of his television set, and it was not uncommon for members of the Royal Family to feature in his nightly reveries. 'The Queen was lovely, as she always is, in my dreams,' he told Heinz. In life, it seemed, as in art, he was invariably drawn to the rarefied end of the spectrum. The 'common' man would always be a stranger to him and – in many ways – the 1960s appeared to have passed him by entirely.

Curry's nationalistic pride was authentic – and unfashionable – but no one had expected him to win in Japan. After reclaiming his British title, Haig Oundjian had travelled east as the British Number One. All the pressure had been on him. For years, his father had been urging him to quit; warning him that prejudice against the Oundjian name would always block his way. In Sapporo on the first day, despite having flu, he'd been just one place off the bronze medal position after seven of eight compulsory school figures.

It just blew me. I was already nursing a fever. Me, fourth in the Olympics. Oh my God. I just blew it and completely bottled the last figure. Even though I went on to do the best free skate of my life, it didn't matter. I'd gone back to ninth with that one figure which meant there were eight to free skate after me and they never give top marks if there are eight to come. They hold them back. John Curry fell over on or missed both his triples and got higher marks from the British judge than me. You can't refute that can you? My father always said I was never going to make it. This is the British way.

It was to be Haig Oundjian's last hoorah. Hampered by an old ankle injury, he withdrew from the following month's World Championships in Calgary and would never skate competitively again. No longer restrained, he went public to lambast bias in the marks of British skating judges. 'When John came eighth overall, the British judge has him fifth. When I come overall third, the British judge has me fourth. What does that tell you, event after event?' When the National Skating Association banned him for a year, he told them he'd already quit. Perhaps his father had been right. The British 'way' had got him at last.

———

Curry had been inspired by Sapporo. Alison Smith had been inspired by John Curry. Although the NSA had been unable to pay for her airfare, the two friends had stayed in touch by telephone throughout. 'We had some special music we both liked to listen to and I'd open the window in my Richmond flat and put it on full belt so it would fly over there to lift him.' From the moment he returned, the race was on. By 1976, the date of the next Winter Olympics, he would be 26. One last chance. There was nothing else he could do.

'There should be nothing less than perfection,' he told Nancy. 'At the moment I am so inspired I could explode with what I feel to be inside me. I want to work and work for – something!'

Tirelessly, Curry threw himself into the challenge. It didn't make him any easier. There were still filthy arguments between coach and pupil. 'She felt his cruelty,' says Heinz. 'He could be really, really hard – really scary – and Alison suffered from it a great deal.' Unlike previous coaches, however, Smith had taken the time to work Curry out. If a storm was coming, she could often with Heinz's covert help circumnavigate the worst of it. And should the storm actually break, she knew how to make Curry laugh:

> For instance, John hated back paragraph brackets [one of the compulsory school figures] and I'd see the mood he was in before the lesson so I'd think, let's really get him in a mood. It's supposed to be perfect circles and he'd probably miss the axis of the turn by half a foot and I'd stop him and put him right, then next time half a foot became a foot, so I wouldn't take any notice, then he'd miss it half a foot on the other side. So we played this game and I'd say you've got to go round six times and of course he was laughing inside, then suddenly we'd both be openly laughing about it.

No one had ever manipulated Curry before. 'Without Alison,' he admitted in 1987, 'I would not have been able to make it because Alison held me up during the hardest period ... because she liked the way I skated ... without her it would not have worked out.'

> Was he temperamental? Yes. Would I let him get away with it? No. Three hundred and sixty-five days of the year, maybe ten he was extremely difficult, but I had other students to teach, so had to be able to switch off and carry on. If he started being silly and doing the opposite to what I'd told him to do, I'd let him do it. I'd say I'm obviously more interested in winning than you are. But then John's a genius. You're always going to have these ups and downs. When he knew he'd lost the battle I'd get a bunch of flowers and a letter apologising. He was a totally class act.

Curry had found the dream coach – a contemporary coach; ears and eyes open to the modern world. Every day, usually for around five hours, he would work on the ice. On at least two days a week he was also continuing his London lessons in modern and classical dance. In September, he'd even performed at Coventry Cathedral with 14 girls from the Elmhurst Ballet School. 'Needless to say I am the only male in the entire production unless you count Albinoni who wrote some of the music,' he informed Nancy. 'Tonight I had dinner in the school dining room with about seventeen girls!! That's a lot of women even for me.'

It helped that there were no significant distractions elsewhere. Although John's evenings still revolved around London's gay clubs, he very rarely came home with company. 'I've never had so many good glances from people, even the leather ones,' he told Heinz after a night in the Coleherne: 'I made a date with a boy about my age and I'm sure you would approve. Last week I saw him somewhere dressed in leather and we smiled at one another but he was with someone dressed as a cowboy … I came home alone (as bloody usual) … Love and miss you John.'

Leather clothing – and one-night stands – would subsequently become a feature of John's other life. But in 1972, as December approached, very little got in the way of his skating. Early that month, with Oundjian now retired, Curry effortlessly reclaimed the British figure skating title. He would hold it without interruption until 1975, and only a young tyro called Robin Cousins would ever remotely threaten his perch.

Other, more insidious, things were corroding Curry's state of grace that winter. Like all amateur skaters, his attendance at international events was managed, and underwritten, by the National Skating Association. It was the NSA that planned his trips and booked the flights. It was the NSA that ran the rule over his outfits and his choice of music. And like all such organisations, the NSA accorded the sport's rules with the weight of biblical commandments.

Nonconformists like John Curry unsettled them, even more so when paired with unknown quantities like Alison Smith. Ever since his teenage years, Curry had kicked at skating's codes. Now firmly entrenched as Britain's Number One, he felt empowered to kick them even harder. Only the year before, Curry had fired off a bitter broadside in their direction: 'The English judges don't like me to free skate in black!! I think they are completely wrong because it looks so nice. They want me to have a green suit, all one colour. I suppose I must do it if I ever want to win in England. Anyway, we shall see about that later.'

Battle lines had been clearly drawn. Curry's balletic unorthodoxy on one side; the sport's establishment on the other. There were no formal groups, no identifiable cliques. This was a whispering war, waged between conflicting attitudes, and as the competition season progressed into 1973 it was clear which camp had dominance. As Curry expressed it, 'I felt like I was working a whole year to learn a poem and then having to recite it to deaf people.'

At the World Championships in Bratislava, he'd finished a dazzling fourth but still couldn't silence the negative backchat. 'Curry's art not fully appreciated' was the *Guardian*'s headline, above copy which stated that although 'Curry's graceful skating has earned him the name "Nureyev of the Ice" … there are many who do not wish skating to progress along such balletic lines'.

Even Canada's greatest ice acrobat had stepped up among the naysayers. Donald Jackson was a high-jumping, four-time national champion who'd performed the first triple lutz ever seen in open competition. 'Many judges will not give high marks to someone who makes it look so easy,' he declared. It was a bizarre observation.

In his pomp, Jackson had made it look easy, too. The difference was that the Canadian's performances ran on testosterone while the British skater's did not. Once again, Curry would be required to defend himself. 'I don't think that anything I do is vaguely effeminate or feminine at all,' he insisted, 'I don't think that any movement I do looks bad on a male body.'

Some years later – when his fame was threatening to overwhelm him – Curry would take sweet revenge on Jackson in a television documentary he presented exploring the difference between their two styles. First he shows a black and white film clip of the Canadian skating to a piece of classical music. Next, Curry himself performs to the same recording.

Where Jackson leaps, Curry glides. Where Jackson bustles and grins, Curry beckons sensuously. Where Jackson dazzles and spins, Curry creates fluid shapes. Both men make their craft look easy, but only the Canadian's moves are wantonly telegraphed. And only one man transcends. 'I tried to incorporate the jumps into a framework that was not just preparation jump preparation jump … because I think the jump is much more effective if one doesn't expect it.'

Details; with Curry it was all about details. Every skater choreographed their jumps. Curry choreographed down to his fingertips. Everything he wore and every arm movement was meticulously prepared. Every piece of music he ever selected was chosen for a reason. Historically, skaters had favoured classical crowd-pleasing beats, hoping to land their jumps on a giant chord or a cymbal crash. For John Curry, who had skipped up his childhood stairs to the rhythms in his head, the music was everything. Heinz Wirz, in particular, had always been in awe of Curry's musicality.

> Whatever piece he was using as the basis for a programme, he went to read the books; went to see the plays; and went to the museums to see period costumes. This was always how he wanted it to be. He had one Tchaikovsky programme – 6th Symphony, I think – and he read thousands of things on Tchaikovsky. He had to know how Tchaikovsky felt and only then could he start to put things together. Sometimes he would work on something for two or three months and then abandon it.

Now Alison Smith was fathoming the depths of her student's passion. In a lifetime's disregard for possessions, few things mattered more to Curry than his record collection. And nothing made him happier than music. 'To me the music said exactly what it wanted me to do and I just did it. It wasn't a chore. It was the part I enjoyed most.'

'He'd suddenly fall in love with something like *Cavalleria rusticana* [an Italian opera by Mascagni],' says Smith. 'My father would have bought all the latest hi-fi equipment and I'd come into the apartment in the afternoon and he'd have the headphones on and be singing along. You just don't get that kind of culture now.'

In Bratislava – to predictably negative mutterings – Curry had skated to a piece of sitar music by Ravi Shankar, wearing a jacket picked up on Kensington Market. In December 1973 – at the British Championships in Richmond – he performed his short programme to a Scott Joplin ragtime piano. No one had ever taken such liberties with tradition. According to one national newspaper, his daring had 'caused a sensation'. Some audience members had even laughed out loud.

In a letter to Nancy Streeter, Curry confirmed as much. 'They laughed and smiled all the way through and clapped a good deal. The judges on the other hand were shocked by the overall "fem" effect.' It was true. For many British officials, this was all too much.

'I must say I did enjoy shocking those old fogies,' said John. But the 'fogies' were growing restless. 'General laughter during the compulsories is unheard of,' grumbled one of them. It was time to do something about Curry and Smith.

A few weeks later – as they were leaving for the 1974 European Championships in Zagreb – a letter arrived from the NSA. Inside was a cheque for £20, and a letter requesting that Curry desist from skating to the Scott Joplin soundtrack.

> We started laughing. We were furious about it. It was a fantastic programme. John had tap danced and done a change foot sit spin all to the beat of the music. Wonderful, but the NSA didn't like it. It was too advanced for the old fuddy-duddies. So we changed it for the Europeans – he did all the elements without using his arms – and he still got a standing ovation. In the end we spent the twenty quid on tickets for the ballet.

Ever since his Davos exhibitions, Curry had sensed that the public were way ahead of the administrators. Unacquainted with skating's rulebooks, audiences followed their hearts and this ethereal Englishman stirred them. In 1970, while winning the St Gervais International, he'd noticed 'a few people moved to tears by my slow section'. In Prague the previous November, a Czech audience had been roused by his Indian dance. Finally, in Zagreb, the passion of his skating had decisively got through to the judges. He hadn't won – he'd got the bronze medal – but for the first time in a major tournament Curry had finished on the podium.

He should have been happy, but he was not. Throughout the previous year, Curry's inexorable march up the rankings had been mirrored by a deepening sense of solitary desperation. After the champions tour of 1973 – the obligatory post-tournament circus – he'd returned to his private darkness. This was the old John Curry, beset with anxiety.

> I long to feel something permanent in my life; some reason for myself. Think back to when we were 17 and 18 … It seems not long ago but it was SEVEN years … I came to your room and listened to some music. We were strangers then, Hene. There must be something more to living than what I feel. There must

be fire not only warmth. When I skated on the tour I felt so wonderful. I felt alive. The whole of my body and my soul lived for those minutes. Since then I've been waiting for something; just sitting feeling nothing again.

It's not much to want to feel alive is it? Youth is such a glorious, precious time and my youth is spent waiting. Every day should be full of life.

In London, Curry had friends, but not partners. A charismatic young Welshman called Roger Roberts had drifted into his orbit but, as with Julian Pettifer, no one seemed sure whether he was a lover or a companion. 'John told me he was the most beautiful person he'd ever seen,' recalls Penny Malec. 'He said I had to meet him and, yes, he was a truly lovely person. Very much at ease with his sexuality. Laughed all the time. I even met a couple of Roger's boyfriends. One was black, the other Asian, which John was a bit iffy about. John would have said, "Oh, Roger likes black boys". He could be very sniffy when he wanted to be.'

For the next 20 years, the two men would stay close. While Curry lived in London, Roberts was a housing officer in Brixton. When Curry moved permanently to New York, Roberts took a job running a basement restaurant off Times Square. If any letters passed between them, none have survived. In due course, both men would be consumed by the AIDS epidemic, and when Roberts died before him – in truly grim circumstances – Curry was devastated.

John had once said to Heinz, 'There seems to be no end to my loneliness.' Even Nancy Streeter was no stranger to his hopeless sense of isolation. Earlier in the year, during his exhibition tour, he'd reached out to her as never before:

Do you think that it is my fault that I feel lonely – even when in the midst of all this hectic activity? Is it because I don't let people come too close to me – by people I mean people one just sees every now and then and does not really know. I am very lonely. I'm neither fish nor flesh and the sun is too bright – the shadows too dark. The other skaters look on at me as a strange being. I love skating but the judges see my skating as symptoms of homosexuality. They really do. It is not easy to be judged by a pack of fools who know nothing of art. I feel out of step with a hostile world. What should I do? I'm sure all the trouble is all inside myself.

Skating was to blame. Since childhood, Curry had isolated himself and isolation was its consequence. Sacrificing his adolescence had rendered him socially naïve. When he was away from the rink, his prickly hauteur often turned to shyness and his sexuality compounded the constant nag of detachment.

> I try to be a very private person. I think that's partly due to the solitary life learning to skate. I was always pretty private as a child. The ice was a world where I could go and be free and alone and that suited me. Maybe it's because one is shy that one needs that place where one can come out and feel free.

One critical aspect of John Curry's fortunes had finally improved, however. For the first time in his life he had some money.

––––––

Curry was no stranger to uninvited advances from older men. But Ed Mosler was different. Moments after his fourth place finish in Bratislava the previous February, Mosler had sought the Englishman out. As Curry fretted, the balding stranger peppered him with compliments. 'Your skating has given me a great deal of pleasure over the last three years,' he told him. 'I'd like to help you.' Puzzled – and understandably suspicious – Curry politely steered the stranger away. The following day, Mosler was back. '[He] walked up to me, laughed and said: "You don't really know who I am, do you?" and I had to admit that I did not.'

Few Americans skaters would have made the same mistake. In Cincinnati in 1848 Ed's great-grandfather Gustave Mosler had founded what became the largest safe-making company in the world. It was a Mosler vault that guarded the nation's gold reserves in Fort Knox. In Washington it was a Mosler safe that housed the Declaration of Independence and the Bill of Rights. After the family business was sold in 1968, Ed Mosler had turned his energies – and his fortune – towards less commercial pursuits. Firstly, his vast collection of mechanical money boxes, and, secondly, his near-obsessive love of ice skating.

By the early 1970s, Mosler's largesse – channelled through a charitable foundation – had already helped dozens of American skaters. No targets were ever set, no stipulations were ever made and his only return appeared to be the pleasure he took from excellence. Few major tournaments were not marked by his discreet presence, and, without exception, the skaters seemed to love him.

Unmarried and softly spoken, Mosler – with his square, jowly chin and drooping nose – offered an antidote to the poison of competition. He was also fiercely loyal. Whenever one of 'his' skaters won a medal, it was rumoured he presented them with an engraved Tiffany decanter filled with melted ice from the winning rink. If they'd finished first, tiny flakes of gold would be dispersed in the liquid. If they'd finished second, the flakes would be silver.

That Curry had no idea who'd approached him was not surprising. Until Bratislava, Mosler's cash oiled only American wheels. Anything else seemed absolutely contrary to the rules. For years he'd been quietly admiring John Curry while feeling powerless to intervene. In Czechoslovakia, for whatever reason, Mosler had broken this long silence with an initial offer of £500 for Curry's travel and training. More was likely to follow. 'Rather dazed' was Curry's reaction. His days demonstrating cash registers looked to be over. 'From that day on, I really didn't have to think about money.'

Back in London there was a cool response from the National Skating Association. A British winner backed by American cash might become embarrassing. On the other hand, the NSA had little money and seemed incapable of finding Curry a sponsor. 'There was some feeling that it might be better if I went on … skating on cornflakes rather than actually accepting money from an American,' he said. In the arguments that followed, Curry's stance prevailed. Muddling through on the generosity of friends was over. Mosler's money immediately started to flow.

Within a year, Curry was showing the benefits. At the European Championships in Zagreb, his new focus, Smith's nous and Mosler's dollars had together notched up their first significant medal. Four weeks later – in March 1974 – everything went disastrously, and inexplicably, wrong.

Arriving in Munich with Alison Smith for the World Championships, Curry found his name being talked up as a favourite. From distant threat, he'd finally surfaced as a genuine contender. It was a prospect that turned his stomach to slush. Ever since his teens, he'd been hamstrung by nerves. Now, as the world's best skaters poured into Germany, Curry's self-confidence slumped. Struggling to sleep – and plagued by anxiety dreams when he did – he could see nothing clearly except the certainty of failure.

'He started to get a bit depressed at that particular point,' recalls Alison Smith. 'He was uptight with the fact that he hadn't been able to train the new programme enough. He also didn't think the NSA wanted him there because he was gay.' To lift him, Curry had summoned Heinz Wirz from Switzerland; and from New York, Nancy Streeter and her daughter Ellen were already on their way. For once, whatever happened next, he would not be alone.

After the silent ritual of the school figures, Curry was lying fourth. After the short programme of compulsory jumps, he'd dropped down to sixth. No one had ever seen him skate so badly. No one had the remotest idea why. Only a brilliant free skate could save his pride, but Curry – in his own words – was now 'paralysed with fear', unable even to recall the steps to his own salvation.

High in the packed stands of the Munich Olympiahalle, Nancy and Ellen Streeter looked down in disbelief. 'It was agonising. It was like he was going around and around in slow motion. Mum and me were horrified. He just got worse and worse and then gave up right there. Awful. I was amazed he even got seventh,' says Ellen.

As the East German skater Jan Hoffman kissed his gold medal, Curry told Ed Mosler that he could no longer accept his money. He was quitting. It was over. Calmly, Mosler told him: 'There were a few moments in that programme that I thought were exceptionally beautiful.'

> My reaction was that there could not have been one-thousandth of a second that was all right. Mr Mosler insisted that there were a few moments which he described as some of the most beautiful skating he had ever seen. Unconvinced, I told him that I was sorry that I had wasted his money and that I could not accept any more of it and that I was going to give up.

It was a full-blown crisis without any obvious cause. According to Meg Streeter, Nancy's youngest daughter, Curry later alluded to 'something traumatic that had happened to him the night before; something on a personal level that had unravelled him'. According to Curry himself – in one uncorroborated account – the unravelling had been caused unintentionally by his brilliant Canadian shadow, Toller Cranston.

After attending a preview of Cranston's Munich programme the previous evening, Curry claimed he had found himself 'choking back sobs', having 'just witnessed the future of skating'. 'He [Cranston] was dressed in black and was in white face make-up with a tear painted on one cheek. For four minutes he skated like someone possessed.' By the following day – in front of thousands of spectators – Curry's veneer of superiority had dissolved. Just as it had done in Toronto three years before.

'Did John see my programme beforehand?' asks Cranston. 'I have not a clue. I was in my own bubble and I was also hanging by a thread, as I had so bombed in school figures.' Nevertheless it would be Cranston not John Curry who dazzled Munich. Theatrical, thrilling, unconventional, his performances crushed not only the Briton but everyone around him. Although it had earned Cranston only a bronze, the Canadian's visionary athleticism had plundered Curry's bearings. A black despair settled on the Englishman's camp. 'The day after the competition my mother and I had lunch with him,' recalls Ellen Streeter.

> He had this depression over him. Everyone was like doom and gloom at the table. No one knew what to say. No one was talking. John just had his head down and I blurted out that I had a new boyfriend and I was going to live with him in Atlanta. John looked horrified. So did my mum, so we ended up talking about that and not skating.

A few days later, back in Manhattan, Nancy was still deeply concerned about what Curry might do. In New York, she'd known only happy John. His darkly troubled alter ego had come as a shock. In a letter to Heinz Wirz she wrote : 'His skating in Munich and his state of mind are still very baffling to me and I suspect they are to him too ... I was able to say [to John] that I hoped he would not make any decision right away and would consider all the possibilities.'

As he stood alone in Munich airport, Curry's resistance to one of those 'possibilities' was under assault. Twice before he'd turned down Holiday On Ice. Now, just a few hours before flying to London, they'd sought him out again. In a hastily scribbled note to Heinz, Curry explained what was happening: 'Skee Goodheart [the owner of Holiday On Ice] talked me into going to Paris today as his guest … I must admit it is very flattering … I wish I had someone with me. I'm such a babe in the forest of wolves and bears.'

After two days of corporate arm-twisting – and a ringside seat at an ice show – Curry remained unconvinced. 'I saw the show and can honestly say it was awful. All the skaters were totally blank of any expression. The costumes were dreadful, lighting was ill-planned … the sets were laughable … there is more dignity working in any job no matter how little one earns than in being in one of those shows.'

After an evening meal in the company of a skating dwarf, Curry had seen enough. Despite an offer of $500 a week, they could shove their razzle-dazzle. 'It was fun but only highlighted the sordid sort of life one has to lead in an ice show. There is no beauty or refinement in this life, only brashness, vulgarity and tastelessness.'

Two weeks later, Curry's post-Munich despair deepened. If Paris had been depressing, the post-Championship tour was worse. Seething with resentment, he expressed his angst in his correspondence:

> It is such a bore to travel alone, without a friend, without a lover or anything … Next week I should go to Italy, then on to Japan to the USA to Sweden. That would mean me being away a whole month with skaters. Well, I'm not going to go … Why should I spend even one hour of my life wandering over the globe with a group of people who mean less than nothing to me? I'd rather be miserable in peace at home. I'm fed up with skating and skaters. They are such an artless bunch of morons.

Within days Curry was heading back to London, desperate for a tonic. For some time, fissures had been opening in his friendship with Alison Smith. Munich had undoubtedly widened them. A few months before, he'd told Nancy: 'I've had enough from Alison. FULL STOP. If the worst comes to the worst, I'll live in a hotel.'

Now he was crammed unhappily into a new bedsit listening to the stereo record player Nancy had provided for him. 'I must say I've been a bit blue lately,' he admitted. 'I guess that living alone takes getting used to just like everything else.'

It was hopeless. Nothing he did seemed to lift his spirits. Even a trip to see his mother had plunged him further downwards. 'Coming here is like taking a sidestep out of my real life – there is so little here with which I can identify. It is eight years since I lived at home and naturally one grows away. Here I mark time.' And later: 'Every now and then I get a huge fit of the blues over the Munich skating and I feel retched [sic] – really retched.'

By April, he'd had enough. Popping a letter in the post to Nancy, he made his way to his Manhattan bolt-hole via an exhibition skate in Japan. 'Please try and understand how I feel. I'm totally panic-stricken. I've never doubted my skating like this. I am sorry that nothing has gone to plan but I hope that when I arrive in New York I'll feel more like myself and not the failure I feel myself just now.'

By 19 April he was with the Streeters. He would stay with them for three desperate months. 'He was good at running away,' says Penny Malec.

Four

'The Hermit of Denver'

If it hurt Rita that John was choosing New York over Birmingham, she would never say. On every measure, her son's choice made absolute sense, but – despite Rita's now permanently brave face – her dismay must have been intense. The boy she'd driven to 6 a.m. skating lessons, with a winter coat slung over her nightie, was passing over the Atlantic horizon. 'I'm sure John was often rough with Rita,' thinks Penny Malec. 'He talked about how difficult she was to separate yourself from.'

Without fail she would always get a Valentine's Day card from him – likewise a note at Christmas and birthdays – but her Sutton Coldfield maisonette was no match for either Nancy Streeter's Manhattan apartment or her intuitive, artistic instincts. And unlike Nancy, she could rarely even afford to watch John skate in Europe. 'If there was jealousy then, somehow they all got past it,' thinks Meg Streeter. 'Mum and Rita had a good relationship. She came here, and Nancy went there.'

From the spring of 1974, however, New York effectively became Curry's permanent home. There would be very little room in it for his yesterdays. 'Nancy loved him and took him in,' explains Penny Malec. 'They were very rich – which he liked – and gave him the sort of life which he thought he ought to be living. I would also say he had more of a home life with the Streeters in New York than he did anywhere else.'

For almost the first time in 17 years, he'd packed away his skates. No early calls. No school figures. No barking coaches. Just occasionally, he'd slip across to the Sky Rink, where the paying public would stand back in awe, but Curry's energies were mostly consumed by dance. If a class was recommended, he'd try it; modern, classical or jazz. If a ballet came into town, he'd be in the audience. Nothing stood still in New York anyway.

'Being such an up and down person it is strange to feel so tranquil and at ease,' Curry confessed. 'I have the feeling that this is going to be one of the golden years of my life. In a way it is frightening to be so happy because one knows it cannot last.'

Energy seemed to flow down New York's avenues and straight back into his feet. To expiate it, he joined a gymnastics class at the New York Athletics Club. He watched Nureyev dance at the city's Metropolitan Opera House. He gaped at Anthony Dowell and Antoinette Sibley and swooned at 'three pas de deux which moved me more than any dancing I've ever seen'. Back in London with Alison Smith he'd often melted at Fonteyn, but this was different. In New York he felt liberated. In Britain, he'd felt crushed.

From very early on, Nancy had known what Rita did not. 'I wasn't his mother and we are New Yorkers,' she explained. 'We take it as it comes.' In the beginning, needing her to understand – but possibly lacking the courage to spell it out – he'd given her a copy of *Maurice*, E. M. Forster's tale of homosexual yearning. Not for the first time, or the last, Curry was employing code to avoid direct revelations. 'We were not so close that he felt he could always open up to me. However, I did sometimes find that John, and also many of his friends, found it easier to talk about their lives with someone who was not so close. It was a lonely existence, I guess.'

Incrementally the picture also cleared for Nancy's three daughters. Ellen had found John's copy of *Maurice* on her mother's bedside table and started reading it. 'Before then I really didn't get that men and women could be attracted to each other.' Gradually, and with no discomfort, the penny had dropped.

The Streeters embraced John emphatically, and without judgement. New York – on a grander scale – had done the same. With every visit he'd loved it more. Cushioned from Manhattan's darker corners, Curry saw only a city proud of its artistic pretentions. In New York it was all right to talk about ballet or dance. Better still, it was all right to be gay. After two months, Curry's post-Munich blues had blown away and he was charged with fresh conviction.

'There was something about his single-mindedness which was compelling,' recalled Nancy. 'But it was so important that he got things right in his head. Not the feet. If you have the capability but not the mindset, it won't happen.'

With barely 18 months to go to the 1976 Olympics, Curry's challenge was a formidable one. In Munich, his 'head' had reduced him to a hopeless quiver; his school figures – the mandatory shape tracings in the ice – remained inconsistent; and although his free-flowing programmes were admired they still fell short of the technical standards required. Jumping wasn't a choice, it was an obligation, and he would win nothing until it was mastered. Those that he could do he often performed desultorily and the triple loop – in which the skater takes off and lands from the same backward edge – was still beyond him.

In the time that remained – with the right team – Curry believed he could eliminate all these deficiencies. But, as he surveyed his options in mid-1974, the biggest obstacle to success seemed insurmountable. In the Munich World Championships the winner, Jan Hoffman, had been East German. The runner-up, Sergei Volkov, was a Russian. In the previous year the top three places had gone to government-sponsored skaters from Eastern bloc countries. In 1972 – and in every European Championship since 1969 – the outcome had been virtually the same. By the tiniest of increments, skaters like Curry – and Toller Cranston – were slowly changing the game. But between them and success was an Iron Curtain they somehow had to dismantle.

It wouldn't be easy. While no one doubted the ability of Eastern bloc skaters, the outcome of few sports seemed as vulnerable to abuse as figure skating. Traditionally, scores had been awarded by a panel based on each member's subjective appraisal of a performance. Finding nine judges capable of doing this impartially seemed impossible. Under pressure, many appeared too afraid to shed partisan affiliations. To neutral onlookers – and growing television audiences – the results could often be baffling. On the same night that mediocrity struck gold, virtuosity could vanish without trace.

Everyone had their explanations, but most Western skaters – and Curry was no different – believed corruption was poisoning their sport.

'It isn't Bill versus Joe,' he claimed in 1976.

It's Britain versus East Germany or Czechoslovakia … The judges are judging the countries unfortunately. They can't do it to an absolutely blatant degree but if there's any room at all where they can fiddle it [they do]. If there are five Eastern judges judging … you know the Western skater doesn't stand a chance. The most important day in a competition was the day they drew the judges. I would just sit there counting East, West. One for East Germany. One for UK. And I'd just hope this side won because I knew that I would do well if it did.

For years he'd been offering his elegant alternative to the Soviet tide, and yet still – backed by block-voting – Eastern European athleticism stood in his way. He understood that judges felt safer with the textbook vaulting prowess of men like Volkov. He understood that brilliant showmen like Hoffman ticked all the required boxes. What he couldn't comprehend was why anyone in their right mind would like watching it. Or how he could permanently tilt the way sufficient judges thought.

'I don't think the Russian men can skate,' he told the BBC.

Of the ones I've competed against there isn't one who has a line in his body. They are technically like bulldozers. They have no refinement. It probably sounds horrible but they are so crude and so unmusical … no quality … I know the Russian skaters better than most and I know how bad they are, and I know that they won't take a ballet class …

For once, Curry was not entirely alone. After one major tournament, Toller Cranston had branded his Russian rival 'a hammer thrower' who had skated 'like a meat chopper'. The former British judge Sally-Anne Stapleford – a six-times UK ladies champion – thought that most Eastern European skaters showed 'no passion and no life'. 'If you took out the jumps and just watched what was left you'd be bored to tears,' she suggests. 'Music meant nothing. Light and shade meant nothing. Skating is not just a sport. It's an artistic sport.'

Imperceptibly, the Soviet monopoly was faltering. Even if some judges demurred, audiences undoubtedly loved Curry's silky lines. Given the right guidance, despite his three months' hiatus, Curry might yet turn the waverers around. Steered cleverly by Nancy Streeter, John Curry crept back. 'I came to the decision that I was not going out of skating through the back door. I was going to make changes. I was going to put right everything that everyone said was wrong with my skating.'

He had scarcely a second to lose. Everything had to be right. No distractions. No weak links. To jump like a winner he would turn to a master. To penetrate the political labyrinth of international judging, he would turn to a legend. Sadly, there would be limited space in this plan for Alison Smith. After almost four years, their partnership on the ice was petering out. Anchored in London by her father's ill health, Smith felt unable to join her friend in America. And America was clearly where Curry intended to remain. 'I wasn't going to leave my father,' says Smith. 'I just couldn't do it, so I said to John, you have to go. Just go … It was extremely difficult.'

Privately, Curry was probably relieved. Events had moved fast in Alison's absence. Thanks to Ed Mosler's free-flowing financial support, two of the skating world's most sought-after luminaries had signed up to his mission. In June he was booked to be in Lake Placid for six weeks with Gus Lussi. By the autumn he was expected in Denver to start work with Carlo Fassi. Both men were giants; and both had stepped enthusiastically into a role that had proved beyond at least five previous incumbents.

———

The village of Lake Placid – 250 miles due north of New York – is a place of few distractions. Sheltered by the Adirondack Mountains, its 2,600 residents have always favoured physical pursuits over cerebral ones. While its hills are not high, they are unprotected from the north and, during the endless winters, Whiteface Mountain invariably lives up to its name. For decades, Lake Placid has been a magnet for fresh-faced action-seekers and since the 1930s, for skaters with gold on their minds, it has been a place of work.

Like Perren and Gerschwiler, Gustave François Lussi had been born in Switzerland. As a child he'd wanted to be a ski jumper, but had lost his nerve after a fall. In 1915, aged 17, he'd emigrated to the United States, washing dishes in a Manhattan hotel before taking the skills he'd learned on a frozen Lake Lucerne up to the fast-growing winter resort of Lake Placid. By 1924 he'd mentored his first champion. By 1932, he was watching the luminous Norwegian figure skater Sonja Henie win Olympic gold on the ice where he now coached. By the late 1940s he'd refined a method of teaching that had aspirants begging him to stop hunting moose and tell them what to do.

Sequestered in the Adirondacks, Lussi hadn't just embellished the skating manual, he'd rewritten it. His spins were so fast it was said NASA sought him out seeking solutions to the nausea suffered in orbit. Together with his American protégé, Dick Button, the Swiss guru had fabricated entirely new techniques and jumps – the flying camel and the flying sit spin, the two-and-a-half aerial turns of the double axel, and in 1952 the world's first three-revolution jump, the triple loop.

Just three days before his death – aged 95 in 1993 – Lussi was still giving lessons. 'Dedication beyond feeding, sleeping or living' was all he demanded. 'If you are great enough, you are going to win.' It was precisely what John Curry needed to hear. The perennial question when he arrived in Lake Placid on 16 June 1974 was whether John Curry would listen. What followed, however, was little short of a sporting miracle.

At 75, Gus Lussi didn't believe in wasting time, not when there were animals to track, edelweiss to plant and antiques to collect. On their first morning together, Curry was ordered to run through his jumps. 'He was far from impressed … and told me bluntly we would have to start again from scratch. You can't put a roof on a faulty foundation [said Lussi]. So, deeply chastened, I agreed to go back to square one.'

The following day, Curry was led out across the town's vast Olympic rink to a marked-off section of ice 'no larger than an average sitting room'. Expecting to stretch out and soar, the Briton was confined. Until he could perform flawless rotating jumps inside this 20 × 30ft 'box', nothing else would happen. Lengthy run-ups were forbidden. Momentum could be generated only within the designated patch. Lussi, surely, was senile. 'Triple jumps on a piece of ice I could not have fitted a school figure on to; what trick was this? There began then, on that portion of ice, a most drastic reassembling of everything I had been taught.'

It was as unceremonious as it was ingenious. Not even when he was a child had Curry fallen like this. Thirty or 40 times a day he clattered to the ice in an undignified heap. Every night, as he nursed his battered rump, he cursed this latest in his collection of ageing Swiss sadists. Every day, the same challenges confronted him. How could he attain elevation using only muscular coordination? 'My embarrassment knew no bounds ... nearby were ten-year-old girls doing things which seemed beyond [me]. I fell and I fell and I fell.'

After three weeks, Curry was in despair. 'The evenings away from the rink were spent in abject misery thinking about the misery on the rink.' Even the simplest jumps were now failing him. Five years before, he would have walked. Somehow in Lake Placid, against all his instincts, he was still clinging on. 'John realised that he was never going anywhere unless he did this,' explains Haig Oundjian. 'That's the power of the spirit. The spirit that says you can rise up. John said, "I have to change myself to do this." It's a huge life-changing moment.'

And when it came, the moment was sublime. As he prepared to quit, Curry threw himself into a jump that had thwarted him for days. For the first time he seemed to hang magically in the air, allowing his rising body to complete two rotations before landing sweetly on his extended leg. From behind him he heard a single pair of hands clapping. It was Lussi ... 'watching me with just the suggestion of a smile at the corner of his normally stern mouth. "Good," he said simply, "now we can begin."'

For the first time in a month Curry was smiling again. Living in Lake Placid had suited him. Although it was summer, and the snows were long gone, he'd thrived on his own in the mountains. In his room he played Mozart and Leonard Cohen. At the weekends, the town's orchestra gathered beside the lake to play tunes from their classical repertoire. All through July, hikers and fishermen filled the hotels, and, as the snowline retreated, the air buzzed to the sound of carnivorous flies and chainsaws.

Since so few of Lake Placid's rustic charms challenged his concentration, Curry built swiftly on his first gravity-defying moment of flight. By the end of summer, his entire jumping technique had been dismantled, rebuilt and enhanced. Lussi's stipulated mission statement – dedication beyond living – had been met unconditionally. Rarely had Curry gone so long without a flounce.

Working with the septuagenarian visionary had done more than refashion his skating. It had refreshed his temporarily deflated ego. 'All those people who had giggled at me began giggling less and looking more. I was no longer told that at my age it was impossible to change. I *had* changed. Mr Lussi's trick had worked.' The peculiar thing was that in their six weeks together, Curry had only ever seen Lussi in shoes, never skates. And rarely, in all his later years, would anyone else.

Oddly, it would be Alison Smith who bore first witness to the refashioned John Curry. After their split she'd taken a senior coaching job at Jaca in the shadow of the Spanish Pyrenees. And since they'd parted on good terms, John travelled from New York to join her in Spain in early August. 'She has never looked so well,' he wrote. 'She is brown as a berry … her skin is clear and her hair looks healthy again.' After just a few days, however, he was already beginning to doubt the wisdom of his visit.

In Lake Placid, with Gus Lussi, Curry had controlled himself. Working alongside Alison Smith – now more a friend than a coach – the scarcely buried diva was stirring. 'Today, for the first time I felt myself slip again and recognised the old traits,' he told Heinz. 'It is awful to feel the tranquillity of the last few months just melting away.' Alone in the Adirondacks, Curry had found inner balance. He couldn't let it slip now.

> These last few months have been among the best of my life. I've lived in great style, in beautiful places, skating to my heart's content … being away from Alison and Richmond has been very calming. Being away from the gay world has also had a very soothing effect.
>
> It is not Ali's fault and it is not mine either. It is just the way of it … but I feel she is a child playing in an adult world. It seems unnecessarily cruel. I hate the way I am. There are some good aspects but they are not nearly good enough to make up for all the rest. There is more debt than credit in my account.

For three weeks, Curry and Smith persevered. Just enough of their old chemistry remained intact and Curry's devils were invariably hushed when he was skating. With Alison's help, he finally mastered the triple toe loop. Working alone, he'd also plotted a new routine. 'It is very modern, athletic and highly masculine in form,' he told Heinz. 'As it is I shall probably lend it that special curry flavour of half-baked effeminate slush that has characterised all my other works.'

As the sun sizzled over Jaca's medieval walls, Curry deepened his tan and made plans to visit England. Rita had booked a summer cottage in Cornwall. His brother Andrew would be joining them there. On the way, John had stopped in London, firing off a letter to Nancy before catching the train to Penzance. 'Spending those few days in London made me realise how few friends I have there,' he wrote, later adding: 'I know that I do cut myself off from people and that having done this for all these years it is not surprising I now find myself rootless in the big city.'

In Cornwall, Curry's memories returned to his childhood. Rita had rented the clifftop bungalow near Sennen, which they'd stayed in 20 years before. Inside, running hot water had replaced bedroom bowls and basins. Outside, the sweeping view of the bay was unchanged. 'This is a house that I'd one day like to own,' he told Nancy. 'It is very modest but has a truly happy feeling to it. I cannot remember my father ever being here and when I think back on times spent here they are simply good times.'

By day, Rita and her two sons would walk the sands and watch the waves roll in from America. At night, John would compose childlike doodles of Hell's Angels in leathers and post them to Switzerland, replete with familiarly gloomy contemplations:

> There are so many awful people everywhere; the gumblie bumbliness of people is dreadful … Living on a boat in the middle of a silent sea and having special friends on very short visits every now and then would be fine. But the visits would have to be short … Your nasty friend. John

It was perhaps as well he was due back in the United States. In Spain, and then England, he'd begun drifting back towards the undertow. On 6 September, Curry flew into JFK airport, picked up a hire car and pointed it west towards the Rocky Mountains. Although he'd rarely travelled outside New York State, no one questioned the scale of his mission. Three days, and 1,800 miles later, he was standing under the Colorado sun with the great Carlo Fassi. 'It would be no more than the truth to say that at that time I did not like Mr Fassi and Mr Fassi did not like me. We shook hands without either of us smiling ... and then I departed to settle in.'

———

With his dark sideburns, deep-set eyes and Italian breeding, Carlo Fassi had the unblinking flamboyance of a Mafia don. It was a look that suited him well. Carlo Fassi was a player and John Curry had met his match. Born in Milan in 1929, he'd been the Italian champion ten times and a European champion twice before settling in the Dolomites to mould young female skaters into winners. One of them – a fair-haired German girl called Christa von Kuczkowski – had become his wife.

Side by side, Carlo and Christa had developed their coaching skills together, and by the early 1960s they'd swapped the jagged peaks of northern Italy for the Rocky Mountains of Denver and Colorado Springs. After a plane crash had robbed the United States of many of its leading skaters and coaches, the Fassis were deemed vital to the sport's domestic recovery. By 1968 they'd groomed their first US Olympic champion in the form of 16-year-old Peggy Fleming. By 1974, they had John Curry racing halfway across America to be gilded by their Midas touch.

Simply to be in their presence would help him. Judges took notice of who was on the Fassi roster and who was not. Carlo always made sure of that. In a sport infected by politics, Fassi was a master politician; a professor of spin. Every national judge knew who he was and he knew every national judge. No one dared to ignore him and at major tournaments Fassi prowled backstage tirelessly, gathering information and raw intelligence with forensic zeal.

Since he was fluent in several languages, few judges escaped his Lombardian charm. Fassi could speak perfect German to a judge on his left, while smooth-talking an English judge to his right. Nor did he care on which side of the Iron Curtain he was operating. 'The East Germans were our greatest rivals but he was unafraid of them,' remembers one of his American champions. 'At competitions [there] he would walk right up to their judges and referees and ask, "What's the talk?", "What's in now?", "What are you looking for?"'

Fassi was smart because he had to be. In a sport of fine margins plagued by suspect judging, every nugget of gossip was precious. Every slender opportunity to promote one of his skaters had to be grabbed. If a little gamesmanship could give him an edge, then so be it. Even Alison Smith, now watching ruefully from afar, deferred to his guile. 'John made the right move at the right time because it was all politics then and Carlo was *the* politician,' she says.

Whether Curry actually liked Carlo Fassi was immaterial. By September 1974, he was going nowhere without him. Whatever pleasure John had taken from baiting Arnold Gerschwiler would not be repeated on the Italian. Where Gerschwiler had been old school and weak, Fassi was streetwise and shrewd. In tandem with Christa – 16 years younger than her husband – he was also a brilliant coach; every bit as meticulous about the details of skating as he was about the politics. 'My husband was a little bit hesitant at the beginning but he really learned to love him,' says Christa. 'We'd been worried he might be a little highly strung – high-maintenance – but he really was not at all.' Provided he behaved, Curry could not have been anywhere better.

Sitting a mile above sea level, on the western edge of the High Plains, Denver is a city of sunshine. In the long summers, the streets can fry at 41°C. From October to April, snow growls through the southern Rockies, dumping over 50 inches even in a quiet year, very little of which stays long. Even when the sun is not shining, the warm chinook winds melt it quickly. It was an environment well matched to Curry's oscillating psyche. Within a few days of unpacking his skates, the mutual anxiety that had preceded his arrival was vanishing fast.

In the thin mountain air, Curry blossomed. Everything the Fassis did seemed to have a purpose. Consistency suited him. Routine kept anxiety at bay. 'I started to feel marvellously alive,' he enthused. At any one time the couple would be working with around half a dozen students. If Carlo was busy with one of them, Curry would work with Christa. Likewise, when Christa was busy he'd train with Carlo. Nothing was left to chance. Neither of them, Curry soon realised, was any softer than the other.

Sometimes on the ice Mr Fassi would look at something I'd done and say: 'This is a really hexellent figure. Hexellent! Hexcellent'. And invariably Mrs Fassi would then say something like: 'Oh no no. Just look down here. There's a slight double line; just here. Look Carlo'. I could not get past her with anything.

For the first time in years, Curry's behaviour was blemish-free. There was a steeliness about Carlo which compelled him to silence. Although he was by nature laid-back – and a master of savagely funny anecdotes – his languid manner concealed a formidable Latin temper. The meteoric American teenager Dorothy Hamill – a student of Fassi's at this time – had good cause to remember it. In the middle of a training session, after 'acting like a temperamental spoiled brat', Fassi had ripped her music from the rink-side record player and 'flung it across the ice like a Frisbee'.

Like Curry, Dorothy Hamill had found relief from family tension on the ice. Like Curry, her father had been a hard-drinking undiagnosed depressive. Just for once, the British skater had met someone whose childhood appeared almost as compromised as his own. Under the Colorado sun, the peevish teenager from Connecticut and the fine-spoken 24-year-old from Solihull made a connection. Quietly, under the watchful eye of the Fassis, both of them were being calmed in the presence of a 'new' family.

Although Curry had his own apartment, he'd become a welcome fixture at the Fassi's home. Dorothy Hamill was the same. 'Christa loved being a mom and homemaker and every night there was a family dinner in their house,' she wrote in her autobiography.

> They had two children at the time. Everyone was expected to pitch in and help, including me. Life at the Fassis' gave me a first glimpse into how normal happy families behave ... I didn't feel homesick for my own family because our home life had never been quite like this.

By mid-autumn, Curry's sense of wellbeing was being expressed in superlatives. 'Ecstatically happy,' he said. 'Skating could not have seemed easier ... Perfect ice, and Mr Fassi always in the same mood; a half-wit could have done it. All I had to do was skate, and perhaps for the first and only time in my life, skating was absolutely easy for me. Even in New York it had never been so easy.'

The Fassis, too, seemed delighted. 'When we knew him he was always alone,' says Christa. 'I'm almost sure the years he spent with us were the best years in life. I had kids and he loved them just as they loved him. He cooked. He was always there. He'd fix stuff. He was family. This was when he was happiest.'

The British wunderkind Robin Cousins understood perfectly why Curry was so content. Some years later, when John was dazzling Broadway, it would be Robin's turn to pursue Olympic glory, and, like his older shadow, he too reached out to Carlo and Christa. The Fassis, he said, never imposed their own artistic vision. They had no need to show Curry how to skate. Their job was to teach him how to win.

> We were all taught to work with what we had to offer. Carlo would package and hone what you wanted to do. He'd also manipulate you without you really knowing you were being manipulated. He'd say, do what you want to do but do it the way the judges will appreciate it. There was no reason not to trust them implicitly. You felt you could not be in better hands.

It would work for Robin Cousins. In Lake Placid – watched by Gus Lussi – Cousins won his Olympic gold in 1980. Back in 1974, however, as the winter tournament season approached, Curry still had much to do. In the Adirondacks, Lussi had tackled the deficiencies in Curry's jumping. Inside the Colorado Ice Arena – charging his student just $9 for a 20-minute session – Carlo Fassi was preoccupied by Curry's recalcitrant school figures; a discipline that made even the steeliest competitors quite so nervous.

Surrounded by nine judges – in chapel-like silence – skaters traced designated shapes in the ice. If the blade wobbled, the shape was lost. If the trailing foot dragged it might scuff, or damage, the line of the figure. Even the sound of the blade on the ice would indicate mediocrity. A clean single note invariably came from a perfectly sliced pattern beneath an upright blade. If the foot trembled, slicing shavings from the ice, judges were drawn to the tell-tale rasp. 'Figures are like scales to a piano player,' says ex-judge Sally-Anne Stapleford. Finally, John Curry appeared reconciled to their mystic cadences.

If it was Fassi who engineered this mellowing, it was a master stroke. Further afield, however, there was even better news. Under pressure, figure skating's lawmakers had belatedly acknowledged the absurdities of their rules. During the early 1970s, the much-derided school figures had been worth 40 per cent of a skater's final mark. In 1976 – precisely when John would be at the Innsbruck Olympics – that value would be lowered to 30 per cent. Another 20 per cent of the score would come from the short technical programme and the remaining 50 per cent would be determined by the extended musical routine upon which Curry had always lavished such time. It was a small but significant shift. If the paying public wanted to be entertained – and they did – then the odds were moving decisively in Curry's favour.

Up in the mountains, as snow began to fall, Curry's sense of wellbeing persisted. A young family who shared the same apartment block had welcomed him as a friend, and in breaks between lessons Curry would help their two young children build crude igloos and grinning snowmen. 'That was as much a family life as the Fassis [for him],' recalls Dorothy Hamill. 'She would cook for him and have a cup of tea with him when her kids were at school. I'm sure it was lonely for John, because it was for me and I was there with my mom.'

It was only in the long evenings that Curry's composure faltered. Mindful of his reputation, the Fassis had lodged him in rooms directly across from the rink. There could be no excuses for tardiness, but the arena was out of town and Curry's social options were limited. 'I've just heard *La Traviata* on the wireless,' he told Nancy. 'Oh I'm so happy I have that lovely black box – a voice in the wilderness.' Eventually Carlo Fassi would lend him a television, but the city's gay scene had eluded him. The occasional snowball fight with his neighbour's kids was about as good as it got.

'I am at home feeling very lonesome and frustrated. The rink and my apartment is way out of town,' he told Heinz.

My Nun of Richmond days may be over but now I'm the Hermit of Denver. My lessons with Mr Fassi are really great. I like him even though I should not like him at all … The only possible distraction is that there are no distractions. I do 4 figure patches every day and 2 free skating sessions. And that is IT. If I did not work myself to a standstill, I'd be very unhappy here ... when I was in London and New York I did not go out either. Sometimes I wonder if it is all worth it.

After six months as a 'hermit' he was about to find out. In early December, Curry travelled to London to defend his British title. Only Robin Cousins came close. Two weeks later he was back in New York to spend Christmas with the Streeters. Once again, his mood rocketed skywards. 'New York looked so beautiful. I've never loved that city more,' he told Heinz. 'Sometimes I feel I shall burst with shear [sic] ecstasy. When I'm there, there is a voice whispering in my ear – "Here, anything is possible, there is always a chance, always a chance". One day I shall live in New York.'

In a thank-you letter to Nancy Streeter he was no less ecstatic: 'I don't think I've ever been sadder to leave the city than I was this time. It was so strong a feeling I could have very easily have just said "No, I won't go". It is strange that I am so enchanted with New York. I love being with you. I love being a part of your family.'

Manhattan had worked its seasonal magic. By mid-January he'd returned to the High Plains, enjoying a delirious surge of energy he couldn't quite explain. 'Mr Fassi and Mrs Fassi and I; no problems,' he told Heinz. There were just two weeks left before the 1975 European Championships in Copenhagen and he had never felt fitter or happier.

> Everything here goes well and I'm so happy skating and skating my heart out. This is what I've wanted all my life and the most wonderful thing about it is that now I have it I want it even more. I am so lucky to have this wonderful love in my life and even luckier to be able to live it out like this.
>
> I don't know where my energy comes from. I do six or even more [school figures] patches per day and I free skate twice and I still want to do more and more. Stamina here [at altitude] is very difficult ... I am running to help my condition ... We have been lucky in our lives haven't we? Keep well. Love John.

Only one thing blackened this otherwise serene horizon. Shortly before Christmas he had written to Alison Smith in Spain. Although she was surely in no doubt, Curry informed her that he would be travelling to Copenhagen with the Fassis, and that her role as his coach was formally over.

'It was not an easy decision to reach and not an easy letter to write … she has done so much for me as a person and a skater. As yet I have not heard from [her]. She must be upset but I still feel I'm right.' Satisfied that he had acted correctly, Curry, Carlo and Christa made their final preparations for Denmark. It would be the first significant test of his progress. Unless he'd managed to shake Munich out of his system, he was finished.

———

As a teenager, John Curry's physique had been impressive. In his twenty-fifth year it was a form worthy of Michelangelo. Where other skaters had bulk, Curry had line. The torso was perfectly triangular, descending from straight shoulders to a waist that allowed no fat. The legs were long – although he decried them as short – encased in muscle which was conspicuous but never grotesque. It was a body designed for grace, not feats of brute strength.

It was typical of John Curry that he could never see it like this. 'I'm the wrong shape for a skater,' he later told the BBC. 'Long body and short legs. There are certain movements that no matter how I twist myself they just look horrible. We have to disguise this as best as we can. There are certain movements which exaggerate the length of your leg and there are certain movements which make them look shorter. What you wear makes a tremendous difference.'

Curry's attention to detail had always been impressive. It was inevitable this would extend to his costumes. For years, his letters had been festooned with sketches, for shirts and dancing suits. While 'guarding against any blatant hint of indecency', he understood the challenge: to appear in outfits that complimented his music (and his shape) but gave no ammunition to his nameless critics. It was an almost impossible line to walk.

Curry's instincts were stylish and minimalist; blacks and blues in preference to the sport's prevailing obsession with 'sequins, spangles and nylon lace sleeves'. Had he opted for the glitter, Curry's fragile stock would have fallen. By choosing to ignore it, he merely opened himself up to more criticism. It was a dilemma even the fastidious Fassis had overlooked.

Curry's bid for European gold in Copenhagen had started well. After the school figures – for which he'd chosen plain black trousers, gloves and a thick sweater – he was among the medals. The following day, in the short free-skating programme, Curry opted for an outfit he'd designed himself, a tight-fitting electric-blue leotard and trousers overpainted with a white 'vapour trail' spiral, which uncurled around his body from the right wrist to the hip.

When Curry entered a spin – he was skating to Stravinsky's *The Rite of Spring* – he looked like a dazzling human top. When he came off the ice, to giddy applause, he was lambasted by officials of the International Skating Union: 'I was told that I must not wear the costume again as it had influenced the judges against me. The form-fitting line, which was entirely innocuous, had startled them'.

Alongside Alison Smith, he'd found himself in similar situations. Either his music had been too 'faggy' or his skating had been too 'feminine'. 'We didn't tell people to fuck off in those days, though,' says Alison. 'We were taught to respect authority and that's what we did.' Carlo Fassi was the same. Realpolitik was his middle name. With just his long free programme to go, Curry had fallen back to sixth. The 'vapour trail' outfit had to go. In the hours before his final skate, out came his 'good old navy-blue'.

Between them, Fassi and Curry had fixed it. Placated by his costume change, the judges devoted their attention to the Briton's subtle brilliance. Five minutes later he was clutching the silver medal that would yank him back from obscurity. The year before, in Munich, officials had taken Curry to one side and told him he was finished. One performance in Copenhagen had neutralised establishment negativity.

'It was a sweet moment for me,' he said; made sweeter still by closer scrutiny of the results. Only the Russian Vladimir Kovalev had bettered him. Floundering in his wake were six skaters from East Germany, Hungary, Czechoslovakia and the Soviet Union. At a critical moment, Curry had driven a wedge into the heart of Eastern bloc dominance. The strategy he'd drawn up in New York the previous summer was working. Gus Lussi had polished the tricks. Carlo Fassi's endorsement was ripping away the blinkers.

Mr Fassi is wonderful. He intimidates the judges in such a way.
Everybody knows he knows more about skating than anyone

else. He goes up to them and says. 'My John. He's skating so well. You should see this. When he comes out of that triple jump watch how his skates come down. You watch this. You watch that'. The judges have to listen to this barrage but the thing is, they actually do then see it when it comes to the point.

The following month – at the 1975 World Championships in Colorado Springs – Curry won bronze and his renaissance was complete. Two Russians had beaten him, but he was officially the third best skater in the world. It was the fourth-placed Canadian skater, however, who had become Curry's biggest worry.

––––––

Ever since Toronto, Toller Cranston and John Curry had circled each other like respectful boxers. Although connected by a passion for the fine arts, they were distanced by the strictures of competition. 'John and I were different yet the same,' explained Cranston. 'Neither of us was the boy next door. Both of us laughed at ourselves, yet we were both absolutely convinced about our destinies. Unfortunately we wanted the same thing and two people can never win the same Olympic gold medal.'

In tournaments, Cranston's performances were electrically charged with theatrical emotion and technical risk. Most skaters performing the so-called Russian split jump brought their skates up to their waist. Cranston's invariably contorted up to his shoulders. 'Toller was angry. Toller was bizarre. Toller was extremist,' says Haig Oundjian. 'John was ballet and classical. Toller was weird, but they were both very artistic ... and Cranston was a much better jumper than John.'

In his own words, the Canadian was a 'mystical child left on the doorstep by folkloric creatures' who'd gone on to become a 'self-invented renegade artiste'. Whatever he was, modesty played very little part in it. His autobiography *Zero Tollerance* opened with a prologue entitled 'The Genesis of a Legend'. 'I think of myself as being androgynous,' he wrote. 'And not really of this world.' Like Curry, he'd wanted to be a ballet dancer at the age of six. Like Curry, Cranston had unerring faith in his own rebel instincts. And like Curry he was an imperious national champion.

I felt more, suffered more and tried harder than anyone. I was under a microscope. I lived by extremes. At the same time, I cultivated a persona that exemplified strength and confidence, but it was false. I wasn't always a victim. Often I invited controversy. I was uninhibited in a day when lack of inhibition was virtually unknown; uninhibited in interpretation, original moves and body language – which I felt was inherently neither male nor female.

The words might have been Curry's. There were even persistent rumours that Cranston was gay – and that Curry and he had enjoyed a brief fling. 'I'm not sure they didn't,' says Oundjian. 'He and Toller had a love-hate thing.' Alison Smith had her suspicions too. 'Something happened around Munich. I don't know what it was. They'd had a good friendship but after Munich they were not in each other's pockets so much. Why? Maybe someone tickled the wrong guy's stick? I just wouldn't get involved with it.' John's long-time confidant Heinz Wirz, however, thinks not. 'I would be surprised if they had ever had a love affair,' he says. 'I'm convinced John would have told me about it. As far as I remember he didn't like Toller at all.'

By March 1975, that feeling was entirely mutual. Cranston found his rival's skating 'as cold as an iceberg' and Curry had been badly rattled by the Canadian's verve. As he collected his bronze at Colorado Springs, the two men could barely look at each other. From what the bemused Canadian could see, his old rival had come down from the Rockies with 'a disposition makeover', a 'Jekyll and Hyde metamorphosis'. 'Even "good morning" was no longer in his repertoire.'

'Only a few things have ever intimidated me,' says Cranston, today a painter living in Mexico. 'One of them is Rome. The other is John Curry. He always made me feel uncomfortable. At one time I was actually friendly with him and then there was this about-face. He ceased to communicate with anyone. He was austere, aloof, rude, but it was very clever and it pushed the buttons of the other competitors.'

Undoubtedly, Curry had changed. He was still a nervous competitor, but the Fassis had bolstered his fragile self-belief. Emboldened by their rink-side presence, he had developed his otherness into a valuable tool. If his attitude to Cranston had cooled after Munich, it was simply because he'd seen the Canadian outperform him so brilliantly there. The rudeness that blanked Toller Cranston wasn't a misunderstanding; it was a strategically deployed weapon in Curry's arsenal.

Beneath the Briton's icy reserve lay a ruthlessness that Toller would always struggle to match. 'I was a lousy competitor,' admits Cranston. 'Being creative was more important than winning.' With less than a year to go to the Olympics, his British counterpart had found a way of fusing both. 'He had the tenacity of a rusty old nail. You can't be a wimp and be the Olympic champion.'

Curry's regal demeanour dovetailed perfectly with his grander purpose. Within days of meeting Nancy Streeter, he'd promised to win the Olympics and establish his own company. Toller Cranston's fatal flaw was that he neither shared, nor needed, such a singular goal. Even before John Curry's journey to Denver, Cranston claimed the Fassis had approached him offering 'free lessons, ice time, and even my own car ... to defect to Colorado'. If true, the fate of both men might have been different. Out of loyalty to his long-standing Canadian coach, however, Cranston had declined. A few weeks later Curry – with no such qualms – had stepped unknowingly into his place.

For the time being, their rivalry was put on hold. The two former friends – together with Eastern Europe's finest – would not resume formal combat until the 1976 Winter Olympics and the World Championships, now both less than 12 months away. Before the 1975 ice skating season ended, however, it required one last duty of its star turns.

Curry's loathing for the annual Tour of Champions was extreme. Everything about it incensed him, from the dreary company of his fellow skaters to its lack of financial reward. 'He said it felt like they wanted him to be in a circus,' explains Christa Fassi. 'He didn't want to be a circus animal that was paraded around.' Nevertheless it was Carlo who persuaded Curry to join the springtime tour of the United States, insisting 'it would be political suicide to refuse to go in the year before the Olympics'. 'So off I went,' scoffed Curry, 'dressed in my sober little black outfits and trying to persuade Toller that I was still his friend.'

By mid-March, after a 'gruelling succession of one-night stands', the circus had reached Canada. Nothing about it had softened

Curry's repugnance. In the American venues, audiences had accorded him grudging respect, before showering the ice with bouquets for home-grown stars like Dorothy Hamill. Then, if it were possible, in Vancouver things got even worse.

As Curry stood alone under a spotlight waiting for his music, all he could hear was a chorus of boos. It wasn't an unknown Englishman these people had paid to see. It was their larger than life Canadian national champion, Toller Cranston, whose every spin was greeted with flag-waving applause. As Curry would later remember it:

They started a steady chant and began to bang their feet on the floor and I could stand it no longer. As I left the ice, an empty Coca-Cola can was hurled at me, and I went to the dressing room, took off my skates and left for the airport. Even if it meant I would not be acceptable to the Olympic Committee, I had no intention of staying any longer. I swore I would never foot in Canada again.

———

For a few weeks, Curry hid from the flak at the Streeter apartment in New York. Over the years, his private circle of intimates had grown there. More than London, he now regarded the city as his home and Nancy's discreet presence at both the European Championships in Copenhagen and the Worlds in Colorado Springs had cemented her place at his side. Even that hitherto sunny relationship, however, was fraying at the seams.

With so little to report from west Denver, the skater's letters to Nancy had become shorter and less frequent. Those that he sent were often either requesting or thanking her for money. During his time in New York, Curry was also torn between his desire to meet men and the importance of not offending his hosts. It was a balance he was signally failing to achieve. In mid-May, shortly before Curry returned to Britain for a brief exhibition tour, the tensions at East 72nd Street broke the surface. In a letter from London, Curry reviewed what had happened:

You feel that the person I was died, and with him died all his feelings and loves. You feel that my love for you has died. In the several talks we have had over these weeks, I have repeatedly told you that is not so Nancy, but still you don't believe me. Lately you are seeing me for the first time at my own full strength. I'm recovered from my broken heart and my broken skating and my broken mind. And I guess this is me in one piece. You are seeing me lately through less rose-coloured glasses. It is inevitable that as time, YEARS, go by we begin to see one another as the people we are.

Although Nancy's half of this correspondence has not survived, it isn't hard to imagine her distress. Curry's 'breakfast bombshell' – as he called it – was not only peevish, it was cruel and devoid of gratitude. 'I'm not going to appologise [sic] for staying out late and one, or fifty one lovers. In the same way I'm not going to appologise for having brown eyes and skating to 'Rite of Spring'. This is all me. However I am sorry if I have given you reason to doubt my feelings (and it seems I have).' As the letter wound up, Curry wrote:

> People often say I'm your son – I've never felt this is quite the right way of putting it, but there is something I like in it. I think we are friends. However what I'm trying to say is having sons can be as painful as having daughters or mothers. See you very soon Nancy. PS In case you had not noticed this letter is TEN pages long.

By early June, Curry was back in Denver – and his 'difficult patch' with Nancy appeared to be over. Once again, however, the skater's correspondence had dried up. This time, it was Nancy's turn to pen some home truths. In a letter – now lost – she rounded on her friend for his coldness and neglect. Mortified, Curry sent back a note so stripped of aggression, it read like the confession of a penitent.

> You said you felt I'd withdrawn from you and at the same time taken for granted all that you and your family, and the security of your household have given me. Well Nancy, this is a side of myself that I guess I shrink from even thinking about. People have said things like this to me before. Pat Dodd once said to me

in an emotionless voice, 'You are a great user of people, John'.
My mother tells me I only like people with money. It is not a
terribly attractive picture is it?

In mitigation, Curry blamed sexual boredom and loneliness. 'Just
lately the parts of my life do not fit together. I feel as empty and
broken as I've ever felt,' he said, later adding: 'It's kind of funny
to think that most of the millions and millions of people could
never even think of winning a medal in the Olympic games, but
most of them can and do find someone to make them feel alive for
a while.'

Curry badly needed a break. Under scorching skies, he pointed
himself west, passing through the Utah deserts and Las Vegas,
before checking into a seaside hotel at Laguna Beach, California.
Everything about it thrilled him. At dawn the coast was draped in
chilly mist. By mid-morning clean Pacific light had exploded right
down along the coastline. Of the five surf-stroked beaches, one was
almost entirely gay and, in a joyous letter to Nancy, Curry frothed
with happiness:

> I've never seen so many beautiful people in one place – in fact
> I've never seen such beautiful people anywhere, ever. Perhaps
> even more sensational is the fact that all these hundreds of people
> are gay and behaving just as any young people would on a beach.
> There is lots of flirting and people playing volley ball and frisby
> [sic], some walking hand in hand, lots of people playing in the
> surf – everyone just being themselves like anyone else on any
> beach anywhere except all these people are homosexuals.

He had never seen anything like it. And outside of California – with
very few exceptions – nor had anyone else. 'How good it feels to be
oneself in broad daylight, not to be in some dark smoky bar in a
deserted backstreet, some time when normal folk are fast asleep.'
For a few days Curry wandered between beach fires and gay pool
parties, one hundred-strong: 'Like a scene from the last days of the
Roman Empire (American style).' When company dried up, he
walked for miles through the night along deserted starlit beaches.
'I'm glad we can be honest with each other,' he told Nancy. 'It's
worth a lot isn't it?'

By the early autumn, after spending several weeks in California 'the hermit of Denver' was back in Colorado. For the next six months, allowing himself very little time off, he stuck dutifully to the agreed plan. Only rarely would he deviate; and, when he did, the old private frustrations burst through. In late September he'd found himself in New York fantasising about leather trousers and a place of his own:

> Thoughts of giving into my desires took me to a shop called the 'Leather Man'. The assistant helped me very well and I tried on some trousers. They fitted me well and I felt very good in them, however I thought I'd save the money for my HOME ... I had one little adventure but it was difficult to get away from Nancy ... Mr Mosler has been very nice to me and we have become friends. His [Manhattan] flat is like a dream come true ...

Just as he'd promised in Bratislava, 'Mr Mosler' had kept the funds flowing. Curry, in return, had become an industrious – if sometimes, tardy – pupil. 'John was not the hardest worker,' says Christa Fassi. 'But then he didn't need to be.' Inside the Ice Arena off West Evans Avenue, it was his unfailing creative intelligence that impressed them the most. 'Skaters are very immature most of the time,' she remembers. 'John was a breath of fresh air.' Only once in 18 months had he misbehaved. 'Fortunately, he was smart enough to stay away until he came out of it.' Fortunately for all of them, the end was getting nearer.

Just one facet of John's preparation remained unresolved: his nerves. In Colorado Springs, at the World Championships, despite 'shaking like a leaf in a hurricane' he'd held it together 'by pure consciousness and willpower'. There was no guarantee he could do it again. In his own words, 'something had to be done'.

———

In the late 1950s Werner Hans Erhard – born John Paul Rosenberg – had been selling cars in St Louis. By the early 1970s he was running a 'self-empowerment' empire with centres in Aspen, Honolulu, New York and Los Angeles. In a country with a weakness for the glib platitudes of life-coaching, Werner Erhard had struck pay dirt. He was slick, charismatic, persuasive and an open admirer of Scientology founder L. Ron Hubbard. He was also extremely lucky.

The fast-wilting appeal of flower-power's sloganeering had beached an entire generation of disillusioned neo-hippies awash with cash. Erhard Seminar Training – or EST as it became known – tapped into both their money and their feelings of post-1960s dislocation. When it all eventually wound up in 1984, amidst accusations of brainwashing, EST had more than 250,000 disciples. Even today, on websites for diehard believers, John Curry is offered as incontrovertible proof of the efficacies of the Erhard way.

At the heart of the EST pitch was a promise to 'transform one's ability to experience living'. Reaching that Zenlike state, however, would require students to endure a soul-stripping, four-day course of mind-numbing intensity. Upon arrival, wristwatches would be removed from delegates. The 15-hour daily workshops that followed were punctuated by a single meal break alleviated only by rationed pauses for the toilet.

No one could speak unless spoken to; no water was allowed; delegates were referred to as 'estholes'; the chairs were famously uncomfortable; and the onstage rhetoric consisted largely of machine-gun aphorisms fired either by the eloquently plausible ex-car salesman from St Louis or his carefully prepped acolytes. 'What is, is and what ain't, ain't' was one of them. 'The truth is always and only found in the circumstances you've got' was another.

Few cities were as curious and welcoming as New York. Among Manhattan's chattering classes, EST was a regular topic of dinner party conversation. Nancy Streeter was an advocate. So were a number of Curry's friends within the dance world. Urged to try it as a cure for his nerves, John checked in at a Manhattan hotel for an introductory seminar. Despite loathing the people – and the messianic hectoring – he handed over $250 for two full weekends of training. 'There are rare moments in my life when a course of action seems not only right but inevitable – almost preordained,' he said. The Olympic preparations would have to wait.

It was an extraordinary impulse. With Carlo Fassi drumming his fingers in Colorado, Curry had gone walkabout. For the next two weeks, instead of carving school figures his prized student would be weeping confessionally among 225 total strangers. 'True enlightenment is knowing you are a machine' ran one EST truism, but, amidst the fatuous Californian-style psycho-babble, there were shards of genuine wisdom, which seemed to help the troubled skater.

Erhard's core mantra was that individuals must take responsibility for what they are; displaying 'a willingness to acknowledge that [they] are a cause in the matter'. At the emotional climax of the course, 'students' in batches of 25 took part in the 'danger process', standing silently in line before a vast room of people while EST staff tried to provoke a reaction from each one in turn. 'The real secret is whether your ego runs your life or you do,' claimed Erhard. 'The only way you can transcend your ego is to accept responsibility for it.'

For a controlling individual like John Curry these were pertinent observations. It was also remarkable that he had engaged in such searing, albeit private, disclosure. At the raw heart of his difficulties, EST taught him, were repeat patterns of behaviour over which he should exert command. Since he alone was responsible for switching them on, he should, and could, learn how to switch them off. In the afterglow of epiphany he appeared transformed.

'It brought me a new kind of freedom,' he was quoted as saying. 'I was no longer plagued by nerves … I was buoyant, eager to do my programmes and very sure of myself. Even more important was the fact that I was no longer lonely. I felt high all the time.' 'He was completely changed,' says Heinz, another 'graduate' of EST. 'Absolutely changed. He really was a darling man again. I mean not for long, though. He soon got back into his ways.'

In early December 1975, Curry got his first chance to put EST to the test. The first signs were not good. Back in London he'd retained his British title by a controversial whisker. There'd been no nerves, but he'd skated like a novice. 'He had a hideous championship, one of the worst skates of his career,' recalls Robin Cousins. 'He fell. I beat him in the short programme and the long programme and he still won.'

Everyone knew why. Curry himself had railed against 'pre-ordered' results at big tournaments. This time he'd been a beneficiary of them. This close to the Olympics, it would have been unhelpful if Curry had lost. The judges knew Cousins would come again. Their current champion almost certainly would not. Blind eyes had been turned on his mistakes. Publicly, Curry blamed his lacklustre performance on a desire not to peak too soon. Privately, he saw nothing that undermined his faith in EST.

Precisely what had passed between Curry and his American mentors was never divulged. Among friends he would sometimes describe how they'd invited him to pretend that he was either inside a strawberry, or that his blood had been replaced with orange juice. Many years later he was quoted as saying his 'private thoughts' had been 'scattered across the floor for everyone to see'; that 'a central core of strength' had emerged afresh from the 'emotional rubble'. In view of the timing – whatever had happened inside the Hilton Hotel – it was hardly surprising just how deeply Curry had been affected. Almost exactly ten years before, John's father had been checking into a Paddington hotel with a bottle of chloral hydrate. Given what lay ahead of Curry – and knowing what his father had already missed – the skater's emotional susceptibility would have been preternaturally high. Quite simply, EST had found him at the right time and – whatever it had done – he would always be thankful for it.

That Christmas, Curry joined the gathering around the tree at the Streeter apartment. With three lively 'sisters' around, it was easier to shut things out. 'John did not like Christmas,' explains one later confidant. '[He] spent most Christmases alone, allowing himself to be coerced only on rare occasion by close friends to do otherwise. I don't recall why he did not like this particular holiday, but he didn't. I think all the celebrating was somehow depressing to him.' From Nancy he got a shirt with the message 'EST IS BEST' stitched into the front. 'There are times when things just don't add up,' he told her in an emotional thank-you letter. 'And at those times I think of you.'

By late December, after dazzling Madison Square Garden with two exhibition performances, Curry was back in Denver, sporting a tight perm (which his mother loathed) and the gleaming eyes of a zealot. Any irritation the Fassis might have harboured over his absences were never aired. There was no longer any time for recriminations.

Ahead of them, between January and March, they had the European Championships, the Winter Olympics and the World Championships – the most important 50 days of John Curry's life. Not until it was all over did Carlo Fassi, with an Italian shrug of his shoulders, pass comment on EST: 'Everybody has got to believe in something, so I let him believe in that,' he said. As always, the arch-manipulator had played it with style.

With winter approaching, Curry got back to work. There had been more 'little adventures' in New York, but nothing serious had gelled. Such would be the pattern of his life. 'He never really had a soulmate,' said Nancy Streeter. 'He was always very sad about this.' Over the months – after their summer spat – John's trust in Nancy had strengthened. The vicissitudes of his private life were no secret to her and his struggles would be her constant sorrow.

On New Year's Eve 1975 in the family's Manhattan apartment, Nancy Streeter, not for the first time, couldn't get John out of her mind. Around her were her family. Only the day before, John had rung from his Colorado apartment for a chat. At her side was the plant-holder he'd left for her Christmas present. In return, she was thinking of buying him a new canvas skate bag as a late gift. As the crowds gathered in Times Square to usher in the New Year she picked up her pen:

> It is wonderful to see you skating so well. You have a big job to do these next months – but you can do it. You can win, John, and you know you can, and that you want to. It was very good to talk to you yesterday and know that your EST strength has helped you. It is remarkable isn't it, what EST has done for you in so many ways; that you are so much happier with yourself and with other people; and that you reach out to others is so wonderful.
>
> Even though you have disappointments, and you have had more than your share these last weeks, don't let them discourage you and draw back in to yourself. This has not been one of the greatest years for me but what you have done, and our friendship are among the good things in it.
>
> Geneva is just around the corner. I am so looking forward to it and will try to be your exemplary friend and skating mother – I will be on my pills so should be calm and collected. Again – happy and successful 1976 – and that means on beyond March for whatever comes in this new year. With my love Nancy xxx

Nobody yet knew it, but 'on beyond March', John Curry would be one of the most famous men on the planet.

Five

'That Olympic business'

John Curry returned to Denver buzzing with more than Werner Erhard's soothing truisms. For months he'd been fretting about his extended musical programme for the three defining tournaments that lay ahead. Suddenly, in an extraordinary way, the conundrum was solved. Somewhere mid-flight between Manhattan and Colorado – according to the myth he subsequently peddled – Curry experienced a revelation.

During a 20-minute burst of creative electricity, he mentally plotted every second of a five-minute routine that would shortly be watched by tens of millions. The music was by Ludwig Minkus – from the ballet *Don Quixote* – and without even stepping on to any ice, he could feel every movement deep in his bones. 'From that moment, I could always do it; it was very strange – as if someone had waved a magic wand over me.'

Sadly, the truth was rather less exotic. In Spain the previous summer, Alison Smith had watched Curry doodling with the same *Don Quixote* music every day. ('He was mad with me,' she laughs, 'because he wanted it for the Olympics and I told him he should stick with the stuff he was doing.') Curry, as always, would not be told. Between Spain and the Sky Rink, he had continued to experiment. Familiar moves from earlier routines were re-sequenced into a new pattern. Edits were inserted into the Minkus music at key points. Point-scoring jumps were carefully accommodated around the rise and fall of the score.

When it all finally came together – no matter how he mythologised it publicly – the outcome was more of a climax to a life-long process than a convenient single revelation. Wherever it had come from, it was brilliant. And even Carlo Fassi – still smarting over Curry's absenteeism – couldn't hide a smile. Not only was the programme incandescent, it was also cunningly competitive, cut precisely to the Italian's pragmatic design. 'Very basic, but effective,' Curry wrote later.

> I set the programme so that no one could miss the difficulty of what I was doing. In fact it was more simple than what I'd been doing in the previous three or four years, but it was easier for the judges to see ... I don't think it was a sell-out to my artistic beliefs because it was a musical and nicely crafted piece of skating.

From its first balletic skips to its final kneeling pose – left hand on hip, right hand pointing to the sky – Curry had fashioned a work of such gliding energy that the Fassis were unable to find fault with it. 'Normally these things take months,' explains Christa. 'This appeared to have been born on an aeroplane back from New York to Denver. Everything was there in his head. He'd even designed his outfit.' The fact that their skater also radiated nerveless positivity merely added to their joy.

For the next few weeks, every evening at six o'clock, Curry ran through the routine inside the Colorado Ice Arena (or the CIA, as Fassi called it). More than 20 consecutive performances later, he still hadn't fallen. Every rehearsal appeared flawless. Every movement seemed destined. Curry's quest for flow had been rendered with such perfection that, for once, the required elements – the toe loops, the spins and the salchows – looked at ease amidst the surging force of his movement.

> I was always 'on'. Never missing a jump, or two-footing, or missing a beat. The whole thing became something of a lark ... Suddenly I appeared as a very consistent person who could churn out a programme mechanically and the sight began to undermine the confidence of the other competitors.

'It was scary,' recalls Christa. 'Twenty-three perfect programmes. It seemed impossible that he could keep it up and yet then he did another one. It was incredible he didn't run out of steam. But then he'd done this EST course and had come back changed. Completely changed. All of a sudden he had no problems with mental garbage. Before it was always, "I can't do it" or "I'm not good enough". Doubt.'

As the European Championships approached, Curry practised furiously. 'I had decided by then that I was not going to stop any more. I was not going to be tired any more. I *was* tired, but I did not stop. And it worked; everything worked.' Even his closest friend couldn't penetrate this wall of concentration. For the first time since 1968 his letters to Heinz Wirz had ceased and Curry's coterie of influential Manhattan intimates – many of them introduced to him by Nancy Streeter – had been quietly expanding.

The skater with no home, and a passport full of ink, had attained new levels of rootlessness. For almost two years he'd been living in and out of Denver. When asked, he gave East 72nd Street, New York, as his home address. The boy from the West Midlands had become an English skater living in New York – underwritten by an American millionaire whose family made bank vaults. Apart from Alison Smith, his various coaches had been born in Switzerland, Germany, Canada or Italy. Before him, relatively few British athletes had crossed the Atlantic to better their chances. Within a decade, the route map laid down by John Curry would be familiar.

Back in London, Britain's skating establishment twisted uneasily in its seat. Just so long as he won – and didn't wave his arms too much – everything would be all right. Hopefully no one would notice that the man under the Union Jack didn't even have a permanent address in his own country.

————

In the second week of 1976, Curry concluded his final session in Denver and flew to Geneva with the Fassis. Whatever happened now, their work there was done. A few days later, Nancy Streeter arrived in Switzerland to support him. It was the third trip she'd made to watch her young friend compete in the European Championships. This time, she was carrying his New York-made costumes. 'I always feel a responsibility not to intrude on you at a competition either personally or officially,' she told him. 'You make it all very easy for me.'

As it did with John, skating ran deep in Nancy's veins. For the previous two years she'd been president of the exclusive Skating Club of New York. While her husband Frank juggled the Whitney fortune, she – with John's active help – had raised funds for the

American Winter Olympics team. Although she had come to regard John with the possessive tenderness of an adoptive mother, Nancy Streeter brought expertise with her warmth.

In Switzerland she could be both a companion and an adviser. She could organise his laundry, accompany him on icy lakeside walks or review his performances. And, if so required, she would be John's shoulder to cry on. At the Patinoire des Vernets ice arena, however – home to Geneva's ice hockey team – Carlo Fassi had no intention of losing.

After his school figures, Curry was lying in second place. Never before had he carved his shapes with such nerveless accuracy; and yet never before had his way been blocked by such a formidably determined Eastern European contingent. After two years out with injuries, the former World Champion Jan Hoffman was back in contention from East Germany. Alongside him were the two Russians, Sergei Volkov and Vladimir Kovalev – World and European champions – together with a watchful posse of Soviet advisers and spin doctors.

Amidst rumours of dirty tricks, Carlo Fassi urged Curry to stay calm and concentrate on his skating: 'Never fear the Soviets when you have the CIA behind you.' By the following morning – after John Curry's public practice session for his compulsory short programme – Fassi had unpicked a 'plot'. Embedded within Curry's two-minute routine the Russians had detected a so-called illegal move and approached each of the judges – 'with the obvious exception of the British judge' – insisting that the Briton should be downmarked when he performed that evening.

It was a depressing development. All Fassi's skater had done was insert an elegant backward leaning spread-eagle ahead of a stipulated double axel jump, one of the six so-called prescribed elements. Nothing had been missed out. Curry had merely been striving to bring beauty to the prosaic.

> Our informant was in fact a Russian teacher who felt that the whole campaign was so unfair that he was determined to try and prevent it. Carlo Fassi's plan was very simple. 'Keep practising the programme exactly as you have been doing it. Change nothing. But in the competition itself, don't do it; don't do the spread-eagle. Just skate backwards and go straight into the double axel'.

That night, skating to Rachmaninov's *Rhapsody on a Theme of Paganini*, Curry followed Carlo Fassi's orders to the letter. No rules were infringed. The offending move had vanished from the programme. 'Panic registered on numerous judges' faces,' recalled Curry. 'Where was the illegal element? ... I had skated quite well, the judges were flummoxed and there was general uproar. The Russian contingent was plainly amazed and mystified. Then the marks came up and a great wall of average marks left me in second position.'

It was just like he'd always said. Skating was rigged. The judges were only there to put their own skaters first. Even if he skated like a 'moron' he'd never win. For the next 24 hours, Curry braced himself for more disappointment. Guided by Carlo Fassi he'd chosen not to protest. 'You can't win that way,' Fassi had told him. 'You will have to skate twice as well in the long programme. You can do it.'

It was time to unveil the *Don Quixote*. Watched by more than 7,000 people, Curry slid out under the blanket lights of the auditorium. Wearing black boots and a tailored sleeveless black-green one-piece, he stood perfectly defined against the ice. The front of his outfit was cut low. Narrow straps rose over his shoulders, framing a silk coffee-coloured shirt tied loosely at the neck. The outfit had been made and designed by the New York illustrator Joe Eula, but the inspiration was all John Curry's.

Five minutes later – for the twenty-fourth time – Curry had completed his programme without error. 'Very determined, very tight, no mistakes' was his verdict. As 14,000 feet stamped their approval, the judges went into a huddle. 'They were having some kind of frantic discussion and finally my marks came up. They were still average and I was suddenly weary of the whole thing.'

For the next half-hour, Curry sat disconsolately backstage while the remaining skaters completed their programmes. Failure here would be ruinous. As the last music ended, and muffled applause dwindled to silence, Curry prepared to leave. Suddenly 'Carlo came bounding around shouting: "Ya got it. Ya got it".' Almost 20 years after persuading his father to let him skate, the Englishman was European Champion. Kovalev, Hoffman, Volkov and the rest had been humbled. Finally the aesthete and the athlete in John Curry had found perfect expression. He had arrived. And he had arrived – in part – courtesy of a judge from Czechoslovakia.

For the first time ever, according to Curry, an Eastern bloc adjudicator had defied the party line and marked decisively in favour of the Englishman. It was, as John noted, a 'very dramatic turning point', but then Curry's portrayal of the East-West schism had always been born of bitterness, and was thus hopelessly simplistic. By degrees, rapprochement had been coming for years. Like everyone else, the Russians could recognise genius, too. And they had always loved a dancer.

During the early 1970s, he'd enjoyed summer weeks skating exhibitions for appreciative crowds in East Germany. The fleet-footed Oleg Protopopov and Lyudmila Belousova – the pioneering 1960s Russian pairs skaters – were high on his list of heroes. In 1975 in Copenhagen, while travelling to an event by public bus, Nancy Streeter had been daringly entreated by a female Russian judge. 'Give John my best and wish him well for tonight.' Long before that, at an event in Calgary, Curry had ripped off his skates in a temper and torn the tongue from a boot. It had been a Russian – Vladimir Kovalev – who then ripped the tongue from his own boot and handed it across in silent homage.

By 1976, almost everyone acknowledged that Curry was single-handedly redefining his sport. It was not until Geneva, however – through small acts of courage – that the results reflected what he had already done. Although he'd probably have won anyway, the story of the dissenting Czech judge, Josef Lojkovic, added intrigue to romance, more so because he too had apparently vanished swiftly into the night.

It was only later during an exhibition tour when we were in Brno, that a man came up to me in the street and said, with the aid of an interpreter: 'I am the judge from Czechoslovakia who put you first'. To which I replied rather lamely: 'Well thank you'. For less than a minute the strangers exchanged awkward pleasantries. 'I got into trouble but what I did was right,' the Czech insisted before he, too, shuffled into the darkness. I never saw him again but he it was who made the vital difference to everything that followed.

In Britain, John Curry was still an unknown. Since the mid-1960s, football's popularity had been on a rising curve, and television time for figure skating was sparse. By mid-January 1976, however, all that was about to change. No country fixates more on its unexpected glories than Britain. And watching events unfold from her home in London, John's friend Penny Malec had been witness to a sudden national awakening.

'I was practically hysterical,' she wrote to John:

> After the compulsories all the papers and Alan Weeks on the wireless were saying that the marks were unfair again, so I sat down last night [before Curry's *Don Quixote* free programme) just gibbering with nerves ... you were so wonderful that I calmed down – especially when the artistic marks came up with that lovely band of 5.9s across the screen. When the final results came up we just screamed and danced around the room (doggo barking with joy).

The domestic press had woken up to a story. Twelve humiliating years had elapsed since the British sniffed success in a winter pastime. Home-grown historians might brag about the Briton who'd invented slalom skiing, but we still weren't terribly good on anything slippy. Back in 1964, Robin Dixon and Tony Nash had unexpectedly won Olympic gold in the two-man bobsleigh. Before that, in the 1920s, the British men had won a gold medal at curling, but by the time it was formally recognised in 2006 the team were long dead. The only skating medal had been Jeanette Altweg in 1952. Since then, nothing.

For lots of reasons – and not all of them about skating – John Curry seemed interesting. Not only was he a rare British champion, but, for a sportsman, he seemed cut from peculiar cloth. With the Innsbruck Winter Olympics just four weeks away, Fleet Street prepared to satisfy the swell of public curiosity. The age of the paparazzi had yet to dawn, but John Curry's life in the shadows had but days left on the clock. Sensing what was to come – and to seal off their skater from the outside world – the Fassis moved their camp east into Germany.

Under the gaze of the Zugspitze mountain, the Bavarian resort of Garmisch-Partenkirchen would enable Curry to decompress without distractions. For one week, lodging at the Hotel Zugspitzen, he had the ice to himself. Nancy Streeter was already back in New York, glowing with the memory of her time with John:

> Everything seemed to come together – the costume, the beauty of the long program, the audience's response, the press … and most of all you, with your confidence and lack of nervousness and the beauty and strength of your skating … I'll never forget the excitement of learning you had won, seeing you on the podium as the British flag went up; the flowers – all the rest of it. As well, I just loved being there, being part of the 'scene' and being with you and doing all the little things – tea, TV, talks, Geneva walks – even laundry duty.

Few people knew Curry's frailties better than Nancy. Since victory in Switzerland, his mood had slumped. Being told how marvellous he was would help until the adrenalin returned. Being told that American television was also waking up to his talent would help even more. It wasn't a cure, but Nancy's letters, always fizzing with can-do energy and mumsy advice, seemed to calm him: 'Just don't let people get at you there even if it means Mr Fassi or your team leader have to be brutal to your public and press. I can see you smile and say "Easier said than done, Nance", but this really is important.'

Instinctively, she had seen the storm coming. In North America, the big television networks were clearing their schedules for the Olympic figure skating. The immense battle for the men's gold – with Cranston, Curry and Kovalev in contention – would lie at the heart of their coverage. So, too, would the fortunes of 19-year-old Dorothy Hamill, already a national treasure and the runaway favourite to win the ladies' event. Even allowing for time differences, John Curry's skating would shortly be seen by tens of millions. 'This won't be easy and the pressure will be very great but I know you can handle that and that you can do it.' Again and again, Nancy accentuated the positive.

Curry's slump had been mercifully brief. By late January, Hamill had joined him, Carlo and Christa at the Hotel Zugspitzen. During the day, if it got too cold, Fassi sent Curry from the ice. In the evenings, there were raucous meals at the town's restaurants. 'There is nothing wrong with me,' he reassured Nancy by letter. 'I'm just tired. I think I'll take a sauna this afternoon. Since our arrival I have eaten so much cake, potatoes, soup, bread, meat, cream and ice cream.'

Fassi's military-style planning and discipline suited him. Weakness of any kind did not. His EST training had also reasserted itself and he was sleeping ten hours a night. 'We were like a small family group,' remembers Dorothy. 'We were Carlo's kids.' Seven years before, Curry had wrestled with Arnold Gerschwiler in the blizzards of Davos. Now he was enjoying 'the happiest winter of my life'. 'It was fun even though we worked very hard [and] the organisation never flagged.'

By early February it was time to forsake the log fires of a Bavarian pension for the utilitarian bedrooms of the Olympic Village. Two hours across the border, the representatives of 37 nations were gathering amidst high security in Innsbruck. By the time Curry arrived, the British team were already settled in, but 'there was no demur'. No other individual carried such realistic hopes. It didn't matter that he kept his distance. 'Even in a room with a hundred people he'd still be on his own,' explains Robin Cousins, Curry's junior partner in the 1976 figure skating 'team'.

Personal space would be key. Nothing could be allowed to break into it. Every day at 7 a.m. Cousins pulled on his winter woollens and braved sub-zero temperatures on the outdoor training rink. If Curry was already there, the two men spoke little. 'There was an acknowledgement, but that was all,' remembers Cousins. 'We had nothing to talk about. Nothing in common. I only ever saw him at the rink. Never at the village.' Small talk had never suited Curry. In Innsbruck, few people were allowed near. Not even his mother.

At this point, no one would have begrudged Rita a little jealousy. Ambition – and American sponsorship – had drawn her son into the embrace of a surrogate family. And although it helped that Nancy Streeter telephoned regularly, Rita had spent years being kept away from events at which Nancy was now a regular spectator. Apart from one early trip to France, she had never seen John compete at the highest level. It was an indignity unworthy of the crucial early role she had played and John's motives for keeping his mother at a distance seemed woolly at best.

My mother's always talked about coming to an international competition in Europe – Europeans or Worlds – and I always used to say 'Wait till next year when I'll be doing a bit better' because I would have hated her to come and see me come in seventh or fifth or whatever. That would have been miserable. So as far as I was concerned, she was always waiting till next year. But this year she was very strong and said, 'I'm going to come to the Olympics'. And I said, 'Fine. That's great. It'll be lovely to see you there'. But we made an agreement not to see each other before the competition simply because I'm not used to having her around before competitions.

Ever diplomatic and respectful, Nancy had stayed away. In her place she air-mailed scented freesias pressed flat by her favourite dance books 'topped by Nijinksy for extra good luck'. No one ever questioned John on Rita's absences or why, unlike the effervescent Nancy, she would not be privy to the 'tea, TV and talks'. Having waited so long, Rita was happy enough to be included at all. Along with Andrew, and a handful of Solihull friends (the 'Birmingham XI') she'd saved up £400 for a two-week 'package tour', and set up camp in nearby Seefeld. Every now and then she spoke to John on the telephone, but there would be no direct contact until it was all over.

As Rita settled in, curiosity about her son was growing fast. Under pressure from the British (and foreign) press, who knew virtually nothing about him, he'd given an impromptu virtuoso press conference. Some of the questions had been about ice skating. Many, however, had not. Looking on, the British Olympic team officials had shuffled uncomfortably. 'Why did your father object so strongly to ballet?' he was asked. 'Oh,' said John. 'For the perfectly obvious reasons.' The inference, although heavily disguised, was abundantly clear. Insidiously, the pressure was building.

The following day, newspapers worldwide began to carry articles sketching out his journey from Acocks Green to Innsbruck. The *Guardian* announced his plan to form a 'theatre on ice' once the Games were over. In the *Observer*, the athlete-turned-writer Christopher Brasher declared that 'John Curry will break through a barrier of British inhibition – the belief that ballet dancing is not manly.' In the *Daily Mail*, the brilliant sports journalist Ian Wooldridge was more artful in his selection of words. The only one missing was 'homosexual'.

> Despite his soft curly hair, chiselled lips, gentle voice and the graceful arcs he describes with his hands when he talks about skating being removed from the rough world of sport and elevated to the realms of the performing arts, he has thick armour plating just below the surface and a capacity for swift waspish repartee ... It is no secret either that his Soviet rivals, intending to rattle him, mock his gentle mannerisms. Curry not so much shrugs it off as makes it perfectly clear that their very existence on earth is to him a matter of supreme unimportance.

Since very few newspapers penetrated the Olympic Village, Curry's preparations proceeded in ignorance of this ballooning hype. It was a news vacuum that would have damaging consequences. Although Curry was no fool, his guard was underdeveloped. He was also honest to the point of recklessness and, away from the formal structure of a press conference, other journalists were seeking his ear.

If someone asked him a question, he would answer it truthfully. If that someone happened to be an agency journalist from the Associated Press, Curry would answer that, too. Penny Malec called it 'moral consistency'. The concept of 'off the record' was not one he fully understood. In five days' time, that would be a mis-understanding he had cause to regret bitterly.

In the final frenzy before the opening ceremony, whatever Curry might – or might not – have been saying was forgotten. As Britain's one serious medal hope, he'd been chosen to carry the Union Jack into the main Olympic arena. Four years before, in Sapporo, he'd savaged the 'snobs' around him for whom 'the Olympics meant nothing more than the price of a bobsleigh holiday'. In Austria it – or he – clearly hadn't got any better.

'I heard the same crass remarks and the same brand of cynicism that had scarred the Ceremony before. Nothing seemed to have altered.' Instructed to walk four metres ahead of the British team, Curry happily maintained 'a twelve-foot cushion between [his] idealism and the ribaldry behind [him]' ... 'I was suddenly out of earshot, and I no longer cared about the belittling; for better or worse I was in a nationalistic vacuum of my own devising.'

Ahead of him in the snake of marching flags, John could see the red maple leaf of Canada. Somewhere behind it there would be Toller Cranston. On his day, despite the muscularity of the Eastern bloc skaters, Cranston was surely still the man to beat. What John Curry couldn't possibly have known, however, is that Toller Cranston was probably already beaten.

———

In Canada, only the day before travelling to Austria, Cranston had run through his long Olympic programme for one last time. Everything about it was perfect; too perfect. Euphoria and horror had surged through every movement. 'I was skating the performance of my life. I could do no wrong. In an era when three triples were quite a lot, I think I did seven.' In the parlance of modern sport, Cranston had peaked too soon.

A few days later he gloomily collected his Olympic accreditation in Innsbruck wearing a 'floor-length sheared muskrat coat', and headed for the windblown practice rink. It was no more to his liking than Curry's. Needing badly to emote publicly, he struggled with even the basics. 'I did not make the impression that I wanted to make. I was more concerned with attempting to jump downwind. I couldn't weave my mystical star magic because there were too many distractions.'

Jumps he'd mastered years before stayed trapped in his legs. It was 'like writing with one of my feet,' he wrote some years later. 'When I dove into a snow-drift during the first practise I understood that the skating world was too ridiculous and absurd and I completely lost interest in it.' If it was true – and Cranston's words were written some years later – one of Curry's fiercest rivals was already losing the mind games. But since the two no longer spoke, no advantage accrued to the Englishman. 'What is, is and what ain't, ain't.' Had Cranston known about Curry's EST-induced sanguinity, it would only have made matters worse.

Four days after the opening ceremony, combat was joined. On Sunday 8 February – on a subsidiary rink still surrounded by Christmas trees – the leading skaters ran through their byzantine school figures. On either side of them, motionless judges wrapped in knee-length furs and thick coats looked on. The only sound was the steady hiss of steel on ice. Wearing fitted black trousers, gloves and a short, red and white Norwegian-style sweater, Curry appeared calm and concentrated.

With his eyes on the ice, and his arms raised slightly from the waist, Curry traced each circular pattern of his three mandatory figures in unbroken flowing movements. Behind his blade – and the glossy polish of his black boots – only the narrowest trace of crystal shavings broke the surface. A penitential stillness hung over the proceedings. No one seemed to be breathing. Only the judges' eyes were moving in silent scrutiny. Thirty per cent of Curry's score would come from their microscopic examination of his technique. By the end of the morning, he was feeling satisfied.

Toller Cranston, on the other hand, was feeling miserable. Despite his earlier encounter with a snow bank, he, too, had started the figures feeling confident. For years, the tracings had been his downfall. Arriving at Innsbruck he felt certain he had mastered them. As with his practice jumps, however, that hard-won proficiency had suddenly disappeared. 'I pushed off and then I don't know what happened … nerves or something else … but my eyes filled with tears and I became blind.'

Cranston's first figure was diabolical. The next two were 'a smidge' better. Once the scores were tallied he'd finished the day in seventh place. Without the generosity of the Canadian judge, it might have been worse. 'The Olympic gold medal had just evaporated,' he said. Not so for John Curry who was lying second, sandwiched between the two Russians, Sergei Volkov and Vladimir Kovalev. All in all, a good day's work.

That night, Curry and the Fassis analysed their prospects. A glow of quiet confidence seemed in order. Volkov's lead was an illusion. The young Russian – who Curry referred to as 'the boy' – was a technician not an artist. School figures were his strength, not free skating, and his challenge would fade. Kovalev remained a big threat, and Cranston's theatricality might yet revive his fading hopes. 'Keep quiet, eat properly, and try not to think about the other competitors,' Carlo Fassi advised him. It wouldn't be difficult. 'He never spoke to any other competitors,' remembers Cranston. 'Nothing. It was very effective. We all felt like dirt.'

The following evening hostilities resumed on the granite-like ice of the Olympic hockey stadium. After the scholarly weavings of the figures, the skaters performed two-minute musical programmes packed with seven specified jumps and spins. Of necessity, the musical pace was frantic, with restricted opportunities for Curry's familiar embroidery. 'Rather uninspiring' was his own verdict. Inside the vast ice arena, the public had reached a different conclusion.

Wearing his trademark one-piece suit and beige shirt – and skating to Rachmaninov – Curry had wrapped the required elements inside a package of such panache that flowers had showered down from an ecstatic full house. 'The most elegant skater I have ever seen,' the American ex-champion Dick Button told the watching millions. 'Until this year he's never been able to pull it all together between the ears … but he's taken on a course in learning to discipline his emotions … and all of a sudden for the very first time he's been able to compete under pressure.' Even the media had now heard about his Erhard Seminar Training.

As Curry stepped off the ice, frowning darkly, Carlo Fassi gripped him in a playful bear hug. There was still no smile. Seconds later, Curry's marks flickered across the electronic scoreboard. Despite a handful of near-invisible technical flaws, almost every judge had carded him 5.9 for artistry. Clapping his hands, he bowed his head for a kiss from Christa. With both Volkov and Kovalev underperforming, only Cranston stood between Curry and victory in the short programme. Overnight, however, the Canadian extrovert's skating had been thrillingly recalibrated.

> I wore black, the colour I always wore for the short program. I skated with such veracity (or ferocity, or velocity) that I destroyed everyone, and I won with a 6.0 from almost every judge. I then pulled from seventh to fourth which put me in medal range – although I still felt like a failure.

Wearing a one-piece black suit, with sparkling shoulders, and a plunging neckline, Cranston had dazzled to the music of Johann Strauss. Although his highest score was a 5.9 – not six as he claimed – there had been no trace of negativity in his performance. On American television, commentators drooled over its 'bizarre and exotic' flair. 'He's an artist on and off the ice,' viewers were told.

Only the East German and Czech judges had failed to see it that way. If he was going down, he was doing so with style.

But it had not been enough and he knew it. Although he'd vanquished Curry on this second day, it had been only by a whisker. The Englishman had still shone, and the fading challenge of the two East Europeans had seen him move above Sergei Volkov on the leader board. With just one component left – albeit one worth half of the total mark – Curry was in pole position for Olympic gold. Short of a fall in his *Don Quixote* routine, it seemed that no one could stop him.

The following day – a Tuesday – the competition took a rest. Despite virulent flu that was decimating the village, Curry joined the crowds of Americans watching Dorothy Hamill score a perfect six in her own short programme. Like him, she'd finished her second day in the lead. Wherever you looked, it seemed Carlo Fassi's stardust was proving irresistible. And wherever Curry walked there was a reporter hanging on his tail.

In the press tent yards of patriotic copy were already winging their way back to Britain's newspaper. A country conditioned to defeat was being whipped into a frenzy. Over breakfast the next morning, readers would be informed that 'a nation watches in hope' and that 'into the Olympia Eisstadion tonight, quite alone' (according to the *Daily Express*) 'will come a man facing the great moment of his life. John Anthony Curry.'

Every single paper crowded its pages with similar words. Leader columns dripped with good luck exhortations. Cartoonists were pressed into action. Phrases like triple salchow and double axel were being helpfully deciphered in curtain-raising background articles. Television and radio broadcasts assessed his chances. Images of John Curry – sporting his distinctive perm – were everywhere. Even Curry himself, with 24 hours still to go, was struggling to block out the frenzy.

From all over the world the telegrams had started to arrive. 'It suddenly hit me that day what was happening. There were so many people in England hoping that I would win and the weight of that arrived on Tuesday.' After congratulating Hamill, Curry's clock started to slow. 'Everything seemed to take an eternity. There seemed no way to fill in the time … It was like I had a sack of coal on my back.'

Up in his room he read *Bleak House*, stewed in a hot bath and sat in statuesque concentration behind darkened curtains. Hour by hour, Tuesday tick-tocked into Wednesday. Inside his head, to help pass the time, he ran an imaginary loop of what was to come. He called it visualisation:

> I went into my 'space'; I shut my eyes and took a 'step' outside my body and examined it in very close detail, and found that it was in very good working order. Mentally, I 'played' a film of myself doing my programme (without any mistakes in it) and after that I simply opened my eyes.

On the final morning, Curry headed for one last practice session. Dorothy Hamill was there to watch. Like her English friend, the teenager had an entire nation bearing down on her. 'I was sad because I was not going to be able to watch his final free-skate that evening. There was no TV in our little village bunks and it was going to be on quite late at night. I remember telling him how great his programmes were and how I wished I could do that but I doubt I could express then how amazing I thought he was.' Over a private coffee they wished each other luck. Soon both would be very public property.

By the early evening, the Olympic stadium was starting to buzz. Cocooned in a sheepskin coat, Rita had arrived several hours early to take her place high in the public gallery. Over the previous few days, John had rung her three times. Although they hadn't met, he'd arranged special rink-side spots for both Andrew and his mother, which the pair had declined. 'We came as a team,' she said. 'I preferred to stay as a member of our Birmingham XI.' In front of their £6 seats they hung a huge Union Jack. Down by the barrier, Rita had left a bouquet of white carnations to be thrown on to the ice if things went well.

Under a sky full of stars, Curry was making his way to the arena on the British team bus. Alongside him was Robin Cousins (who would finish tenth) and the team leader, Eileen Anderson, 'the grande dame of skating' as Haig Oundjian called her. 'She was very fond of John and she loved telling this story,' says Oundjian. 'Around 9 p.m. she looked out of the window and said, "John look, it's a full moon". John goes "Oh my God stop the bus". The driver stops the bus. John says to Eileen, "You must go out, turn three times and bark at the moon." So this woman in her sixties, set upon by John, goes outside. "Woof woof woof." Comes back on, and John says, "Thank God" and falls back in his seat.'

Backstage at the arena, Carlo Fassi was conducting a more grounded master class. At the draw for the evening's skating order there'd been a setback. Following one skater's withdrawal, Curry's name had emerged first. Historically, the opening free skater was always marked low. With competitors still to come, judges liked to hold on to their big scores. Curry's lead suddenly looked as vulnerable as his nerves. Carlo Fassi saw it differently.

> [He] said in a rather loud voice, 'That is wonderful! He gives so much pressure to the others'. And with that we left. We did not even bother to see where the others were skating. 'Hexcellent. Great. They will be so nervous after you skate,' continued Mr Fassi in earshot.

It was nothing they hadn't planned for. Secretly in Garmisch, Fassi had meticulously groomed Curry for every possible place in the starting order. No crevice was left into which Curry's anxieties could creep. Every minute of his build-up had been allocated, from the times of the Olympic buses to the moment he put his skates on. 'I was not nervous in the slightest degree,' said Curry. 'It was extraordinary.'

Skating first had never troubled him anyway. In the past, it had minimised stage fright. Here, he might even have won before the others started. In the final few minutes, as 10,000 people craned forward in their seats, Curry composed himself alone. Once again, he was wearing the dark green jumpsuit and the wide-collared shirt – along with the tiny black belt that (in Toller Cranston's bitter description) encircled a waist so slender it 'piqued his inordinate vanity'.

At a nod from 'Mr Fassi' he made his way to the ice and circled uneasily. When his name was announced – 'John Curry of Great Britain' – a huge roar ripped from one side of the stadium to the other. Battered by noise, under the bludgeoning glare of the floodlights, Curry skated smartly to the end of the rink furthest from the judges and pulled up by a plastic glass wall measled with the bruises left by ice hockey pucks. Extending both arms, and looking skywards, he held his pose and waited. And then it began.

———

As the music starts, Curry declares his intent. A skip, a sideways step, a delicate semaphore of arms, and he is gliding towards his first triple spin. No effort is visible in what he does. His back is redwood straight. His fingers curl and fold like petals. By the time he touches down his right foot he has rotated his forward moving body three times in little more than a second. Only when he pauses to take in the first gale of applause does it become apparent that something subtle has shifted in the dynamic of the evening. That man down there on the ice – under the scrutiny of 20 million British television viewers – is winning before it has begun. If there is a competition here, then this spectacular young stranger is already above and beyond it.

As he sets off again, skipping to the flow of the Minkus score, Curry's furious confidence is proving infectious. The audience can enjoy it now. It seems impossible that he will ever falter or fall. It doesn't matter that skating's mystifying glossary is beyond most of them. Pioneering art often transcends understanding. Tonight it is the spirit alone which moves inside people. From a wally double flip, Curry melts into a triple jump, landing with such deft precision it's as if the ice has dissolved.

Barely a minute has passed. The rout continues. Curry's unbroken thread of willowy movement now softens. Behind the applause for his jump, the music has slowed. In the place of bombast comes romance and elegant yearning. Curry swoops and spread-eagles, raising first one arm and then the other, before an elegant clockwise spin leads him off across the rink in immense soaring strides. After his third triple jump, there's a surprise. Even the television commentators notice it. John Curry is smiling. From now on it is easy.

Second by second, he is working his way through the *Don Quixote*. Twenty-four flawless performances but none of them quite like this one. After a cross foot spin in which his rotating feet never leave their spot, the music changes again. Waltz music. A charge of gleeful energy pulses through Curry's routine. He skips and shuffles. He clasps his hands behind his back and rocks mischievously from side to side as the audience turn his smile into a joyous community clap-along. 'Look at that. Extraordinary,' says the American commentator. 'He never succumbs to pure theatrics.'

Everyone is with him. Whoops and ecstatic yells puncture the constant clapping. Untold pairs of eyes are following him round and round. 'I love having people watch me. I love an audience. I skate to them not to myself,' he says. No skater has ever had an audience like this. With less than two minutes remaining, a harp arpeggio cues a camel spin. Curry's hands slide to his waist as he rotates ten times on his anchored left foot. For the first time the music pauses – a bar of orchestral silence before the rustic pizzicato that propels him in thrilling, skipping steps the full length of the ice. His arms rise and fall precisely to the beat. A wave of exuberant delight bursts across the arena.

Momentarily, everyone has forgotten just how difficult skating is. No one is adding up the lonely hours that became weeks, or the solitary months that became years. No one is seeing the seven-year-old child at the Birmingham Ice Rink. No one wants it to stop, but it must. With the music winding up, he vanishes into the blur of an anti-clockwise sitting spin, somehow switching feet after five rotations. Within seconds he has stretched out of it and dropped to his haunches once more for a sit spin in the opposite direction. As he switches feet, the toe of Curry's blade catches the ice. It's his first mistake, but no one has noticed. On American television, the commentators are awe-struck. 'We've never seen skaters that can do this kind of thing. What an artist. He is on. He is so on.'

Only seconds remain. The music swells to its fiery crescendo. Curry orbits the rink tossing in double spins and split jumps, before his final soaring spread-eagle. As the cymbals crash he crosses his arms across his chest before opening them up like a crucifix. His legs are parted wide; the blades are pointing in opposite directions; and the line between them is ruler-straight. Leaning back into gravity, he begins to carve a circle.

Music and motion now seem so gloriously synchronised it is pointless to resist. The ovation has already started before Curry exits the spread-eagle – with a theatrical flourish of his arms – and hurls himself into his final double jump. After a dainty hop into a kneeling position, it is over, four minutes and fifty-eight seconds after it started.

Curry kneels on his left foot. His right arm is folded high over his head. His left hand is on his waist. A spray of flowers slides past him on the ice and a boyish grin breaks out all over his face. For a moment he looks ten years younger than he is. Over his shoulder, Carlo Fassi, at rink-side, is hopping and clapping. More and more bouquets are piling up near Curry's feet. No one seems to want to stop applauding. To make themselves heard, even the commentary teams have to shout. 'One of the finest moments of skating I have ever seen and he knows it.'

He knows it too and he is happy; as happy as anyone has ever seen him. He waves. He bows. He smiles. But he leaves the bouquets. With his chest still visibly pounding, he stands up and skates towards the noise.

———

Before he stepped off the ice, Curry felt certain he had won. Nothing, not even the crackle of camera flashbulbs, had distracted him. As Carlo clutched a bunch of yellow orchids, Christa clamped John in a congratulatory embrace. With few exceptions – one of them being the Canadian – the Olympic judges had been seduced. Almost every score was a 5.9. Whatever 'Cold War' bias still lingered had been blown away and for the remaining competitors the game was up. For Toller Cranston, a bad Olympics had just got worse.

As he made his way into the arena, the backstage corridor was blocked by British team members shouting, 'He's won, he's won.' Through the PA, Cranston could hear the announcer telling him to take to the ice immediately. 'I saw the absurdity, the surreal twist … I'm going to be disqualified because I can't walk the last five feet to the ice … I think I even chuckled.' Even before his troubled journey to the rink, however, Cranston had already made what he called a 'fatal mistake'.

Much as Cranston had derided Curry's outfit – 'extremely conservative meat and potatoes' – the Englishman's contemporary cool had triumphed. Cranston, on the other hand, had opted for a peacock-blue one-piece, complete with embroidered leaves and beaded flowers. Once again, the neckline was low. It was a look Curry loathed. And it was a look that had had its day. 'It was something I never did,' said the Canadian. 'Usually I wore black, the colour of omnipotence and total destruction.' Cranston was also carrying too many pounds. 'With all the free meals that one has at the Olympics, I was starting to gain weight, so it didn't really fit me. I had to perform with my stomach sucked in.'

When he stumbled on his first triple toe loop jump, any lingering hope Cranston might have had died with it. No amount of soaring split jumps to a Prokofiev score could save him. When the scores were counted, he'd pulled himself up into the bronze medal position behind the Russian Vladimir Kovalev. 'God knows I tried my best, but I was on the down and Curry was on the up.' The Englishman had plundered his Olympic gold.

For Curry, there were tears but no champagne. 'He wasn't the sort to jump up and down,' explains Christa. In his dressing room, he wept quietly as bedlam reigned outside. While reporters rapped on his door, he loosened his boots and prepared for the medal ceremony. In the auditorium, the lights were being dimmed and the red carpets rolled out. Under a volley of military trumpets, Curry tiptoed to the podium, grinning shyly. Traipsing behind him were Cranston and Kovalev.

'Standing on that Innsbruck podium … John was but six inches higher than I, yet he was on Mount Everest and I was in the gutters of Calcutta,' recalled Cranston. 'He had won; I had lost. He had graduated; I had failed … I don't believe that he congratulated either Vladimir or me.'

With the gold medal around his neck, Curry stood motionless during the British national anthem. It was to be his last moment of Olympic calm. In Britain, live or on news bulletins, his victory had been watched by almost half the nation. Photographers were banking up rink-side wanting his picture with Rita. Radio reporters with microphones were shouting for his attention. Every payphone in Innsbruck was occupied by a journalist ringing through his copy. Every telegraph wire into Switzerland was zinging with congratulatory telegrams. By the morning, they would be piled up around his bedroom door in boxes.

Telegrams from royalty and cabinet ministers; telegrams from publishers wanting his life story; telegrams from his past. Solihull School wished him 'heartiest congratulations'. 'All at Weetabix' – for some reason – wanted him to know they were delighted. The pop singer Anita Harris and the Royal Ballet were 'thrilled'. So was

Denis Howell, the Minister for Sport. 'Please phone,' he urged. Elton John was stunned: 'Would love you to be one of my guests at my concert.' Werner Erhard of EST told him his win had created 'space for people everywhere' and from Eric Morley, at MECCA bingo, there was the offer of unspecified work. From two anonymous enthusiasts there was merely: 'Congratulations Nureyev on ice'.

Among the cryptic, the weird and the anonymous – and the unsolicited felicitations from strangers – there were the ones that mattered. From New York: 'Your performance golden terribly proud love nancy'. From Heinz Wirz, 'Tonight you showed us all what art and beauty in skating can be stop I am so proud of you and proud to be a friend'. And from Penny Malec in London: 'We are bursting with joy'.

Two days later the letters would start to arrive. Proposals of marriage. Expressions of love. Random photographs and curious drawings. An early Valentine from a nameless New York admirer. Letters from schools, letters from well-wishers, letters from people he knew well and from people he'd never met. Few would ever be answered. Most were not even opened. By the time the flood of correspondence struck the Olympic Village, Curry was already in mental flight; no longer just an Olympian, but that rarest of things in 1970s Britain – a publicly 'outed' homosexual sportsman.

———

There had been no post-ceremony party. For the first time since arriving in Switzerland 11 days before, Rita was able to wrap her son briefly in an overdue embrace. Like so many others in the village, she'd succumbed to laryngitis. Either that or she'd lost her voice shouting 'We want six' to the judges. 'Finally, he's got his style of skating over to the world,' she told the *Daily Mail*, but the 'words were less spoken than croaked'. Quietly, John slipped away to find a telephone. In New York, it was early evening and the Streeters were getting ready to dine. 'Oh my God,' he told Nancy, 'I'm missing my favourite dinner.'

There would not be much time to celebrate. For several days, John had been meeting a journalist in the competitors' café. 'I had never seen anyone skate like that before,' explains New York-born John Vinocur, now of the Paris-based *International Herald Tribune*.

'I thought there might be a story.' Vinocur's brief was an enviable one. Providing he generated intelligent pieces of broad international appeal, his employers, the Associated Press (AP) agency, gave him free rein. Already this Olympics he'd filed copy on the mindset of downhill racers which, like everything he wrote, AP had syndicated to English-speaking news outlets around the world. Backing a hunch that John Curry could win gold, he'd asked the Englishman for an audience. The Englishman had said yes.

In an age before personal managers, no corporate eyebrows were raised. Curry was lonely and liked to talk about himself; an attention seeker who craved privacy. He was also alarmingly frank. Over several cups of coffee, their talk drifted naturally from skating to Curry's sexual orientation. 'I've got into various scenes,' Curry told Vinocur. 'I'm not a promiscuous person but I've got friends and I like to go out. I talk. I look. If I need to explode I can go on a three-day binge in Greenwich Village. I've had a lover and it was OK but now I have friends. It's nice too.' Curry was clearly not talking about women.

'I found myself telling him things I had kept deliberately suppressed for years,' Curry said later. 'He asked me if I was happy and I said no, I didn't think so. I lived in a homophobic world and I was a homosexual which made it very difficult.' The American had his scoop. By accident or design Curry's 'secret' was coming out. As soon as the Englishman's gold medal was confirmed, Vinocur called up his news desk and told them to 'move' the story.

As the champion dozed, it sped around the world like a virus. By the following morning, it was starting to surface in news outlets from London to Los Angeles. By Friday, it was everywhere. 'My fight to be different' headlined the *Daily Express* with glee. 'Britain's gold medal star explains his very personal lifestyle'.

Much later Curry would insist that he'd been betrayed, and that his unguarded candour had never been intended for publication. 'With the medal it seemed that I had acquired all the trappings that went with it; the chains as well as the ribbons. Well, so be it – but it is a foreign jungle to me,' he'd said. It is much more likely, however, that Curry knew precisely what he was doing. 'He was fed up with denying it,' thinks Penny Malec. 'He let it out deliberately.' Unsurprisingly, John Vinocur agrees. Curry's subsequent protestations, he insists, were a smokescreen.

'These were not off-the-record conversations,' he insists.

> No way. The whole thing was absolutely standard journalism.
> There was no expectation of copy approval either. He knew I was
> a reporter; we met more than once and we had a cordial relationship
> in which I at no time felt like I was transgressing into areas which
> were uncomfortable for him. He seemed quite relieved if anything.
> I liked him. None of this was fraught. It was all the most natural
> thing. The quotes were scrupulously what he said.

When Curry rose on Thursday morning he had no hint of what lay ahead. The world's newspapers would not reach Innsbruck for several hours, and most had gone to print long before Vinocur's revelations rattled off the wire. The *Daily Mirror* praised 'Golden Boy Curry' who 'makes all the rest look like men on stilts'. The *Daily Mail* raved about 'the ice–cold golden boy'. The *New York Times* spoke of Curry's 'triumph against the old guard'.

Everywhere, the reportage had captured the previous night's mood of emotional wonderment. Even the most hard-bitten reporters had been moved. Ian Wooldridge in the *Daily Mail* spoke for them all. 'John Curry gave us precisely what he said he'd give us – an exhibition in skating as a new modern art. Amid the carnations and the gasping recognition of his commanding brilliance, he just looked up with a smile which said "I told you so". Supercilious, I think, is the word for it. We forgive him that. We'll forgive him damned nearly anything for the way he did it.'

Within hours of waking the next morning, however, the news agenda had shifted. This was no longer just a sports story. As Vinocur's article bled out, national celebration – in some quarters – was mutating into something more prurient. Although the timing of the telephone call is unclear, Curry had been reached by a British tabloid newspaper offering a six-figure cash sum for his 'unexpurgated' story. 'I felt sick to the pit of my stomach,' he later told a friend. 'I knew that I would never, ever, as long as I lived be able to trust anyone again.'

By mid-morning, having abruptly ended that telephone conversation, Curry was on his way to Seefeld for a pre-arranged lunch with Rita, Andrew and the party from Birmingham. Rarely had the Alps looked so magnificent. Every tree was sagging with snow. Enormous icicles ran down from the eaves of wooden chalets framed against a cloudless blue sky. Wrapped in a duffel coat, he entered his mother's hotel looking 'deathly pale'. 'The lines [in his face] induced by remorseless training were almost vertical ravines,' noted Wooldridge, who'd been invited along with a *Daily Mail* photographer to observe. 'Uncharacteristically, for he is by nature a courteous person, he was nervy, snappy and abrupt. "DO come on", he instructed his mother, "I'm EXTREMELY hungry". It was 12.42 p.m.'

Over lunch, Curry's mood brightened. For a couple of hours, the dog-tired ache where his adrenalin had been was forgotten. In the late afternoon light he walked quietly through a nearby forest with Rita and Andrew. He told her that there might be something unpleasant brewing in the papers. 'But I don't think he went into any more details,' she says. If he'd intended to say more, Curry pulled back. Like everyone else – if she hadn't worked it out already – his mother would find out the details through the papers.

By the time he got back to Innsbruck, matters had escalated. The AP article was now running on the front page of the London *Evening Standard*. Under a picture of Rita and John, millions of commuters were absorbing the headline: 'Would some fool say, He skates like a gay? ' 'All along during my career,' it quoted him as saying, 'I've wanted very much to talk to people frankly about skating, about my view on things but I've lived fearing these idiots.'

Curry's opportunity to 'talk frankly' was nearer than he thought. Trying to face down the onslaught of media interest was proving impossible and a press conference had been hastily arranged for eight o'clock that evening in Innsbruck. As a growing army of reporters took their seats, Curry telephoned Carlo Fassi for advice. 'Just be honest – tell them something but not too much and then they will go away.' Next – perhaps inevitably – he called Nancy Streeter in New York.

'He was so disappointed and anguished that this was all people were interested in,' remembers Nancy's daughter Meg. 'I believe she said: Do what you think is right and if you think you are ready to handle it, then be true to yourself. If this is what you are, then bring it forward.'

Flanked by Olympic officials, Curry entered the press room and took his place behind a forest of microphones. Slowly, his interrogators danced around their subject. Not one of them seemed able to be direct. This was new for them too. Coming out was rare. Coming out in public was surely unique. There was no real precedent for what one writer praised as his 'act of social courage' and almost every question was phrased as a negative. With £10,000 of American money behind him, had he really been skating for Britain? 'Of course,' came the reply. 'But I love America. I love the attitude that before you start all things are possible.'

'Slowly the questioning got around to words like "virility" and "masculinity",' wrote Ian Wooldridge in the *Daily Mail*. 'Curry heard them coming and smiled at the room's discomfiture and said simply, "I don't think I lack virility and what other people think of me doesn't matter".' Warming to his subject, Curry admitted that he'd had affairs and gay lovers but 'had nothing new to say about sex'. 'Do you think that what I did yesterday was not athletic?' he snapped at one reporter.

> When the official conference was over he was put under private questioning. He crossed spread hands like a boxer and said 'Finish' ... It was John Curry's second stunning performance in 19 hours. He had taken on the world's hard newsmen and beaten them at their own less artistic game.

Publicly, Curry declared that it had 'passed off satisfactorily'. Privately he was shattered by it. According to one version of the day's events he immediately returned to Seefeld and finally opened up to his mother over brandies from the mini-bar. Rita Curry, however, proffers no recollection of that meeting. 'If he did, I think that's something I've shut away,' she says. At the time, in a magazine interview, she was more forthcoming. 'He rang me up and said "I'm sorry Mum, but it's not really the way it's printed." For me that was enough ... what they said isn't true anyway. But in any case, I can't see that it matters."

Rita knew but didn't want to know. Her relationship with John wasn't configured for detailed confidences. She could never be what Nancy could be. She couldn't pretend to be comfortable with any of this. But neither would she make things difficult. Even when he was dying, Rita never questioned her son's choices; never asked for details if none were supplied. There was no reproach, or criticism, in her silence. John had always been free to make his choices. Just as she could always choose what she believed.

In Innsbruck that was not proving easy. The morning after John's press conference, a British journalist had telephoned her and read out the contents of John Vinocur's agency report. Does your son have any girlfriends, she was asked? 'I don't know, he doesn't tell me,' she was quoted as replying. What do you think of the 'gay' tag that he has carried? 'All this gay talk is pretty irrelevant, don't you think?' she countered. 'I want John to be judged for what he does on his skates. His private life is his own business. He is strong-willed enough to make sure it does not affect his career.'

It was extraordinary. Less than 48 hours after Britain's 'golden boy' had won his Olympic medal, Curry's character was being filleted in full public view. Even if he had conspired with Vinocur to 'out' himself, he could not have expected this. His mother's telephone 'interview' had made the Saturday papers under the headline 'My beautiful son's gay tag by Mrs Curry'. Elsewhere – as far away as Chicago – there were coded pieces on 'the haunted hero', 'gay blades' and the 'man with pink skates'. Only Christopher Brasher, writing in the *Observer*, seemed capable of intelligent perspective.

> When everybody had telephoned their story [after Curry's press conference] and discussions broke out in many languages around the bar, opinion began to emerge that it was John who was normal and that it was we who were abnormal. By which we meant that he had spoken with the honesty of modern youth and was prepared to admit that what is known as his 'lifestyle' had brought him many problems. However much the law has changed, the minds of most of us are still full of taboos.

Only Rita really knew it, but courage was in John's DNA. It had been there when her husband had escaped from a German stalag. It had been there when she had kept going alone. In Vinocur's article, her son had spoken of a lifelong fight to be himself:

> When I started to skate I had a coach who used to grab my arm and push it back to my side when I finished a movement with it in the air ... When you're seventeen, people have the idea that they construct you somehow. This man wanted me to skate in a

certain way and when I didn't he beat me. Literally beat me. And there were more humiliating things. He sent me to a doctor as if there were something to treat.

Curry had defied them all. Arnold Gerschwiler; gone. Armand Perren; gone. Peter Dunfield; gone. And now when Curry waved his arms, the sky rained flowers. He'd won the fight to construct himself, but at a cost, and by Sunday 15 February he wanted to be anywhere but Austria.

The 1976 Winter Olympics was closing. Dorothy Hamill had won her gold medal and Carlo Fassi's twin triumph was complete. Only one duty remained: the exhibition performances by all the medal-winning competitors. Usually this was the formal requirement John resisted. In Innsbruck, however, he embraced it with cathartic relief. After the water torture of public scrutiny, it would get him back on the ice. Carlo and Christa Fassi had never seen him skate better.

Dancing to Rimsky-Korsakov's *Scheherazade*, Curry abandoned the wit of *Don Quixote* for a programme that shimmered with brooding intent. There were no skips or smiles. This was elemental and furious. Curry seethed with 'everything that [he'd] heard and read about [himself] in those few mad days'. Forgoing his usual make-up – 'someone will think its effeminate' – he'd poured what remained of his energy into four searing minutes. 'I suppose I was fighting a lot of things,' he said. 'After that, the flags came down and everybody packed up and went home.'

Only one man packed his bags faster than Curry. At the closing Olympic party, Toller Cranston had arrived wearing a gold lamé ski suit, a black velvet fedora and several black scarves. 'I could have been Jesus Christ wandering in the desert. Never have I felt so alone, so much of a failure, so heavy of heart.' In his own words, 'that kind of failure ... becomes more monumental as time goes on'. Within a month, he would get his chance for revenge, but the scars from Innsbruck were all too visible.

> Today I would have to be dragged by the hair, heavily sedated and handcuffed to ever watch those Olympic tapes again ... But think; Curry won fair and square and had a horrible life and died. I lost, and am still alive and continue to be creative.
>
> So who won? Who lost?

Six

'The fairy for the tree'

As the Olympic circus dispersed, Curry headed for London. Six months had passed since he'd last been there and he was both curious to experience fame and desperate for a bolt-hole. All around him the media fallout was still swirling. With no one to help, he'd started to drown under a wave of unopened mail and unsolicited calls. In Britain, surely, he could lose himself and take stock. It was time to fall back on an old friend.

Ever since they'd met at Richmond Ice Rink, he'd stayed close to Penny Malec. Like all of Curry's enduring confidantes, she was plain-speaking and utterly trustworthy. Since she also now lived with her mother in Richmond, Penny was the perfect solution 'I was an outlet. He'd tell me stuff,' she says. 'He was a terrifically loyal person.'

Throughout Olympic week, nursing flu, she'd watched him win gold from behind the sofa. 'It was just like *Doctor Who*,' she explains. 'I couldn't look.' A few days later, Curry had called her from Innsbruck and told her what plane he'd be on. 'He said there'll probably be a few people but I'd really like you to meet me. I must have said OK, but I was quite cross about it. I put on a woolly hat and a big scarf so no one could see me and then the cameras started to flash.'

When Curry had last been in London, few people had known who he was and his personal life had been exactly that. All that had changed and he was now a national curiosity. Sadly he would soon discover that, in some quarters, the veneer of public flattery was wafer-thin, and that beneath it lay cheap innuendo and ridicule. 'My bubble has been broken,' he lamented to Alison Smith. 'I've got no reason to get up in the morning.' For every observer who admired the skater's courage, there was another who was privately unsettled by him. Legalising homosexuality was one thing. Liking it – or those who practised it – was something else entirely.

'The fact that he was judged so harshly at the time of the Olympics really mattered to him,' says Penny. 'I remember sitting on a train with a man and a woman and she said, "Oh look there's a picture of John Curry, isn't he a brilliant skater?" and the bloke said, "Ugh. He skates like a woman."'

Behind the locked doors of Penny's Richmond flat, Curry was finally able to draw breath. Outside, whenever anyone left, they would be accosted by reporters. Inside, the telephone rang constantly, and even Penny's appearance at the airport had made the national newspapers. On a picture caption she'd been described – presumably with heavy irony – as John Curry's girlfriend. 'One time a journalist got hold me on the phone and more or less said – are you sleeping with him? John came out of the sitting room like a bolt of lightning and snatched the phone out of my hand and put it down.'

As the siege slackened, Curry ventured into the city. It was, he said, 'like being in an insane asylum.' Everywhere he went his distinctive hairstyle was recognised. 'People ran out of shops; cars would stop right in the middle of traffic while the drivers got out; taxi drivers held up the traffic to let me cross the street; it was really most odd and rather bewildering.' Although 'panicked' at first, Curry found the public's apparent warmth much less disturbing than expected. He was, after all, a man who enjoyed being looked at.

Very soon, to his mother's relief, Curry's footballer perm would be gone. It was only there because he'd lost so much weight during training the previous summer that 'the sight of [his] own skull in the mirror had depressed [him]'. By having it curled, he'd hoped to present a more 'cheerful and healthy look, even though I was neither'. What London's star-struck shoppers took to be normal was merely the transient consequence of Curry's vanity; and of his lifelong obsession with his weight.

For the first time in months, however, Curry wasn't even training. Drinking tea in Penny Malec's flat, he had put his immediate future on hold. In 16 days the World Figure Skating Championships would begin in Gothenburg. If Curry competed and won, he would have taken the European, Olympic and World titles, all inside 50 days, a feat that might never be repeated. The Englishman was keen. His pragmatic Italian coach, however, was not. As far as Fassi was concerned, their work was done; what you have, you hold. A defeat in Sweden taint the noble perfection of Olympic triumph. He was giving Curry's stablemate Dorothy Hamill the same advice. 'After you win, you quit and you go home and that's it.'

As Curry left Innsbruck, he'd fully intended to follow Fassi's advice. After a week in London, he was no longer so sure. For years he'd resented the need to be a sportsman. Hidden away in Richmond, Curry was unexpectedly missing its certainties; the smell of an empty rink at dawn and the growl of an Italian accent. Competition was all he had ever known and on both sides of the Atlantic precious sanctuaries were being violated. Over in New York, even Nancy Streeter had been tracked down by British reporters. 'I guess all this is the price of fame,' she wrote. 'Come home soon – so many things to hear about.' Privately, his thoughts turned towards Gothenburg.

As he agonised, demand for Curry's presence was growing. In Birmingham there had been a civic reception. Advertisers wanted his face on their products. Women's magazines wanted his life story between the knitting patterns. Promoters wanted him in their theatres. A publisher wanted a book. With no agent, Curry felt unable to sift good from bad, and almost every enquiry was ignored. On Friday 20 February, he weakened. Wearing a paisley tie, and sitting next to Manchester United's Sir Matt Busby, Curry had agreed to speak in London's magnificent Guildhall for the Valour in Sport Awards. For days, he'd been crafting a speech on the theme of courage. Penny Malec was there as his guest. Not even compulsory figures had rendered him so nervous.

After the endless toasts and votes of thanks, Curry rose from his seat. The widow of racing driver Graham Hill, killed three months earlier, had just sat down. In his hand was a speech covered in frantic crossings out. 'People at that moment were ready to listen to almost anything that I might utter,' he said. For the next few minutes, Curry tore into the poverty of British sports funding. 'Training in Britain was impossible,' he said. 'Half my time was spent dodging other people. The ice was all right in the morning at six … then a school arrived. I owe a debt of gratitude to my American friends … [and] unless something is done the British people condemn their sportsmen to an endless prospect of wasted courage.'

In every corner of the Guildhall, leather seats creaked and mayoral chains rattled. This wasn't the definition of courage they'd had in mind. Amidst polite applause – and a military fanfare – the winners and the dignitaries filed out. But for some last-minute revisions, it could have been worse. Curry's fury with British facilities had been diluted for his Guildhall audience. Following the press coverage the previous week, it wouldn't do to alienate everyone. 'England loves me right now,' he told Nancy. 'It's all quite overwhelming.'

By the time Curry returned to Penny's flat, he'd made his decision. Whatever Fassi said, he was going to Gothenburg. That evening, he rang his coach at his training camp in Helsinki. 'Please don't come,' pleaded the Italian. Within hours, Curry was bound for Sweden determined to show that Innsbruck had not been a fluke and to prove to himself that he 'could again face the possibility of *not* winning'.

> I thought there was a chance that I might not win but I didn't really mind actually. I just felt that if I didn't go I wouldn't be much of a champion. I thought if I'd won the Olympics and turned round and said I wasn't prepared to face them all again it wouldn't be much of a gold medal either.

Between London and Helsinki Curry penned a note to Nancy Streeter. 'Don't be afraid. I'm not. I'm excited and looking forward to it. I made it into *Newsweek* and *Vogue* is next on the list. It is all very exciting. Offers are coming from all directions.' As the plane banked over the expanse of snowy forest, he paused. Amidst the media carnage, something durable had emerged. 'Mother has been WONDERFUL about everything. We talked about my being gay and she was so kind and understanding. That has been one of the greatest things to come out of the Olympics. You can imagine how relaxed and easy I feel now.'

Nevertheless, after nine days of inactivity, Curry had set himself a huge task. 'A week without skating at that level is too long,' says Dorothy Hamill, who, like John, had ignored Carlo Fassi's advice. 'I was pleasantly surprised when he turned up in Helsinki. I wouldn't be surprised if he'd thought, "If Dorothy can do it so can I. What have I got to lose?"' After a week together in Sweden, however, the Italian felt certain Curry was about to lose everything.

Above: The only known picture of John's father, Joseph Henry Curry, aged around 35. 'It was very easy to start arguments.'

Top right: John (*left*), Michael and Andrew Curry, 1951. 'A melodious infant with a zest for the blessings which cushioned him.'

Above: John Curry, aged 10. Public schooldays. 'He was in a different world. A square peg in a round hole.'

Right: Rita and John in the garden at Acock's Green. 'Everything about it was grand.'

Above: Schoolboy John on a frozen mere at Aldeburgh. 'My father told me awful stories about people falling through the ice.'

Above: Second place in an early competition in Solihull. 'I liked winning, principally because I disliked losing.'

Right: 'As a child moving towards his teens, a girlish delicacy hovers across his features, but already he is classically handsome.' A teenage Haig Oundjian holds the winner's trophy as Curry finishes second.

Opposite top: 'I fluttered my hands – like birds – and I would win. The other boys were extremely upset.' *(© Curry family)*

Bottom: Teenage kicks. 'Once at the rink, I rather dreaded going home again. In skating I was happy.'

Left: 'After four difficult years, when I was sixteen, my father died. He had seen me skate twice.'

Below: Haig Oundjian, Curry's first great British rival. 'He talks non-stop about motorcars, places he has been to, and girls. All very hearty.' *(Picture courtesy of Haig Oundjian)*

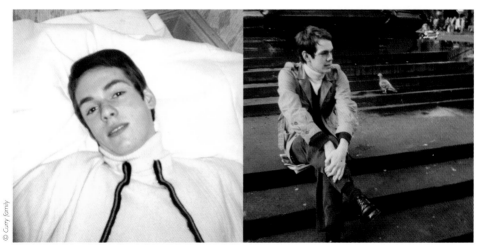

Above: John, London 1969. 'Do you think I shall ever be happy?
Everywhere I go I get miserable very quickly and I don't think anyone will ever love me.'

Below: Heinz Wirz, Curry's first serious lover and lifelong friend. 'When you come back to England I want to marry you. I want you to drink my blood and I your's.'

Picture courtesy of Lorna Brown

Left: Heinz Wirz and a sullen Armand Perren, Curry's first full-time coach. 'He was strange – a nightmare really.'

Left: Lorna Brown and John play bedsit *Romeo and Juliet*. 'He said he loved me but we were just beautiful friends.'

Above: New York, early 1970s. Nancy Streeter with John. 'We all became close very quickly,' said Nancy. 'It just fell into place.'

Above: Toller Shallitoe Montague Cranston. 'I lived by extremes.'

Below: February 1976. Carlo Fassi (*left*) with John and Christa Fassi. 'The unblinking flamboyance of a Mafia don.'

Above: Innsbruck, 1976. American Dorothy Hamill and Curry prepare to do Olympic battle.

Left: European, Olympic and World champion. 'An exhibition in skating as a new modern art.' (Courtesy of Sepp Schönmetzler)

Below: Rita and Andrew Curry flank the shell-shocked Olympic champion. As they do, 'news' of his sexuality is being wired around the world.

Above: BBC Sports Personality of
the Year. 'The whole furore took me
completely unawares. I almost panicked.'
(Picture by PA/EMPICS)

Right: Impresario and manager
Larry Parnes. 'Larry makes me feel
uncomfortable. I'm not sure that our
contract will be a very long one.'

Above: Julian Pettifer in Vietnam — a picture found amongst John's effects. 'It frightens me to think about him marrying a girl or not loving me any more,' wrote Curry.

Left: Penny Malec. 'He was lost, hungry and poor. I was magicked by him.'

Below: The 'triumvirate': Roger Roberts and William Whitener photographed by Curry at the Statue of Liberty.

Above: Early 1979, on holiday in Egypt with Ron Alexander. 'Bad on stage and a bad influence on John off it.' (© *Curry family*)

Right: 1979, summer life on Fire Island. 'Every day there seemed to be perfect.'

Above: 1977. Icarus: mocked in Bristol, praised in London. 'A sublime essay in the dizzy joy of flight.'

Left: L'Apres midi d'un faune. Curry swoons with Cathy Foulkes. 'He was always 100% the faune. He was transformed. He didn't even look like himself.'

Above: Mid-1980s. Curry acquires wheels. 'He drove poorly. Absolutely terribly, with no conception of what was going on around him.'

Above: David Spungen. 'A ceaseless spring of positive energy.'

Below: 1984. With Elva Clairmont. 'Charming, literate and wickedly funny.'

Right: JoJo and Curry in China. 'They very much loved one another, but whatever was going on there, John had not come to grips with it.'

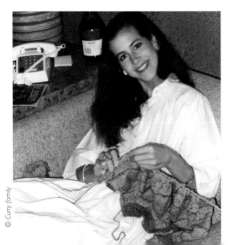

Above: JoJo Starbuck and Curry vamp during Tango Tango. 'On the ice, they seemed propelled by authentic yearning.'

Left: Cathy Foulkes. 'A bit of a Pygmalion thing.'

Above: *Brigadoon*. 1980. 'I'm sure he was in pain 24/7. Unfortunately he was on display from day one as being behind.'

Top right: Curry with ballet dancer Anthony Dowell. 'The John and Tony Show,' said the *New York Times*. Finally, John gets his chance to dance.

Right: 1987. Curry on stage in *Hard Times*. 'He knew he couldn't act terribly well.'

Left: 1992. Back home with Rita. Selling his story, and distressing pictures, to survive.

Below: 'If you truly want to understand John, just look at his needlework.'

dise in a garden,
else on earth.

JAC

All the old certainties were gone. Idleness had robbed him of his appetite. Inertia had dulled decades of polish. 'There was nothing I could do, not even if my life had depended on it. For once my long-standing discipline totally disappeared. I never completed a practice programme. I would fall over, or miss 20 things in the first 30 seconds.' From the sidelines, the Fassis watched in despair. Nothing he said could change Curry's mind. Two days before the competition began, Carlo, Christa, Curry and Dorothy Hamill shifted camp to Gothenburg. Once again, the newspapers were waiting.

Every time he trained, radio and television crews congregated rink-side to watch. Convinced that he was being bugged, Curry refused to communicate with any of them. As Fassi begged him to concentrate, Nancy Streeter flew in from New York. Shortly afterwards, John appeared to calm down. 'He looks confident – practising wearing a T-shirt proclaiming "Smile" – and should have no trouble achieving his goal,' noted Sandra Stevenson in the *Guardian*. As the competition got underway, no one around the worried Italian couple shared her confidence.

Apart from the Canadian Toller Cranston, all the skaters – even the indefatigable Eastern Europeans – seemed stale. A strange ennui had infected the event. After the school figures, Curry was clinging on in second place, behind the Russian Vladimir Kovalev. No one could understand why. To Cranston, it felt like a scandal was unfolding.

'As my figures got better, my marks sank lower, and as their figures got worse, their marks climbed. Curry was shaking with nerves,' he insisted. 'It was the most terrible school figure ever traced in the history of figure skating ... I think that many people knew that Curry didn't deserve his placement, but he was the Olympic champion and, well, they gave it to him.'

Had they been on speaking terms, Curry would probably have agreed. Judges were drawn to winners. Conservatism was endemic. He'd said as much himself: 'the final results of the previous year are almost always exactly reproduced in the results of the following year so that means for every year in memoriam whoever came first, second and third in one year will come first, second and third in the next.' As Olympic champion, Curry was now the beneficiary of a system he'd once lampooned. For Cranston, none of this was any consolation. Very recent history was repeating itself.

Just three weeks before, Cranston had dazzled the Olympics with his short programme. In Gothenburg, he'd done the same. Under the glare of nine judges, a lacklustre Curry had followed him out on to the ice, touching down a trailing foot within seconds of starting. When the scores were totted up, the Englishman was somehow still holding on to second place behind Kovalev. Toller Cranston, lying fourth, felt doomed.

> There was darkness all around me. I didn't see a way out ... I foresaw no career whatsoever – only a loss of face, a loss of persona, a fall from grace. That was what I was up against going into the long program ... I couldn't understand why the judges had held up the guys who had fallen and given me only a smidge of a lead. So I pulled up to fourth. Big deal.

Within 24 hours, as Cranston had feared, the World Championship was Curry's. During a stunning long programme, the Canadian's brilliance had elicited a 'drumbeat of approval from the whole stadium'. But Cranston had heard none of it. All he could see through a wall of 'nausea and apathy' were nine judges 'like hungry vultures ready to pick my bones clean'. Once the Minkus music started, the Canadian's efforts had been forgotten. As Curry danced his *Don Quixote* routine competitively for the last time, the Swedish audience swooned. Back home in Britain, millions around their television sets did the same. Carlo Fassi had instructed him to 'go out there and smile' and he had never skated it better.

'Gone was the uncertainty which had pursued him through the earlier sections,' proclaimed the *Daily Express*. 'He rediscovered all his delicacy as the audience clapped him on as he lifted the tempo weaving his magic. He was no longer the prisoner of his own art, but the absolute master.'

Flanked by Carlo and Christa, and clutching an enormous floral bouquet, Curry had shuffled nervously as he waited for the scores. A perfect six (from the British judge) for artistic merit – and eight 5.9s – detonated thunderous applause. As Carlo punched the air, Christa clapped her hands wildly and bent double in jubilation. Turning calmly to his coach, Curry leaned forward to shake the Italian's hand. Since leaving Denver in January, the trio had won the three biggest prizes in men's figure skating. It was over. Job done. Time to settle the bill and get out.

'Carlo was business,' says Dorothy Hamill, who, like Curry, would be leaving Sweden with a world title.

> He taught whoever it was and then moved on. That's the way of the professional coach. You invest all this with a certain skater, then they turn pro or quit, so it's who's next? Much as I adored Carlo I always had the feeling that it was business. It was a job. He was getting paid. He was very involved but he also knew that after the Olympics or whatever these skaters would get on with the rest of their lives.

On the podium, Curry had wept. There would be no more tournaments now. 'No more 6 a.m. patches', as Nancy Streeter had told him. 'For so long this had been the only life I had known,' he said later. 'The door was closing for the last time and I would never be able to go through it again. It felt like a kind of death.'

As Curry was wiping his tears, Toller Cranston, who'd finished fourth, was staring into a Gothenburg canal holding the skates he'd always worn for his school figures. Nobody could understand why he'd been scored so meanly. 'Their only fitting resting place was a Swedish sewer,' he explained. 'They hit the surface, floated momentarily on the sludge, then disappeared from view.' Neither Cranston nor Curry would skate competitively as amateurs again.

Once again, the chequebooks were out. Within hours of Curry's victory, several lucrative options were already on offer. 'I shall never join Follies or Ice Capades,' he had promised Heinz 12 months before. But in Sweden he was wobbling. Alongside the gush of telegrams – 'You are inspiring. I love you,' wired Werner Erhard – came a string of temptations. Senior representatives of the world's three major ice show conglomerates arrived separately at Curry's hotel bearing flowers and gifts. 'Curry ponders over offers,' claimed the *Guardian*. For years, he'd been promising a radical new 'theatre on ice', but he hadn't a clue where to begin, and he hadn't a penny to his name. Back in London – and aware of what was happening – Penny Malec was urging him to shelve his principles temporarily and cash in.

'It was the closest we ever had to a row,' she says.

> After he won he was inundated with sponsorship deals for vast
> sums and he looked at them and said, 'I'll do Weetabix because I
> eat Weetabix'. I said; take it and make all the money you can this
> year, go with Holiday On Ice and then you'll be in a position to
> do what you want to do and won't have to deal with people who
> don't have your vision. He said, 'No way am I prostituting
> myself', but if he'd put the money in the bank he'd have been
> free. I've always thought he was wrong.

Feeling spooked and out of his depth, Curry turned to Heinz Wirz
for help.

> He asked me if I'd be his general manager and I'd just started to
> become a successful [skating] teacher in Switzerland. I told him I
> didn't know if I was capable of doing it and I think John was very
> very disappointed. I think he needed someone who was on his
> side but I was not the guy to do that. I knew nothing about
> finance. He told me he was sad because I was the only one he had
> real confidence in at that time.

Uncertain what to do, Curry fled. For the next three weeks, he
burrowed deep into the champions' exhibition circus; rolling into a
different European city every night; performing to music he loved
in outfits of his choosing. Historically it was an obligation he had
always loathed. After Gothenburg, it saved him. No longer pursued
by men clutching contracts, Curry flourished where previously he
had wilted. 'Lo and behold I had the best time I could remember,'
he said. 'Every night I did my Olympic programme – plop, plop,
plop. All fun and no problems.'

During a break in London – a few days before travelling on the
Eastern European leg – he'd picked up a letter from Nancy Streeter.
Everyone was certain he would quit the tour. Everyone was
expecting him back in New York within days. A 'welcome home'
party had even been planned at Nancy's apartment. The EST
people were going to be there and she was pestering for his flight
details. The party would have to wait. 'So – on to the next venture,'
she wrote. 'Things may seem a little confused at the moment. Take

your time. Things will fall into place. You will have an independence you have never been able to have before. A lot of people are interested in your future … Won't it be nice to have some leisurely time?'

It was all much too much, too soon. After an emotional gala performance at Richmond Ice Rink – complete with champagne quaffed from a presentation goblet – Curry vanished back into the tour. Eighteen exhibitions in 20 days; standing ovations wherever he skated. Zagreb. Brno. Kiev. Leningrad. Nothing fazed him; not even the winter deprivations of Eastern bloc railways.

As he headed deep behind the Iron Curtain, spindrift billowed across a landscape drained of colour. In Czechoslovakia, frozen snow banks trapped his train for 30 hours. Entering Russia, some of his luggage was lost. In every hotel, there were rumours of KGB listening devices. As other skaters dropped out, Curry soldiered on. If he had lovers – which seems highly unlikely – he told no one. Every day, and every frozen mile, was buying him precious time.

He told an impatient Nancy:

> I am anxious to skate for a public who live under a very different set of rules than our own … While I detest the idea of skating for people who consider my way of life as degenerate, there will be many who will enjoy maybe a little hope because of me. You know that I believe every person should be able to live as his heart leads him. I'm doing what I feel is right this time. So please understand and please forgive me once more. I know you will because I know you love me. Please know that I love you.

By 21 March he was in Moscow; journey's end. Salt-streaked buses patrolled frozen streets. Ice-breakers chewed a ragged path along the Moskva River. It felt right to be bowing out here. All his skating life he'd fought to overcome the Volkovs and the Kovalevs; perfectly groomed specimens propelled by an all-conquering patriotic hunger. Dick Button liked to call them the 'Russian mafia'. To Toller Cranston they were 'hammer-throwers'. Whoever they were, all John Curry wanted to do now was stir their hearts.

> I found myself determined. I was going to go in there and show them! I was there and I was still kicking and they were going to have to look at me. All the rows of stony faces in the Official Box

were trapped in their seats while I was out there on the ice. It was a delicious moment to relish. The actual Russian people themselves do enjoy my skating, strangely enough. I even did an encore, which is something I very seldom do. But it was Russia. I was happy it was all but over and those people who had tried to stop me all those years were having to go on watching.

Midnight in Moscow; that was the end of my amateur career. It was over at last.

The following morning he wrote a final letter to Nancy Streeter, before heading back west:

I wanted to cry because it was the last time. Saying goodbye to all the eastern skaters was sad and they represent a whole part of my life – and the thought of not seeing them again moves me more than I anticipated. Today I feel a little hollow inside. I'm uncertain of the future and tired. It's time to go home to New York.

––––––

At about this time in a west London penthouse flat overlooking Baden-Powell House a brand new colour television set was re-running pictures of Curry's recent successes. The beak-nosed man watching them was intrigued. He knew a thing or two about pretty boys. He knew even more about camp.

Across the hallway, his enormous bed hid behind fluted columns and shimmering drapes. On the mantelpiece were the ashes of his beloved Alsatian dogs, Prince and Duke. Everything, and everywhere, seemed drenched in eau-de-Cologne. Only the television – or the gleaming stereogram – broke the silence. Thick creamy carpet swallowed almost every other sound.

Laurence Maurice 'Larry' Parnes – also known as 'Mr Parnes, shillings and pence' – was a West End legend. As a teenager, he'd worked for his father's tailoring business in Kent. In his twenties he'd bought a share in a seedy Soho drinking hole on Romilly Street, where he'd latched on to the post-war possibilities of show business for adolescents. By 1956, he'd 'discovered' Tommy Steele in a Regent Street club. Five years later, at just 31, he had a business that was turning over a staggering £500,000 a year.

Dubbed the 'beat Svengali', Parnes had a formula that was shameless. Flamboyantly gay, he had always craved money and the company of very young men. Through pop music he'd discovered the perfect route to both. Regardless of their sexual orientation, the most handsome ones – presupposing a modicum of talent – were groomed by him for stardom. Reg Patterson, Ron Wycherley and John Askew became Marty Wilde, Billy Fury and Johnny Gentle. Ray Howard, Terence Williams and Clive Powell became Duffy Power, Terry Dene and Georgie Fame.

At a time when most agents took 10 per cent, Larry Parnes insisted on 40 per cent. 'It costs me £40,000 a year for four years to make a star' was his justification. 'At the end of the fifth year, you get your money back.' By Christmas 1962 a recording of 'Telstar' by Billy Fury's backing band, The Tornadoes, had sold 1,300,000 worldwide with recording costs to Parnes of a paltry £300. He was forming plans for his own record company – even a movie business – and as the royalties poured in so did the country houses, the racehorses, the mohair jackets, the designer dogs and the reputation for unsavoury invitation-only parties.

By 1976 – as he stood dumbfounded by the vision on skates – Parnes was finding it much harder to add to his fortune. Since The Beatles, musicians knew what they were worth. Nobody fell for the slick patter and the shiny suits any more. In 1969, he'd gone back into tailoring with three men's boutiques branded 'Sir Larry', opening the first one – in Kensington High Street – with a male model sitting naked in a foam-filled bath. For the second, in Portobello Road, he'd put a pyjama-clad male in a double bed, alongside Larry's very own design of plastic Roman togas and 'off-the-shoulder' lace shirts.

Along the way, Parnes had staged a play on homosexuality set in a Canadian prison and acquired a lease on London's Cambridge Theatre, enjoying frisson-free success with popular musicals which never quite thrilled him like the 1960s. Watching John Curry had rolled back the years. Reading about his dreamy plans for a professional 'theatre of skating' had given him a notion, and, when Curry returned from Moscow, Parnes invited his fellow Virgo to lunch. By the end of it, he was obsessed.

'He wanted John because – like everyone else – Parnes fell in love with him,' says Penny Malec, who at John's request, had attended all their early exploratory business meetings. Neither had any experience of a man like Larry Parnes. After a lifetime secluded in ice rinks, Curry had strayed into unfamiliar territory. No one could flatter quite like Laurence Maurice Parnes; and no one enjoyed flattery quite like John Curry. 'I must say I liked your red plaid shirt,' Parnes told him in a letter after watching a BBC documentary on the skater's triumphs. 'Where did you get it? Your interview was superb and I have never seen you more relaxed.'

It was more oily than seductive, but Parnes was in a strong position. As the owner of a West End theatre he could function as both manager and impresario. In London, he could offer Curry a home at the Cambridge for his still fuzzy 'theatre of skating'. Overseas – if Parnes was to be believed – the 'beat Svengali' had the cash and the contacts to turn the skater into an international superstar.

It was a tantalising package, which Curry was in no state to assess. Three weeks on the road had worn him out. Three days' bombardment from Larry Parnes had left him confused. From New York – via Nancy Streeter – he was also hearing of more professional possibilities. 'Sorry to land all this on you but as a conscientious secretary I really have to.' To make matters worse, Curry had a letter in his pocket which had stirred up old guilt.

Since the trauma of Seefeld, he had barely seen – or spoken with – his mother. In mid-March she'd been in the audience at his Richmond exhibition gala, but 'as people were very anxious for autographs' they'd met only briefly over breakfast the following day. If it was a situation Rita was prepared to tolerate, that didn't extend to her Birmingham friends. On 31 March one of them, Dorothy Fantham, let fly.

> Whether you realise it or not you have a happy knack of hurting your mother very much. I doubt whether you would even realise this ... Rather she would prefer you to think her as being cross with you or something like that. I suspect she will never let you know. However this I have to say, for when we shall see you again God knows and I really feel you should look deep into your heart and ask: 'Do I really try to repay in some measure the love and support my mother has given me all these years or do I just do my duty call and think that is sufficient'.

It was a lacerating letter, written by a woman who'd made fancy dress costumes for John as a child and who still worked in the accounts department of his late father's fast-declining factory. After Innsbruck, she'd even taken on John's fan mail, little of which remotely interested him. 'Don't you care John?' she asked. 'I know you are tired but this is the life you have worked for, surely that is your reward. My scribble is caused through emotion … I still feel there is a great barrier between your feelings and your home … Remember. You will still need your old friends.'

A day after receiving it, Curry was on his way to America. Parnes could wait. Everyone could wait. Nancy Streeter had rearranged her party. 'Not long now, the champagne is waiting,' she'd told him. After the previous year's friction, their relationship was back on track. In New York, with her to guide him – whatever Rita's friends might think – he'd find a way through this morass of possibilities.

Every day a new one seemed to be tossed on the pile. According to one newspaper, he was seriously considering three Hollywood film scripts. According to another, he'd been offered a recording contract. 'It was as disturbing to be potentially rich as it had been to be potentially poor,' he said some years later. 'I found myself worrying for days over the difference between 2.5 and 2.55 million.'

This wasn't true. John Curry's name was wanted, but not at any price. Despite his persistent snubs, Ice Follies had returned with an offer of $6,200 a week for a three-month tour skating in nine major American cities. Alongside his name at the top of the bill would be one of his idols, Peggy Fleming, the 1968 Ladies Olympic Champion. It was all very tempting, but Curry hesitated. Too many things were still swirling around. Larry Parnes was offering to fly out for a meeting in New York. Even the American über-agent Jerry Weintraub was reporting an interest. 'I don't know who to trust any more. The whole thing turns me off,' he told Nancy.

After a few weeks kicking his heels in Manhattan, Curry went back to Britain. By the end of the year, he'd become an incessant transatlantic commuter. 'Life just seems to go on here,' he grimly reported back to Nancy. 'Nothing new really happens and somehow the days pass and everyone gets a little older.' Once again, however, Larry Parnes had lured Curry into the cloud of aftershave at his Cromwell Road penthouse. Although there was no apparent physical connection, the two men got on tolerably well. 'There was a bit of dreamer left in his soul,' was Curry's later assessment, and by the end of month they had reached an accord. For a trial period of six months, Parnes was to manage John Curry's affairs for an undisclosed percentage.

> Larry is very kind and thoughtful but he makes me feel very uncomfortable and I'm not sure that our contract will be a very long one. Once again I find myself wondering if I really want all of this. I just don't know. I want to live and be happy, love and be loved, and it just isn't happening right now. When you have wished, hoped, worked and dreamed and it all comes 'true' and you are still not happy it is very unsettling. Right now I'm not sure what I want and I don't know what to wish for any more.

It was fortunate that the infatuated Parnes was not privy to these thoughts. Business relationships for John would invariably be defined by what he alone got out of them. There was either John's way or there was no way at all. Any number of discarded skating teachers could testify to that. Temporarily blinded by Curry's imperious charm, Parnes had lost sight of basic business principles. He had presumed himself to be in control, but he was not.

———

In the short term, at least, the partnership showed promise. Curry's stalled progress once again began to fizz with possibilities. In early June, he'd been awarded an OBE – 'all very nice and harmless' – and in a smoke-stained London gambling club, flanked by tables laden with champagne and lobster, Curry and Parnes had appeared before journalists to unveil a spectacular plan. Under a fusillade of flashbulbs, the man who'd created Billy Fury unveiled what the *Guardian* dubbed 'extremely ambitious if unspecific plans for a world tour' taking in Europe, Australia, South Africa and the United States.

Venues were to include the Sydney Opera House and the Kennedy Center in Washington, DC, but neither had been booked. Six months' intensive rehearsals were about to begin, and a tour of British theatres would commence in the late autumn. However, no dates had been set, no venues agreed and no skaters had been hired.

Curry himself would supposedly be on a six-figure salary and flown by private jet to every engagement. When the tour was over he would have earned £350,000. All of it was Parnes bluster on an epic scale. Even the broadsheets were sceptical.

As bemused hacks attacked the Moët, Curry tried to explain his lifelong vision for a show fusing classical ice dancing with specially choreographed new work. The background noise in the casino grew louder. Parnes's overblown bubbly was going flat. Pressed for specifics, none were forthcoming. Curry's only definite booking turned out to be a one-night stand at a Bournemouth ice gala on 27 June and a Christmas special for London Weekend Television. Even a possible television commercial had been canned. 'I'm only doing [Bournemouth] for the money,' he confided to Nancy, adding ominously that 'things just aren't working out right now'.

Since Moscow, Curry's skates had festered in their bag. Three months on he could no longer afford that luxury. It wasn't how he'd dreamed it, but – of necessity – his first professional appearance would be at a seaside resort on the south coast of England. It was everything he loathed; sequinned splendour in a provincial hell. Ahead of him on the summer bill, the Ice Follettes would be performing 'Viva España' and after the interval Hami Brown would be wowing the holidaymakers with 'A Wee Drop of Scotch'. Only two chinks of light shone through.

During his bedsit years, Curry and Linda Davis had held hands and danced at the skaters' ball. Since then, they'd lost touch. Under pressure from her mother, Linda had turned to the money-spinning glitterball shows and, when John had won the Olympics, she'd been watching backstage on a portable television at a huge Wembley ice panto. When he turned up in Bournemouth, Davis was skating on the bill wearing a figure-hugging spangled catsuit. The hesitant girl with a crush had matured into a dark-haired beauty with a smile as dazzling as her outfit.

Alongside her was another old friend, Lorna Brown. She too had lost contact with John. She too had succumbed to the professional lure of the holiday ice spectacular. Backstage, posing with the Bournemouth ensemble for photographs, Curry stands out among the pink satin in plain black trousers and his tan-coloured Olympic shirt. By his side, Linda Davis shines and sparkles. Her arm is wrapped around the tanned body of Lorna Brown, who is naked but for a gold-braided thong and a tiny bikini top.

'It was amazing to have him in that show,' says Linda.

> He came down and said, 'I'm going to skate to "Greensleeves" in my own spot'. I really don't think the audience knew what they were looking at. It was so beautiful. Most of the rest of the show was just feathers and tinsel. Lorna was in her scanty bikini. We had comedians in between and then at the end of each part we had John. I think he did it just for us actually. Just for me and Lorna.

After one night, Curry was gone. Before leaving, he'd told both girls of his plans for a 'theatre of skating'. If it ever happened, he'd be in touch. 'I was the first person he asked to be in it,' says Lorna. 'Of course, I said yes.' Bit by bit, the shape of something promising was starting to emerge. Back in London, he turned, with reluctance, to the Christmas special he'd promised LWT. 'The thought of what I'm going to do gives me little cause for excitement,' he confided to Nancy. 'The truth of it is I'm spoiled and lazy.'

It was to his advantage, however, that 1970s television was not constrained by a quest for ratings. When LWT had asked John Curry for a one-hour special, they had imposed no conditions. Curry could choose the music and the costumes. He could even nominate a favoured choreographer, opting for the Irish dance teacher Norman Maen, a man whose later triumphs included pairing Rudolph Nureyev with Miss Piggy for *The Muppet Show*'s rendering of *Swine Lake*.

Equally happy with puppets or people, Maen was an unabashed populist with a classical touch. Television studios were his natural habitat. Handling divas – even foam rubber ones – was his business. During his career, he'd worked with Gene Kelly, Lisa Minnelli and Julie Andrews. When Curry raged about the size of his studio ice rink – less than 30 square metres – the Irishman had the know-how to calm him down. 'Working with Norman Maen is really great,' reported Curry with evident relief. 'He is a very talented man.'

It was a risky pairing. Curry had never shared decisions with a dance choreographer before. Maen had never created for the ice. In a few short weeks, however, they had crafted numerous works of enduring beauty. One of them – a highly charged erotic duet skated with (a pregnant) Peggy Fleming to Debussy's *L'après-midi d'un Faune* – would go on to become Curry's most haunting post-Olympic crowd-pleaser. Others cast him in a jazzy mould; riffing seductively around a hall of mirrors to the drawl of a saxophone wearing a trilby, a tie and black-striped trousers.

By mid-August, the show was complete. Everyone – including John Curry – seemed content with it. Working on such a tiny 'rink' had opened his eyes. It had taken a skilled choreographer to unlock the steps, but expressive movement was possible without a vast expanse of arena ice and he was eager for more collaborations. The news from Larry Parnes, however, was not good. No more bookings had come in and the world tour was looking doubtful. 'Despite everything I feel totally isolated here [London],' he wrote. With nothing to do, Curry flew directly back to New York. By the time he reached Nancy Streeter's apartment the tour had collapsed completely.

Only Parnes knew how real it had ever been, but, with still no sign of his theatrical debut he and Curry were no longer on speaking terms. From her Bournemouth flat, Lorna Brown was frantic for news. 'I've heard so many different stories,' she told him. 'But I don't take much notice, not until I hear from you. I have to know if I am wanted and if the show is going on.'

From his mother there was bad news of a different kind. After years of managed decline, his father's old company was on the brink of liquidation. 'I wish it would just fold and leave her free,' he'd told Nancy Streeter. 'Naturally mum is loath to "give up". Anyway it highlights the fact that she will have to be supported.' Suddenly it wasn't just for himself that Curry needed to be out there earning money.

―――――

Under warm September skies, New York offered welcome distractions. Over the years, Curry's circle of male companions there had grown. Through the dance classes he'd found friends in the ballet world. Through his continued presence at the Sky Rink, he'd found others. Periodically, the possibility of romance would flicker. Mostly, however, it did not. The previous winter, it had been a close fellow skater, Brian Grant, who'd urged him to try EST. Intimate Italian suppers and Valentine's Day cards had followed – 'Skate beautifully xxx' – but so far nothing else.

It had been the same back in his early London days. People looked, but seemed disinclined to go further. In conversation, Curry could be loquacious, indiscreet and savagely amusing. But he could also be overpowering, moody, and a master of the hurtful put-down. In either mode he was intriguing, but not everyone was seduced. 'Let's just say he did not suffer fools gladly,' says his brother Andrew.

Since Heinz Wirz – and Julian Pettifer – he'd had good reasons for solitude. Training for competition had necessitated focus, which was not conducive to relationships. In New York, he finally had the time but nothing was happening. In his so-called 'magic city', the familiar ache of loneliness was back; one he masked with his closest Manhattan friends, long afternoon teas and excursions to the theatre with Nancy Streeter, and the gnawing fear that time was being lost.

Ballet dancer Billy Whitener understood how he felt. 'New York is a city of many lonely people,' he explains. 'It's easier to fit in there if you're lonely than in other places.' Some years before, Whitener had taken his teacher's advice and risen early to watch the English skater everyone was talking about. 'He was practising at Sky Rink and I knew immediately what I was seeing.' The two had quickly become 'very tight friends'. Whitener had met Curry in Europe before the Olympics, and sent a jubilant postcard from St Louis to Innsbruck after watching him win gold. 'Words seem superfluous right now – actions and feelings are more potent – so I've been sending you regular energy doses instead.'

Like Heinz – and Roger Roberts – Billy Whitener would prove to be one of Curry's most steadfast companions. In the early autumn of 1976, he would also prove to be one of the most influential. As Curry sulked, Whitener was in Brooklyn rehearsing with Twyla Tharp, the Indiana-born choreographer with a reputation for unlikely creative fusions. As a child Tharp had worked at her parents' drive-in movie theatre on Route 66. Aged just 24, she'd set up her own New York dance company, attracting praise from critics for her 'technical precision coupled with streetwise nonchalance'.

No movement was out of bounds, from boxing to classical ballet. 'Art is the only way to run away without leaving home,' she would say. By the mid-1970s, Twyla Tharp was a rising force of modern dance. Ahead of her were Hollywood movies, Broadway shows, Emmy awards and 19 doctorates. Already behind her was a ballet – *Deuce Coupe* – set to music by The Beach Boys, which Curry had seen and loved. 'It was the ballet [which] for me says so much about how I felt it *should* have been when I was young,' he explained. To Billy Whitener, Tharp and Curry seemed like a 'creative fusion' in waiting. All he had to do was bring them together.

That didn't prove difficult. Curry's diary already had a gap in it he urgently needed to fill. In November, he'd promised to perform at an Olympic fundraiser in Madison Square Gardens. Sixteen thousand people would be watching him – his biggest ever audience – and the deadline was just eight weeks away. Since a new work would require money – which Curry didn't have – the skater had turned for help to the man organising the event. Ed Mosler had never yet refused him. As both men would benefit from a Curry–Tharp collaboration, Mosler wouldn't, and didn't, refuse him now.

A few weeks later, a slender dark-haired figure arrived at the New York Sky Rink to watch Curry go through his moves. Although Tharp couldn't skate, she'd prepared carefully by watching tapes. 'I've got three hours,' she said. 'Show me everything one can do in skating on the ice.' If Curry was doubtful, he said nothing. However dysfunctional the process, this wasn't yet the time for a tantrum. The next day, Tharp came back with some suggestions.

> She put together a combination of steps that had never been done on the ice before; they were a totally new way of moving on an ice skate. And they all worked. This floored me; I could not believe anybody could do that. Also, I could not believe that after twenty years I had not thought of it myself.

For the next few weeks, Tharp and Curry rehearsed furiously on a New Jersey rink. All the clichés and heroic jumps had been discarded. Skating to Albinoni's Trumpet Concerto in B Flat, Curry swapped razzle-dazzle for single, unbroken movements of such grace they seemed miraculously grafted to the rise and fall of the horn. Nothing mattered to Curry more than this. After the clipboards and the jingoism, this was skating as it was meant to be, jostling for its rightful place as an art form. Or so he hoped.

Recharged by Tharp's unorthodoxy, Curry turned back to the repentant Larry Parnes, dashing off a letter setting out a blueprint for a London show that would fill seats and, he presumed, make both of them some money. A few days later, a relieved Parnes telephoned his approval to the Streeter apartment. His only caveat was that the show must be staged at his own Cambridge Theatre. Curry's enthusiasm immediately slumped.

> I marked off an area of ice on the rink in New York. Every day I skated only on this area; the same size as the stage at the Cambridge … I became more and more disheartened and frustrated, but I did discover that eventually if I made certain modifications, then I could do quite a lot on that space. In fact my technique in some things had to be altered radically.

Once again, Nancy Streeter steered him through. Over a pot of tea, and with the leaves falling in nearby Central Park, the pair considered Curry's dwindling options. Very soon, public curiosity in him would have dribbled away. The grandiose touring ice shows were unlikely to come knocking again, and he needed cash. By working with Norman Maen, he'd established what might be accomplished in a tiny space. Nothing about Parnes was perfect, but Curry couldn't afford to walk away. A few days later, the dates were set. Curry's long-cherished Theatre of Skating would open at the Cambridge Theatre, London, on 27 December.

Almost overnight, Curry's 'lazy' days became crammed. Breaking off from rehearsals with Twyla Tharp, he flew to London to draw up lists of skaters, choreographers, directors, and costume designers. With barely eight weeks to go, quick decisions were vital. Not all of them would be good ones. Over in New York, a full house at Madison Square Garden was looming. Nothing could be allowed to spoil it. The Cambridge would get his full attention, but only after he'd taken Manhattan.

As ticket-holders gathered at the Garden on 15 November, the pre-show bustle concerned *Don Quixote*. Two hours later, when they returned to their limos, Curry's piece of Twyla Tharp craft – now formally christened *After All* – had supplanted it. Although the

New York Times later derided it as 'a solo in love with itself', the crowd had bellowed in rapture, demanding that even Tharp herself take a bow on the ice. Wearing only white, Curry had delivered on his promise. Skating didn't have to be a barrage of stunts. 'Curry was thanking America last night,' wrote the *Guardian*. 'He was also, however, repudiating the specific nature of his achievement, the fact that he had triumphed as an athlete.'

If it was Ed Mosler's last gift to John Curry, it was a glorious one. If it was Curry's symbolic expression of thanks, that, too, was magnificently expressed. Either way, his performance of *After All* had marked a corner. Under pressure, he had concluded his triumphant night with a final grudging performance of his Olympic routine. The applause had been loud, but it had been far louder after Twyla Tharp's piece. As he flew back to London yet again – 'back into England's chilling damp arms' – he no doubt wondered whether Britain would feel quite the same way.

Tucked off Shaftesbury Avenue on Earlham Street, the Cambridge Theatre was a leftover from the West End's golden era. Just like five other London playhouses, it had opened in 1930, at the hedonistic midpoint between two catastrophic wars. Unlike its contemporaries, however, the Cambridge had always struggled. Since 1967 – when Ingrid Bergman had starred there in *A Month in the Country* – it had been run as a rather dismal-looking cinema. From the street, film-goers entered what looked like a giant slice of grey cake. Once inside, they were greeted by sickly red paint, monstrous candelabra and a frieze of bronze nudes in exercise poses. It was an aptly butch motif for its current leaseholder.

By 1976, the fate of the Cambridge was resting with Larry Parnes. It was from there, staffed almost entirely by young men, that Parnes ran the LPO, the Larry Parnes Organisation. And it was at the Cambridge that the promoter hoped John Curry would instigate a creative revival in the failing theatre's fortunes. It was a substantial ask of a 27-year-old man who had never worked the professional stage before, and whose chosen medium had never been attempted under a proscenium arch better suited for music hall comedians. To his credit, Curry was back from the United States with what passed for a hopeful smile. From mid-November until the following March he would scarcely see the light of day and by the end of it, his smile had been consigned to history.

Curry had never been in a team, let alone recruited or led one. Temperamentally and creatively, he was a loner. Making the right commercial choices – against limited time and budget – would prove a challenge. Conceding even an inch of control, while governing his impatience, would prove beyond him. From the very beginning, backstage problems began to accumulate. For his director, he'd plucked Peter Darrell from the Scottish National Ballet, a man with a formidable creative reputation, none of it earned on a frozen sheet of water. To augment the choreography he'd recruited yet another stranger to the challenge of ice.

As creative director of the Royal Ballet, Kenneth MacMillan was both a legend and a luminary. Where dancing was concerned, however, slippers and not skates were his artistic weapon of preference. Within days, Curry was already quietly regretting his choice. Almost certainly, so was the choreographer. Much as Curry loved MacMillan's selected music – 'Feux Follets', or 'Will-o'-the-Wisp', a piano study by Franz Liszt – it was nearly impossible to skate to. Instead of creating flow, it tied his feet in knots. 'I always assured him I could manage it,' said Curry. 'But technically it is something of a killer.'

Every choice Curry was making felt like a statement. The mundane practicalities of fashioning a hit show for Larry Parnes seemed of little or no concern. If he was to be judged seriously as an artist, then the production credits had to impress, whether or not they were right for the job. If any of this worried Parnes, he didn't show it. In his office, behind a haze of cigarette smoke, the 'beat Svengali' kept his head down and sold the advertising space in the project's glossy programme. Things were looking up. All he needed now was a show people would watch.

By late November, Curry was ready to begin rehearsals. Alongside his backstage team, he'd assembled just six skaters. On the tiny Cambridge stage, there simply wasn't room for any more. The three men were from the United States – Paul McGrath, Paul Toomey and Bill Woehrle. Of the three girls, two were from Britain. Lorna Brown, to her intense relief, had finally been given her chance. So, too, had Jacqui Harbord, a raven-haired, plain-speaking show skater, who'd performed with Heinz Wirz and known John casually since the late 1960s. Of them all, however, it was the third female, a waiflike American, who intrigued the most.

At 19 years old, Cathy Foulkes was a virtual unknown. She'd won no medals, and her highest place in a major championship had been a lowly eighth. 'I was not even a blip,' she admits. 'Not even a tiny little blip.' Only John Curry knew why he'd chosen her. Four years before, he'd watched this girl skate near her home town of Lexington, Massachusetts. In some raw way – even at 15 – she'd embodied his vision of how an ice ballerina should look: petite, miraculously slender and born with such gentle features a single glance could tell a story.

It didn't matter that she couldn't jump or spin like a champion. In Foulkes, Curry had found an intelligence of emotion, which could never be taught. Now that the moment had arisen, he picked up the phone to her coach. An audition had followed in Boston. 'We were skating together for a week and it was clear we heard music similarly.' Out of nowhere, with less than four weeks to go, she was in London. Gradually, over the next eight years – until the dream turned rotten – Cathy Foulkes would become his constant friend and ally; 'a bit of a Pygmalion thing'. She would rarely skate with anyone else, and she would be the only skater he could never part with.

'In some strange way John had a snobbism about class maybe,' thinks Cathy.

> Jacqui and Lorna came from a very working class background. But my mother is an Andrews. Her first cousin twice removed was Thomas Andrews; the man who designed the *Titanic*. My family was Irish establishment. Entrepreneurs and statesmen. My parents were educated in England and my father went to Cambridge.

Foulkes herself was no intellectual slouch. She read books, listened to music and studied the world. When Curry called, she was midway through a law degree. Years later, when Curry's theatrical dreams had all collapsed, she went back and finished it.

On the morning of Monday 29 November, Curry gathered his six-strong troupe together at a dance studio in Floral Street, Covent

Garden. Under the eye of teacher Joyce Graeme, they clasped their hands around the barre, and commenced what would become their daily warm-up ritual of ballet stretches. If it was unorthodox, no one was sniggering. Each skater was on a weekly wage of £300 and few of them had seen money like it. Questions were neither encouraged nor advisable. Already, everywhere they looked there were problems, and Curry's intransigence was at the heart of all of them.

'He didn't know what he was doing. People got frustrated. He was frustrated. There were huge problems with Larry Parnes and him, and he in turn took his frustrations out on the company,' recalls Jacqui Harbord.

> He wouldn't speak to you for ages, and his favourite thing was to moan, 'Oh no Jacqui, that's not really skating'. It was feathers out, sequins out. Pointed toes and sustained edges in. Fantastic. All very clever and ballet-oriented, but the public don't know anything. The public want to see you do a fast spin. He had no experience of shows whatsoever. Everything was very intense. He would expect this and this and this and it would dissolve because it couldn't be done.

Keeping his own ego under control had never been easy. Now he had six more. Under the growing pressure, Curry's composure crumbled. Always friable, he became fractious and visibly flustered. Only he seemed to grasp what he was trying to do. Even the Scottish director seemed lost. To Peter Darrell, it seemed obvious that Curry – Britain's Olympic golden boy – should enter the stage in the manner of a star. To Curry, that was an abomination. Fanfares were for ice shows not art. At his insistence, he would enter anonymously and without noise. 'It was a silly thing to do,' he admitted later. 'But at the time I thought I was right.'

At the theatre – as the gremlins multiplied – the air became combustible. '[It] is rather like a bomb site,' he told Nancy. 'Pipes, workmen, debris of all kinds everywhere.' Space was so tight that the miniature rink had been built over the pit. Four rows of seats had been removed, and instead of a full orchestra Curry had been reduced to a small house band on a specially erected platform. More worryingly, the water was refusing to freeze and the first week's rehearsals were being walked through amidst the red velvet of a downstairs bar. Under Curry's controlling eye, every tiny detail was becoming a flashpoint. 'I think he felt empowered with his three medals. He probably felt he was above everything at that time,' explains Lorna. 'He wanted everything his way.'

As a child he had pushed tiny paper 'actors' around his home-made toy theatre. Nothing had prepared him for this. From New York, he had invited Joe Eula – the man behind his Olympic outfit – to design the costumes. When they arrived, they were ridiculed. 'He'd made this thing which looked like an under-slip, then he gave me this rag at three hundred quid a yard for a belt and I got really mad and said I'm not wearing that, so we stitched in some silk instead,' says Lorna. Jacqui Harbord had felt the same: 'I looked like I was in a silk sack tied up in the middle with a belt. The [designer] had just freaked out and rushed back to the States. We had to get someone else to finish them off. John's big idea had blown up like a balloon in front of him. He was higher than everyone else but hadn't the experience to carry it through.'

Fierce arguments had even broken out over the colour of the girls' boots. Lorna and Jacqui had arrived with the traditional beige. John had insisted on white. After experimenting with white, Curry suddenly panicked after being told the girls' feet looked like 'clubs of ice'. 'He then wanted beige but not Holiday On Ice beige,' says Jacqui. 'I went out and got a Max Factor pancake, which I mixed with shoe dye and showed it to John. We changed the white to a soft ballet-pink beige. He was happy.'

'All will be fine,' Curry wrote wearily to Nancy. 'Though I don't quite know how.'

'He picked on everyone,' says Harbord.

> Like he'd often zero in on me. Everything we were doing was so alien so I used to say the show was like amateur hour in Dixie. After that my nickname became Dixie. He had no respect for anybody who had any experience and he shot himself in the foot so many times to prove himself right.

It was hardly surprising that Curry drifted towards Cathy Foulkes. Lacking experience, she generated no friction and made no demands. On and off the ice she had slowly become his favourite.

'I was his raw material,' says Foulkes. 'Maybe a little bit of a muse to him. I think that was problematic for some of the women who were more experienced.' She was right. But although both the other girls had seen it coming, Lorna, especially, found marginalisation deeply wounding.

> From the start, Cathy was completely into John. It was like John was her reason for being. Everything revolved around him. Even though she hadn't done much ballet before, she'd be in every show, from first to last. She was very willowy and long and some of us were envious because it was obvious he put her into the most beautiful piece.

Ever since recording his LWT special – due to be broadcast on Christmas Day – Curry had been wondering whether to reprise *L'après-midi d'un Faune*. But since Peggy Fleming was back in America, he needed a new partner. Lorna Brown hoped desperately that it would be her. As teenagers they'd shared a bed and acted out *Romeo and Juliet* together. Surely no one was better placed to play the female foil to the erotic yearning of Curry's weird woodland creature.

'I'd loved that piece since I was a child,' she says sadly. 'I had the whole fantasy in my mind. It was something I'd thought about for years and years and years.' When the part subsequently went to the American newcomer, Lorna Brown was devastated. 'I was perfect in terms of proportions for him,' thinks Cathy Foulkes. Seeking consolation, Lorna inevitably blamed the disappointment on her own weight.

> I wasn't fat, but John liked women to be very very skinny. It got so I was afraid to eat in front of him because he'd look at me and I'd think, am I too fat or something? ... Cathy was incredibly skinny ... I remember going for a meal with him and Cathy and he said to her, 'Well, I hope you are going to eat something' because she was picking pieces off a pizza. Literally, almost like tweezering pieces of food. She was so devoted and in tune with him as I would have been if he'd asked me. I just think he wanted me to be longer and thinner.

For Curry – amidst the backbiting and stress – there were occasional distractions, not all of them welcome. In mid-December, he was presented with the BBC Sports Personality of the Year Award by Lord Mountbatten, beating British racing driver James Hunt in the public vote. Unknown to most, Curry's televised handshake with Earl Mountbatten of Burma had been his second brush with royalty that year. In July, the Royal Yacht had berthed off New York for the 200th anniversary of the Declaration of Independence. On board had been the Queen, and the OBE she'd carried across the Atlantic for her private time with John Curry.

'He was thrilled,' says Penny Malec.

> He was on his own. He wasn't in a herd of people. He had a proper conversation with the Queen and she then said that people on the ship would really all like to meet him. So he went on a tour and the thing he remembered in the kitchens was that the royal vegetables were all in little rows. He'd have really liked that. Vegetables neatly lined up in serried ranks.

Shortly after picking up his BBC award, Curry turned up as a nervous guest in a double-breasted suit on Michael Parkinson's Saturday night chat show. 'Had I not won [the Olympics] this year,' he told the watching millions, 'I'd just be another crackpot.' Rudolf Nureyev had been on the same bill, but – for whatever reason – they were interviewed by Parkinson separately.

Backstage, the imperious Russian had quizzed the skater about his upcoming Cambridge Theatre show. Who had designed the costumes? Curry told him it was Joe Eula, the same New Yorker who'd concocted his Olympic outfit. Nureyev was unimpressed. 'Toilet paper,' he snorted. Curry's upstart art form had been put in its place. A few days later it would be Curry's turn.

At the Sports Journalists' Association Christmas awards, hundreds of celebrities, hacks and sports stars jostled for the free wine. Haig Oundjian, Curry's old rival, was there. So, too, was Frank McLintock, the Arsenal FC captain. Towering above all of them was Joe Bugner, the heavyweight boxer. In a dining room almost entirely free of women, locker-room testosterone prevailed; cigar smoke plumed towards the ceiling; and bowties and belts were loosened in anticipation of a rowdy night.

That year's big winner – John Curry – was late. When he finally arrived, and began inching towards the top table, the evening's comic turn was midway through his repertoire of seedy gags. 'It's good to feel the Christmas spirit among us all,' he quipped into the microphone. 'Here comes the fairy for the tree.'

Like many in the room, Haig Oundjian was horror struck. 'I turned and saw John's face. It broke my heart.' According to another witness: 'There was a little embarrassed laughter, a lot of mutterings, some booing and jeering and Eric Morecambe [one half of comic duo Morecambe and Wise] stepped out of character by shouting "Disgraceful".' Unable to escape, Curry received his award in near silence. As the function ended, he turned pale-faced to Oundjian and told him he was finished with Britain. 'He said, "I'm leaving. I can't stay here any more".' It had been, Curry later told an associate, 'one of the most hurtful incidents in my life'. Only the Cambridge Theatre show was now keeping him in London.

On Christmas Eve, *The John Curry Theatre of Skating* squeezed in its first, and only, full dress rehearsal. Three days later, on 27 December, the inaugural incarnation of Curry's long-cherished fantasy was unveiled to a packed, and expectant, Cambridge Theatre. Standing in the wings, a huge gold ring on his left pinkie finger, Larry Parnes was beaming. Curry's Christmas Day ITV special had pushed up demand for tickets. No other West End show was exciting quite so much interest. If he was secretly nervous about Curry's singular brand of 'entertainment', it was forgotten as he watched punters shelling out for the show's glossy programme.

Backstage, Curry had also temporarily pushed away all doubts. Bouquets of white and red roses littered his dressing-room table. Nancy Streeter, just in from New York for opening night, had sent freesias. Bottles of multi-vitamins and Korean ginseng – a habit he'd acquired in New York – jostled for space alongside telegrams, tubs of make-up and 'gentlemen's soap' by Chanel. At his feet were the leather skating boots he'd softened in pans of boiling water, each with a square cut from its heel to help him 'dance'.

Two hours later, as 1,100 people filed from the Cambridge and the cast partied in the stalls bar, an air of puzzled euphoria hung over the company. As he had feared, Curry had visibly struggled during his Liszt solo. In the subdued opener, 'Scenes of Childhood' – set to music by Schumann – the tiny stage had felt ludicrously cramped for six people in motion. Flowing movement had been impossible and the skaters had flirted dangerously with the footlights. Although sections of it had gelled – like the jazzy nod to Fred Astaire – Curry was left with an ominous feeling of anti-climax; a feeling compounded by the *Guardian*'s savage overnight critique:

> In the narrow confines of the Cambridge Theatre, these skaters, even the wonderful Curry, seem like caged birds rather than the wild nightingales they ought to be … and much though Curry's own skating (and to a lesser extent that of his companions) has benefited from the balletic influence, their 'line' cannot rid itself of those heavy skates. As an art form, skating has something to offer, but it is all a bit like ballet in big boots.

Not everyone had been so brutal. *The Times* had found it to be, rather patronisingly, 'a jolly good show'. Others had praised the 'simple, effortless elegance' of its leading man. No one had effervesced, however, and faint praise appeared to be the norm. Among the skaters – or some of them – a feeling of despondent *schadenfreude* prevailed. 'One of the crits said the set looked like the inside of a fridge,' recalls Harbord. 'To me, it looked like a blue box. Very minimalist. A couple of trees. I felt it was all so misguided of John. All he had to do to open the show was that famous little step from the Olympics and he'd have had them in his hands.'

Only when it was over would Curry acknowledge his mistake. As his show settled into its run – and as 1976 trickled away – he was unprepared to make changes. Eight times a week, the lights dimmed and Schumann's hushed piano ushered in the skaters. Through repetition, Curry mastered the footwork required of Kenneth MacMillan's choreography. Through practice, the production achieved consistency and flow. Night after night, however, only one dance transported the audience where they'd expected to go.

L'après-midi d'un Faune had been included only at the last minute; too late even to be mentioned in the programme. Thrust into the role, teenager Cathy Foulkes had learned her part in just one afternoon. She would have ample time to perfect it. Over the next eight years, she and John performed *Faune* together hundreds of times. In the process their friendship would flower and deepen. It was, and still remains, one of Curry's most powerful and personal works of theatrical genius.

As it begins, Curry – the faune – stands alone at the back of stage. A melodic ripple of flute stirs his forest slumbers. He moves forward into the light, where – in the daring leaf-coloured body stocking designed for later shows – he seems totally naked. Every secret ripple of his body is visible. 'You could hear a pin drop,' remembers Cathy.

As the music swells, the faune's body unfurls, moving faster and more freely under the warmth of the sun. Suddenly he is gone, and a young girl in white, a nymph – her long tresses spinning – enters the glade. Like the faune, she has come to be alone, but when the faune gives chase, they touch and they dance and their bodies lock in such tender unison there can be only one shuddering erotic outcome.

'When we did that, he was always 100 per cent the faune,' says Foulkes.

> He didn't even look like himself. He was transformed. He literally looked like a creature. Sometimes when he grabbed my hand it took my breath away. It never felt routine. There's a part where the two ripple through in synch together and there's clearly masturbation implied. And he was right up against me. Two bodies plastered together. It felt like masturbating.

As the music slowly ebbs away, the bereft faune appears to defy the laws of physics. Skating slowly forward on his right foot, his arms and left leg fully extended, Curry slows and stops. Suddenly, without any perceptible effort, he begins to move backwards along the same line on the same foot. Night after night, audiences were stunned by it. 'It was the first time I had done any partnering where real feeling was called for between partners,' admitted Curry. 'It is the most satisfying of the works I have done. I enjoy it the most.'

For the skater, it was also a piece thundering with buried meaning. Every performance consumed and overwhelmed him. As the nymph flees, the faune is left to dance alone. Although he searches, she does not come back. Hidden within mesmerising code, Curry had opened a tiny window on his life. Not knowing this, audiences simply tuned in to the near-indecency of its passion. 'There was an eruption every night,' remembers Cathy. 'I always think that others questioned why John cast me in the nymph role – a total novice to professional skating. In the end I think it was obvious to all.'

But not even the *Faune* could save Curry's show. As the winter months dragged on, the audiences tailed away, deterred by poor weather and patchy reviews. With nearly one in three seats unfilled, Parnes began to sense danger. Staging a skating show in a theatre had been expensive and the risk was all his. Every empty seat was hitting his profit, company morale was low and Curry's mood was dragging it lower. 'Being Mr Nice is fine,' John confided to Nancy. 'But to get anything done one has to throw a fit. Fit throwing can be rather exhausting.' Relations between the manager and his client were also in freefall. At her flat in Richmond – where Curry was still periodically camping out – Penny Malec bore witness to her friend's rapid decline.

'His nature changed,' she explains.

> He was corrupted by rage. He got bitter in a way that he hadn't been. He wasn't a bitter kid at all. He thought his show at the Cambridge would change attitudes, and it was corrosive and personally disappointing that it didn't. He also couldn't believe that all these people he'd given this amazing chance to would turn up five minutes before curtain and he'd be there two hours before the show. People never lived up to his expectations of them.

On 12 March, to the secret relief of everyone, the Cambridge show folded. Right from opening night Parnes had harboured doubts. Curry's show was too intense, and the skater's fears about the small stage had turned out to be correct. After 87 performances, when the lights finally went out on *The John Curry Theatre of Skating*, it was exactly 12 months since he'd stood on a podium in Gothenburg.

Four days later 'the fairy for the tree' was in New York.

Seven

'Dangerous appetites'

John Curry was in pain. For over 20 years, every joint in his body had been under daily attack. Since the age of seven – in the arthritic gloom of ice rinks – he'd twisted and jumped almost every day of his life. Few skaters escaped unscathed and most would eventually nurse corroded hips or crumbling knees; quite often both.

John Curry's athletic young rival Robin Cousins had been unable to kneel since he was 15, and had the first of eight knee operations two years later. By the time he'd reached his mid-fifties what was left of them was – in his own words – 'shot to shit'. Curry's balletic style had minimised the destruction, but in the days following the end of the Cambridge run – wallowing in bruised pride – he was publicly feeling every hurt.

> Sometimes I feel as if my whole body is seizing up. There have been nights when I can hear my joints and bones clicking above the sound of the music. I have tendonitis in one arm where a girl skater has to grip tightly when I lift her and I've been so tired that it has been an effort to get dressed … I have gone on twice with food poisoning … I cannot be ill myself because it has been my name which has been bringing in the public … one hears such dreadful stories about sportsmen ending up arthritic cripples … it scares me to think I could wake up one morning and never be able to skate again.

Curry's spell at the Cambridge had amplified more than his physical distress. Under pressure his secret insecurities had, at times, transformed him into a crushing, autocratic bully. When he was a competitive skater, only a handful of intimates – like Nancy, Heinz and Alison – had ever engaged with these hidden complexities. Now he was a professional, running an embryonic company, the circle of witnesses was widening, just as the public gaze was intensifying.

Somehow, Curry had persevered and delivered flashes of brilliance, but the effort had taken a horrible toll. He'd lost weight, and had required two hot baths, a daily sauna and regular massage to keep going. In a *Guardian* profile – presciently headed 'Agony of the ice man' – Curry sounded worryingly hollow. 'When I've washed the winter out of my system everything will be alright,' he'd said, adding that 'at the moment I hope to go on skating till I'm 35, but who knows?'

Larry Parnes knew. While Curry recuperated in the USA, his besotted manager was scouring London for a bigger theatre. Despite its limitations, Parnes had been heartened by the Cambridge experience. In a grander venue with a bigger, breezier production, the promoter felt certain he could claw back his losses. It was a fatal misreading of his client's indifference to Mammon. As Parnes prepared a spring relaunch built around Curry as a mainstream, family entertainer, the Olympic champion was declaring that 'money has never been my god'. And as Curry dreamed of Covent Garden, Parnes struck a deal with the Soho home of lowbrow schmaltz, the London Palladium, a building with ice in its illustrious past.

In the nineteenth century, a 'national skating palace' had stood on the site in Argyll Street. Since 1910 – in a rebuilt Edwardian masterpiece – it had become the premier venue for West End variety. Judy Garland, Frank Sinatra and Bing Crosby had all performed at the London Palladium. It could seat over 2,200, had a revolutionary revolving stage and boasted a private phone system that allowed the big-money occupants of boxes to call one another. Only Elvis Presley had ever refused to perform there, and even Curry was too focused to do that.

By mid-March, a new schedule had been agreed. Terrified that the skater's popularity was fading, Parnes had booked out the Palladium for July and August. Ahead of that, he'd arranged a two-week run at the Hippodrome in Bristol. Casting would start in late April; rehearsals would begin a fortnight later. It was all happening very quickly. 'Just thinking about it makes me feel nervous,' admitted Curry. 'But then, I'm nervous before anything new. I would push a disappear button if I could.'

Curry's fears were not without reason. Under pressure from Larry Parnes, he'd conceded that his Cambridge show may have been too serious, but neither crass vulgarity nor crowd-pleasing frivolity were acceptable alternatives. In February, he'd appeared on *Desert Island Discs* choosing just one contemporary track ('Cuddle Up' by The Beach Boys) amidst a raft of classical pieces. Around the same time, a planned *This Is Your Life* on the skater had (perhaps wisely) been shelved. From all directions, the signals were the same. Curry would amend, but he could not be changed. His old friend Penny Malec watched developments through her fingers.

> John was unwilling to see either the Cambridge or the Palladium as a star vehicle, which was naïve if not idiotic given his celebrity. He wanted to turn the Palladium into Covent Garden, regardless of the business side of the venture. I think Larry tried hard to please him – I remember getting taken to Jonathan Miller's *Three Sisters* at one of Larry's theatres and then all of us meeting Miller, who looked down his nose at us while both he and John jointly looked down at Larry, who was struggling with all the high-mindedness ... Although he liked the fame and the things money buys, I really don't think John was interested at all in making money for himself and this must have been inconceivable to Larry.

Blind – or indifferent – to the risks, Parnes ploughed on. The Palladium would be bigger in every way than its forerunner. In gushing press releases, he promised 12 skaters, over 80 costumes, new dances and even a harpist on the ice. *The Theatre of Skating II*, as he called it, would cost £140,000, and its star – according to one comically inflated estimate – would be earning £350,000 a year. Although the figures were fanciful, the blunt reality behind them was not. Parnes had dug deep, and Curry, newly back from the States, urgently needed to shake off his transatlantic torpor.

'A wave of depression, the like of which I have not experienced for many a year enveloped me as I left New York,' he wrote to Nancy Streeter. 'Thursday here was unimaginable. I am "reviewing the EST training" starting next weekend. It was either that or the gas oven and I really detest the smell of gas.'

As always, time was tight. From the first show, Cathy Foulkes, Lorna Brown, Paul Toomey and Jacqui Harbord – a self-confessed 'witch and a bitch' – were retained. Bill Woerhle and Paul McGrath – with whom Curry had repeatedly clashed – were not. To her unbridled joy, there was a spot for Linda Davis, the girl from the Bayswater boutique. There was also a place for David Barker, the blond-haired Londoner with whom Curry had enjoyed a one-night stand in France. As auditions continued, the final places were hastily filled up by talented, but inexperienced, newcomers. One of them would have an immediate impact on the show's reluctant star. Very little of it, claim Curry's surviving friends, was for the good.

In the official programme for *The Theatre of Skating II*, the career details alongside the photograph of Vancouver-born Ron Alexander took up very little space. As an amateur skater, he had achieved nothing. As a professional, he'd made up the numbers at nightclub shows from Vienna to Las Vegas, mostly as an 'adagio' pairs skater – a muscular set of shoulders whenever acrobatic lifting was required. Unlike his lacklustre curriculum vitae, however, Alexander's mugshot lingered on the eye.

'John was desperate for people,' remembers Harbord. 'I showed him a picture of Ron who was a great mate of mine but just wasn't very talented. I knew John needed men and Ron was a big strong, handsome guy. John fell in love with the photograph.'

With his dark curls, square jaw and aquiline nose, Alexander had the looks to go with his body-builder physique. He was also sharp-witted, combative and gay. If the girls had privately questioned Curry's selection criteria for male skaters at the Cambridge, Ron Alexander confirmed it. Nothing Curry had done was remotely within the Canadian's range. When it became obvious the two men were sleeping together, nobody was surprised. 'Ron was an opportunist,' thinks Harbord. 'When he found out what was required of him, he ended up living with John. He ended up playing that part.'

Apart from his friendship with Julian Pettifer, there had been no lasting 'other' in Curry's life since Heinz Wirz. The adult skater of 1977, however, bore little resemblance to the bashful youth who'd cruised London's gay clubs alone. Ever since his teens he'd been needy and prone to extreme mood swings. Now, through celebrity, had come an expectation of dominance – to be exerted by Curry over both his art and his new lover. It was a dangerous expectation. Alexander was no wallflower, and their two turbulent on-off years together would be distinguished by bitter rows.

In one crucial aspect, however, they were a perfect match. After years of self-deprivation, Curry was not uninterested in the wilder trappings of 1970s fame. 'Cocaine. Parties. This is all happening within a few years of the first gay pride march. It's like the Berlin Wall coming down for gay men,' explains Foulkes. 'It's like, great, you know? People feeling alive. Finally gay guys could party.' As Curry experimented, Ron Alexander embraced the role of willing accomplice. 'I think that John knew the dark places before Ron entered the scene,' points out Harbord. Either way, it was all about to get a great deal darker.

———

On 9 May, at Twickenham's world-famous film studios, the new troupe gathered to rehearse on a sheet of belatedly laid ice. 'Oh it is all such a worry,' he told Nancy. 'Only three weeks to put this thing together. It is frightening.' After the now mandatory ballet warm-up, Curry took command of proceedings. Immediately, the Cambridge veterans could see how much had changed. Only the captivating *Faune* duet and Norman Maen's slinky *Jazz Suite* had survived. Everything else was new, or a work in progress. And all of it had John Curry himself at centre stage.

From the opening fireworks of *Le Valse Glace* – in which Curry showcased his tricks dressed as a Ruritanian prince – to the wholesome show closer *Winter 1895*, the new programme appeared, at first glance, to be everything Curry had previously dismissed. Hamming it up as a Cockney pearly prince – or 'pearly queen' as Lorna Brown dubbed him – was not exactly high art. Being on stage for two hours of a two-and-three-quarter hour show was hardly the act of a reluctant star.

Every facet of the programme, however, was studded with variety, invention and good taste. The music ranged from Drigo and Debussy to Arthur Sullivan and Thad Jones. And discreetly sandwiched between the mandatory humour was the piece which – to Curry – mattered the most. And which to Larry Parnes made absolutely no sense whatsoever.

For years, Curry had dreamed of an ice ballet in which a skater might appear to fly. During his last trip to New York he'd discussed the idea with the American choreographer John Butler. When their brainstorming threw up the fable of Icarus, Curry was thrilled. Apart from Peter Pan – another Curry favourite – no story could have been more perfect, or more tuned to his painfully unfolding myth than that of the man who yearned to fly only to fall back to earth after venturing too close to the sun. In 1977 – by inviting audiences to swap the wing-melting sun for his own Olympic gold – Curry would be presenting the story of his life so far; and unknowingly, the terrible story of what was yet to come.

> One of my beliefs has always been that everyone wants to fly too close to the sun – wants to get something very badly – and when they do get there, they usually find that the thing they want – whether it is the sun, or whatever golden object one might think of – is their ultimate undoing.

Larry Parnes was horrified. For two months he'd been distancing the Palladium show from its earnest Cambridge prototype. Curry's vision for Icarus – with its specially commissioned contemporary score and sophisticated costumes – risked undermining whatever progress he'd made. It would also be costly to stage, squeeze limited rehearsal time and extend an already bloated production. Thus far, Parnes had granted Curry his every whim. This time, he would not. Unless Curry paid for it himself, *Icarus* was out. To his amazement, the skater called his bluff. Curry footed the bills and *Icarus* stayed in.

Across at Twickenham – with Kirk Douglas filming on an adjacent lot – rehearsals continued feverishly throughout May. The schedule was unforgiving, and Curry's intransigence on *Icarus* added strain to tension. Not only were the new ensemble routines complex, but Curry dominated each of them. 'He was the focal point of everything,' explains Harbord. 'It was a walk in the park for the rest of us. We didn't do anything. It was boring for everyone except John.' Ominously, the pressure on their leader was building.

'It was not easy,' he admitted later.

We were preparing five pieces and remounting two with what was basically a new company. The time pressures were great and it fell upon me to be involved in nearly all of this work in one capacity or another; either through learning three new pieces, choreographing two others, or rehearsing the remainder. My concentration and effort were spread over a very large area.

Soon, the old cracks began to reappear. Twelve-hour rehearsals left the skaters fractious and weary and any sign of weakness was pounced on. When Lorna Brown's foot became infected, she'd switched from ladies' boots to men's simply to keep going.

At some point I'd been standing there with John, who was choreographing this dance with a harp and he said, 'Well, don't just stand there like a pudding'. I had to go off crying and demand that I was sent to a doctor. I said, 'Take me out of this number, the whole show' and stormed off. Then the next day, I was a bit scared to come in, but it was like nothing had happened. It was terrible.

For Linda Davis, fresh from her Wembley ice panto, Curry's erratic behaviour was disappointing.

He was very strict; very harsh on a lot of us. You mustn't be a minute late, and there'd be only a strict 15-minute break. To get to the rehearsal in Twickenham involved a bus and a taxi and we had to be there at 8.30 every morning. One day my bus didn't come and he went crazy. He had no idea about those sorts of things. There was a side of him that was very naïve. He didn't think that I might have to get help for my son, and that my husband was a pain in the bum. He didn't understand any of that. He went bananas ...

For Curry there had never been anything else. Pain and inconvenience had not been obstacles for him and real art required discomfort. Nor was he particularly interested in what his troupe thought of him. In a letter home, Cathy Foulkes wondered 'perhaps if we act human towards him, he will act human towards us'. But since there was little personal investment in any of this,

that seemed unlikely. On the ice, provided his skaters learned
quickly, he would remain calm. Off it, in the canteen queue for
his beloved sponge pudding and custard, all his ire would evaporate
anyway.

Among Curry's befuddled skaters the bruises lingered longer.
Doubt and fear fostered gossip and mute dissent. The girls especially
craved approval, but struggled to get past Curry's growing regard
for Foulkes. 'John didn't like women like me, whereas Cathy
wouldn't say boo to a goose,' says Harbord. 'She seemed to lose
weight just to skate with him. She'd eat a yoghurt a day whereas
Lorna was just not his type of person and got terribly upset by it all.
Me, I just thought John was a bit stupid. The whole thing was
awful.' As the talk swirled, one issue united all of them; Curry's
supposedly clandestine affair with Ron Alexander was putting the
entire show at risk of ridicule.

In his self-funded folly, Curry had cast himself as Icarus and Ron
Alexander as his father, Daedalus. It was a decision no one could
understand. At best, the Canadian was a passable, chorus line skater.
At worst, he was a shuffling novice, hostile to the discipline required
to meet Curry's stratospheric standards. For a piece in which Curry
had staked both cash and reputation, it seemed an extraordinary
blunder, one that was compounded as John Butler's vision for
Icarus began to emerge.

Nothing about it seemed straightforward. The Palladium
band was too small for the original score and all work had to
stop while a new one was written. When he was tossed into the
air by Ron Alexander, Curry panicked, noting drily: 'I am not
the world's bravest pair skater. I would rather be the thrower than
the throwee.' The fabric wings that Curry strapped to his arms
created severe wind resistance, and his outfit looked like a bikini
assembled from chamois leather patches. Fuelled by Toblerones
and gripped by anxiety, Curry pressed on. 'One is scared but one
is also excited by such departures,' he said. Watching from the
sidelines, as Curry flapped and fretted, Linda Davis was feeling
uneasy.

> It took John ages to master the wings contraption. It was all very
> modern with very skimpy outfits. I personally thought, perhaps
> they're going too far but I wasn't going to talk about it outside

the rink. My little boy was only four at the time and he came to rehearsals twice and I remember thinking that this one was really only for grown-ups.

———

Even as a child, Curry had nursed a weakness for leather. His mother remembered him making his own leather waistcoat, around the time he'd spent his birthday money on that pair of winkle-pickers. In London, he'd hung around Earl's Court's notorious leather pub the Coleherne. And six years later he was lusting after a custom-designed highway patrolman's jacket – 'with regular collar and epaulets' – from Langlitz Leathers, 'the finest motorcycle clothing in the world'.

Nothing epitomised the late 1970s gay stereotype better than a zip-up biker's jacket. It was the Village People. It was New York. It was gay pride. But with John Curry, it was also the one visible clue to something more troubling. Heinz Wirz referred to it as 'his dangerous appetite'; a private need for extreme sex, something which his adventurous new partner Ron Alexander seemed eager to satisfy.

'I think Ron was staying at a flat near White City,' recalls David Barker.

> One day I was summoned there and I think we had sex – Ron and I – and then he said, John's very interested in leather sex and because I knew so much about it, could I give him a few tips. So I gave him my tips on leather sex – sado-masochism, whipping, bondage, all that sort of thing – and Ron tootled off and told John. But John himself couldn't come to ask me. He had to ask through Ron.

Everybody knew. But it was never – and could never be – discussed. Increasingly, Curry's activities were becoming compartmentalised. Admission to one box by no means guaranteed access to another. At best, his closest friends caught glimpses or heard rumours. But nobody ever got the whole picture. Whatever turmoil lay buried behind his choices was known only to Curry himself. The others, like Jacqui Harbord, could only speculate.

John was going through a lot of problems at this time ... The
S&M thing was certainly one, but then we all knew what John
was like. This was what Ron provided for him. Lorna knew that.
I knew that. We'd known John since he was ten and he didn't go
for nice young people. He went for older people who were awful.

Linda Davis's queasiness was not misplaced. Increasingly, Curry's
work was tossing out clues. In later years, he would perform to
Khachaturian's 'Spartacus' with his arms bound to his naked upper
body. 'Absolutely there was a message there,' insists Wirz. 'He was
the slave as Spartacus was and in his sexual orientation he was very
much a masochist. He also told me he tried to skate tied up for the
whole programme but it wasn't possible.' In *Faune*, he'd visualised
his loneliness. Through the homoeroticism of *Icarus*, Curry was
reaching out again. Small wonder Parnes had refused to pay, or
that, privately, he feared a box office disaster.

By mid-June, the troupe was ready. At a packed Bristol
Hippodrome, the curtains opened with the 'whizz-dashery' of a
smiling John Curry in tight white pants and waistcoat, shamelessly
showboating for applause. Gone was the sombre intensity of the
Cambridge. In its place was a populist menu illuminated by Curry's
impeccable taste. Only *Icarus* stood in the way of a resounding hit
show.

Wearing a huge, floating silk cloak, Curry had entered the stage
under a giant hollow sun. As the story unfolded – and as Ron
Alexander flopped self-consciously in the background – 'boos and
hisses' could be heard coming from the auditorium. Not since
Vancouver had Curry felt so humiliated. According to one review,
his costume had resembled a 'leather nappy'. According to another,
it all 'went on far too long'.

'*Icarus* was two men skating together, one of them in a scanty
leather g-string,' says Lorna Brown.

Looking back, it was very gay, but at the time we didn't think it
was a gay thing. We just thought of it as being very contemporary.
John would never have let a woman go out and be that naked.
For a photo-shoot, he once told me off for wearing a pink ballet
leotard, beige tights, and hair in a little bun. 'Ugh. You can't have
your photo taken like that,' he said. 'You look like a stripper.'

After 16 performances in Bristol, the production moved to London. As the liquid stage set hard inside the Palladium, Curry's nerves were sizzling. Parnes clearly wanted *Icarus* dropped and, by miserable coincidence, the skater's new show would open just as Nureyev and Fonteyn were dancing on stage barely a mile away. All his life he'd worshipped Fonteyn's 'infinite qualities'. He wasn't quite ready for his own ice-bound form of dance, to be viewed in direct comparison. And he was certainly in no mood for platitudes. 'I remember walking into the Palladium with him and musing on who and what had been there,' remembers Jacqui Harbord. 'I said to John, "Think of that. This place is just steeped in history." He just looked at me, and walked off.'

There was another possible reason for John's foreboding. Across in the States, his old rival Toller Cranston had reappeared in his peripheral vision. On 19 May at the Palace Theater on Broadway, the Canadian had dropped into his own eponymous ice show aboard an illuminated star clad in 'a black beaded jumpsuit cut nearly to his navel'. Unlike the Englishman, Cranston gleefully embraced his own fame. In interviews, he had also lampooned the intensity of Curry's alternative brew. 'His Twyla Tharp piece was totally bland ... anti-skating ... it didn't make sense at all ... I am sick of this pseudo-intellectualism in dance where very obscure things are often a substitute for greatness.'

Curry could live with Cranston's knockabout abuse. Curry had the medals, Cranston did not. What troubled him more were the Canadian's half-empty houses. Despite emphatic reviews, Manhattan's notoriously picky theatre-goers had stayed away. 'If we had been a musical or dance company there would have been queues around the block,' moaned Cranston. 'It's hard for people to accept something that's different.' After a four-week run, his show had expired. By the time *The Theatre of Skating II* opened in London on 4 July, Cranston was grimly totting up his losses in a $900-a-month apartment.

Curry need not have worried. Bristol may have sniggered, but London swooned. In every newspaper, the critics spoke with one voice. 'Curry appears a unique and mysterious being and one absolutely not to be missed,' raved the *Financial Times*. 'A star personality of astonishing theatrical charisma,' gushed the *Herald Tribune*. 'Nothing short of sensational ... world-class entertainment,' boomed the *Daily Mail*.

Almost inevitably, nothing garnered more compliments than *Icarus*. It was, said one smitten reviewer, a performance of 'heroic poetry [which showed] that skating can, in the hands of a master be an act of real, expressive force'. 'You forget about the skating virtuosity and watch it as ballet,' said another. According to the *Mail*'s legendary theatre critic Jack Tinker, it was 'a sublime essay in the dizzy joy of flight'.

It was precisely what Curry needed to hear. Across the city, Nureyev and Fonteyn were enjoying 15-minute curtain calls, but the Palladium had become London's hottest ticket, with Curry alone its indisputable draw. However hard they worked, no one else in his cast could match his spell. In one review, a fellow skater was described as a 'stalwart lady homing in on [John Curry] like a homicidal blancmange'. In another, the show was marked down for its mediocre 'pit band' and for a flawed 'bill devised to keep as many different people as happy as possible'. Only Curry escaped tarnish. Once again he had found redemption through his disdain for compromise.

'The ultimate and lingering image is of him as a solitary figure,' wrote Clement Crisp in the *FT*. 'His abilities are so far in advance of those of his colleagues, his ambitions and interpretive powers so much richer, that his becomes the isolation of the truly innovative artist.'

John Curry himself, however, was taking little pleasure from his triumph. In a long letter to Nancy Streeter, which he insisted she kept secret, he told her he'd asked Parnes to 'reduce the Palladium season to 4 weeks or however long it takes to recoup the money spent on my show – then I am finishing and returning to the US to make my home and my life', adding, 'Everyone else tells me that it is much better than the Cambridge production – well it may be, but I don't care for it as much.'

Like it or not, for another three weeks Curry's show was unstoppable. After each performance, the stage door was snarled by autograph hunters and flowers choked every dressing room. There were private lunches with Princess Margaret and invitations to Buckingham Palace. Well-known thespians and dancers streamed into the Palladium to see it. One of them, the English actor Alan Bates, had already been spotted at the Cambridge Theatre in March. Out of a casual friendship, something enduring and intense – but elusive – was slowly stirring.

'Years before, we'd seen his naked body wrestling in the film *Women in Love*,' recalls Heinz Wirz. 'When John told me he'd seen Bates in a London play, I told him he should have taken me! Although I've no real idea how they met, they would eventually become very close friends. I'm sure they eventually loved one another.'

Very few of Curry's intimate relationships lasted long. Of those that did, none would be protected quite so fiercely as the one with Alan Bates. When Curry was floundering in America, Bates would suddenly appear at his side. When Curry was dying, Bates would be there to prop him up. Since neither discussed it publicly, and since no letters appear to have survived, the precise nature of their affair died with both men. Bates had been a public figure, married with children, and John Curry had no wish to embarrass him. For almost 20 years, their story lay deep beneath the radar. And in the summer of 1977, Curry already had distractions enough.

Performing had usually recharged Curry. Success at the Palladium – possibly boosted by other stimulants – seemed to knock him off balance. When he was on stage, unnoticed by audiences, his behaviour had become periodically erratic. Away from it, as well as plotting to curtail the run, he had a lifestyle that was raising eyebrows. The two things were almost certainly connected.

'One night we were skating together,' recalls Brown,

> and he reached out his arm to me so our hands were touching and then he sniffed very loudly. Snorted in fact. I started to snigger, then he started to snigger and we laughed all the way through and tried to make it look as though I was crying. Afterwards he said we must never do that again … On other nights, he would say terribly rude things in my ear during a very intense piece with the harp on stage … maybe something about someone in the audience … and I would just smile and keep going.

When the theatre emptied, nobody – apart possibly from Ron Alexander – seemed too sure where Curry went. After years of on-off lodging with Penny Malec, he'd moved (courtesy of Larry Parnes) into a large furnished flat off Kensington High Street, in Marloes Road. ('Very grand and good for him,' Penny told Nancy

Streeter. ('Breaking the umbilical cord and getting him into it was a slightly painful experience but I'm confident that he'll be happier once he's used to being on his own.')

If he was feeling tired, Curry would unwind there with a marijuana joint. When the adrenalin was still pumping, he would wander among Soho's backstreets. 'Ron had once taken me to an all-nude review – *Oh! Calcutta!* – just to shake me up a bit,' recalls Foulkes. 'But I was a teenager then. John had a nightlife which I was unaware of.'

Perhaps inevitably, Curry seems to have dabbled briefly with cocaine, the decade's drug of choice for entertainers with surplus cash and a need for chemically induced energy. Few stimulants, however, were less suited to the pinpoint accuracy required of ice skating than this one. And no drug could have been more likely to short-circuit Curry's already precarious state of mind. Years later, in words attributed to him, the skater recalled the terrifying feeling of decline:

> I had always been a very secure performer but now I found myself falling. No one except Ron knew about my nightly excursions, so my deterioration was put down to depression and fatigue. I knew I was on a dangerous course, but I desperately needed the measure of escape it afforded me. It gave me a kind of happiness … I couldn't stop.

Almost halfway through an eight-week run, Curry had become an accident waiting to happen. On 26 July, it happened. According to the *Guardian*, he'd been beaten up on Earl's Court Road 'walking home at about 10.30 last Sunday night with friends'. There'd been no arrests and there were precious few details. Curry himself was said to be under sedation, having collapsed at the end of his Monday performance. Until he was fit, the Palladium was offering free tickets and refunds to disappointed customers.

No one knew what to believe. Nothing quite like it had ever happened before. For a major West End show to lose its star was a catastrophe. For the cast, and production crew, there was the sudden vacuum of speculation, not helped by the inconsistencies in Curry's accounts of what had happened. The ever-alert Lorna Brown had been one of the first to glean any answers. Barely an hour before the doomed Monday performance she'd found him by the ballet barre 'all cut up and bruised-looking and shocked'.

> He said he'd been to get a Chinese takeaway or something and then somebody attacked him. I didn't believe it because he was sexually involved with Ron Alexander then, and I don't know what sort of places they'd go to. I think John got led the wrong way.

Heinz Wirz – staying with Curry at the time – had seen the bruises too. 'Pretty bad,' he remembers. 'I don't know if that wasn't a proper beating up. He was in agony and I thought then it must have been in one of those sexual experiences but I'm not sure and John would not say.'

For the next week, Curry recuperated at his Marloes Road apartment. Apart from the facial injuries, there was severe bruising to his back, which specialists had urged him to rest. Across at the Palladium, the show stuttered on with an understudy but no one was under any illusions. Without Curry, there was nothing to sell. *Faune* and *Icarus* were withdrawn from the running order in his absence. However hard he fought it, a star was what people paid to see. Without one, ticket sales collapsed.

For Larry Parnes it was a body blow. Since the Cambridge, his relationship with Curry had been awkward. By refusing to fund *Icarus*, he'd allowed their different visions of theatrical skating to become irretrievably polarised. With critical opinion behind Curry, Parnes probably sensed he was losing his man. On top of that, with Curry bedridden, Parnes was losing money. Somehow the ugly rumours had to be stopped. A week after the incident, Parnes summoned reporters to the Palladium. There to enlighten them 'looking exquisite and extremely fit' was a recovered John Curry.

It had happened – he told the journalists – shortly after leaving an Indian restaurant, but there was no explanation of why he'd been attacked; or why he'd failed to report it to the police. 'What can you do?' he pleaded. 'There were a thousand people about and the attacker had gone. I just wanted to go home and get my nose fixed up.' It was a plausibly thin account, beyond which Curry would never publicly go.

Whatever had happened in Earl's Court, Curry's life had reached one of its periodic crises. Publicly, Parnes was still telling people that *The Theatre of Skating* would shortly be touring the United States; and that Curry himself was seriously considering a film script – a romantic drama. But almost all of it was nonsense. When the Palladium show resumed, Curry opted out of the afternoon matinée and for as long as he skated his back would never fully recover from the mysterious assault. More significantly – although as yet mistily – he must have known Parnes would soon be joining his pile of human discards. 'If John didn't like something he would never forgive it,' says Lorna. 'We could have run the Palladium for a year but they fell out. That's all we knew. They fell out.' As always, however, Curry already had his safety net in place.

———

At 26, David Singer was a young New York lawyer dreading a life measured out on Wall Street. And then he saw John Curry skating to Twyla Tharp's choreography at Madison Square Garden. Overwhelmed, he'd sought Curry out backstage. 'John mattered,' he explains. 'I told him I'd welcome a chance to produce a show for him in New York. I was a real devotee. I felt I had good taste and could make distinctions. He said that if I was serious I should come to London.'

Singer was deadly serious. In the early spring, with fellow producer Charlotte Kirk, he'd flown to England to watch Curry perform. Flattered, but seemingly clueless about his 'contract' with Parnes, Curry had urged the pair 'to work things out with Larry'. Larry Parnes, however, had absolutely no intention of sharing his prize asset with two American strangers.

After meeting them he told Curry that the pair had neither the experience nor the funds to produce him in North America. David Singer, for his part, had been equally unimpressed. 'I felt like I needed a shower after being with Parnes,' he says. 'He was not someone to do business with. He was greedy and I didn't trust him. He asked inappropriate terms and asked for an inappropriate role if I was to work with him.'

Privately, Parnes was rattled. John Curry wasn't a naïf like Billy Fury. He was smart, he was stubborn and he was fickle. He'd also signed nothing. ('I don't think I'd sign for the Pope,' he'd once told a reporter). Any interest from New York, however vague, was guaranteed to unsettle him and since the 'assault' and the euphoria of opening night, he'd seemed even more distant. It was time for a Larry Parnes grand gesture. Soon after Curry returned from his convalescence, further 'details' were released concerning the pending 'world tour'. In a state of high excitement, Cathy Foulkes wrote home, saying:

> Rehearsals are to begin mid October in New York and will last about 6 to 7 weeks. Then we'll tour the US, east and west and then go to Australia for the Adelaide Festival. [John] asked us all to think about whether we wanted to go and let him know. Last night there were a whole bunch of U.S. backers over to see the show ... John did Faune and Icarus. His back was killing him.

Parnes alone knew how real any of this was. John Curry no longer seemed to care. Whatever happened – and whatever Parnes conjured up – he and the 'beat Svengali' were finished. Curry had wanted out of London for several months anyway. Provided he could navigate through the legal issues, the skater had decided to pair up with David Singer in New York, whatever it took. The hurdles in his way, however, appeared significant.

Parnes owned the *Theatre of Skating* 'brand', and had bankrolled key elements of its choreography. Unless he relinquished control, Curry faced rebuilding a new show from scratch. David Singer appeared untroubled. 'After talking it through with John it became apparent that working with Parnes was not necessary. The rights were not impossibly sewn up. We didn't need Parnes at all.' Meanwhile, the Palladium show limped on.

Everyone had noticed how quiet Curry was. Since his week's absence, nothing had been the same. Although he continued to perform supremely, the show's invulnerability had vanished. Backstage, bitter grumbles resurfaced. Curry's relationship with Jacqui Harbord had never been warm. After his injury, it got worse. 'She was a great showgirl and John hated vulgarity,' explains David Barker. 'I remember once at the Palladium she'd been sitting in the wings with Ron Alexander with a huge dildo and everyone on stage could see this and was laughing. John was horrified.'

During his absence, it had been Harbord who reorganised the show's music. 'I kept it open. He didn't count on that,' she says.

> It was a black mark against me, but I don't regret doing it. While he was off, people who'd bought tickets to see him were told they could come back for free when he'd returned. But he never gave them the opportunity. At the end of the run there were people who'd been cheated. He would have done brilliantly well if someone had been there to manage it all. But he was just not good at handling people.

Curry's affair with Ron Alexander was also under strain. Performing *Icarus* – for each of them – had become an exercise in professional restraint. 'They were always arguing,' says Barker. 'John came up to me one night and said, "David, you're going to have to do it this evening". I said, "John, I don't know anything about it". He said I was going to have to do it, but thank God it didn't come to that.' As Alexander's 'throwee', Curry's vulnerability had also become a nightly hazard. From one night to the next, he told close friends, 'I would never be quite sure how far or how hard I would be thrown.'

By late August, it was all over. After 60 performances the refrigeration was switched off, the cast said their farewells and Curry flew to New York. Before leaving, he took a satisfying last kick at England courtesy of the *Daily Express*. 'If I loved being in London, the way I love being in New York, I would stay here,' he explained. 'It is as simple as that … In America, your individual merits are respected.' He hadn't mentioned 'the fairy for the tree'. He hadn't really needed to. 'With one leap John Curry frees himself of Britain' ran the headline. By 10 September, he was back in Manhattan. It would be seven years before the London public saw him in action again.

Escaping from Larry Parnes wouldn't be quite so easy. Or so swift. The much-touted world tour had evaporated, leaving only a trap. If he turned up in a new show using any of his Palladium material, Parnes had intimated he would sue. Without serious cash, Curry couldn't afford new choreography. It was a dilemma foreign to his experience. 'When he came up against people in business he would not bend,' says Penny Malec. 'So people started to hate him and that made him crawl back into his shell of self-righteousness.'

Frustrated, Curry stewed angrily through the autumn. Back in his London apartment, Larry Parnes did the same. Without his backing, Curry's theatrical vision would have been stillborn, and, since he'd genuinely believed in Curry's project, the entrepreneur was entitled to his disappointment. 'I suspect that both Parnes and John thought that they could manipulate the other for his own purpose and each was enraged to fail,' thinks Penny. 'But John got paid and prestige while Larry lost money and probably credibility among his peers.'

Curry was now 28. For the first time in over a year he had time on his hands. As they so often did, feelings of fatigued numbness crowded in. 'One really does look around some times and wonder what it is all for,' he told Heinz in September. 'My love life hasn't been terrific and when the professional satisfaction isn't there, there's not much left except a constant slog which makes you very tired, but not very satisfied.'

In Manhattan to help break the impasse Curry had engaged the services of Berlin-born celebrity agent Robert Lantz, a New York legend whose clients included Yul Brynner, Bette Davis and Leonard Bernstein. No one could hustle like Lantz. Few people had a better feel for the delicate flower of fame. Or, as he liked to put it: 'A bad haircut can be a catastrophe of biblical proportions.' Shortly before Christmas – almost certainly following advice from Lantz – Curry made his move to end the stalemate.

In a letter sent to his ex-Palladium cast – all still awaiting news of more work – Curry informed them that 'unforeseen difficulties' had required him to postpone all his plans until autumn the following year. 'It seems that the change of production company makes it impossible for me to do the show as it stands and it will be necessary to replan it almost completely. For this reason, I must ask you … to seriously consider any offers that may come your way.' In a handwritten postscript to Cathy Foulkes he added, 'I am so sad to write all this. There seems no end to the problems and I have not the words to tell you … Keep safe.'

If Parnes had ever been serious about legal action, he wasn't now. He'd never really owned Curry anyway. It was business. It was pride. Nor was he the only one to be cast overboard. Whatever plans Curry was hatching no longer included Jacqui Harbord. Not everyone had received his newsletter from America. Like Parnes, Harbord had already been shown the exit.

Every night at the Palladium she'd admired *L'après-midi d'un Faune* from the wings. Sadly for her, however, the admiration was not mutual. 'After the Palladium I received a pack of photographs from him saying he wished me luck but he would not be taking me to the USA.' Whatever happened next, both she and Parnes were out of Curry's story for good.

———

In the winter, New York can be a glorious place. Cold nights, under skies stripped of cloud, plate the leaves of Central Park with frost. Along the corridors of stone and steel, tempers and temperatures fall slowly away. Unencumbered by his own recent pressures, Curry relaxed, too. After years of semi-permanence, Manhattan felt like home. Among his tight circle of friends, the smiles and the dark humour returned. A refresher course in Erhard Seminar Training was even booked into his diary. 'He loved this period of his life,' recalled Nancy Streeter. 'He'd made a little money. He was in his late twenties. He was independent.'

After the years at the Streeter apartment, Curry was finally equipping a place of his own, a ground floor apartment along 221 West 13th, just a few strides down from Seventh Avenue, opposite what is now the Lesbian, Gay, Bisexual and Transgender Community Center. A few blocks away were the coffee bars and galleries of Greenwich Village.

Along the district's leafy sidewalks it wasn't difficult to believe that everyone was an artist, a poet or a dancer. Nowhere could have been better suited to Curry's momentary state of drift. Rarely – if ever – had he stopped. Here in his own sparely furnished place, soothed by the occasional lungful of cannabis, he could enjoy a life void of decisions but almost permanently blessed by good company.

Despite their rancorous arguments, he and Ron Alexander were still lovers. Brian Grant, the male model and skater who'd turned Curry on to EST, lived nearby in the Village with his partner. By the end of the year, Curry's friend Roger Roberts would have relocated permanently from London to New York. When he did so, he'd share a high-rise apartment on West 43rd Street with Billy Whitener, the dancer who'd introduced Curry to Twyla Tharp. It was hard on Nancy Streeter, but her ex-lodger now had his own circle. And for the time being, loneliness was no longer a concern for John.

'I saw John almost every day,' says Whitener.

At that time I was at the Brooklyn Academy of Music and on the way back through Manhattan I'd stop and have tea and cookies with him in his lovely apartment. I got very used to it; the English need for mid-afternoon sustenance. It became a custom, a habit. We listened to music, I'd help him select pieces … New York suited him. It suits lots of artists. There's friction. There's dialogue. Creative ideas are spawned and circulated. There's plenty to do. We saw lots of shows. Lots of ballet. We went off Broadway, on Broadway. *Sweeney Todd* with Angela Lansbury, I remember … In Greenwich Village, John became a New Yorker.

From his home in Switzerland, Curry's oldest friend, Heinz Wirz, watched with concern. He'd never understood Ron Alexander, and knew Curry's weaknesses well. 'I said to John, "I'm not sure if I like Ron" and he said, "Oh you don't know him". But in New York, I know, John had dangerous appetites. He wrote and told me about this party and that party but it was dangerous.'

At nights, as in London, no one really knew what Curry was doing. Not even intimates like Billy Whitener. 'He went to different gay bars than me,' he explains. 'He'd won his medals but I was still rehearsing so didn't stay up too late. We'd bar hop for a while but I had to go home early. The seventies were dangerous.' Nowhere were they more risky than a short cab ride from Curry's rented brownstone.

In 1974, the Anvil nightclub had opened in the heart of the nearby meatpacking district. Two years later, it had been joined by the Mineshaft. No two institutions better exemplified the unrestrained excess of pre-AIDS New York. And it seems Curry – and Alexander – were known at both.

'There was a lot of pressure on him. He needed release,' thinks Whitener.

I think John got into some dangerous territory in terms of his own emotional landscape. You want to push things to the extreme so you have something to say on stage, and New York is lively.

There are all sorts of people. We were pleasure seekers. We were handsome. We were on stage. We were on display. We had a good time. And to be a loyal and true friend to John sometimes meant looking aside. We lived life to its extremes … there was always something wild and unbridled about his gift.

At the Anvil, naked go-go boys jigged on a stage to disco beats. At the Mineshaft, the options darkened. Denim and leather were the dress code. Cologne was forbidden. Once inside, down in the dungeons and cells, the rules petered out. Along one wall, punters knelt to service the disembodied erect penises which emerged anonymously through a line of 'glory holes'. In a blackened cellar, men so inclined took it in turns to be urinated upon in a bathtub. Sado-masochistic sex and group sex were commonplace. No one seemed to care. No one asked too many questions. 'The Anvil made the world quiver and quake,' recalls Cranston. 'And Curry would go there.'

To what extent he participated will never be known. In the dawn light, few attendees broadcast their nocturnal preferences, and in this respect the skater was no different. In 1978, most people in the Mineshaft wouldn't have known who John Curry was, and by the mid-eighties AIDS had turned off its lights for good. By then, with most of their former clientele already dead or dying, New York's grimmest dives had been silenced for ever by the arbiters of public health. And long before that, Curry's burgeoning fame in New York had required him to keep away.

Whatever need his activities satisfied – and how precisely he satisfied them – remained known only to himself. As a confused teenager, he'd craved 'normality'. As a man, he seemed bent on punishing himself for the lack of it. Only one tragic link was visible between his secret world and the one on public display. Underlying both was the same persistent sense of unhappiness; the same ache of dissatisfaction. And underpinning all this was the conviction that, as an artist, he had not even begun.

At the start of 1978, Curry still appeared paralysed by his problems. For the first time in two decades skating had not dominated his winter months. Harsh lessons learned under Larry Parnes, however, had chastened him. In business, he was learning the value of patience. Discreetly, he had contacted choreographers Norman Maen, Kenneth MacMillan and Twyla Tharp, seeking permission to use their earlier collaborations in a possible new production. Since Parnes had no hold over their work, each had agreed. Crucially, the priceless *Faune* was back in the fold.

By mid-February, the two Americans who'd visited him in London, David Singer and Charlotte Kirk, were formally operating as his producers. Writing from a Broadway office, Singer had alerted key cast members (like Cathy Foulkes) to the possibility of a summer tour which would require May rehearsals, to be followed by 'a winter tour of even grander proportions (including a Broadway engagement)'.

After a few months, unable to secure the finance, this too had started to collapse, leaving only the distant prospect of a New York run in December. Frustrated, and running low on cash, Curry offered himself to the Sky Rink as a teacher. By early June his New York School of Skating was ready to run. All it needed was a launch party.

Even by New York standards, John Curry's 'Gala Summer Evening on Ice' was a shimmering affair. Sipping 'cocktails at sunset' and nibbling chocolate-coated strawberries, the sold-out house of 650 boasted the cream of Manhattan party-goers. A-listers like Lauren Bacall, Paul Simon, Liv Ullmann, Andy Warhol, Carrie Fisher and Mikhail Baryshnikov chinked flutes with socialites and tycoons.

Tickets had cost up to $100 each. Nancy Streeter was there. Ed Mosler, too. Members of the New York City Ballet were employed as ushers and the lofty *New York Times* had given it an entire half page. 'Mr Curry is devilishly handsome,' it reported the next day, adding that his 'virtual unknown' status in the United States looked all set to change.

For 40 minutes, Curry – with eight other skaters – had thrilled an audience replete with sliced cold veal and spinach quiche. As a showcase for his skating school, it was a success. As a sales pitch for Curry himself, and his embryonic new production, it was a masterstroke. With Kirk and Singer's help – and his agent Robbie Lantz's contacts book – the Englishman's presence in New York had been announced. No one had been disappointed. As always, Curry's cryptic dance with Cathy Foulkes had moved onlookers to tears. But for once it had been another duet – with a brand new electrifying female partner – which had stirred most of the post-Gala chatter.

If John Curry was a 'virtual unknown', the 27-year-old Alabama-born JoJo Starbuck most decidedly was not. As a skater, she was a former Ice Capades star and a veteran of two Olympic Games. As a public figure, she was one half of the so-called 'golden' marriage to the idolised Pittsburgh Steelers quarterback Terry Bradshaw. Few men in American football earned more at the time. No sporting sweethearts garnered more headlines.

Sassy, smart, and attractive, she seemed ill suited for John Curry's lofty vision. Toller Cranston, on the other hand, adored her. 'A showgirl. A show-poodle,' he averred. 'All legs, teeth, rhinestones and blonde hair. Real star quality, a huge personality and a work ethic that was dazzling.' On paper she epitomised the starlit sequins and tinsel Curry loathed. And yet here she was, at the Sky Rink Gala, stealing the show and sporting a huge diamond ring cut in the shape of a football.

It wasn't Curry's choice that she was there. A shrewder brain had seen to that. By the time of the Gala, David Singer had secured a venue – the Felt Forum theatre, at Madison Square Garden – for a two-week run before Christmas. A glamorous American on the billing would surely protect everyone against box office embarrassment. Less than a month before the Sky Rink Gala, Singer had picked up the phone to Louisiana. 'What time do you want me there?' said JoJo.

It was a serendipitous call. Unknown to Singer, Starbuck was lonely, bored and unhappy. During the football season she hung out in Pittsburgh. After it was over she was marooned on a 480-acre cattle ranch near Shreveport. 'I was so painfully lonely there,' she now admits.

> I came from this amazing world of crazy friends. Like Toller.
> Great careers. Putting gorgeous costumes and dresses on. And
> then all of a sudden I'm on a ranch in the middle of nowhere
> surrounded by cattle. There wasn't even another house. Terry
> loved animals. I loved ballet, Broadway, the theatre. There was
> nothing for me there. Nobody got me, and I didn't get them. I
> felt a big chunk of me was void. I couldn't wait to be wanted
> again ... and then I got this call.

Within days she was in New York. Within two weeks she was ice dancing with John Curry in front of the city's elite. 'It was like that old song,' she says, '"How Ya Gonna Keep 'Em Down on the Farm (After They've Seen Paree)". It was a kinda like that. A total blast.' Starbuck was fresh, modern and dripping with sexual charisma. Out on the ice, under her spell, every gram of Curry's frosty reserve disappeared. Nothing he'd done before had generated such erotic heat. No dance would ever prove quite so popular as the one he premiered with Starbuck at his gala.

It had been a Danish-born choreographer – Peter Martins, of the New York City Ballet – who'd stitched together their sleazy Latin extravagance, a number wholly at odds with the skater's previous repertoire. This was no *Icarus*. *Tango Jalousie* – or *Tango Tango* as it became known – was slutty, sensual and gloriously commercial. 'It had a hip quality,' recalls Singer. 'But I think he resented it. I think it was more lowbrow than he wanted. It also took on a disproportionate degree of success for his company. JoJo's jump at the end always brought the house down. I don't think she missed it ever.'

Few of Curry's works were quite so shameless as *Tango Tango*. Wearing a tight black matador's suit and slicked down hair, Curry vamped alone before JoJo swept in wearing a slash of purple satin over exposed thighs and shoulders to lock eyes and arms with her lover. As the music built, the ghosts of Fred and Ginger stirred. On the ice, the couple seemed propelled by genuine yearning. Together, they glided, they waltzed and they spun, and after JoJo's climactic jump she beckoned her man meaningfully off stage.

At Curry's summer gala, the audience had brayed with delight. Over the next six years, thousands more would do the same. If it was 'lowbrow', Curry was stuck with it. If he resented Starbuck's evident popularity, he was lumbered with that, too. During the summer months of 1978, plans hardened for his run at New York's Felt Forum and JoJo's place in it was now guaranteed. In the meantime, he knuckled down to his twice-weekly teaching responsibilities. Up at Sky Rink, 15 students, of all ages, were awaiting his instruction. Almost without exception, they were terrified. Among them was Nancy Streeter.

'Patience was rather difficult for him,' she recalled.

> He didn't easily appreciate that people didn't do things as quickly as he did. However, I went along and I learned more in those six

weeks of summer than I ever did in years. He also made me work harder than I'd ever done before. I'm really not sure how much longer I could have survived.

By late summer, Curry had fulfilled his teaching obligations. Although briefly reactivated the following year, his heart had never been in it. From the start, it had been little more than a stopgap and in October rehearsals for the Felt Forum were ready to begin. From the Palladium show, Lorna Brown, David Barker, Paul Toomey and Cathy Foulkes had been retained. So, too, had Ron Alexander. Linda Davis had been invited, but felt unable to leave her young family in London. In her place, Curry had reached into his past and found Patricia Dodd, the lissom Canadian with whom he'd once shared an innocent bed. Alongside her, in a 12-strong company, there was also a spot for his New York friend Brian Grant, an unaccomplished skater with even less experience than Curry's on-off Canadian lover.

For an artist so fixated on standards, the inclusion of Grant and Alexander was curious. Either it was a spectacular act of friendship or Curry simply knew he would shine brighter in their company. Any bashfulness about his star status had by now entirely vanished. His new show was to be called *John Curry's Ice Dancing* and his new publicity guru, Bobby Zarem – the mastermind behind the 'I Love New York' campaign – was busily turning him into a Manhattan celebrity. Gossip columns twittered regularly about his activities, and in November a documentary aired on public television promoting Curry's upcoming new work. 'I did all that Olympic business,' he explained to viewers, 'specifically to get the chance to do this.'

Away from the cameras, however, Curry's cheery demeanour was being tested. Unlike Larry Parnes, Kirk and Singer were not afraid to challenge the skater's aesthetic. 'We had our own ideas. We were present. We did what we had to do,' admits Singer. 'I was there at almost every rehearsal. We wanted to have an impact. We needed the show to be fun as much as classical.' But there was worse.

To Curry's horror, JoJo Starbuck's name had been inserted in big letters under his on the posters and hoardings. A 'creative supervisor' had also been appointed to hand-hold production. And since rehearsal ice was being shared with the New York Rangers, every day began with a tetchy pre-dawn bus ride through the waking city to Westchester. Outside the rink, the leaves turned red. Inside it, the mood – as David Barker recalls – could be black.

> They hired these famous choreographers and they thought we were all trained ballet dancers and we were not. We were ice skaters and some of the rehearsals were excruciating. These people didn't know anything about ice skating. There was no connection … They had one number, this big cardboard magic box, and we had to be in it and stick our arms and legs out. It was dreadful. Who'd want that in a Broadway show? It was a nightmare.

As rehearsals progressed, fault lines formed, exacerbated by Curry's new-found reluctance to share the limelight. Feelings of personal diminishment fostered insecurity; constant revisions unsettled the cast; and to the newcomers, Curry's behaviour was proving an unpleasant revelation. In sly asides to Dodd, Curry carped about Starbuck. 'All I got from John about her was negative. He'd been told, "You're not an American, you've got to have an American". When they were doing *Tango Tango*, I sometimes wondered if he was tempted to throw her out of the wings.' None of which alarmed Starbuck herself. 'John didn't need me and maybe didn't want me, but I toughed it out because I wanted to be in on this. Suddenly I was learning so much beauty again … so no matter how John treated us – and everyone was hurt by him every day – I was thrilled to be part of the experiment.'

No one questioned Curry on the ice. Out there, away from the barrier, there was no challenge to his control. However much Barker derided it, 'the cardboard magic box' (from a routine called *Scoop*) would stay. So too would *Faune* and Twyla Tharp's *After All*. Despite Singer's best endeavours, Curry's lofty instinct still drove proceedings. To his credit, *Icarus* had been quietly dumped. But so, too, in Machiavellian style, had numerous ideas from his new hands-on producers.

'When we were up at Westchester, I was cast opposite JoJo in a piece,' recalls Patricia Dodd.

> Ron came up to me and said that John wanted me to really fuck up because he really didn't want this piece in the show. The

producers were watching and he only wanted what he wanted and this was – for John – a tacky, vulgar piece. So I did. I went in with no energy and fell once or twice. Basically, I was bad but it had to be hush-hush and although the choreographer was looking, and might have had some suspicions, it was dropped.

Had David Singer known of Alexander's role as Curry's stooge he would not have been surprised. Without Curry's backing, Alexander would never have been cast. 'I thought he was an awkward man who didn't belong in that group,' says Singer. 'He was bad on stage and a bad influence on John off it. I also think he was ambivalent about John. Through bad judgment or maliciousness, he could hurt him.'

Unknown to Singer, the feeling was entirely mutual. In a hilariously indiscreet letter to Jacqui Harbord started just 24 hours before the Felt Forum show opened, Alexander branded Kirk and Singer 'full of shit and fuckups'. 'Parnes, although a shark, left John alone,' he added. 'Kirk and Singer … are always hanging about … [and] are totally incompetent assholes.' It was a letter which gleefully blew the lid off life inside John Curry's seething troupe of talents. Whatever his limitations as a skater, Ron Alexander could clearly scratch like a cat.

> Patricia comes off very well in the show with a dramatic solo part in the opening … however Patricia feels that John begrudges her this small success in the show. He does have some competition from JoJo Starbuck, as against his better judgement she has remained although he treated her like shit for 3 weeks to the point where she wanted to leave … David Barker freaked out the day before we did our first preview and walked out, creating some small havoc …
>
> Lorna is not pleased with her lot either. She has nothing with John and feels wasted … and is becoming most boring with her complaining about her knee, and back and head. I have a lot of time for Looney [Lorna] but she can be such a pain in the ass … Pat and her have been sharing an apartment [and] Pat wants to leave because of Lorna's never ceasing ill temper and selfishness … If the show does not continue past December 3rd I will go to

Portugal for 2 months to do a dancing nightclub offer ... how awful that would be.

Alexander wouldn't get to Portugal. On 21 November, Curry had opened at the Felt Forum theatre in front of 3,500 people. As always, his dressing room had been swamped with flowers and telegrams. Carlo and Christa Fassi, the dancer Anthony Dowell and Ed Mosler had sent their good wishes. So, too, had both his brothers. Even JoJo had penned a cryptic message; 'To my passionate tango partner. You drive me mad.'

Two days later, when Ron Alexander finally sat down to finish his interrupted letter to Harbord, *John Curry's Ice Dancing* was surfing a tidal surge of acclaim. 'I'm tempted to tear up the beginning as it really isn't too positive, but it's the truth and I will let it stand. The reception we've had after 11 performances has been incredible with bravos and standing ovations every night ... John could not have had a bigger, or better triumph.'

According to the *New York Post* the show was 'a knockout, a mindbender, a unique concept'. 'Delicate, charming and delightful' was *Variety*'s verdict. Even Anna Kisselgoff, the doyenne of Manhattan's art critics, had been impressed. 'Everybody should see him, and now they can ... a brilliant beginning.' Amidst the bouquets, however, there were reservations and prescient doubts. At the early previews, Curry's quest for contemporary edge – replacing *Icarus* with Robert Cohan's ultra-modern *Myth* – had badly backfired. 'The one out and out fizzle in the show,' wrote one critic. 'Totally senseless,' added another. By opening night *Myth* had vanished from the running order, and *Variety* was sounding an ominous note of warning.

> Curry is asking for recognition for ice ballet into the top cultural ranks and cutting off the kind of audience that take the kids to ice shows to see stuffed animals and maybe get a ride on the kiddie vehicles ... It's recalled that ice shows had several starving years before the big money came. Curry may experience the same.

As snow piled up in Central Park, few of Curry's cast were looking that far ahead. At $375 a week the pay was good, and the pre-

Christmas mood was high. On the opening night, celebrations had drifted from a Chanel-sponsored party to Studio 54 – the city's legendary disco club – where champagne and Quaaludes had been on offer amidst half-naked dancers.

After the first weekend alone, box office receipts were rumoured to be $125,000. Sniffing takeover potential, executives from Holiday On Ice had even attended the show and stories were recirculating about either a three-month European tour or a two-week run in Chicago. 'It now seems clear anything can, and probably will happen,' Alexander told Harbord. 'But one can be sure that John will be looking out for himself.'

When the Felt Forum run ended – on 3 December, after just 21 performances – it was clear that New York wanted more. 'We were very hot,' recalls JoJo. 'Andy Warhol, Bianca Jagger, Kris Kristofferson. These people would come and see us, and then we'd go and see them in their shows. One night we had Katherine Hepburn and she couldn't find her car after the show, and got lost trying to find it, and even that was in the paper. Everything was in the paper. Bobby Zarem was an amazing publicist.' With demand still high, the skaters would not get long to recover. On 19 December, the show reopened at the Minskoff Theater.

From the beginning, there were danger signs. Christmas was approaching, always Curry's least favourite time of the year. During the two-week break – while Ron Alexander had been laid up with blood poisoning – Curry had secretly consummated his friendship with Brian Grant at a romantic tryst in New England. Back in rehearsals, Curry was clearly troubled by the Minskoff's smaller stage. Twyla Tharp's *After All* needed reconfiguring, and the choreographer had been recalled to restage it.

'I seemed to have lost my nerve,' he subsequently explained.

> Twyla kept asking me to skate right into the front corners of the stage, but I would chicken out before I got there. She was incensed, telling me that I was going to ruin the piece. Finally I lost my temper and deliberately skated into the orchestra pit. 'Is that what you wanted?' I demanded. Twyla stared in disbelief, gathered her things and turned to leave the auditorium. 'I don't work with children,' she said.

There were problems for Curry's co-star, too. According to the *New York Times*, JoJo Starbuck's husband, Terry Bradshaw, was refusing to allow her back for the Minskoff performances. Only the threat of a lawsuit had apparently got her on a plane. 'Terry's southern and those men tend to be a little more old-fashioned,' Starbuck told a reporter. 'He's home alone and he misses me.' A few years later their marriage was over. 'Getting back into skating didn't help,' she says now. 'He was seizing his moment. I was seizing mine ... I was 25 going on 14 when I married him.'

Predictably, Curry's Broadway debut had drawn strong notices. Posters mushroomed around the city – 'back by popular demand' – and celebrities joined the hunt for tickets. Diana Ross, Johnny Mathis, Ted Kennedy and Woody Allen were among those paying homage, each one intrigued by this putative, new art form and mesmerised by this charming Englishman's nightly tour de force. 'Only *The King and I* was as big as us on Broadway that holiday,' recalls David Singer.

By Christmas, with demand still high, the run was extended into the New Year. And when JoJo took a weekend break to watch the Pittsburgh Steelers, Lorna stood in (to critical acclaim) and danced *Tango Tango*. At last she had enjoyed her golden moment with her childhood Romeo. Sadly, for her – and for all of them – it was a prelude to the end.

A week into January, ticket sales collapsed. Broadway's perennial post-Christmas slump had begun and the rush into the Minskoff suddenly looked ill-judged. With insufficient publicity, Curry's problematic status as an 'unknown' was exposed. 'He was not yet a bona fide ticket-selling star,' admits Singer. 'And he was very difficult to market because he was not a flashy skater. He didn't like to jump. He was about something better and more important.'

More alarmingly, Singer's leading man was drinking liquid protein to combat weight loss and getting only four hours' sleep a night amidst persistent rumours about cocaine. 'I remember at his flat in New York he'd say, "Can you roll me a joint? Can you get me this drug? Can you get me that drug?"' claims Barker. 'Like the star telling the underling to get the thing for him.' As the producers weighed up their options, the skater's mysterious demons broke loose. Midway through an evening show, watched by 1,500 people, Curry crumpled to the ice during a sit spin.

'No one had seen John before the show,' says Lorna.

> Then he came on like he was drunk and went sideways into a sit
> spin and sat down and put his arms out to the audience. Then
> Ron came and picked him up and took him off. All this in the
> middle of a New York show with a big audience. He was all over
> the place. The curtain closed and there was an announcement
> and next thing his understudy rushed on and looked like a
> comedian, and we went from shock to hysterics. You couldn't
> help but laugh.

Amidst the chaos backstage, Curry was revealing little. 'Someone
mentioned that he'd been taking muscle relaxants,' says Lorna. 'He
was crying like a baby.' 'I think Ron or someone had given him
something,' says Patricia Dodd. According to the show's stage
manager, Joe Lorden, Curry had been out late the night before.
Shortly after his collapse he had also been spotted leaving by a back
door with Ron Alexander. Both had been fully kitted out in black
leathers. 'I said, "John, you can't leave. Your name is over the title.
This is your show." He said, "I'm going" and didn't come back. I
had to cancel that night and we closed a few weeks later.'

Whatever had happened, neither Curry's producers – nor his
ferocious agent – were laughing. Rather like his London 'mugging',
the fall had seriously exposed the skater's fragility. 'This was not an
insignificant event,' says Singer. 'It affected my confidence in the
situation. We were talking about touring but with a show like this,
he is the show.'

After 23 nights of standing ovations, *John Curry's Ice Dancing*
folded on 14 January 1979. With no prospect of a tour – or any
further work – the company was dismantled. Few of the 12,
including Lorna Brown, would ever skate with Curry in front of an
audience again. 'It didn't take the form of a break-up,' explains
Singer. 'It took the form of an absence of business. We simply
didn't have a financial proposition for him.' For Curry, it was
another cruel lesson in economics. Unless it could make money, his
infant new art form was doomed.

Among the debris, however, a more alarming picture had
emerged. In both London and New York, Curry's temperament
had disintegrated under pressure. Although the work he'd produced

was often sublime, the emotional toll on his fellow artists had been high. Each one acknowledged his genius. Most would gladly return. But not one of them really knew him, or knew what he would do next. As the troupe dispersed, the suspicion lingered that somehow Curry, in each city, had deliberately pressed the self-destruct button.

If so, he was not short of reasons. Curry had been drained before New York. After two months of daily performances there – in which he was rarely off stage – he was beyond exhaustion. Box office gloom and a handful of negative reviews had reinforced his own crippling artistic doubts. 'Maybe when Curry feels more secure,' observed one critic, 'he will risk presenting more serious works.'

Far too often he seemed unhappy; his material was still uneven and the skaters around him were mismatched. Some of them – to his eyes anyway – looked too fat. Others simply couldn't dance. Just as it had done in London, a suffocating shroud of expectation had descended, complicated by his 'dangerous appetites' and his traumatic love life. As the Minskoff went dark, mingled with the confused disorientation of failure, there came a deep unheard sigh of relief. It was over, and he was out.

Before January was done, as blizzards stalked Broadway, Curry put himself on a plane bound for Egypt with Ron Alexander. Neither he, nor anyone else, had any idea when – or if – he would skate again.

Eight
'Daddy says no'

The beach, which seems to go on for ever, looks south. Along its entire line, hissing breakers crumple on white sand. Grass-tufted dunes back up against sun-greyed boardwalks that run to each horizon. Beyond the snaking walkway, connected to the shore by private paths among the salt-blown marram, hide elaborate timber houses, fronted with fields of glass that drench each room with warmth, allowing the far-travelled Atlantic air to flood in.

No one knows how Fire Island got its name. In the 1970s, everyone knew how it had got its reputation. Over thirty miles long – yet never more than 400 metres wide – this stubborn spit of crushed shells had become a legendary haven for America's homosexual young. It had no roads, few cars and only a handful of permanent residents. Access, by ferry or seaplane, was awkward, ensuring privacy for the thousands of men who flooded there every summer; streaming out of Manhattan, through Long Island and across the Great South Bay to the source of its dangerous heartbeat, the tiny hamlet of Fire Island Pines.

In the summer of 1977, John Curry had found his way there too. Over the next few years, he would return whenever he could. Nowhere else soothed him like Fire Island. Nowhere on earth allowed gay men to fashion a structured lifestyle so comprehensively devoted to pleasure. Daily life there represented a reward for their long battle for tolerance. Barely ten years before, electro-shock therapy was still being prescribed in the US to 'decrease same-sex attraction'. As it was for the Atlantic zephyrs, Fire Island was a welcome refuge; somewhere young men could unpack winter-long frustrations.

As a child, Curry had thrilled to the surf's roar in Cornwall. On Fire Island, among valued companions, the wind tugged his devils away. During the summer months, in a spacious waterfront rental, there would be no skates, and no box office disappointments. Instead there would invariably be Billy Whitener and Roger Roberts – the two loyal pit props of his Manhattan life – supplemented, at times, by a string of passing visitors. The male model Brian Grant was often there. So, too, were Cathy Foulkes, Nancy Streeter and once – from Britain – Curry's dependable brother Andrew.

'He loved the beach,' recalls Whitener.

> Sometimes the house would be full. Other times, it was me and John. Or me, Cathy and John. Or Roger, Cathy and John. It was an entourage. Usually the same people. A bunch of friends. John was very generous. He paid most of the rental and I paid some of the bills because I could. I didn't want to rely on his generosity. There were no freeloaders. John was picky. What did we do? A lot of cooking, and John absolutely loved the beach and there were moments he wanted privacy. More than I did, he needed that. Sometimes he'd retreat.

With no set routine, the friends drifted in and out of the sun, together or alone. 'I'm out for a walk,' read one note signed off by Whitener with his drawing of a ballerina. Two hours later, he returned to find a message underneath it from Curry and Roberts – 'Hi. We are walking on the beach' – complete with their own tiny cartoons of an ice skater and a rippled body-builder. During these long days, Curry's slender torso tanned. It was important to look beautiful. Everyone else on Fire Island always did. 'Roger was especially good-looking,' says Whitener. 'Very, very funny. Delightful. Intelligent. He worked out at the gym before it became so popular. At Fire Island you saw people with developed upper bodies. Chicken legs, we called them. Roger rode a bicycle round New York so he was developed all over. A beauty from head to toe.'

Amidst the household goods, the local store sold postcards of bronzed, semi-naked men. At 5 p.m. hordes of them gathered at the Pavilion bar for 'Blue Whale' cocktails laced with Curaçao. As the sweet liqueur painted their tongues blue, they moved on to the legendary weekend tea dance, bouncing to disco music till dawn in sleeveless white T-shirts, spilling out across the moonlit sand where the surf still boomed.

'Every day there seemed to be perfect,' says Foulkes.

Gay people nude on the beach having a great old time. Very free. Sunny. He wasn't working and the pressures were gone. Very communal and he liked that. This was another side to John. More relaxed and a little happier ... I went to the tea dance but if he was going out late at night, he would put me to bed. There was clearly something he didn't want me to know about, or be exposed to. He was protecting me. This 'other thing' would happen much later at night.

On Fire Island – for everyone – there was nothing to fear. This was life at full throttle. No chance of a crash. Few people were chasing relationships. Mostly it was about sex. 'It wasn't our priority to have a regular partner,' explains Whitener. 'We were sowing our oats.' 'Everyone slept with everyone else,' adds writer Felice Picano. 'No one in their twenties or thirties was monogamous at all. Even guys in relationships fucked other people.'

Amidst the dunes, under a constant sun, this new freedom tasted delicious. One summer's day, Picano had been transfixed by a stranger running along the beach in his shorts. 'Who's this guy with the cool rear end'? Soon after, they were lovers. 'The interior matched the exterior,' he says. 'John Curry was a beautiful man.'

I saw him every day in the week that summer. We had sex together. We had a fling. He told me he was sharing a house but I never went to his place. We always met at mine. I'd go down to the harbour and pick up a newspaper, or have breakfast and I'd see him there. He didn't go to the afternoon events too often. Because of his celebrity, I think he kept a low profile. But he seemed very lonely. In fact, he was always alone in the week. He was very masculine; very straightforward; a nice guy who seemed to have things on his mind. Not a camp or gay cliché. It was a moustache butch community and that wasn't his look.

It didn't last. Very little on Fire Island was ever intended to. Even the tide-lashed land itself seemed poised between sunshine and drowning. In the late 1970s, as Freddie Mercury lookalikes oiled their pectorals and Donna Summer 'felt love' in the Ice Palace, doctors in New York were pondering the early signs of a 'rare form of cancer' exhibited by homosexual men. No one was getting too alarmed, and it wouldn't merit a headline for another two years. Out on Fire Island puddles of sea spray dried on the ocean boardwalks and the dance music still rumbled until sunrise.

—————

When Curry returned from his Egyptian holiday – in mid-February 1979 – the beach villas of the Pines were still boarded against the winter storms. Not till the spring would the party kick off again. Until then, Curry was marooned in his own darkness. Although Ron Alexander was still around, their relationship remained unsteady. At his Greenwich Village apartment – decorated in beige and grey – Curry fought sleeplessness by night and welcomed select visitors by day. Cathy Foulkes loved its 'impeccable minimalism' and its huge collage assembled from schoolchildren's desk blotters. 'A sort of Calvin Klein home,' she says. Patricia Dodd had once encountered Alexander there emerging from the bathroom in leather cowboy chaps. Others escaped with Earl Grey and a Rich Tea biscuit.

Artistically Curry was snared in a conflicted web of boredom and doubt. The shows in London and New York felt like failures. Neither had matched his vision. Both had suffered from restricted stages, artistic compromise and a lack of money. Welding his noble aesthetic to business imperatives had nauseated him. The physical and mental strain had taken him to breaking point, and his fantasy of a permanent company of ice dancers now seemed pitifully remote.

Had he been rich, it wouldn't have mattered. But Curry's financial outlook was bleak. Although Larry Parnes had offered 50 per cent of net profit – plus a weekly fee – it wasn't clear how much profit there'd been, if any. Nor would his income from the Minskoff sustain him for long. Curry wasn't broke – and had generous friends – but he needed to work. Indolence had its attractions, but returning to England in defeat did not. Radical options were under consideration.

During his first summer on Fire Island, an eight-seater seaplane had splashed down on the ocean as he sat alone on the beach. From inside stepped the English actress and comedienne Millicent Martin, alongside her American partner, voice coach Marc Alexander. 'We waded ashore with our suitcases over our heads,' remembers Martin. 'When John saw my feet he said, "Your feet, your feet, you've got beautiful feet." I'd trained as a dancer and he'd spotted them.'

The two had first met at a celebrity-studded 1976 New Year's Eve party in St John's Wood, London. A few months later, when Martin turned up in a New York show, Curry had been the first Englishman she saw. The weekend on Fire Island, including a visit to a tea dance, had followed soon after. It was a friendship that pointed the way Curry had secretly always wanted to go. If he couldn't skate, he would act. And if possible, finally, he would dance.

On paper, the plan made sense. Curry's bones were sore, and increasingly he moved in theatrical circles. Back in England, the dancer Gillian Lynne, soon to be the choreographer of *Cats*, had become a close friend. Clandestine contact with Alan Bates had continued, and a London agent had been retained to help find suitable parts. In New York, Curry had been taking acting lessons, and – be it ballet or Broadway fodder – he rarely missed a new show. The reality of his declared ambition, however, presented him with significant personal obstacles he would have found uncomfortable to acknowledge.

Nature – and public schooling – had endowed Curry with a reedy, aristocratic voice. It was a misfortune compounded by both his manner and his naturally introspective personality. As a dancer, he possessed what Lynne called 'his natural, beautiful line'. But as a budding actor, other than stunning looks and name recognition, he had little to offer. It was a challenge his various coaches took on with limited success. Among them was Millicent Martin's new husband, Marc Alexander:

> He was ultra-introverted. Painfully shy. You had to pull every single thing out of him. When he was on the ice the centre of him would emerge and there was this grandeur. Off it, he'd close down. So I'd work on his voice and projection and be almost like his psychiatrist. But his voice was very tight because when you close up like he did, it affects the vocal chords. So I'd show him how to punch out his voice; how to make sure he didn't stop breathing when he got frightened. Because if you don't breathe on stage, you die.

Back in his apartment, Curry laboured dutifully through sheets of exercises ('Imagine smelling a beautiful rose and drink in the odour WITHOUT RAISING THE SHOULDERS'). In both London and New York he now had agents prowling for work. In the meantime, there were always the dance classes; the indestructible remnant of the dream his father had sought to demolish. 'He still often went for those dancing lessons,' says Heinz Wirz, 'but I think each time he went through the door he knew that "daddy says no".' Ironically, however, as he approached his thirtieth birthday, it would be dancing that suddenly catapulted Curry out of the doldrums.

Since his first London shows, Curry had forged a friendship with the Royal Ballet's principal dancer, Anthony Dowell. The two men were well met. Although Dowell was slightly older, both were intensely private, and both were driven by relentless artistic curiosity. Curry had watched Dowell dance many times and Dowell, in return, had designed Indian costumes for an aborted ice *Suite for Sitar* at the Cambridge Theatre. By the time Curry was resident in Greenwich Village, his friend was performing regularly with the American Ballet Theatre in New York. By early spring 1979, he was in a position to make one of John Curry's lamented fantasies come alive.

Every year, the ABT staged a so-called 'million dollar celebration' to raise funds at the city's Metropolitan Opera House. Then and now, no venue in New York conveys status like the Met and few audiences were more high-recognition than this one. Ahead of them, as they poured across Lincoln Center Plaza, was a night of dazzling world-class entertainment. Nureyev would be dancing with Cynthia Gregory. Makarova would be paired with Patrick Bissell. But it would be the odd couple from England who brought the house down.

Wisely eschewing classical ballet, Curry and Dowell stunned the Met with such a witty homage to Fred Astaire, the *New York Times* promptly tagged the evening 'The John and Tony Show'. Dressed in top hat, tails and white bow tie, the two men had tapped and shuffled with an aplomb that even Nureyev's performance couldn't match. 'One trusts that Dowell will don a couple of silver blades and repay the compliment,' suggested the *New York Post*. Whatever nameless terrors gripped Curry beforehand had not shown. Steered reassuringly by Dowell, he had danced in public for the first time.

Over the coming year, Curry and Dowell would reunite to perform *Top Hat and Tails* at gala events in Washington, Chicago, Los Angeles and San Francisco. 'They are a tempting tandem,' observed one newspaper, but this was a double act with no serious future. By the summer of 1979, Curry was back on Fire Island after reluctantly rerunning his skating class for star-struck pupils at New York's Sky Rink. Dancing with Dowell had been good for his American profile, but he was no richer for it. A sense of drift hovered above the cloudless skies off Long Island.

For some time Nancy Streeter's influence in Curry's life had been fading. Although he would go to her when he needed something – and never forgot her birthday – he no longer welcomed her advice. When she visited him on Fire Island, it would be less as a confidante and more as a spectator; a cruel state of impotence, which made her friend's apparent aimlessness almost impossible to bear. In July, no longer certain of Curry's ear, she had written him a long letter but couldn't muster the courage to mail it. After her death it was found, unsent, among her effects.

> What do you really want? Do you want to continue doing shows? Do you want to teach? Do you want to change completely and do something different? If this is it, you better get started and be very realistic about your talents as your name and fame will only last so long … You are tending to drift. 1) Fire Island whole summer 2) Not really skating 3) Not really dancing 4) Not doing much. Are you willing to listen to anyone?

As the days shortened, and Fire Island fell silent, Curry returned quietly to New York. In a letter to Cathy Foulkes – the only former cast member with whom he stayed in constant touch – he wrote plaintively: 'I am back in the city now … the summer is over and hopefully we shall all be working soon. It has not been easy. The skating is the simple part.'

It was hard to fathom what he meant. No new backers were looming and Curry's 'theatre of ice' was effectively dead. Exhibitions and one-offs were now his only work. In November he previewed a new 'skaters' waltz' at Madison Square Garden. The following month, he and Foulkes reprised *Faune* to a live orchestra at the well-remunerated Christmas 'Pops On Ice' in Colorado Springs.

'All this clean air and clean living is for the birds,' he told Nancy in a cryptic postcard. It was the curious end of a year to forget. The next one would start with a tumult of memories.

———

In mid-February 1980, the Winter Olympics juggernaut came to Lake Placid. Almost six years had passed since Gus Lussi put him through hell there on a square of ice. Nancy Streeter was right: fame was fleeting. Curry's own golden night in Innsbruck already seemed like someone else's life. This time, another young Briton had been marked for figure skating glory. Like Curry before him, Robin Cousins was arriving under the protective embrace of Carlo and Christa Fassi. And like 1976, the British media was feasting on his chances.

From an American television network's commentary box, Curry watched proceedings unfold. Cousins was undoubtedly brilliant – and destined for gold – but his vigorous style was not to Curry's liking. Nor did John have any aptitude for broadcasting. While the director bellowed down his earpiece – 'say something, say something' – Curry leaned back and purred, 'let's just watch the beautiful skating.' However much they paid him, he would never deface excellence with facile microphone burble. He was also rather troubled and deeply preoccupied.

As the 1976 champion, Curry had been invited to perform at the Lake Placid closing ceremony. Rather than revisiting his triple jumps, he'd reunited with choreographer Twyla Tharp to fashion *Three Fanfares*, a modern programme set to the music of Strauss, Albinoni and Copland. It was a characteristically bold proposition. Robin Cousins had just topped the podium with a glorious display of athletic power, but Curry's offering would pointedly showcase his own classical alternative. As a packed Olympic arena awaited his entry, his nerves crashed back in.

Caught on video, it is almost impossible to watch. Standing by the barrier – wearing a powder-blue top over a white shirt – Curry looks tired and hollow-eyed. As he rocks from foot to foot, he stares down at the ice, picking his fingers. When he finally looks up, sucking in deep breaths, his face is ghastly white. And when he walks, head bowed, on to the ice, all confidence seems drained from his stride. Only when it begins does everything flow seamlessly back. Free of figure skating's rulebook, Curry floats and flows and builds to an exuberant trademark spread-eagle, which drives the audience up from their seats and pushes a smile of relief on to his face.

Not everyone had enjoyed it, however. 'I don't know what it was,' Carlo Fassi was reported as saying later. 'But it certainly wasn't skating.' By taking his art into a sports arena, Curry – perhaps deliberately – had underscored his own isolation. 'It may have been at this point he realised how alone he was in what he'd set out to do,' thinks a friend, Charles Cossey.

Shortly afterwards, when Larry Parnes contacted Cousins suggesting a money-spinning 'skate-off' against Curry at the Royal Albert Hall, the idea was laughed off the table. The two men shared Olympic immortality – and their paths would cross again – but Curry and Cousins shared little on the ice, and nothing off it. After Innsbruck, Curry had publicly confronted his homo-sexuality. After Lake Placid, Cousins headed happily off to cash in with Holiday On Ice. One man was relishing the spotlight. The other, temporarily, was trapped in the shadows, unable to secure the platform he craved.

In the spring, with no long-term plans in sight, he flew to London where the Queen's Ice Rink in Bayswater was celebrating its fiftieth anniversary. Temporarily reunited with JoJo Starbuck, he'd given an invited 500-strong audience a dazzling taste of his truncated Broadway show. Nothing at the Palladium had ever steamed hot like *Tango Tango*. And no-one at Queen's was still sitting when it was over. 'They [Curry and Starbuck] knocked a restrained stuffed shirt audience for six,' proclaimed *The Times*. 'This was tango unlike we have ever seen.' Much as they howled for more, Curry had refused all pleas for an encore. The hit of the evening,' said another review. 'Curry has advanced the frontiers of ice dance.' It was a stop-gap, but it would do for now.

With nothing in the United States to rush back for, Curry lingered in Britain. Fire Island would not be throbbing until July and, since Egypt, his affair with Ron Alexander had slowly faded away. Eager not to waste time, he linked up with the actor George Baker – known later for his Inspector Wexford television role – and knuckled down to more voice coaching. Once again, in the company of the jovial

Baker, his wife and daughters, Curry had temporarily found another surrogate family. Between the lessons, he'd also found time to be best man at the choreographer Gillian Lynne's wedding in Chelsea – preceded by a restrained three-man stag night – before hopeful developments in New York lured him back in early summer.

———

Together with his father, the infant Curry had been an admirer of thigh-slapping theatrical musicals. 'I acquired a taste for them very quickly,' he remembered. 'We saw everything that came into town.' Just so long as his son only looked at the dancers, Joseph was happy. Fifteen years after his father's death, however, John Curry was not only dancing in New York – at a show his ill-fated parent would have adored – but he was also wearing a kilt.

Most musicals are dogged by improbable plots. *Brigadoon* is no different. Since premiering on Broadway in 1947, its unlikely brew of bumbling American tourists and star-crossed Highlanders has attracted both ridicule and rapture. Once disbelief has been dispensed with, it tells the story of a Scottish village that appears out of the mist only once every century. But after its triumphs of 1947 – and a Gene Kelly film – the musical had surfaced almost as infrequently. By 1980 it was deemed ready for a major revival. All it needed was a star's name over the door in lights.

Long before it opened, however, Curry's proposed involvement was causing problems. The director, Manchester-born Vivian Matelon, was in favour of him. The musical's revered choreographer Agnes de Mille was apparently not; and few people on Broadway ever tangled with 'Miss de Mille'. Although 75 years old and impaired by a recent stroke, she carried the whiff of *Sunset Boulevard*. As a child, like Curry, she had been forbidden by her parents from dancing, despite which she'd worked with Dame Marie Rambert, before choreographing hit shows like *Oklahoma*, *Paint Your Wagon* and *Carousel*. In the 1940s, she'd added *Brigadoon* to her credits and for the part of the villainous Harry Beaton – with its highly complex sword dances – she wanted a professional dancer who could act, not an ice skater who could do neither.

'His name got him the job,' insists the show's stage manager Joe Lorden. 'Vivian was smitten with him. Liked him a lot. Thought he'd be a terrific Harry Beaton. Miss de Mille was not crazy about his dancing. She went along with the director and the producers, but she was not pleased with his ability.'

Soon after rehearsals began in late August, Curry's presence had split the cast. Many of the trained dancers were irritated by his lack of expertise. Others – like understudy Tom Fowler – were moved by his courage. 'He did seem like a fish out of water,' says Fowler, who wisely avoided a tempting 'romantic link' with the skater. 'Some had compassion for him. Others felt he should not be there. I wanted to help him in any way I could. It wasn't his milieu. It wasn't his world. He was lonely. He just didn't fit in ... Something could have happened between us but I would never become involved with anyone I was in a production with.'

Even for stage-hardened, ballet-trained stalwarts, *Brigadoon*'s Scottish dancing represented a hefty challenge. For the inexperienced Curry, it fast became a confidence-sapping ordeal. Admonished by the grey-haired Miss de Mille from her chair, he battled to master dizzying sword dances plagued by screaming calf muscles, a weak back and battered toes. 'He was man down from the beginning,' recalls dancer Amy Danis. 'I'm sure he was in pain 24/7 as indeed many of the men were ... but unfortunately he was also on display from day one as being behind.'

It was a situation fraught with risk. To help him, Agnes de Mille had refashioned much of her original choreography. Curry's dubious Scottish accent had also been laboriously overhauled. But the skater was unused to public humiliation, and histrionics were never far away. 'It was very challenging for him to have his voice heard,' says Fowler. 'He was self-conscious about how he sounded on stage. Once or twice he became absolutely exasperated and had to leave a rehearsal.' 'Rumours would go through the company that he was pitching a fit about something,' adds Danis. At a press conference to promote the show, Miss de Mille summed up her own feelings with acid aplomb. 'As a dancer,' she said, 'John Curry is a wonderful skater.'

By the time, *Brigadoon* previewed at the Saenger Arts Center in New Orleans, on 20 August, expectations were low. In his dressing room, Curry uneasily surveyed the usual gush of flowers and telegrams. 'Knock 'Em Dead' from Whitener and Roberts. 'Thinking of you' from Anthony Dowell. As had always happened before, however, the skater's onstage professionalism successfully masked the tumult which lay beneath. Not only was the production warmly reviewed – with a standing ovation for Agnes de Mille – but Curry himself was singled out by the New Orleans press for praise.

His Harry Beaton, said the *Times-Picayune*, displayed 'the dangerous neuroticism of a spoiled child'. As a review of Curry's performance, it was exemplary. As a summation of Curry's persona, it was even better. Two weeks later, after a well-received spell in Washington, *Brigadoon* was ready for its eight shows per week run at the Majestic Theater on Broadway, New York. Everyone was optimistic. There was no reason it couldn't stay there for a year. Publicly, Curry appeared settled. Privately, in a letter to Cathy Foulkes, he was expressing his doubts.

> We ... will move to NY next week – the very idea gives me a cold flush. Things I hope, prey [sic], are in fairly good shape. We shall soon find out – the idea of being reviewed for dancing and acting by Broadway critics gives me horrors. Still, I guess I can live through it ... I'm getting used to the idea of living alone – STILL miss Ron. Am well. Think of you often. I do hope we shall skate more.

By early February, after only 133 performances, *Brigadoon* had shrunk back into the mist. Despite strong notices, Manhattan's theatre-goers had not warmed to Lerner and Loewe's dated Caledonian frippery. No one was blaming John Curry. In New York, once again, the critics had dripped honey on his performances. 'Compelling energy,' said one. 'The exhilarating sword dance is brilliantly executed by a balletically perfect John Curry,' crooned another. Behind the scenes, however, the skater's periodically toxic behaviour had stretched the company's patience to the limit. 'As far as a Broadway show went, he simply wasn't disciplined enough,' says Joe Lorden.

Barely 12 months before, it was stage manager Lorden who had mopped up after Curry's perplexing fall at the Minskoff. Five weeks into *Brigadoon*'s Majestic run – on 27 November – he was doing it again. Almost everyone, including Amy Danis, had sensed it building. 'Once we'd got to Broadway he was spending a lot of late nights out; burning the candle at both ends; and coming in the next day just not up to par; unable to do a good show.' The unspoken twin nightmares of the Anvil and the Mineshaft were stirring.

> There were moments when he was physically hurt and it wasn't because of the show. He'd come in bruised and stuff and I was so young I didn't really know what was going on. Maybe it was all so overwhelming this was all he could do to relax. I know he wasn't happy. I knew he wasn't taking care of himself. I don't think he realised what was required to do something of this difficulty eight times a week. I don't think he ever got to the point where he could enjoy it.

At the matinée performance on Thanksgiving, Curry snapped. During the climactic scene in which he threatens to leave Brigadoon, he threw his dagger on stage, where it quivered, blade down in the boards. Curry then walked into the wings, got changed and left the theatre. 'I had no idea what was going on in his head. His mood swings were incredible,' says Lorden. 'He was unapproachable.' No one knew what had triggered his strop. Other than Lorden, no one in the production had seen anything like it before.

In his absence, an understudy played Beaton's corpse (the face carefully obscured by a blanket) and later stood in for the walkabout star during the curtain call. If the audience noticed, it never reached the ears of the press, and by the evening Curry had returned. 'Although the cast were really upset, I embraced him and we had turkey and stuff between the performances ... but word got out and it damaged the show.'

Curry never repeated his behaviour. Nor did he ever explain it. By February – when *42nd Street* eased them out of the Majestic – there was no one left to explain it to. On a newspaper photograph of himself dressed in a kilt, Curry drew horns and a devil's tail. Around the head of his co-star Marina Eglevksky he inked a halo. For the second time in a year, he'd been party to a Broadway collapse, and his bankability as an aspirant actor had been crushed. If it was a devastating blow, it was also an entirely predictable one.

It didn't matter how often people told him he was good. Unless Curry believed it – and he rarely did – there was little pleasure in anything; and therefore no incentive to continue. 'He had the feeling that it wasn't worth doing unless it was perfect,' says a friend. 'And that's a problem, because things are not perfect.'

Even in the chaotic minutes after winning Olympic gold – with the world drooling at his grace – he'd telephoned a friend and asked: How was I? Six years later, under sustained and self-imposed pressure, his doubts could only be temporarily suppressed before they blistered and burned. Only on Fire Island was he ever truly free of them. But, like everyone else, he needed to work.

———

Overnight, New York had lost its shine. The summer was still months away, and Curry had nothing to do. In November he'd skated an exhibition at Madison Square Garden with the three-times world champion Peggy Fleming. He'd also skated alone most mornings at Sky Rink during the winter. But without *Brigadoon*, Curry's solitude was horribly amplified and his relationship with Nancy Streeter was no longer an available solace.

In October, still feeling estranged, she'd penned another heartfelt letter to him. For a second time she chose not to send it. 'I hope we can work out a friendship that takes into consideration the new interests and directions without wiping out the past which still holds good memories.' It was a plea that Curry never heard. Loyally, she'd stood and applauded his Harry Beaton, but the skater's mind was clearly wandering. After the shutdown, in mid-February, Nancy received a terse note informing her that he was returning to Britain. 'I have been feeling very reclusive lately and I am going to go home soon. I am looking forward to a change of pace and scene.'

For the next few weeks, Curry laid low. Out of sight, his disappointment quickly faded. After a short spell in London, he returned to New York, where there was an early rapprochement with Nancy. 'I'm pleased that you have managed to talk,' Rita wrote confidentially to her. 'I do not understand his wording of intrusion into his life. I'm quite sure that would be your last thought.' There was also news on the work front; some good, some bad. Starting in September, he would be performing in a Shakespeare play in England. That was the good. Before that, he had to go to China with Toller Cranston on a televised exhibition tour organised by the ubiquitous Dick Button.

By the 1980s, Button had become a significant player in international skating. A five-times world champion himself, he was not only the hugely respected television voice for every major competitive event, he also ran his own company, Candid Productions, packaging glossy professional ice events for American, and foreign, broadcasters. With so few outlets where top skaters could make serious money, Button's position was a powerful one. Thus far, Curry had survived without his patronage. By early June 1981, devoid of alternatives, he had succumbed. By the time his party reached Beijing, almost everyone else was wishing he hadn't.

Relations between Cranston and Curry had been contaminated for years. In China – complicated by the presence of JoJo Starbuck – their animosity ensured a trip from hell. 'JoJo had to cling to John professionally and kowtow to his every whim,' claimed Cranston. 'But my impression is that she did not like him (admittedly this is not the way she remembers it). She preferred me. So JoJo ended up between a rock and a hard place. To be honest with John and me, it was … between a landmine and a grenade, and at any second – well, you just never knew.'

For Starbuck it was especially tough. As an amateur, she'd forged a 'fun camaraderie' on the circuit with Cranston. On the flight into Beijing, however, Curry had talked openly to her about his father. Appearing to favour either skater would suddenly be awkward; never more so than on the tour bus with only two spare seats left – one next to Cranston, the other next to Curry. 'Toller would be sitting behind John, so John couldn't see him indicating that I sit with him, not John. So I think I stood …'

'Every day, every hour was ruined by John's froideur towards me and mine towards John,' remembered Cranston in his 1997 autobiography.

> As hot and muggy as Beijing was, every day was chillier than the last. If I wished to address Lord Curry, I needed an intermediary. Face to face conversations were out of the question. JoJo was the designated diplomat whose trip was completely destroyed by having to perform in this capacity.

Nevertheless the tour had its moments. During the rehearsals, over 20,000 people crammed into the city's stadium to watch. During the televised exhibition, there was an audience of millions. 'We were mice on the Chinese scale,' mused Cranston. 'One felt inferior and insignificant.' In their time off, there were trips to Ming tombs and the Great Wall followed by interminable banquets where freshly tapped monkey brains were served; and where JoJo and Curry posed for photographs, with cigarettes drooping from their mouths. 'I confess those particular brains were wasted on us. They were never sampled,' quipped Cranston. 'The dinner ended precipitously. All of us, without prompting, fled into the Pekinese night.'

———

Restored to the ocean sun Curry rode a bicycle up and down the creaking boardwalks, and prepared elaborate meals for his friends. Nowhere else did his life have such structure. Away from it, possibilities and confusion lay in every direction. Reluctantly he'd let go of his Greenwich Village apartment. 'Packing up has been intense,' he told Nancy. 'Still it is all for the best ... I'll let you know my next stop – as soon as I know it myself.' By September, he knew where that was. In place of an Atlantic beach-house Curry had a room in the Victoria Hotel, Nottingham. Instead of the ocean's roar, he had the growl of city traffic on Milton Street.

As a teenager, Curry had dreamily read *Romeo and Juliet* with Lorna Brown. At the age of 32, the Olympic gold medallist had been offered the part of Puck in *A Midsummer Night's Dream* at the Nottingham Playhouse. For a seasoned thespian, it would have been an intimidating prospect. Pictures of Judi Dench, Peter O'Toole, and Ian McKellen lined the theatre's foyer. Nottingham itself was a proud city of culture. As a boy, D. H. Lawrence had strode its broad Victorian streets. In his own youth, Curry had skated there. But he had never trodden the boards; and he had never been so exposed.

He told the *Daily Mail* shortly after arriving:

> I am still surrounded by people who tell me everything I do is a mistake. To most people the only thing that matters is how much money you get and that you appear to be terribly successful ... those who [truly] succeed just put everything aside and say 'This is what I am going to do' and just keep walking to that goal.

Richard Digby Day, the theatre's director, had faith. For years he'd nurtured the unwavering premonition that one day he would work with John Curry. Separated by five years, both men had attended Solihull School. As a television viewer, Digby Day had been entranced by Curry's Olympic performance. He'd also been among the audience at the Cambridge Theatre, and, like Curry, he was gay. 'So when I got the call from his agent I wasn't a bit surprised. We went off and had tea together, got on well, and I offered him the part.'

By late September, Curry was shuttling alone to the theatre for private acting sessions with Digby Day. 'Rehearsals are going well and very happily,' he told Nancy. 'Next week the full cast begins.' Before they arrived, Curry's voice badly needed to be strengthened. There was no power in it, and he struggled with the unfamiliar rhythms of Elizabethan dialogue.

What Curry delivered, however – without tuition – was the darting grace Puck's magic required. Wearing an all-black costume he'd designed himself (a suggested thong had been wisely rejected) it was a performance that immediately won over doubtful critics. 'He is lithe and graceful with a come hither personality,' concluded the *Financial Times*. Audiences were impressed. So were his fellow cast members.

'His voice was rather fey and inexpressive,' says Malcolm Sinclair, who played Oberon. 'But he had a natural Pixie-like quality and a very sharp sense of humour. He was also as bright as a button and had an impressive insolence about him. A "take me as you find me" side to his personality.' There were no diva-like tantrums; no mystery disappearances; no temptations.

'Life in Nottingham certainly is different to NYC,' he told Nancy. 'Fortunately I am busy, but when I'm not it is dreary.' As a favour to the Victoria Hotel, he would periodically hang around in the lobby to be seen by other guests as they checked in. In return, he got his room for nothing. It was a necessary bonus. Curry's Equity fee was next to nothing and his name was not even over the theatre door.

Dreary or not, Nottingham had temporarily humbled him. Before the production closed he invited a Fleet Street reporter into his dressing room and articulated his feelings. After the Olympics, he said, 'it was as if I had walked out of a dark room onto a blazingly lit beach. Everything I thought I had missed wasn't just available, it was thrown at me. So naturally I went through a period when I wanted to play more than I had, because basically I had never played at all.' It wasn't the first time he said it – and as usual it was heavily coded – but Curry's hint of a lifestyle shift was intriguing. All around him, a dreadful change was coming.

Four months earlier, as Curry bronzed himself on Fire Island, the *New York Times* had reported 41 cases of Kaposi's sarcoma – a rare and unusually aggressive cancer – affecting gay men in New York and California. By the end of the year a total of 270 cases of severe immune deficiency had been reported among male homosexuals in the United States. Of those, 121 had died. In late October, as the news drifted around Manhattan's gay community, Curry flew back into New York and picked up his skates.

———

There was money to be made on ice in the early 1980s. Thus far, John Curry had been too high-minded to seek it out. In 1981, as Christmas loomed, he was weakening. For the first time in the sport's history, the American circuit was awash with household names. Excited by saturation Olympic coverage, the television millions wanted more than a single competition once every four years. Figure skating – for its one and only time – was big business and people like Toller Cranston, Dorothy Hamill, Peggy Fleming, Janet Lynn, Robin Cousins and John Curry were its stars.

Dick Button had seen the way. In 1973, he'd run the world's first professional championships at Landover in Maryland. With insufficient big-name skaters, the fledgling project had faltered, but eight years later Button was back and the US television networks were slathering for the rights. With broadcaster money in place, the high recognition skaters rushed forward, seeking a long overdue cheque after decades of grant-supported self-denial. 'Peggy Fleming kept saying, "Well, I don't want to lose my Olympic gold medal." And I kept telling them they'd never lose their medals,' says Button. 'They would never be former or past. They were Olympic champions. Period.'

To shelter fragile egos, the competition – which was staged in December – was organised around a team format. But, in truth, this was no competition at all. 'A little bit of a circus,' thought Hamill. Nobody truly cared, or even remembered, who'd won. Many of the skaters were unfit, and regarded the professional format only as a long overdue payday.

'It was a way of cashing in,' insists Cranston.

> It was the house of horrors. After we'd competed at events like the Olympics we all coasted on our laurels. Never practised and always out of condition. It was showbiz fuelled by celebrity. We were card-carrying members of a golden generation but it was as phoney as wrestling and participating in phoney shit was as an anathema to me as it would have been for John Curry.

Nevertheless, bolstered by a reported fee of $45,000, Curry had been seduced. After a short spell in Boston recording *Peter and the Wolf* for American public television, he turned up at the Capitol Center in Landover for the second of Button's revived professional extravaganzas. Every fibre of his being resented it. Only his lack of money was keeping him there. Although, on paper, he was joint captain (with Dorothy Hamill) of the so-called 'All-Stars', he had no intention of subjecting himself to scrutiny by a judging panel. Curry would skate only as an exhibition skater and under no circumstances would he perform in the team uniform.

'He obviously didn't want to be there, didn't seem to like any of us and refused to speak to his fellow competitors,' remembered Cranston. 'Directly before the competition, he refused point-blank to wear the assigned uniform and threatened to flee to the airport. Somehow, a deal was struck and John consented to wear part of it.'

Years later, Cranston accused Button of 'personal weakness', saying he'd 'caved in to every one of John's little demands'. Behind the scenes, Button had seen it differently. 'I had to call his [Curry's] agent and say, "John will never work again if he walks out on this." I couldn't have it. All this complaining about costumes … like a child who has a tantrum … he'd left his room, walked out of rehearsals and the hotel had lost his room. I told the agent that he'd better get his ass back here.' As always, Curry – even under duress – had skated beautifully, but he would never return to Button's circus.

Yet again, Curry's compass was spinning. In December, he switched on the Christmas tree lights at New York's Rockefeller

Center. In February, he reluctantly joined the CBS commentary team for the European Championships in France. If he'd been a dancer, Curry told a journalist bitterly, he'd have 'gone from flower to flower picking the honey' with work at all the major ballet companies. As a skater, there were no ready-made equivalents. Either he built up his own productions, or his art simply did not exist. In between times, he would do what he could, short of wearing a ridiculous costume. And every month, while the good money was there, he would send a cheque to his widowed mother for $900.

On Fire Island the previous summer, as he sat alone on a jetty, Curry had received a visitor. Not a stranger; Elva Clairmont's was a face he knew. Forty-four years old, dark-haired and attractive with a broad, smiling mouth, she had first met him in 1975 at the World Championships. Since then she'd managed Toller Cranston before their partnership imploded amidst vicious legal and financial acrimony. 'Elva was charming, literate, immensely articulate and wickedly funny,' recalled Cranston. '[She] always said, "Tell people what they want to hear and they'll go for it every time."' Cranston had gone for it and ended up wishing they'd never met. In due course, so would John Curry.

'He was really down in the dumps at that point,' she says. 'I asked him what he was doing and he said, "I'm wondering what it would be like to drown". So I thought I'd better just sit there and talk to him because the water was deep and he was never what I'd call a happy person.'

This was no chance meeting. Clairmont had a keen entrepreneurial brain aligned to a thrill-seeker's indifference to risk. She was also passionate about ice skating, intrigued by the untapped commercial value of characters like Curry and Cranston, and intent upon breaking Dick Button's stranglehold on competitive professional skating events. If she could secure an Olympic champion, her plan would acquire momentum and gravitas, and, after that, anything was possible.

Over lunch in Manhattan she unfurled her seductive vision. In the long term, she saw a permanent skating school grooming child prodigies, while Curry's own ice ensemble company performed in theatres worldwide with a live symphony orchestra. More immediately, her plans centred on a lucrative rival professional championship – better paid than Button's, with an emphasis on 'the artistic and performance values of the skating'. It was a brilliant pitch which ended – according to Clairmont – with tears 'welling in his eyes'. Once his obligations to Dick Button were through, he would join her. All she had to do was call.

If entrepreneurs like Larry Parnes had seemed an alien species to Curry, suddenly the waters around the skater were infested by them. Elva was persuasive and committed, but had no money. Behind her were two aspiring players who did. Michael Cohl was a Canadian-born concert promoter whose clients would ultimately include Frank Sinatra, Michael Jackson and The Rolling Stones. Alongside him, New Yorker Steve Leber was a rock band manager who'd produced an arena version of *Jesus Christ Superstar*. Both men were intrigued by John Curry. Both were persuaded by Clairmont's $5 million three-year television deal for Pro-Skate, her proposed North American skating grand prix. To get things going – but with caution – the pair drizzled backing into the enterprise.

After an extended hiatus, the seductive possibility of his own ice dance company had been revived, and it was Elva Clairmont who had made the difference. Without her, he would surely have run from men like Cohl and Leber. Cranston had felt the same. 'I wanted someone to be nice to me,' he wrote. 'I wanted a certain kind of affection. I wanted someone to tell me the things I wanted to hear. Elva obliged.' All Curry's life he'd been drawn to fiercely intelligent mother figures, and Clairmont – with two teenage sons of her own – could play that role; a maternal shelter from commercial imperatives he had no wish to understand.

Alongside her in Pro-Skate was another critical lightning rod. At six foot plus, David Spungen was a mustachioed human bear, with a rich baritone voice and a ceaseless spring of positive energy. Shortly before he and Elva had met, Spungen had been working for Button's Candid Productions. 'He was just a runner,' spat Button years later. Everywhere, it seemed, the stakes – and the temperature – were rising.

For months, agents had been on a feeding frenzy. A feral bidding was underway and one by one, at huge expense, all the headline stars had been wrenched from Button's grasp. 'A $25,000 deal would suddenly became a $200,000 guarantee,' says Spungen ruefully. Curry's presence alone would earn the skater over $120,000 before Christmas. 'We'd made it to the big time,' explains Spungen. 'But we were a multi-million dollar company with no money.' Intoxicated by the thrill of the chase, no one seemed concerned. In March, 1982, with John Curry, Dorothy Hamill, Toller Cranston, Peggy Fleming, Robin Cousins, JoJo Starbuck and Janet Lynn all on the roster, Pro-Skate was ready to roll.

Over the next few weeks, sponsored by Labatt's beer, the fledgling professional tour played in five Canadian cities. Against all the odds, Curry appeared happy. Not even the vulgarity of a sponsor (something his contracts usually forbade) seemed to wobble him. Unlike Cranston and Cousins, he had stayed out of the men's 'competition', and appeared only as an exhibitor; skating ethereally to Beethoven's *Moonlight Sonata* in Vancouver, the city where they'd once pelted him with drinks cans. Well paid and royally indulged, Curry now had a sparkle that proved contagious, never more so than among a group of women.

'He was at his best,' remembers JoJo.

> We'd go out for dinner with Dorothy and Peggy and he would be funny and charming with that biting wit. All four of us on the back seat of a limo, and when we got out we'd be saying between us how sexy he was, and what a hunk he was. Were we wasting our time? Yes, but you can appreciate a handsome, dashing man and he had tremendous sex appeal. He wanted us to adore him and we did. He played games with the men and with the women. What if? Maybe if? Could it happen? I'm not the only girl who was thinking that way. A lot of girls were thinking that ... and he had the body of a Greek god.

———

For the first time in his life – as Pro-Skate's first tour ended – Curry had funds. The previous July, the statement for his personal company – Frozen Assets Limited – showed a balance of just $3,650. By the end of 1982 his monthly gift to Rita had risen to $1,200, and his balance had soared to $93,000. Very little of it was being spent. During his spells in New York, he was once again living at 'Hotel Streeter'. Such possessions as he had were in boxes, and by late July he was living out of a suitcase at the Highcliff Hotel in Bournemouth, England; a reluctant star in a shoestring summer ice show.

'[It] is a singularly depressing experience,' he wrote to Nancy.

> Most of the amateurs should not be performing anywhere, let alone in a paid entrance show. In addition to the lack of quality work, there is a notable lack of audience. There has been virtually no advertising and consequently most performances have about 25–35 people in attendance. All most depressing ... Only one week to go – the time cannot pass quickly enough.

Nothing could have been further from Fire Island. On England's south coast, Curry had few visitors, and, after the Atlantic, the English Channel looked like sludge. Only one thing had illuminated Curry's forlorn summer. Before leaving America, he had slipped into a Manhattan cinema to watch Steven Spielberg's latest film, *ET*. 'It made such a huge and profound impression on him,' says Richard Digby Day. 'Sometimes his instincts would come up with something curiously sophisticated; sometimes it was all quite childlike and innocent. Of all the things we ever saw together, that film affected him most.'

If *ET* had touched a nerve, it was understandable. There were painful echoes for Curry in its fable of a lonely alien infant, separated from his parents and desperate for home. There was familiar sadness, too, as the extra-terrestrial is hounded and probed by confused scientists. 'He wrote me a very long letter largely about that film,' remembers the theatre director. 'I suppose he lived such a transatlantic lifestyle. In the end you wind up like the alien, not knowing where you belong.'

By the autumn, Curry was moving again. In September, he spent a week in Toronto recording *The Snow Queen* for American public television. This was more like it. Alongside a stellar cast, Curry shone in a work of 'ballet-like fluidity'. Two months later, he was back at Madison Square Garden with Pro-Skate for two days of televised professional competition. Once again, he was on his best behaviour. In front of a full house – but no judges – he skated alone to Ravel's *La Valse* but stayed aloof from the so-called sport.

As it transpired his 'team' had won, but in their hearts everyone knew it was of no consequence. However hard Button, Clairmont and Spungen strived, however brilliant the skating, only Olympic victory truly mattered. Everything else was just show business masquerading as sport. Publicly, Curry talked the competition up as 'filling a void'. Privately, he decried it. With his contractual duty as 'official spokesperson for Pro-Skate' dutifully honoured, Curry headed for a week in the Caribbean.

When he returned just before Christmas, Clairmont's Fire Island pledge had taken a huge forward step. The two most perplexing and productive years in John Curry's life were about to begin.

Nine

'With an angel'

For a man of such polar contradictions, John Curry chose his favourite places well. When the sun shone, Fire Island and Cornwall suited him perfectly. When it didn't – when the snow fell – he would choose the mountains of Colorado. Given his bitter memories of Davos, it was an odd choice, but at 8,000 feet above sea level the tiny ski resort of Vail was about to provide the laboratory for his last, epic experiment on ice. Among the clouds, he would forge the ultimate expression of his vision. But the effort would expose his mental frailty – and his cruelty – like never before. And when it was over he would be broke, drained and determined never to skate again.

In the first days of 1983, no one could see that coming. Galvanised by the success of Pro-Skate, Clairmont had moved with reckless speed. When Curry returned from holiday, he was to find a startling offer on the table. Backed by Steve Leber – with a little support from David Spungen's credit card – Elva felt ready to help Curry establish a permanent company in his name: the John Curry Skating Company.

Albeit well-intentioned, it was – in almost every respect – a formula for the perfect business storm. Although Clairmont and Spungen had a surplus of belief, they had a hopeless shortfall of capital for a project of this magnitude. Nor did they have any firm offers of work, despite which Curry was already asking for absolute creative control and a year-round group of 12 skaters, backed by an ice engineer, musical director, costume designer and company manager. Without Curry, his two partners had nothing. Saying no was not an option. Glorious optimism had blinded them just as it had blinded Parnes. Everything now hung on a difficult man with a lamentable track record and, henceforth, everything that he wanted he would have. Unknowingly, they had created a monster;

a diva machine, which Spungen himself would shortly have to control.

> John's statement was 'I've got one more shot and I want to do it with you guys.' That was important to me. That mission statement by him became the thing that weighed down on Elva and I to make a lot of decisions that were for the good of going forward as opposed to making business sense … We thought at the very worst if we can't tour, we could get a TV show out of it. We had no money. There was nothing. We just ploughed ahead.

Curry had needed no second invitation. For him, it was a near-fantasy last-chance scenario. As artistic director of the grandly named *Symphony On Ice*, he would be exposed creatively but the financial risk would lie elsewhere. He would also ask, and keep on asking, for whatever he wanted until someone said no. By mid-January, he was contacting his first-choice skaters. By the end of the month, Spungen's credit card was creaking with the cost of 13 airfares to the proposed company training camp in Denver, Colorado. The roar of expectation was deafening. Above its thrilling clamour, no voices of reason could be heard.

This time, Curry was choosing his 'corps de ballet' with more care. There would be no place for Ron Alexander, and Brian Grant was not even considered. Nor, to her great distress, was the ever-loyal Lorna Brown. Curry no longer had time for women who did not resemble ballerinas. 'I was devastated,' she admits. 'I was the thinnest that I could be, but that was my big thing with John. It wasn't the skating. It was food.'

Old faces and new ones were heading for the Rockies. Each was infected by the same sense of impending adventure. No one had done this before. Something magical was brewing. They were young; they were getting paid $300 rehearsal money a week, and they would be working with John Curry. Among them were Minskoff survivors Cathy Foulkes, JoJo Starbuck and Patricia Dodd. At Denver's South Suburban Ice Arena, they would be joined by, alongside others, the pairs skaters Keith Davis and Shelley Winters; Tim Murphy, an Irish-Italian 21-year-old from Boston; and the five-times American champion Janet Lynn.

Her presence alone was evidence of how Curry had been flexing his muscles. In 1983, Janet Lynn was an American superstar who, during the mid-1970s, had been one of the world's highest paid athletes. In Curry's eyes she had no equal. But she was also expensive, semi-retired and reluctant to work away from her Denver home. To make it work, Curry had waived his own fee to cover hers, but the entire operation was still moving 1,600 miles to accommodate this one member. Overnight, Denver had become a necessity not a choice, and, if there was one, none of this had featured on a business plan.

Within days, Spungen was dashing west to join them. For the next two years, he would rarely stray from Curry's side, plugging leaks and pumping up deflated egos. Already there was a crisis. To defray rising hotel costs, an exhibition performance had been scheduled in Denver, for which Curry was demanding a New York choreographer and a full set of cast costumes. With outgoings already spiralling, his options were limited. Either he pulled the plug prematurely or he caved in to the skater's demands. Wearily, Spungen reached for his credit card. What credit couldn't patch, however, was Curry's fragile mood.

After overhearing homophobic remarks from local ice hockey players, he'd fled from rehearsals and was refusing to return to the arena. Back at the hotel – in a tearful confessional with Spungen – Curry blamed loneliness, and the terror of failure. He also pleaded to be taken out of Denver. 'There was no way to say no,' explains Spungen. 'Managing him was all constant logic and reasoning. If a problem would come up I'd call Elva in New York and she'd say, "Take a deep breath and go talk to John." I can't tell you how many times I did that.'

Within a few days, the entire caravan had been relocated. Following a frantic series of telephone calls, Spungen had settled on Vail, a purpose-built ski resort with its own ice arena less than two hours west of Denver. Finally the serious work would begin.

———

Out of desperation, Spungen had struck gold. From the moment he arrived, Curry's spirits lifted. Ringed by snow-plastered mountains, Vail was alive with skiers. Every winter, the resort wallowed in around 300 inches of snowfall. Every night the slopes were manicured into runs that heaved with daytime activity. At dusk, as the lifts closed – and the air quivered at -30°C – the bars turned up the heat and let 'happy hour' run on towards morning. Every lungful of mountain air was a tonic. And in every direction, the white-toothed horizon pleased his eye.

As a landscape, Vail was sublime. More importantly, its upmarket facilities dovetailed perfectly with the needs of both Curry, and his watchful minder. Unlike Denver, Vail had welcomed its unexpected guests, deluging Spungen with free ski passes for all, and favourable rates at top quality hotels and luxury condos. Even the ice was near-perfect – and cheap. At $15 an hour, the Dobson Ice Arena was not only a bargain, but its glass walls flooded the interior with natural light. 'Skaters are used to being in cold, dark, windowless prisons,' explains Starbuck. 'We'd be going, "Oh my god, can you believe it?" You could see the sky. You could see the mountains.'

It was time for the hard yards to begin. Before they could be a company, they must each learn to skate again, refashioned in the balletic mould of their teacher. For almost all of them – Janet Lynn had remained in Denver – it would be an exhaustingly painful rite of passage. Every day would begin early – swaddled in layers to combat the pre-dawn cold – with off-ice balletic stretches. After this would come 'class', a highly technical period of study, performed in smaller groups, always watched and driven hard by Curry. Only then would rehearsals begin proper.

'A full measure of concentration is required despite the early hour, inevitable fatigue and soreness,' Cathy Foulkes would say later. 'Anything less invites public humiliation through John's scorn. Dreadful.'

Like all great art, Curry's skating concealed masterful technique. In Vail, his awestruck young company were grappling with its secrets. For even the youngest, and best, of them it would be an ordeal. After eight hours on the ice, many could barely stand. 'It was gruelling. Really gruelling,' recalls Tim Murphy. 'Growing up as a skater, it's mostly about jumps and spins. But what he did was break everything down and shape us into something people would like to watch. In Vail, I was like a pig in poop. I was as happy as a man could be. I had never been happier.'

There was no reason for discontent. Curry was driving people hard, but – so far – with untypical restraint. As the weeks passed, there were few tears and no walkouts. Life in Vail was all but perfect. 'The way we lived was amazing. We kind of owned that town,' says Murphy. 'We were all so full of ourselves. At least, I was anyway. We'd go to a bistro and order bottles of champagne. We kind of took over. We used to skate 6 a.m. till 2 p.m., have our skis at the rink, then run to the lifts at two to see if we could get one long run in.'

Although Curry occasionally skied, he rarely socialised. While his 'kids' (as he called them) crowded into the smoke-filled Sweet Basil restaurant, Curry retreated alone to his room with his records. Only Foulkes seemed to make any impact. 'If he pushed people away, she didn't take no for an answer,' noticed Murphy. 'She made sure he was eating.'

Ever since the Cambridge, their bond had been deepening. Back in Denver, when Foulkes had been ill in the night, it had been Curry who took her to hospital. Up in Vail the two would convene secretly in Curry's room after rehearsals; sometimes for 'tea and cookies', sometimes to climb into bed and read Shakespeare. During rehearsals, he was often brutal to her, and yet no one else enjoyed such intimacy. 'He destroyed her sometimes,' remembers one of the troupe. 'He gave her more kindness and cruelty than anyone else.'

'John moves as no other,' Foulkes wrote in her diary.

> I can watch him skate for hours, totally mesmerised. His fluid transitions from one seemingly inevitable position to the next becomes intoxicating, at times hypnotic. Technically it is the complete mastery of his centre that makes him unique. Every movement is initiated from this point; energy emanates from and flows through it. The visible result is a grace liberated from distractions – in essence a purity. White. The rest of the company is at best ivory, achieving illumination only at odd moments.

In late February, Elva Clairmont flew out from New York to see how Curry was progressing. 'John had blossomed,' she noted. 'He had become relaxed, positive and outgoing, and he exuded self-confidence … On the ice, the company now worked as an ensemble, gliding across the arena in breath-taking formation … graceful movements, soft arms, everything working as an elegant whole.' On a trip up into the mountains, Curry pleaded with her to make Vail a permanent home for a permanent company. Only one component seemed lacking. As yet, there were still no concrete bookings for *Symphony On Ice*.

Unreality loomed again. To 'make payroll', the company had staged sellout 'work in progress' performances in both Denver and Vail, but a proposed tour of the Philippines had crashed. So, too, had a lucrative television special. At an ill-tempered meeting in Toronto, Curry had vetoed the production and walked out after hearing that Toller Cranston might be involved; and that it was to be staged on an Alberta glacier. Despite being under contract, he was also insisting that both Steve Leber and Michael Cohl – the two men who'd underpinned Pro-Skate and Vail – be disconnected from his young company.

Curry's grasp of business had always been feeble. In the de-oxygenated mountain air, it was clearly becoming unhinged. By early March, the project was running on hope. Keeping 12 skaters in Vail was costing $10,000 a week with no sign of any meaningful income. Just how much of this Curry knew – or surmised – is unclear. Some things he was told. Others, he was not. As Clairmont shored things up back in New York, Spungen carefully spoon-fed their solitary asset. 'We'd tell John's "people" and they'd be involved in decisions about whether to tell him A or B.' Bad news always had to be rationed. Sometimes there were things it was best he didn't know.

Pro-Skate, at least, was delivering some revenue. In March, the infant professional series regrouped for a short Canadian tour, and, since most of Curry's skaters were involved, activities at Vail were put on hold. For the younger ones – skaters who'd missed out on Olympic selection – it was a genuine chance to compete and win. Behind the scenes, however, even Pro-Skate was in trouble. Sustained efforts to break into the American arena circuit had floundered, and a key Canadian sponsor had jumped ship. Suddenly Elva's vaunted cash cow had developed a limp and Curry's patience had snapped. Deeming Leber and Cohl to be at fault – and unsympathetic towards his vision – he wanted them gone. After two more exhibition shows in April – one in Vail and one with the peerless Janet Lynn in Denver – Curry said goodbye to his troupe and flew to London. Clairmont and Spungen could sort out the mess or it was over without ever really having begun.

———

In every sense, Curry had never been an easy man to find. Shortly before *Brigadoon*, his acting coach George Baker had air-mailed pleading 'be a dear and answer my questions, otherwise you'll get three pages of Edith Sitwell to do in one breath'. Years had passed since he'd written to Heinz Wirz, and his correspondence with Nancy Streeter had shrivelled. Even his friendship with Penny Malec was in hibernation. 'He'd come and go in my life. He was very elusive,' she says. Or, as Richard Digby Day describes it, 'Obsessively private'.

Back in London, Curry burrowed deep. No one seemed quite sure where he was living. Or who – if anyone – he was living with. Unshackled from his company, he'd finally acquired a Yamaha motorcycle to go with his much-loved black leathers. When feeling brave, he burned up to Warwickshire astride it to see his mother in the sleepy village bungalow he'd bought for her just a few miles south of Stratford-upon-Avon. Mostly, he rode it around London – L-plate flapping – often turning up for meetings in a cream flannel suit, slip-on sneakers and helmet. 'He drove poorly,' says his brother Andrew. 'Absolutely terribly in fact, with no conception of what was going on around him which, considering what he did, I found very strange.'

For a short while, Curry had stayed with Penny, only for them to fall out about acting. 'We had terrible cross arguments about that,' she recalls. 'I said, "Well are you going to train?" and he said, "No, I can just do it" and I knew he couldn't.' After that, he'd taken a smart Chelsea flat, flitting between London luxury and weekends away with friends. 'I had no idea where he was living,' says Digby Day. 'I never went anywhere where he lived; never saw his digs. We always met in public places.'

Gillian Lynne's fine homes in Chiswick and Gloucestershire had become favoured bolt-holes. Few people tolerated him more; or had a better grasp of his fears. Throughout the previous year, her own reputation as a choreographer had soared. In both New York and London, Andrew Lloyd Webber's musical *Cats* had won awards, and sold tens of thousands of tickets. Along Broadway, Lynne had seen the storm that was coming. Within a year of opening in Manhattan, four male cast members – 'brilliant boys' – had died of AIDS. Although worried for him, neither she nor her actor-husband Peter Land, would ever judge the choices Curry made. Life in their company – deep in the English countryside – sparkled with laughter, and it suited him inordinately well.

'You would know when John was going to go off on one of his rampages,' she says.

> Most of the time he was this absolutely lovely, gentle, sweet, person, but then you'd get up in the morning and say hello to him in the kitchen, and you could always tell by the look in his eyes. I'd say, 'Oh Johnny, I hope you're careful'. And then off he went on his bike, after which we wouldn't see him for a few days until he'd come back exhausted. We never asked questions and he never told us anything. He just couldn't help it. Those who have to have it rough and hurt each other, I think it's either in them or it isn't. But his promiscuity didn't go with the taste of the man. I never understood it.

Although they now rarely exchanged letters, Heinz Wirz knew all about what he called his friend's 'promiscuous crap'. Since the late 1960s, the Austrian had watched with growing anxiety. 'I mean he's had everyone sexually, oh yes. An incredible amount of gay lovers. Incredibly active. He would often say he'd been to see Nureyev and they went here and there and had something to eat. I often asked if they'd been lovers and he said, "Oh, I don't talk about that".'

No relationship was more covert, however, than the one with Alan Bates. Few people knew about it, and the two men were rarely seen in public. Although no tangible evidence exists, it seems inconceivable that the two were not in regular contact during this summer of 1983. At the age of 48, Bates was enjoying a golden spell. Playing the spy-traitor Guy Burgess in Alan Bennett's *An Englishman Abroad* had earned him a coveted BAFTA. It was a role he'd been particularly well qualified for. Publicly, Bates was a married father of teenage twins. Privately, and very secretly, he engaged in numerous, secret homosexual liaisons, of which his relationship with Curry was just one.

Within the skater's tight inner circle, everyone knew. Open speculation, however, was discouraged. For the director Richard Digby Day it was, like many aspects of Curry's life, a cause for some concern. 'Bates was a butcher version of John. He would not have been a reliable partner for anyone,' he explains. 'It was not in his nature to be that thing. There was no security there for John.' For Gillian Lynne, there seemed a simple reason for their chemistry. 'I would think sex, wouldn't you,' she asks. 'They were both very special men, very classy men. But it's always the one you can't get easily that you truly hunger for and because Alan was both it must have been absolutely maddening [for Curry] to fall in love with him. That's really not easy, is it?'

It must have helped their bond that Curry was acting again. Thanks to Digby Day, he'd been cast as Orlando in a production of *As You Like It* at the Regent's Park Open Air Theatre. Throughout May and June – in front of 1,200-strong audiences – his travails back in the Rockies were ameliorated by good reviews and the respect of his peers. 'He played the part with very considerable charm and warmth,' says Digby Day. 'He wanted to be taken seriously. He didn't just want to be in light comedies and farces.'

Nevertheless, by July he was back in Regent's Park as Lysander in *A Midsummer Night's Dream*. 'I hate it mostly,' he told Nancy Streeter. 'But the audiences go crazy and eat it up. Such is life … I don't think I'm a very good Lysander, but who knows. Life here in London is pleasant enough. I have had little or no social life, which I guess is fine. The best thing about it all is my motorbike …'

No mention was made in Curry's letters of events in Manhattan. Few gay men, however, will have been unaware of them. Just as the skater was grappling with Shakespearean syntax, banner-carrying Gay Pride protesters were taking to the streets in New York and San Francisco demanding: 'AIDS Research – Not AIDS Hysteria'. Everywhere, tabloid fear fuelled by ignorance was stifling rational debate. As it did so, this mystery virus was leeching ever outwards. In California that month, the first AIDs-dedicated hospital ward had been opened. Within hours, every bed had been taken by dying young men.

Across America, terrified and bewildered homosexuals were going into retreat, and checking the health of their former lovers. On Fire Island, especially, people talked of little else. What had started as an American footnote was rapidly spilling out across the world's front pages. In Britain, the previous year, few people had been interested. By August 1983 it had graduated to a full-blown national scare story. The 'gay plague' – as Fleet Street helpfully dubbed it – was winding back the clock on two decades of hard-won sexual freedom. Already secretive, Curry pulled his fears ever deeper, and drove on. Sometimes it was better not to know.

―――――

From elsewhere in New York there was better news. Curry's cherished vision for Vail was not dead. Clairmont and Spungen had found a new investor. Someone else appeared willing to risk money on the mercurial Englishman. This time it was West Nally, a worldwide company packaging televised sports events, with a long-standing interest in the American skater Janet Lynn. During the Sapporo 1972 Winter Olympics, Lynn's artistry had become something of a Japanese national obsession. If she and Curry were prepared to perform in Tokyo – together with *Symphony On Ice* – West Nally would put $200,000 on the table for three huge shows and a television special. 'The deal was complicated but seemed to suit our mutual purposes,' noted Clairmont.

It was a staggering step forward. It was also a huge amplification of scale and risk. The Tokyo performance was to be staged in January at the modernist Yoyogi Stadium, with live music supplied by the New Japan Philharmonic Orchestra. It would also be shown nationwide on Japanese television. Throughout August – around his performances in Regent's Park – Curry agonised over the details of his new show. This had always been the part he relished. Music. Costumes. Choreography. Skaters. Ideas never daunted him – only people did that – and in London that summer his deep competitive instincts had already been stirring. At the Victoria Palace, Robin Cousins had premiered his own ice spectacular, *Electric Ice*, prompting faint sniffs of admiration in a letter to Foulkes:

> Far too much disco movement. Ghastly costumes … but for all that it was/is an effort and had some merit … Robin sort of disappeared in the crowd and was quite disappointing … He needs space for all the speed which of course he was unable to generate …
> I cannot believe the summer is almost over, and that we shall be back in Vail in two weeks and performing again in about six.

Clairmont's quest for more work had borne more fruit. Starting in late September – as a warm-up for Japan – a four-week tour of

Canadian venues had been stitched together for the company. Once again, it bore the tell-tale signs of desperation. Many of the venues would be small and remote. To get *Symphony On Ice* into Vancouver and Seattle, the promoters had also insisted that Dorothy Hamill be on the bill. Merely securing her services – according to Clairmont – had added $8k (plus expenses) to the cost of those two shows. It was money they didn't have. Equally, without her, they had nothing. Against expectations, however, Hamill had been thrilled to be asked.

Almost eight years had elapsed since she and Curry had left Innsbruck with Olympic gold. After a White House reception and hometown tickertape welcome in Connecticut, Hamill had pursued the big money offered by Ice Capades. While Curry remained defiantly poor but artistically aloof, she'd become a high-earning burlesque ice queen; what she called 'a performing monkey living out of a suitcase'. By 1983 she was 'burned out with the ice shows', living in Los Angeles and married to Dean Martin's son. 'I never had the maturity or the knowledge to even think of doing what John did,' she says. And then the call came in from her agent.

Not for the first time, Clairmont had got lucky. Hamill's disillusionment ran sufficiently deep to override a manager who thought the fee was derisory. 'He would have been happier if I was doing the hula,' Hamill later wrote. 'I tried to explain that it wasn't about the money. Sometimes [my agent] made me feel like a racehorse ... He didn't understand my need to grow.' In June, she had slipped into London to watch Curry performing as Lysander in Regent's Park. After dinner they had skated alone to 'Pennies from Heaven' and a Chopin piano piece on the ghostly midnight ice of the Queen's rink. It was her own private midsummer dream. If Curry wanted her from September, she was in.

Hamill's was not the only new face. From Robin Cousins's show, Curry had poached the versatile ensemble skater Dita Dotson. From Boston, he'd called up the gifted, but inexperienced 19-year-old Nathan Birch. Alongside them were veterans like JoJo Starbuck, Patricia Dodd, Tim Murphy and Cathy Foulkes. The pairs skaters Keith Davis and Shelley Winters had also been recalled alongside Mark Hominuke, Lori Nichol and David Santee.

For the entire 12-strong ensemble, three weeks of furious concentration lay ahead. Whatever balance Curry had achieved in

London rapidly slid away under the pressure. For Nathan Birch, in particular, that meant an induction of shocking intensity. Earlier in the summer – in a letter to Foulkes – Curry had strongly hinted that he harboured feelings for his fair-haired new recruit. As rehearsals got underway, those feelings were buried under the onslaught of a deadline.

'There was not a night I didn't dissolve in tears alone in my room,' recalls Birch.

> There was not a day I wasn't made an example of … I was the newest skater at that point and couldn't pick up a step to save my life. I couldn't skate in a group. I couldn't do anything right. At first I felt completely outcast, but then slowly the others helped me gain a perspective. As a group we were forced to band together and be strong for one another.

Almost every day, Curry singled out a different victim. Only Starbuck and Hamill seemed immune. For the rest, humiliation and ridicule were commonplace. On one occasion, it would be Foulkes in a locker room sobbing, 'Why is it always me, why is it always me?'. On another, it would be Dodd lamenting, 'I am not cold, I am not cold. I'm a warm person.' Everyone took their medicine. No one answered back. 'I used to stand there, not shaking although the inside of me felt like a volcano,' says Lori Nichol. 'I remember crying all the time but it was like skating with an angel.'

'The moment he walked into the rink, the air changed. It got heavy and thick,' recalls Starbuck.

> We'd be goofing around and then we'd button up because we didn't know which guy was going to appear. The lost in thought guy. The 'I'm going to get someone guy'. The fun-loving guy. The beautiful artist guy. But he didn't need to be that way. We were all there for him. No one was looking to skip a rehearsal or sleep in. We were all on his team, just maybe he didn't realise it …

Every one of them felt the same. 'It was exhilarating,' remembers Hamill. 'These women were ballet dancers, and I found it really very difficult and humbling. The ugly duckling inside of me was trying to become a swan.' Out of the endless, limb-jarring hours, movement and music were coalescing into routines of finely engineered beauty. Alongside crowd-pleasers like *Tango Tango*, *Skaters Waltz* and *Faune* were numbers crafted around Gershwin, Copland, Rossini and (as a nod to modernity) Jean Michel Jarre. Not even Curry's perplexing mood swings could pollute what was coming together. 'We were all a bit serious,' explains Dotson. 'I thought what we were doing was beautiful.'

Nothing like this had ever been done before. Ignorant of the shambolic finances, Curry drew hope from Spungen's beaming optimism, and a pioneering aesthetic overrode his gloom. Living for free in Vail luxury, as the trees glowed autumn-red, more than compensated for any passing anguish. Out of the pain, and the endless rehearsals, something magical seemed to be forming. And however hard Curry lashed them – and however tempting it might be to do so – no one was packing their bags.

———

As the first snows peppered the tops of the mountains, a coach wound its way down through the tree line. Back in Vail, Curry's project had been unassailable; untested; beyond review. Ahead of his company, across the plains of Canada, were venues they had never heard of, inhabited by audiences who'd never heard of John Curry. If they could somehow survive the dodgy motels and the clueless one-night stands – if Curry could hold it together for four weeks – then anything might be possible. Away from the security blanket of the Dobson Ice Arena, however, that seemed unlikely.

The plan had been a simple one. A handful of shows in major venues – like Vancouver and Seattle – stitched together by smaller ones in towns like Kalamazoo. There would be no live band, no set and no bespoke lighting. Wardrobe would be a girl with an iron. The music would be played off a cassette and piped through loudspeakers into charmless ice hockey stadiums girded by billboards for beer and burger joints. A few solitary spotlights would follow the action. Or try to. The men would share a locker room. Likewise, the girls. Very occasionally, Curry would have space to himself. Mostly, he would not. It was the vision of hell from which he'd once fled on the 'tour of champions'. But for once, Curry's tantrums were the least of Clairmont's considerable problems.

It was a painful revelation, but outside New York John Curry was a commercial nonentity. As ticket sales bombed, panic-stricken promoters had to choose between cancelling dates, reneging on guarantees or renegotiating the price. Even as the troupe's bus snaked out of the Rockies, performances were being scrapped and the entire itinerary was being redrawn.

To drum up interest, Starbuck and Curry jetted on a crazed publicity blitz, but nothing could fill the lines of empty plastic seats; nothing could disguise the hollow sound of half-full arenas. Had the tour been properly promoted, things might have been different, but it had not been. Twenty-eight venues in around 35 days was too much. Curry's tour bus was rolling through the night into a vast continent of stone-walled indifference.

'It was horrifying,' recalls Tim Murphy.

> We had a series of dances designed for a stage and we were playing hockey rinks with no advance advertising. Zero. So we'd sometimes play to 50 people. All the bells and whistles of a big national hockey league venue and 50 people scattered around. It was a classic out of town run. Very soon we'd be thrown into the most glorious venues in the world but here we were practising in front of Coca-Cola vendors.

Ironically, the ordeal was to be the making of the John Curry Skating Company. Somewhere along the endless highway – and the nail-biting plane flights – a sturdy team ethic was displacing the patchwork of egos which had preceded it. However small the audience, however rutted the ice, each skater always performed to their maximum. Night by night, they grew tighter and more confident. 'You learned to be professional,' says David Santee. 'You learned how to get the job done.' A standing ovation from a few dozen curious farmers had value, too.

'We were in the wrong spot,' Santee adds.

> It was a really rough, tough tour. Very clearly we were a dance company on ice and yet we're in Saskatchewan in the wilds of Canada. There just wasn't the market but even so, we were

getting better and better and better. We had to go to places like Thunder Bay to draw people because it was closer to the States, but I know we played the Edmonton Coliseum and got 500 in a 17,000-seater building. Really tough.

From the beginning, all eyes had been on Curry. No one knew how he'd react. In Vail, it had been easy for him to find solitude on his terms. On the tour bus, that sanctuary would be denied him. He would also be dealing with the setback of ghostly venues, followed, at times, by nights in no-star hotels frequented by prostitutes. For the most part, however, he'd been subdued. In Windsor, Ontario, the brief appearance of Alan Bates had helped and in Vancouver, to the horror of Clairmont, he'd briefly found himself back in the company of his former lover Ron Alexander. 'I remember seeing him as we left the arena in Vancouver,' recalls Patricia Dodd.

> He was by his car at the back of the car park. He'd been to the show and we knew he wanted to be involved. John was looking at me, and he knew Ron was over there, and I knew John knew he was over there, but we just stayed walking – John and the rest of the company. I felt, we can't go back to all that again. The shouting and the fighting.

Alexander had gone for good, but Curry's resurgent feelings of paranoid isolation had not. On a bus journey to Kalamazoo he buried his head under a coat simply because no one had chosen to sit next to him. At the town's hotel, he'd stormed out of the purple-painted honeymoon suite (with mirrored ceiling) insisting the entire company be rehoused elsewhere.

Everyone could see his distress. No one knew how to help. Although Starbuck or Foulkes, might proffer a soft embrace, Curry's alienation went unabated. Nothing they did or said could ever persuade him he was liked, or that their work had any merit. It was Curry's eternal paradox; that he wanted to create but was devoured by the act of creation.

'Skaters are very touchy-feely,' explains Starbuck. 'I wanted to be that way with him, but John was not touchy-feely. If he was in a good mood I'd grab his arm and he'd link up. But mostly his body language said, Don't touch. Obviously I'm flattered if anyone thought I was closer to him than the others. The truth is we all wanted to be close with him.'

If anything, the Canada trip had made it worse. The tighter his skaters bonded, the more excluded Curry felt. And the closer the Japanese commitment loomed, the more terrified he became. 'The tour has been exhausting – nearly over,' he wrote to Nancy Streeter on a card from Manitoba. Fatigue was plucking at everyone's nerves. Were he to flee, Clairmont and Spungen's fragile house of cards would tumble. It was hardly surprising if they shielded him from their catastrophic accounts.

In Windsor alone, two out of four shows had been cancelled, and the promoters had withheld box office receipts as compensation. Although the skaters had been paid, Curry himself had received only a fraction of what he was owed. Everywhere they looked, debt was piling up. 'It was heartbreak,' says Spungen. 'It was a financial disaster,' says the tour's wardrobe supervisor, Gayle Palmieri.

> At first I didn't know if we'd ever finish that tour. I remember feeling so relieved to have got through the first performance. Then I thought, I like these people. Then soon after, I love these people. I never wanted it to stop. They were all so dedicated. And even though John could be really snarky, he loved them a lot. This was family. This was blood.

Silently, and without fanfare, Curry had proclaimed that love on almost every night of the tour. With two torn Achilles tendons, Cathy Foulkes could skate, but barely walk. 'There was no replacement for Faune,' she says. 'I never had an understudy.' Instead, Curry would carry her tenderly to the rink and nurse her through each performance. When it was over she would sink her swollen feet into a bucket of cold water. Without Foulkes, his signature piece was simply unthinkable. Without the ice, he had nowhere to go.

––––––

Whatever pain he was in, Curry's nerve had held. As the tour wound up in November 1983, there was no flight to London; no disappearing act on Fire Island. During the preceding months, Clairmont had networked so feverishly that Curry's prospects had been radically changed. Escape was no longer even an option. The following April, she had secured *Symphony On Ice* a precious run at the Royal Albert Hall in London. Three months after that – in July – the troupe would perform at New York's Metropolitan Opera House followed closely by the Kennedy Center in Washington.

These were hallowed venues. Ever since Larry Parnes had promised him Sydney Opera House, this was the level at which he had wanted to dazzle. Behind the scenes, however, lay a patchwork of transactions that would have shocked even his long-abandoned British manager. To help pay for the Canadian tour, money had been borrowed against the Royal Albert Hall advance. And although the vaunted New York Met had offered a $50k guarantee for a week of summer shows, their insistence on Dorothy Hamill's presence in the troupe had, according to Clairmont, already swallowed up half of that.

Once again, momentum was swamping logic. A show for the Met, demanding newly commissioned choreography, would require months of rehearsal. Every week Curry's company stayed together – either on the road or in Vail – was still costing a minimum $10k. Prestige was flattering, but without sustained block bookings it made little business sense to hold these skaters together. Lacking the courage to terminate Curry's ambitions – and convinced it might yet come good commercially – Clairmont and Spungen drove on.

'There's a madness that overtakes you when you have a dream,' reflects Elva. 'You think this is the time,' adds Spungen. 'It's like, we are in this. It can only happen with him. We've got to push it as far as he'll let it go to keep the company together.'

As Christmas approached, strategy again deferred to necessity. For the final two weeks of December, the company returned to Vail, where the long hours of rehearsals resumed at the resort's ice arena. Both inside and outside, a deceptive wintry calm prevailed. Curry seemed happy, cooking a Christmas Day dinner and handing out cards to his company. Four days later, on the anniversary of his father's death, he arrived at Narita airport, Tokyo, accompanied by his co-star Janet Lynn. Twenty-four hours after that, the city was rattled by an earthquake.

After his rare Christmas high, Curry sagged. Rarely had he appeared so low; or been so far from his comfort zone. As Japanese television crews and reporters swarmed around Lynn, he retreated glumly to his hotel suite. 'I have the most horrible feeling that John is going to fall apart here,' Spungen confided to Clairmont. Nerves everywhere were on edge. Once his hotel had stopped quivering, Curry had gone to the Yoyogi Stadium for dress rehearsals, where a full orchestra in tuxedos sat awaiting his instruction. No black despair could resist this. No expense had been spared. From the outside, Yoyogi was a sixties masterpiece in concrete origami. Inside, each musician sat on a glass stage embedded with glowing lights. Vast grids of spectacular spots and lasers swept the ice. Finally, he even had his own personal conductor.

Two months before, Charles Barker had been a 29-year-old freelance violinist working in New York. After a speculative invitation, he'd flown to Vancouver to watch Curry's company in action. 'It was the most beautiful thing I'd ever seen in my life,' he remembers. 'It was tableaux in motion. Unbelievable. I'd seen ballet a lot, but this was better. Faster. They could glide. I thought great, what have I fallen into? How could I even think of saying no?'

Utterly bewitched, Barker had given up a family Christmas to be in Tokyo ahead of the skaters. By the time Curry led his excited troupe out for rehearsals, he'd been working his Japanese musicians for three days. Everything was ready; from Artie Shaw to Albinoni. Standing in his tails he lifted his baton, and the overture from *William Tell* rolled out across the ice. 'I remember in that dress rehearsal looking over at JoJo and she was clearly filled with effusive delight … they all appreciated what I was doing. They all liked what I was doing.'

That night, *Symphony On Ice* was broadcast live on Japanese television. To the watching millions, it was a triumph. Behind the scenes, it had been an evening of nerve-jangling madness. As he prepared himself, 60 red roses had arrived in Curry's dressing room from a Japanese ballerina. Up in the enormous auditorium, Elva Clairmont had found herself sitting next to the Emperor of Japan's brother.

During the interval – after Janet Lynn and Curry had brought the 10,000-strong crowd to its feet – a number counter had been noticed, rising and falling on the television screen during the live broadcast. The louder people clapped, the higher the number. To enhance the spectacle, a clap-o-meter had apparently been installed in the stadium. Unknown to Curry, Lynn or Hamill, their performances were being rated according to the volume of the applause.

'It was rather humiliating, certainly for me,' recalls Hamill. 'We don't like surprises. Things like that can catch you off guard and I was very upset about it. When I think about it now, I still break into sweats. I had no business to be competing against Janet Lynn for applause.'

As tempers rose backstage, the evening forged on. Undetected by the audience, every skater was battling to make critical, tiny adjustments. Back in Vail, they had mapped out these routines on a much smaller piece of ice. Here at Yoyogi the surface was enormous and the orchestra was isolated at one end. Covering the ground – and being seen – without drifting from the beat was proving a challenge.

For the musicians, too, it was a struggle. During a solo to music by Stravinsky, the Japanese pianist had become so lost that Curry was required to improvise until the musician relocated his part. 'I also did this little solo Gershwin thing,' says Murphy. 'I recall taking the first step and I couldn't see anyone in the audience. It was about 30 feet to the first row. The pianist had a single spot and he looked a quarter-mile away. I felt like I was in outer space by myself. I had never felt so lonely.'

A few hours later, as the company's ladies sipped celebratory champagne in chiffon and silk, Curry was nowhere to be seen. With a sponsor's dinner looming, Clairmont tried calling the skater's hotel room but got no reply. Seriously alarmed, Spungen was dispatched to bang, unsuccessfully, on his door. 'David then went and got the manager to give him a key and went in to find John under his duvet, which was very scary because David thought the worst, as [John] was absolutely suicidal that night; very miserable. He wanted to end it all. A lot to do with his loneliness, I think. The troupe was a family and he was like the austere father who didn't know how to tell them he loved them.'

By Curry's darkened bedside, Spungen had found a postcard bearing the image of Jesus Christ. Alongside it, according to Clairmont's subsequent account, there was a half-empty bottle of vodka and some unspecified pills. 'I told him, "John, John, we're here for you,"' remembers Spungen. 'I would never give up on him because it was my mission to bring him through it.' Once again, Curry came round.

On 5 January, following three stunning shows in Tokyo, the circus moved on for an improbable one-off performance in Hawaii. After Japan's winter chill, the promise of Pacific sunshine visibly lifted Curry's young troupe. From Curry himself, the prospect evinced little more than the monosyllabic grunts of a man in despair.

———

His solo work appeared to be growing in emotional intensity. Away from the spotlights, however, Curry was becoming increasingly remote. Fifteen years earlier, Arnold Gerschwiler had sent Curry to a doctor, hoping to 'cure' his homosexuality. At the age of 34, the skater had mental health issues that undoubtedly merited professional treatment – but none was sought, and Curry's weakness for marijuana, far from engendering a euphoric high, was almost certainly exacerbating his naturally depressive inclination. There was also another, more tangible, reason for Curry's slump. And his name was Keith Davis.

They had met for the first time in 1982 when Davis – and his skating partner Shelley Winters – had competed in the fledgling Pro-Skate championships. As Curry began casting for his new company, the Canadian pair had been priority recruits. From the outset, Clairmont had nursed doubts about Curry's motivation. 'I had a strange feeling that John's interest was too intense to be professional,' she later wrote. 'Keith was a handsome, well-built boy … he was also deeply entrenched in a monogamous relationship with a boy from Ontario. I had a strange premonition that this attraction – if that's what it was – would end in disaster.' Even Winters had seen it coming. 'John had a different agenda when he recruited us. But he was not a stupid man, and he would not have had anyone in his company who was not good enough.'

What precisely happened between the two men is almost impossible to discern. If any letters were ever written they have not survived and Curry's infrequent correspondence with Nancy

Streeter and Heinz Wirz no longer dwelt on his private concerns. What seems clear, however, is that – after a brief and unspecific physical friendship – Davis had lost interest, but Curry had not; and that by the time they reached Japan these unrequited feelings for the muscular Davis had become dangerously obsessional.

'On that earlier Canadian tour we were in hockey rink dressing rooms with a shared bathroom,' recalls Winters.

> I'd gone in to use a mirror and John came in, devastated. Very emotional. Very upset. I went in to a stall to get some tissue and he sat on my lap and I was handing him tissues, saying, 'John you're our boss. I don't think everyone should have a relationship with the boss.' He was upset that a relationship had ended, not on his accord … He was used to getting his own way. When he was shunned, he became incredibly bitter … very mean with a lot of people.

For Winters, it presented a dilemma. Working with Curry was a skater's dream, but her loyalty to her ice partner Davis had been forged over two years of performance skating. Up to a point, she would bite her tongue, but that would prove increasingly awkward. At the Dobson Arena, during morning class, Curry would sometimes address the company with his back turned on both of them. 'A little ball of being really wicked towards us had started,' she says. And when Davis had the temerity to entertain another man in his Vail condo, Curry – communicating through Spungen – ordered the 'rival' to leave.

Behind closed doors, away from prying eyes, the two skaters were locked in a grim, private war. On one occasion, after Davis had apparently slapped his face, Curry was seen sobbing uncontrollably. On another, after Patricia Dodd had been out for a mountain drive with Davis, Curry fell into an irrational rage.

> I thought, 'Oh God, John is thinking we're having a relationship', and he blew up in floods of tears, all over Keith and the frustration. I guess I knew Keith was torturing John with this; and that I was a vehicle. But then John could get obsessed with people. One time, when Ron Alexander had been ill, I heard he put him in New York's most expensive hospital and dropped over $100,000 on his medical expenses.

With rumours spreading that Curry was threatening to fire Davis unless he slept with him, Spungen struggled to manage his star. The skater, he would say later, was like 'a windscreen wiper of volatility' and as the company deplaned at Honolulu airport, Curry's dark side was in the ascendant. Washed by Hawaiian music and garlanded with flowers, the skaters were bussed to a mid-price hotel, which he refused to enter. At the company's expense, the entire party – around 15 people – were moved to the shiny city-centre Hilton, where he vanished into a palatial room while his troupe headed for the surf. 'John wasn't partying or playing,' remembers Starbuck. 'We didn't see much of him there at all.' For Clairmont and Spungen, the perfect storm was now overhead. There were no contingencies in their funding. They were spending money they didn't have. And very soon they would be spending even more.

As the plane's cargo had been offloaded on to the runway, a generator required to make the ice had been damaged. For four days and nights, technicians had been battling to get things ready in a venue without air conditioning. Although it was still working, another day would be required to freeze enough water. The skating surface would also have to be smaller – tiny by their recent standards – and the performance had been postponed by 24 hours. In despair, Curry refused to attend rehearsals, leaving his skaters to restage all the ensemble numbers at the Blaisdell Center without him.

'I quite liked him missing rehearsals,' reflects Winters.

> We could sit on the beach or get a day off. But I knew that people were very worried because John was not answering phones and things. He was so depressed that it would not have surprised us if … well, he was hanging on by a thread and the tip of this iceberg was the relationship he couldn't have. I also think Keith had a 'friend' come visit him in Hawaii …

Perfunctorily, the company duly fulfilled their obligation. On a rectangle of half-frozen slush, Curry had temporarily forgotten his woes, and his fellow skaters had vamped with panache. 'It was nothing more than doing a bunch of circles,' says David Santee. 'It was like doing the Indy 500 basically.' As the audience filed away, a mood of weary finality infected the group. Privately, Spungen was seething over Curry's indifference to the financial strain imposed by his demands. Publicly, he said nothing, preferring to mollify rather than confront. As a result, Curry's self-pity had blossomed. In a plaintive aside, he complained that 'the skaters have each other but I'm all alone', but no one had the courage to tell him why.

'I just wish I could talk to him one more time,' says Starbuck, fighting back tears.

> You wanted to squeeze him and tell him how great he was, but then, he could turn around and be this evil person. I think he loved and hated himself too. It was like he couldn't control himself; as if he behaved in a way to make you dislike him because he felt he almost deserved that.

Hawaii was no place he wanted to stay. The rest of his company lingered on for a week's frolics, but by 6 January Curry was back in New York heading for the 'Hotel Streeter'. As quickly as the smothering gloom descended, it had vanished again. Nothing that had happened in Tokyo or Honolulu remotely threatened his plans for the Royal Albert Hall or the New York Metropolitan Opera House. At those two magnificent venues, he felt sure, people would finally bow down and embrace his vision. It would be good to be busy; better still to be back up in Vail. Somehow, New York had lost its zing and – with terrifying dread inevitability – AIDS had finally reached its fingers directly into his life.

Ten

'Moving on air'

No one yet knew how devastating AIDS would be. Although the death toll was doubling each year, the grotesque figures of the 1990s – when almost 18 million men would be affected worldwide – would have seemed fanciful a decade earlier. Even by 1984, however, the word 'epidemic' was not out of place. As John Curry reviewed his prospects, around 4,000 gay American men were contemplating death from a disease that their own president, Ronald Reagan, refused to publicly acknowledge. Numbered among them was at least one of Curry's former lovers, the New Yorker Brian Grant.

It was Grant who'd briefly prompted Curry to explore EST. It was to Grant that Curry had turned from the turbulent Ron Alexander. In return, the skater had rewarded the male model with a part in his Minskoff show for which he was wholly underqualified. Now the mild-mannered Grant was dying and the disease had reached Curry's doorstep, prompting the first in a series of panic-stricken AIDS tests. Virtually no one was told and the blood samples had been coming back negative. Nevertheless, given Curry's promiscuous track record, it was a disturbing development on the eve of his most important year since 1976.

Somehow, in the aftermath of the Pacific trip, Clairmont and Spungen had survived. However bumbling their business methodology, the skater liked both and trusted their motives. Neither exuded the corporate menace that Curry despised, and – almost without exception – his skaters adored them. 'Elva was like a mother figure to many of us,' insists Nathan Birch. 'I never heard a bad word out of her mouth,' adds Charles Barker. Curry's affection for Clairmont, however, did not extend to the company which had bankrolled Japan. Or, indeed, any private backing, if it came with corporate strings and conditions attached. Only one untested option remained. With West Nally jettisoned, Clairmont and

Spungen felt free to file for 'not-for-profit' charitable status. It was precisely what Curry wanted. 'Not for profit' would remove the canker of business intrusion, leaving them free to apply for untainted sponsorship and government grants. Credibility and creative freedom, they believed, would surely follow. But the application process would take time the trio didn't have. And faced with an onrush of work, the hollow rattle in Spungen's credit pot suddenly didn't seem to matter.

> The smart thing would have been to stop; get the paperwork in order; and only then go out to raise funds legitimately. Instead we gambled on John's name and stayed in rehearsals and that was a mistake. We had no money to support more rehearsals. We'd finished Japan. The Royal Albert Hall was in April. We'd got no money to bridge the gap. But this was our moment in time. This was the Royal Albert Hall ... and we needed $100,000 minimum.

Curry had got what he wanted. But his venture was broke. In Japan, the hotel bills alone had cost $10,000, the airfares another $7,000. Every week away from Vail, the *Symphony On Ice* Canada tour had cost $60,000. Swollen by performance rates – when ensemble skaters were paid a weekly $800 – the talent payroll alone was running at $16,000 a week.

No one seemed able to say stop. To be ready for London, Curry had demanded ten weeks' rehearsals and his skaters were already en route for the Rockies. Nor had anyone noticed that Curry's *Symphony On Ice* performance contract with West Nally didn't actually end for another two years. As Curry travelled up to Vail, Clairmont and Spungen resembled the crew of a runaway train for whom collision has become inevitable. The only issue was how far they could get – and how brilliantly they might burn – before the whole magnificent façade finally hurtled off the tracks.

Given the deep-burning crisis – and his secret health worries – Curry's demeanour in Vail was encouraging. Restored by their break, his company were working well. Despite the risk to his knees, he was also skiing more, often in the company of JoJo Starbuck, and privately he was forming plans to buy a house in the mountains. At weekends, unperturbed by heavy snowfalls, he would drive over two 11,000-foot passes to spend time with his friends Charles and Ann Cossey in Denver, along with their 4,000-strong collection of classical records.

'He had a private suite of rooms in the basement and would go out weekend nights,' recalls Charles Cossey.

> One night, as Ann and I were sitting having a cocktail before dinner, John came in and he was in complete leather drag and we laughed. We'd never seen this before. Tight leather motorcycle pants. He was obviously on his way to a motorcycle bar in Denver. Anyway Ann was laughing and I told her that it was serious drag, not funny drag. Her face changed and she looked at him and said, 'You'd better be careful'.

As April loomed, only Curry's ongoing infatuation with Keith Davis threatened the company's meticulous preparations for London. Midway through the rehearsal period, Curry had packed his bags and threatened to leave. A few weeks later, after more tears, Spungen had talked him out of firing the Canadian on the spot. Every breakdown made his job a little harder, and a lot more unpleasant. No one could be certain what would happen in England. And never had a performance mattered quite so much to the man standing alone at the heart of it.

———

Since the London Palladium, Curry's skates had rarely been seen in Britain. In the seven years since the 'fairy for the tree' slur, very little, apart from acting, had tempted him back. The Royal Albert Hall was different. Then and now, few venues in the world confer artistic status quite like it. Since its opening in 1871 the so-called 'nation's village hall' has echoed to the sounds of Bob Dylan, Eric Clapton and the legendary Proms. Not only was he ready to forgive his home country, Curry was desperate to secure validation in the capital's iconic redbrick rotunda. On April Fool's Day 1984, however, with barely two days to go, the prospects did not look good.

Ever since the Cambridge Theatre, Curry had been wrestling with a fundamental need: ice. Sometimes the surface was too small. Sometimes, as in Tokyo, it was too big. And venues like the Royal

Albert Hall were a law unto themselves. The Victorians had not designed it in anticipation of 14,000 gallons of frozen water. No one even knew if it was technically possible to freeze so much liquid in an oval auditorium; especially when only 48 hours had been allowed for the process. For all its months in preparation, Curry's London show now depended on the two men whose ice had already failed to freeze in Honolulu, Enrico Kossi, and his 21-year-old son Kevin.

For years New Yorker Enrico and his wife had been top skaters with Holiday On Ice. When they had children, they became pairs skaters, too. 'Ice was in the blood,' says Kevin. 'I was basically my sister's forklift truck.' As a hobby, Enrico made portable skating rinks – he'd laid the ice for Toller Cranston's Broadway show – so when Kevin developed an appetite for mechanical engineering, a family business was born. By 1983, it was the younger Kossi who was wrestling with its imponderables. 'In Hawaii I went without sleep so long I fell asleep at my steering wheel on a red light,' he jokes. A year later, he'd designed a bespoke system precisely for Curry's needs. The Royal Albert Hall was to be its first field trial.

To Curry and his fellow skaters, Kevin was 'the iceman'. As the clock ticked down, he would need every ounce of cool he possessed. Into a watertight oval 'swimming pool' he laid eighteen miles of custom-trimmed tubing. On top of this – for 36 hours – he continuously sprayed cold water, which became ice through a process of heat transfer powered by a generator. As the chemical refrigerant Freon flowed through the piping, the water temperature supposedly dropped. Once the ice was 1.5 inches thick, the skaters could use it. Any less than that and their blades would rupture the pipes.

As Kossi had discovered in Honolulu, this was a fledgling science. 'There's a million pieces which fit together and if one piece is broken or missing, you're in trouble.' In London, the problem was far bigger than a dud component. Kossi's system ran on 220 volts and 16khz. The generator supplied by the Royal Albert Hall worked on a different standard.

By the time an alternative supply was found, critical hours had been lost. Instead of rehearsing with Charles Barker and the Royal Philharmonic Orchestra, Curry and his skaters decamped with their audio-cassettes to Richmond Ice Rink. And with Kossi floundering in a pool of slush, there'd been no chance to dry-run the overhead lighting. 'I heard a lot of age criticism of Kevin Kossi,' recalls Barker. '"He's too young." "He doesn't know how to deal with people." That sort of stuff. I thought it was just physics holding him back. That, and time.'

By early evening on 2 April, Kossi hadn't slept for days. Even as people took their seats, hushed by the gleaming disc of frosted white, 'the iceman' could be seen spraying water across patches where his pipes were still clearly visible. Backstage, Curry was displaying masterful restraint. As the minutes ticked away, instead of tantrums he'd delivered an inspirational speech urging courage on a dangerous surface, as Tim Murphy confirms:.

> When situations got tense, he really was a leader. I remember him speaking to us that night. If John said, 'Jump off a bridge' we'd have said, 'There's a higher one up the road, let's jump off that one.' His pep talk that night was very sweet. We knew we were going out there and I remember turning away from it and thinking he's crazy. Half of that ice wasn't ice.

At 7.30 p.m., with Kossi still frantic, Curry stepped out in front of 4,500 people and pleaded for patience. 'As he left the stage,' remembered Clairmont, 'the audience rose to their feet and applauded him.' Thirty minutes later, the waiting was over. As Barker lifted his baton, the theatre fell into complete darkness. Gently blown in by the opening bars of Alexander Glazunov's *The Seasons*, a cluster of nine skaters, each dressed in white, materialised under radiant columns of light.

Across the Royal Albert Hall there was a stunned intake of breath. Gone was the gaudy vaudeville of the Larry Parnes show. Curry's new work was pure and clean, and its opening salvo – appropriately called *Glides* – showcased a company of disciples entirely at one with its master's voice. As the spots rotated across the skating surface, however, something else was becoming abundantly clear. In some places the ice wasn't ice, it was sand. And, in others, the pipes were now within easy reach of a misplaced toe pick.

'I remember being in a goofy number I loved called *Rodeo* – figure-skating cowboys,' says Murphy. 'It was the closest to an ice show thing that Curry ever did. Anyway I'd done a trick and turned round and saw one of the skaters gliding towards the exit … his blade had come off and was hanging on by one screw and behind him was a fountain of purple water spurting through the air.'

As the evening progressed, the surface deteriorated. After landing in slush, David Santee broke an ankle that went undiagnosed for months. During *Glides*, there were so many leaks, people thought it was an effect. 'The lighting in that number was blue anyway,' says Starbuck. 'Then it goes bing … blue glycol … then bing … more blue glycol … so that suddenly it looked like a special blue fountain for this one number.'

Amidst the carnage, there were moments of chilling beauty. Skating alone to the adagio from *The Nutcracker*, Curry had evoked memories of 1976. Performing with Patricia Dodd and Mark Hominuke to a wistful Erik Satie piece, he had so utterly transcended the chemical mayhem that no one noticed Kevin Kossi, a lone figure in black, trying to patch around the edges of his failing surface.

Two hours later, after the climactic *William Tell* ensemble finale, the Royal Albert Hall rose to its feet and Curry ushered the weary 'iceman' on stage to take a bow. 'Curry's ovation,' wrote Jack Tinker in the next morning's *Daily Mail*, 'was a fitting tribute to his inspiration – and in these lamentable circumstances – his courage.' Almost without exception, every British newspaper concurred. 'A show of exceptional standard on a meagre, pitted and waterlogged surface' was the verdict of the *Sunday Times*. 'When the conditions are right this will be a gripping and decidedly classy ice show,' added Charles Spencer in the *Evening Standard*.

If there was a carp, it was a familiar one. Not everyone warmed to Curry's highbrow fare. 'At times the effect is almost stiflingly tasteful,' noted one critic. 'I occasionally longed for a dash of unashamed vulgarity.' Others clearly felt the same. One of the evening's biggest hits had been performed, not to the classical strains of the Royal Philharmonic but to a recording of Jean Michel Jarre's pulsating populist electro-rock. More uncomfortably, the reviews had picked up on the performance of Keith Davis and Shelley Winters. 'A dizzyingly fast and sensual pas de deux full of dangerous lifts and spins,' said one. Sadly, the plaudits would help neither of them. A fortnight later, both had been sacked.

After the alarms of opening night, the ice behaved. Every seat had been sold, and every night that followed was a London triumph. No other show in town could touch it. Princess Margaret had gone backstage with her compliments. Alan Bates, too. 'It was amazingly wonderful,' says Penny Malec. 'If you were at that show you saw what he had always had in mind. Vindication is the word. He and JoJo especially were remarkable. From him, she got class. From her, he got a fabulous sensuality.' After the closing night party, however, Curry's famously brittle euphoria had vanished.

According to Clairmont, Keith Davis had turned up 'with his Canadian friend'. A few hours later, Curry was calling her, insisting that both Davis and Winters be fired that night. Shelley Winters had sensed it coming. 'In London John was unhappy. Very unhappy,' she says. Despite a chronic bronchial infection, she'd skated every night at the Royal Albert Hall and been rewarded with cold backstage indifference. 'He could not have made a person feel worse,' she says. When the run finished, Winters – along with the rest of Curry's skaters – had been given a week off before flying to a bizarre engagement in Dubai. Twenty-four hours before they were due to travel, the company regrouped in a London hotel.

'John then called and said that when I was sick at the Albert Hall, I'd somehow snubbed him,' recalls Winters.

> I said that wasn't true, I'd been sick. He said, 'You are lying'. Now that's not a good thing to say to me. I don't kiss ass too well. When he was being mean and belligerent, I couldn't ooh and goo over John to feed his sadness; his depression. I said, 'No, you are wrong.' I didn't curse or swear. I said it very matter-of-factly. He said, 'You are not going to Dubai; not in my company, baby.' And then hung up the phone.

A few hours later, as he stood in line at Heathrow airport, Keith Davis had been given the same message. 'I told him, John can't look at you,' says Spungen. 'He can't have you in the company.' It was the gutless finale to a squalid business from which only Davis and Winters emerged with credit. Both had been treated disgracefully. Both were owed money. Both would struggle for months with the consequences. 'I was like blacklisted – blackballed. For 14 months

I didn't have a job,' says Winters. 'No one would hire us. It was like we'd dropped off the earth as professionals.'

After the shock came righteous anger. After that, merely empty frustration. When the pair pursued a legal action for wrongful dismissal and sexual harassment, somehow their heart wasn't in it. 'Keith's father worked in a car factory; that's a manly place to be,' says Winters. 'He didn't want to make things difficult for his dad.' Everyone knew the company's cupboard was bare. 'They were bankrupt. There was nothing left. It had already cost me more than I'd have got back. So eventually we cut our losses and that was that.'

Meanwhile, the John Curry Skating Company was on a jumbo jet to Dubai. From their first day, every member had lived in fear of being sacked. Now they had seen it happen. As their plane roared south, Curry's demeanour seemed horribly inappropriate. 'He was in a radiantly good mood sitting with Cathy and talking animatedly to everyone,' recalled Clairmont. 'He seemed to be enormously relieved.' With Keith Davis disposed of, he could relax. He was in control. London had embraced him. But he would never skate publicly there again.

No one seemed quite sure why they were in Dubai. John Curry was a nonentity there; skating shows were unheard of; and a two-night engagement in the desert scarcely merited a 3,400-mile flight, notwithstanding the five-star hotel and tax-free shopping. For Clairmont, it offered priceless experience for the company. For Curry, it was merely a money-spinning curtain-raiser for the New York Met. Just like Honolulu, however, the trip's brevity would be leavened by moments of surreal comic madness.

Upon arrival, the Ministry of Culture had decreed that, to conform to strict religious codes, the male and female skaters would have to perform separately. After an emergency audition, the ban had been lifted, with the exception of a single sultry moment from *Tango Tango*. 'At one point I'd pull him towards me, and we'd be nose to nose touching, glaring at each other's eyes,' explains Starbuck. 'That had to come out of the show. We just looked at each other instead of kissing.'

By early May, Curry and his party were back in the United States. A few weeks later, the skater slipped quietly into a New York hospital for arthroscopic surgery on his knee. While he recovered at Nancy Streeter's apartment, Clairmont and Spungen were in a downtown office battling to hold their company together. Long-term, the prognosis suddenly looked bright. Dubai had paid for itself and ahead of them were bookings in New York, Washington, Boston, Chicago and Scandinavia.

Short-term, however, their finances were terrifying. With no capital reserve, Curry's insatiable creative needs were swallowing cash they didn't have. And yet still nobody wanted to let it go. 'As deep in debt as we might have been, it was all full speed ahead,' says Spungen. 'We'd said we'd get this for him and we were going to get it. There was no stopping us. At the Royal Albert Hall, we'd seen something that had never been seen before. And now, unfortunately, something that has never been seen since.'

All the time, more mouths needed feeding. Not only had Curry replaced Shelley and Winters with a new couple – Bill Fauver and Lea-Ann Miller – he'd also added another four skaters to the troupe. For the first time, Curry's personal resources had been drawn into the maelstrom. After the near-disaster in London, he'd demanded that the company acquire an ice-making plant, a necessity he'd funded through his own company, Frozen Assets. 'When we were in this limbo between profit and non-profit, John had come to us and said that if we ever couldn't make payroll, just let him know … After that, I know we went to him on a couple of occasions to pay people.'

Only a patchwork of loans and promises was holding his project together. £6,000 was still outstanding from the BBC for televising the London show. From a sale of their stake in Pro-Skate, there had been an $8,000 advance, and, following the unexpected arrival of a Diners Card, there was new life in David Spungen's creaking credit. With barely two months before opening night, however, the New York Met's $50,000 guarantee was looking woefully thin. 'We needed help before the financial weight of the venture collapsed on top of us,' noted Clairmont. But help meant staff and staff cost money. Meanwhile, Curry, still relatively sheltered from the stirring storm, mustered his troops back in the mountains.

There had been changes since the winter. To ease Curry's load – and to create a firewall between him and his skaters – a creative manager had been appointed. Before taking the job, Rob McBrien had been a popular teacher at New York's Sky Rink. In Vail, his daily mission was to motivate, organise and inspire, a task he approached with such industrious positivity that the entire troupe responded in kind. He was also the only person – possibly apart from Cathy Foulkes – who could calm Curry down. 'They'd spend a lot of time with each other. They'd read plays together,' says Nathan Birch. 'He was an unsung hero in this process.'

Alongside daily notes for each skater, McBrien would launch morning class with inspirational printed exhortations. 'The highest standards only.' 'Don't settle for less for yourself or the Company.' 'Dig into this fabulous, fun work.' If it was cheesy, no one seemed to mind. After Curry's seesaw moods, everyone clung to McBrien's cheerful disposition like a life raft.

Between them all they had eight weeks. Once again, it had not started well. Behind the scenes, unknown to Curry, the local Marriott had hit Spungen with an unpaid $10,000 bill. At the Dobson Ice Arena, a power failure had robbed them of their first week's rehearsals, a crisis McBrien had calmly averted with a week of aerobics and dance. Whenever Curry wobbled, his new deputy would step in and defuse. With so much at stake, Curry's fragility seemed more apparent than ever. And to newcomers like 21-year-old Adam Lieb, the sight of it would prove both inspiring and deeply shocking:

> He would go to an anorexic and tell her she was fat. He would go to the best athlete in the group and tell him he was not worthy. He would go to the most balletic woman and tell her she was a hopeless dyke. He'd find where you lived and then he'd tear your house down. He wanted you to feel the hurt he was hurting inside. He lived by torment. He was in pain. He was adept at speaking without saying a word. Just his facial inflections could rip you to shreds.

Although the men were not spared, Curry's women suffered the most. For some of them it would require an indifference to self on an almost heroic scale. To earn his respect, each was prepared to endure belittlement and abuse. But since nothing damaged their belief in Curry himself, the aura of a minor cult prevailed. Publicly, disloyalty was impossible. Privately, even the anger and tears could not diminish their faith. Whether or not Curry knew this – and played deliberate mind games to raise performance levels – is unknown. What is certain is that by July 1984 Curry's skating was attaining new highs just as his behaviour was fathoming record lows. Like almost everyone else, Adam Lieb saw no reason to walk away:

> Those that suffered grew because of it. We were only scared because we were begging for approval. When the one that holds the stick that measures your greatness is John Curry, you go with it. All we wanted was daddy's approval. Curry made me a better human being, a better skater, better in every way. It was an epiphany. I owe him a lot.

Patricia Dodd owed him a lot, too; but few were so raddled with doubt as she. A friend since the late sixties, she craved his endorsement, but this was never fully reciprocated. On paper, it seemed unfair. No one in the group had known him longer. Apart from Cathy Foulkes, no one else conformed to his slender ballerina ideal and even she could not match Dodd's grace on the ice. Curry's reward had been her nightly solo, *Blessed Spirit*, skated to music by Gluck, but that alone could not quell Dodd's anxieties; any more than her faultless dedication could guarantee Curry's affection.

'Patricia was always exemplary,' says JoJo Starbuck.

> She was always right on the train with him. She always followed everything he said and could always do it. She was that precise. Once she did an exercise with the whole cast watching thinking how brilliant it was, and he just unleashed the wrath of John Curry on her; berated her; belittled her; and she started sobbing and all of us had our jaws dropping and he told her to get off the ice and out of his face.

For 20-year-old Canadian-born Lori Nichol, Curry's behaviour towards Dodd became her crucial daily barometer. 'If he was being mean to Patricia, then you knew he was in a very bad way,' she explains. Few of the girls needed this weathervane quite like Nichol. Nobody else would be so relentlessly abused by their leader. When Curry recruited her in 1983, she'd been living 'hand to mouth' working double shifts at a pancake house. She'd been just 17 when she had a daughter. Coming to Vail, she remembers, had been 'overwhelming and magical' and yet by July 1984 she alone had become the unhappy focus of Curry's morbid obsession with weight.

During the Canadian tour, Curry had insisted Nichol be weighed once a week. As they prepared for the New York Met – according to Clairmont – Curry had upped that to once a day. To the young skater, this ritual humiliation was mystifying.

> At that time, I was just 9 per cent body fat and I was very muscular strong. Not a typical ballerina shape. Not a ripped body like Cathy or Patricia, but he knew that when he hired me ... It was all very difficult for me. I came from a difficult background and needed that job desperately. One moment he could be so cruel. But the next moment he would compliment me in a very beautiful way and that would make me feel OK for a bit longer.

As their work progressed – as hip choreographers and designers flew out to Vail – the circle of witness to Curry's deteriorating behaviour expanded. One of them, Lar Lubovitch, was a 41-year-old from Chicago, with his own Manhattan dance company, and a dazzling reputation for innovative choreography. Working with the Englishman had been a challenge he could not resist. 'He opened a door that was inspiring for me,' he says. 'Curry was a wonderfully beautiful man.' Nevertheless, Lubovitch was still horrified by what he saw up in the Rockies. 'Tremendous, spontaneous cruelty,' he says. 'I witnessed it many times.'

On one occasion, while rehearsing a solo piece, Curry had launched into a screaming fit ('like some out-of-control infant'), which continued until Rob McBrien shook him by the shoulders and told him to stop. On another, after spotting Lori Nichol in a cafeteria with a lunch tray, Curry had 'come in like a steamroller, grabbed the food off her plate and thrown it to the floor', an incident she no longer remembers ('I blocked things out later to move on with my life,' she explains).

Away from the ice – where Curry's balletic instincts thrilled him – nothing Lubovitch saw endeared the young choreographer to the brooding skater. 'He was very snide with a sneer towards most things.' He also found him to be a bully, and a crushing snob.

> He was a person who had two ways of behaving. One for people who had advantages to bring him; the rich and the famous. Another for those who he basically considered his underlings, his servants; the people who served his purpose from the bottom side. He was not nice to those people at all. He could turn away from one of those influential people where he was being sweetness and light and become a demon, aiming some awful barb at one of his skaters ... He looked to be extremely manipulative, using abusiveness as a means of control ... and yet there was this other side where he'd become very needy, but at what level of consciousness he was operating, who can say?

Out on the rink, Lubovitch and Curry worked well. Together they had fashioned an elegant duet – *Tilt-a-Whirl* – which Curry would perform subsequently in New York with Dorothy Hamill. There was also an ensemble piece set to the music of J. S. Bach. 'Although he could be unacceptably and wildly temperamental while working, he never was with me,' recalls Lubovitch.

> I indicated by my particular gestalt that it would not be permissible ... In my experience, skaters are very childlike, even into adulthood. There's a level of responsibility they haven't reached because they've been told every move to make in their life since they were children. Curry probably had very little interaction with his peers away from the ice. He was socially underdeveloped.

Few people had ever analysed Curry with such lacerating acuity. Or observed him under such ferocious pressure. At the Royal Albert Hall, Curry had been performing to a home crowd that wanted him to succeed. In the build-up to London, no one had asserted a scintilla of artistic control. In New York – and its formidable Metropolitan Opera House – the backdrop was very different. The mere presence of Lar Lubovitch in Vail was a clue to just how different. For its $50,000, as well as Dorothy Hamill, the Met was insisting on three new works integrated within two alternating programmes of work.

Out in Vail, Curry's skaters lived with the daily consequences of this staggering workload. 'What he was producing was towering,' insists Tim Murphy.

> He would start on a new dance in the morning and it would be finished by the evening. It was just amazing. My artistic soul was very happy, but we had a lot of pressure. Daily pressure. We were pushed to our limit every single day. It was like living inside a blender. Things happened so fast and you'd think you were going to punch someone and then you'd see the most beautiful thing you'd ever seen in your life. It was like that every day.

Creatively, Curry was insatiable. After all the false starts, this was the work, and these were the skaters, he'd always wanted. As preparations continued, however, the vaporous foundations of his magnificent enterprise were dissolving. 'Costs were escalating rapidly. Many through circumstances beyond our control,' said Clairmont. A new and pivotal figure had also entered the story. The 'dragon lady' to some, 'fucking scary' to others, she was called Jane Hermann and her presence would send shock waves through the team that had finally brought Curry to the brink.

Jane Hermann was, by any reckoning, a Manhattan alpha-female legend. 'I'm actually a marshmallow,' she once said of herself. If so, she hid her soft centre well. With the pugnacity of a New York cab driver and the business acumen of a Wall Street shark, she worked as Director of Presentations at the Metropolitan Opera House. During the summer, when the opera company toured, it was her job to fill the venue for 16 weeks with work that lived up to her establishment's peerless reputation. No venue took less unnecessary risk or pursued quality with more attention to detail. And absolutely no one took fewer prisoners – or drove a harder bargain – than Jane Hermann. Finally, even the redoubtable Elva Clairmont – battle-hardened by Cranston, Cousins and Curry – had run into a wall.

The two women had met in Manhattan six months before. '[She] had a commanding presence and a striking resemblance to Lauren Bacall,' noted Clairmont. 'Full of crap' was Hermann's rumbustious verdict on Elva, delivered some years later. After a series of meetings, the New Yorker had taken full control. Although the Met had previously deemed ice shows to be vulgar piffle, they would accept Curry for a week, subject to certain conditions. Dorothy Hamill was one of them. 'It was very risky,' admits Hermann. 'But I was a gutsy dame at that time.' She was also adept at minimising that risk and, as Nureyev's American manager, attuned to the fickleness of high-maintenance artists.

In April, Hermann had flown to watch Curry perform in London. Shortly afterwards, alarmed by his threadbare team, she once again exerted her authority. 'Curry had no management,' she says. 'It was just a little pick-up company ... the fact that Elva got as far as she did is much to her credit, but she was an amateur.' Having secured Curry's company a run at Washington's Kennedy Center directly after the Met, Hermann urged Clairmont to recruit a costume designer, general manager and production supervisor of her choosing. They in turn hired 'a veritable army of people', requiring further credit to keep the venture afloat. 'Every asset of David's and mine had already been put into the pot,' admitted Elva. 'We had come too far to turn back now.'

There was reason for hope. Curry's eight New York performances had sold out their 34,000 tickets within a week. Demand was so high that an extra show had been bolted on to the run. A few days before opening night – scheduled for Tuesday 24 July – the company flew in from Colorado, setting up camp in the Mayflower Hotel, while Curry made for the 'enchanted bedroom' of the Streeter apartment. Everything – as always – had been rehearsed to the point of exhaustion, and Curry's mood had steadied.

Over that summer weekend, with the asphalt softening in the heat, every New York newspaper was talking about him. Never before had he commanded such interest. As Curry fever built, at around three o'clock on the Sunday morning, Kevin 'the iceman' Kossi trundled his bespoke ice-making equipment, with its 24 miles of tubing, into the Met. By late Monday afternoon he was in the thick of a full-scale disaster. For the first time in its history, an opening night at the Opera House was about to be cancelled. 'There was a lot of blue glycol fluid that needed to be mopped up,' Hermann drily informed the *New York Times*. But it was much more complicated than that.

From the moment he entered the theatre, Kossi had been in trouble. By some calamitous oversight – of the sort that made Hermann's blood boil – the young engineer had no union card and was promptly enveloped by stagehands ordering him to stop. 'It was very scary,' he recalls. 'I couldn't touch anything. I couldn't even show them how to do it. I could describe what they had to do, but I could not physically demonstrate it.'

As the hours passed, Kossi pressed gamely on. Even as he did so, the nightmare darkened. To help ease the company's financial crisis, he'd sacrificed high-quality couplings for budget rubber hoses and clamps. As the system came under pressure, the joints blew apart. Not far behind them was Jane Hermann. 'They didn't realise the Met was a union house? I must admit – *mea culpa* – I never worked with anyone that dumb.'

Had he needed more publicity, Curry now had it. As the news outlets swooped, Curry and his skaters convened at the venue to watch developments. 'He was so joyful to be there,' remembers Foulkes. 'He wanted us to take it all in.' In the orchestra pit, conductor Charles Barker was rehearsing his musicians. In every direction stretched a vast pool of slowly hardening ice. 'All the way back to Tenth Avenue,' says Hermann, 77 feet wide and almost 100 feet long. None of them had ever seen anything quite so beautiful. 'I went out to the lip of the stage and started singing an aria from *Madame Butterfly*,' recalls JoJo Starbuck. 'I can't sing but I wanted to be able to say that I'd sung at the Met.'

As disappointed ticket-holders were turned away, a mood of happy fatalism prevailed. Just as in London, Curry remained calm. Outside, where expectant crowds should have been milling, members of the company mustered uneasily in their 'street clothes'. 'We were sulking,' says Murphy. 'But Jane Hermann said, "You guys really should not be here … let's go drink a million dollars' worth of champagne." So we had the opening night party without the opening night.' Later that evening, at cocktail parties all around Manhattan, skaters mingled with wealthy patrons, hoping – as Starbuck put it – that 'if we ate, drank and were merry, they'd be gracious and come back'.

It was supposed to have been John Curry's night to remember. So far, it had been like the *Titanic* with the ice on the inside of the ship. The following day, 24 hours behind schedule, it was finally ready for his skates.

———

It was, said Lar Lubovitch, 'one of the most unique and superlative events I have witnessed'. As the Met emptied, on Wednesday 25 July 1984, he would not have found a single dissenting voice. From the opening bars of Glasunov, as Curry's white-clad skaters floated towards them in a skein of limbs, over 4,000 people had been rendered mute. Among them were Nancy Streeter, Heinz Wirz and his former coach Alison Smith. Even in the dressing rooms, they had felt the silence. 'I'm standing backstage at the fucking Metropolitan Opera House,' remembers wardrobe supervisor Gayle Palmieri, 'and I heard the audience absolutely catch its breath and I thought "Holy Shit".'

In front of his orchestra, Charles Barker had sensed it, too.

> This was the vision. This was what it should be. I had the best seat in the house and I watched everything I possibly could. The light was so different; so beautiful. You could see this tableau of figures emerge from the wings and glide to the other side of the stage. It was mind-blowing. Also, most big stages go back 60 feet. This went 100 feet back to the firewall. I saw David Santee skate past the 60-foot barrier and I thought, 'No, this isn't happening. That space doesn't exist'. It was scintillating. Breathtaking. For the first time, everything John had wanted made sense.

For the first time, too, Curry's fusion of moods and textures appeared flawless. Humour and verve had found their place alongside austerity and angst. Athleticism and grace – as he had promised in 1976 – had delivered an icebound alternative to ballet. From Philip Glass to Igor Stravinsky and Leonard Bernstein, Curry's encyclopaedic musical brain had plundered a soundtrack for all ears. 'This was a dream of dancing,' gushed the *New York Times*. Nothing about it merited a negative. Not the lighting. Not the costumes. Not the prevailing sense of artistry and exquisite good taste. And for everyone who witnessed it, one moment stood out above all. As from now on, it always would.

Like Lubovitch, Brooklyn-born choreographer Eliot Feld had never worked with a skater before. After a call from Jane Hermann, he'd flown to the Rockies with a suitcase of warm clothing and a mournful 12-minute Ravel composition on a cassette. Five days later – during which Feld had fractured his hand in a fall – the two men had created 'Moon Skate'.

'John was so sublimely musical,' explains Feld.

> It was the easiest most natural piece that I ever did, and at the end – when we skated it right through – he put his head down and I could see he was sobbing. I asked was he hurt. He said no, something had happened. Something in the music. Something in the dance. Something which had evoked some feelings impossible to describe, and I thought, 'He's in touch with the fucking muses, man'.

Alone, under an elliptical splash of lunar light, Curry had unveiled their creation at the Met. For many onlookers, its ravishing intimacy would prove almost impossible to watch. From the wings, fellow skaters looked on and wept. Nothing they had seen had ever been so raw or so autobiographical. Wearing a loose-fitting, all-white outfit, Curry moved to music of such plaintive simplicity that every steely scrape of his blades could be heard. There were no jumps, no pyrotechnics. At times downcast, at times pleading, his face wet with tears, Curry appeared as if cast adrift on a distant planet. 'He is a lone figure on a glacial plane,' wrote Anna Kisselgoff in the *New York Times*. 'But he is also a seeker [who] seems to be moving on air.'

Alongside his 16 skaters, Curry had shaken the Met to its foundations. 'If dancing is the way angels walk,' wrote one critic, 'then skating is the way angels dance.' 'A new art form is here,' affirmed another. Sadly, not everyone felt lauded. 'There were some not terribly flattering reviews about me,' recalls Dorothy Hamill. 'For everyone else they were great.' It was an unduly harsh self-critique. According to the *New York Times* her solo work had displayed the 'poignant sense of a just slightly tamed colt'. But for Hamill, whose star billing had made it hard to fully integrate with the other skaters, that wasn't enough.

I'm a little on the larger side – not a Cathy Foulkes waif – so there was this delicate piece of music and a costume that didn't suit me – and I felt the way I felt. Not like a swan or a dancer on ice. It made me feel more inadequate; that I wasn't up to that calibre; that I didn't have any business in this theatre ... The choreography was beautiful. I just couldn't perform it at the level I wanted to. It had given me a whole new love of skating, but I wanted to be beautiful and not just an athlete. I wanted to be an artist.

For different reasons, others were suffering, too. As the week-long run reached its last night in a sky-burst of bouquets and glory-grams, Curry's creation was collapsing horribly from within. Over coffee in the Mayflower Hotel, Tim Murphy – one of Curry's most intelligent young skaters – had informed Clairmont and Spungen that he was quitting after their final New York performance. Once the shock subsided – 'he was like one of our children,' said Elva – Murphy agreed to hang on for a few more weeks. He was also asked not to share his bombshell with Curry.

Even today, Murphy refuses to divulge the specific reasons for his decision. Like the entire company, he'd been shocked by the brutal treatment of Davis and Winters. Up in Vail, he'd also been frazzled by Curry's relentless volatility. Unlike most people, however, he'd never felt constrained to speak his mind. 'There was never a time when someone was not in the doghouse,' he explains. 'But I just don't let people speak to me that way. I never had and I never will ... also, I was young and full of dreams.' Beyond that, Murphy is saying nothing.

For Clairmont, his news was cruelly timed. Just a few hours before – by her own account – she had met Jane Hermann, expecting to hear that Curry's triumph had boosted their $50,000 fee. If her sums were right, the Met's net receipts – including the extra show – had exceeded $800,000 and it seemed reasonable to request some sort of bonus. Hermann couldn't see why. 'They quoted a fee. We paid them a fee,' insists Hermann. 'The complete financial risk was mine. If she didn't make as much as she expected, tough titties. What's that got to do with the price of eggs? It's hard to believe I even got away with $50,000 but if I did ... anyway, in normal circumstances they'd have had to pay me to come into the Met.'

'I was dumbstruck,' Clairmont wrote later. 'It was almost inconceivable but it seemed we had managed to sustain a loss on the Met engagement.' As with Murphy's resignation, Curry was not to be told. Anything to stave off the next crisis. Anything to keep him moving forwards. One day soon, they reasoned, the money would surely start to flow.

———

As usual, Curry had taken very little pleasure from success. All he could see when something was over was its flaws. And in those times, all he really wanted to do was to stop. Downcast by the need to start again in Washington, Curry pleaded with Clairmont for release. 'He said, "We've done it now, we don't need to do it any more, let's set up the skating school". I said, "John, no. We can't do that. We borrowed money to go into the Met. We have to keep going." And that was the moment that he started to get a little bit resentful.' All he had ever truly wanted was for London and New York to recognise him. And with their validation secured, Curry's motivation faltered.

There was, however, one dangerous consolation. Among his expanded troupe, Curry had found a place for Shaun McGill, a free-spirited young skater from Mississauga, Canada. ('I'd go out with him to a bar and reel him back with five women attached,' remembers Adam Lieb.) During rehearsals in Vail, Curry and the 21-year-old McGill had embarked on an affair. Everyone had seen it coming. Everyone regarded it with alarm. 'Shaun was like my brother,' says Nathan Birch. 'I remember saying to him, "Please be careful here" and that had nothing to do with disease. It had everything to do with not being a skater in the company and having a relationship with the boss.'

As with Ron Alexander, Curry's affair with McGill would be marked by extremes. Private off-ice turbulence frequently spilled out publicly in rehearsals. 'I always thought it wouldn't end right,' says Murphy, who, alongside Birch, had formed a comradely triumvirate with McGill, which was suddenly broken. For the first time, factions were affecting the male half of his company. To Bill Fauver – the replacement for Keith Davis – McGill was 'a player emboldened by his proximity to John'. 'He knew he'd be taken care of as one of John's friends. He was a pretty good party animal and

I think he was kind of cynical in this process. There was John's inner circle, and there was everyone else.'

It was a horrible way for the Met to end. At a celebration soirée thrown by Patricia Dodd in her cavernous Greenwich Village loft, Curry had been the first to leave. Beneath the happy clamour, sour undercurrents were flowing. In huddled asides, Clairmont pleaded with Murphy for continued secrecy, despite which Nathan Birch had somehow heard the news. 'I was devastated,' he recalls. 'How could I lose my best friend?' 'At that time it was like there was a cloud following us,' says Murphy. Less than one week later, in Washington, DC, it would be hovering over them again; a little blacker even than before.

If New York's air had been baking, Washington was on fire. Outside the mausoleum-like Kennedy Center, the midday sidewalks were too hot to touch. Inside, Kevin Kossi was feeling optimistic. With 24 hours to go, despite 100 per cent humidity levels, his ice looked set to be ready for opening night. At two on the final morning – with the ice already an inch thick – he headed for a catnap in a backstage dressing room.

Three hours later, lightning had struck twice. While he dozed, a giant lighting tower had mysteriously toppled over, rupturing pipes and gouging a deep crater in the ice. As dawn broke, Clairmont and Spungen arrived to review the damage in a state of stunned disbelief. Each of them knew it was worse than a hole in the skating surface. Apart from a sold-out opening show, ticket sales had been slow. Only the night before, they'd given away $5,000 worth of tickets to 'the cream of Washington society', hoping donations would flood back in return. They had not. After a grim telephone check, Clairmont had also confirmed that, as at the Met, her company was operating without insurance.

Amidst the despair, it was inevitable that union sabotage would be blamed, but it was a distraction without any real proof. Only one thing was absolutely certain: for the second time in three weeks, Curry's opening night had been cancelled, and yet another five-figure sum had been wiped off his company's income. 'Elva was like a mum to me,' says Kossi. 'When we missed that opening, I wept on her shoulder.'

Although humiliating, the 'bad' publicity proved beneficial. While Kossi rebuilt his ice, ticket sales boomed. By Wednesday evening, almost every seat had been sold and Curry's creation was the toast of Washington's beautiful people. At the delayed opening night party, the city's celebrities and power-brokers had crammed into the Ritz-Carlton for a glimpse of the hypnotic English skater. 'John stood in the middle of the crowd looking lost,' recalled Clairmont. '[He] turned to the imposing man standing next to him and held out his hand. "I'm John Curry," he said. The man took his hand. "I'm General David Jones, Chairman of the Joint Chiefs of Staff. What do you do?"'

A week later, the company arrived in Boston for a run at the city's sumptuous Wang Center for Performing Arts. During the 'roaring Twenties' its marble columns and chandeliers had made it a cultural epicentre for big band music and vaudeville. During the 1980s, however, ice skating was not such a draw. Advance ticket sales had been as sluggish as Curry's energy. After finally learning that Tim Murphy was to quit following this Boston run, he'd vanished to his room. Among his skaters, the pioneering delirium of the Met was already bleeding away.

'We knew we were in trouble,' says Dita Dotson.

> We were having to postpone; people were having to be paid; and you can't do that if you are not generating funds. By Washington, we were all aware there would have to be repercussions. I think we all realised the momentum was gone; that some of the heart that John had in it was gone; and that he was no longer happy doing what he was doing. His moodiness increased and made it more unpleasant than pleasant. We just looked at it as a bad period that hopefully we would overcome.

As Curry brooded, Kossi's work was proceeding with a smile. Since the Met, he'd bought new couplings and joined the necessary trade union. He'd also formed a tight bond with the male skaters, and a close friendship with Cathy Foulkes. Back in London – after the initial alarms – he'd even spent each evening under the stage in an eighteen-inch gap listening to the skaters above. 'They were channelling angelic energy into an art form,' he explains. 'Every night was like I'd died and gone to heaven on mushrooms or something.' In Boston, for once, the ice had gone in 'like clockwork' and, with a day to spare, Kossi's work seemed done.

Shortly before nightfall – some 24 hours before Curry's opening performance – an electric storm plunged the entire city into darkness. As emergency lights flickered on, Kossi's ice began to melt. Unless he could find a generator, Boston's historic theatre would soon be standing in a lake. After frantic calls, suitable plant had been located at an army base in Maine, to which Kossi set off courtesy of an obliging television news crew and their helicopter. By dawn, he had the equipment in place. Before Curry was awake, the ice was returning to normal. Another near-disaster had been averted.

Just as in Washington, Boston's curiosity had been stirred. Over their six nights, houses had built, and the company's final performance was sold out. As he always did, Curry had performed with a blistering intensity. Whatever burden he carried still slipped mysteriously away once he stepped out under the lights. Away from it, with increasing certainty, the darkness returned.

As a farewell to Murphy, Elva had planned a party to which Curry had not been invited. 'The reasons for Timmy's departure made his presence impossible,' she claimed. Meanwhile, another skater would also be leaving the company in Boston – but not of her own choosing. Adamant that she was still overweight, Curry was letting Lori Nichol go. 'The Wang was my last public performance with John,' she says tearfully. 'You had to be a very strong person in that group. John was a genius but he could be frightening ... These are things I've not thought about in a long time.'

After a two-week break, Curry and his skaters reconvened in Vail. In mid-October, they were due in Chicago, followed by a short tour of Scandinavia. There was work to do, but it was plagued from the start by an ominous autumnal chill. Curry's state of mind, despite the avalanche of critical acclaim, seemed resolutely low. 'Like a stranger to me,' recalled Clairmont. 'Weary and lethargic and unusually offhand.' Increasingly, the task of rallying his anxious company was falling to Rob McBrien, whose effervescent printed handouts battled heroically to lift team morale:

From New York through Boston all of you had at least one experience of real clarity and strength. All of you also had misses, slips, major losses of concentration and 'absentee' performances. SO there is room for improvement. I know you all know that … the moment that you plop your little fanny into the violets and feel ANY part of you is finished and as good as it CAN be, you are a joke. There is NO time to stop improving … God bless all of you.

Invariably now, it would be McBrien, not Curry, who steered rehearsals. Since Boston, most of the skaters preferred it that way. None of them – not even JoJo Starbuck – any longer had immunity from his wrath, and McBrien's calm authority was a reassuringly solid. 'He was soaked in what John wanted,' explains Starbuck. 'He would help us like crazy to be as close to John's vision as we could be. Always so gracious. Always so encouraging. John needed that third eye. He was wearing enough hats already.'

On Curry's behalf, down in New York Clairmont and Spungen were walking on quicksand. Although the venture was now formally registered as a non-profit organisation, each of them was panning for funds to keep it afloat. The situation wasn't without hope. Both the Met and the Kennedy Center had pledged to have Curry back in 1985. The faint outline of a future was taking shape. Short-term expediency, however, was necessitating hasty decisions, one of which would eventually unravel in a horrible way.

In return for a $250,000 bank loan, Curry's two embattled cohorts had reluctantly agreed to hand all future booking arrangements over to the powerful Columbia Artists Management Incorporation (CAMI). In little over six months, their decision would trigger a bitter, and damaging, war of words. Closer to hand, in October 1984 – with Chicago looming – it meant only one thing. With the loan secured, they could pay off some company bills and hopefully get their skaters back on the road. Right now, nothing else mattered.

As always, that would depend on Curry; and on their flight north he'd sat alone in first class 'in studied silence'. At the 'slightly seedy' Chicago hotel, matters had deteriorated. Unhappy with the accommodation, Curry swirled out of the lobby and caught a taxi back to O'Hare airport. Following behind at high speed were Clairmont and Spungen, whose inexhaustible powers of persuasion eventually coaxed Curry back to a room at the Chicago Hilton.

Never had he been so brittle; never had they been so desperate for him to hold it together. For the first time, the entire week's costs were being underwritten by the business. 'We take all the risk, we pay for everything, we take all the profit,' explains Spungen. 'We thought we could do it. One good night would have been enough.' With just a few days to go, however, their gamble was unravelling. For the first time in 30 years, the Chicago Cubs 'were in the baseball race'. No one was interested in a British ice skater and with lukewarm press interest – and insufficient paid advertising – only one in three seats had been sold. To make things worse, Curry had fallen out with JoJo Starbuck.

Theirs had always been a collision of opposites. 'Sometimes the sun was out, sometimes there were lightning bolts,' thinks Murphy. 'Putting that blonde exuberant open-faced American zest for life with stoic-faced John had been perfect.' On the road, in conversation with Elva, Curry had professed a special love for Starbuck. There had even been jokes about the pair making 'Olympic babies' – at which 'he would blush and smile and be shy but of course nothing happened'. That the two were now at loggerheads was troubling. With Murphy gone, Starbuck had taken his role as company conscience. No one else felt emboldened to speak out, and Starbuck's faith-based patience had been under attack since 1978.

During a Chicago rehearsal, after witnessing a verbal assault on Patricia Dodd, she had walked into his dressing room with a Bible, telling him 'he needed a lesson in love and kindness, and that he should read this and this, and that if he wanted to fire me, then that was just fine because at that point I didn't care. I'd seen all these instances. Someone needed to stand up to him. He knew that I loved him, but if you love someone you can't let them go on being that way.'

Curry had not been impressed. When the show opened a few days later in the Arie Crown Theater, *Tango Tango*, his fiery duet with Starbuck, had been axed. 'He was punishing me,' she says. Two nights later, it was back in. Tragically for both of them, very few people were watching. By the end of the week, they had played to more empty seats than full ones. Spungen's 'one good night' had not materialised, and, by Clairmont's calculations, they were now $330,000 in debt. All over Chicago, musicians and hotels were waiting to be paid. Interest payments were looming on their

$250,000 bank loan, and numerous other debts required urgent servicing.

With the Scandinavia tour pressing, creditors were urged to be patient. No new bookings had come in from CAMI. Only goodwill – and Curry's brilliance – was on offer as surety. After a brief hiatus in Vail, however, Curry himself was clearly struggling. Complaints about knee pain were being interpreted as an attempt to kill the concerts. Although he'd rallied after an all-clear from a New York doctor, no one had felt able to tell the distressed skater about the full extent of the catastrophe. 'Too much was riding on our ability to survive the next few weeks … I told him as much as I felt he could handle,' said Clairmont. It was a failure of nerve for which she would soon be severely punished.

Meanwhile, depressed, unhappy, and ignorant of his true circumstances, Curry flew his company to Europe in early November. Within a very few days, he'd be on his way back – alone.

———

As an amateur, Curry had loathed the advertising hoardings around the perimeter of ice rinks. As a professional, his contracts had even stipulated that he would never perform in a venue which displayed them. Just occasionally, he would turn a blind eye. At the World Arena in Copenhagen, however, no one had been told of Curry's veto; and, to the skater's fury, no one seemed remotely fazed by his foot-stamping. From the promoter, the message was unequivocal. The arena's billboards were not negotiable. If Curry chose not to skate, he would be sued.

Never had he felt so bereft of control. 'You could see the fire raging,' says Kossi. All his life he'd striven to be the master of circumstances, which in Copenhagen were suffocating him. Here he was: jetlagged in a half-empty stadium; skating to an orchestra flown in from London; surrounded by adverts for Danish lager. Nothing felt like a glorious pinnacle. After the Royal Albert Hall and the Met, probably nothing ever would. Nightly perfection – or the fruitless quest for it – was exhausting, and Curry was beyond that; driven on by someone else's schedule; his fatigue compounded by the growing nag, as yet unsupported by detail, that all was not well with the John Curry Skating Company.

On opening night, Curry's fuss had appeared misjudged. The skating surface was so vast that the hoardings were lost in the arena's spectral blackness. Although no one out on the ice could see them, Curry was still unhappy. Moments before his 'Skaters' Waltz' with Starbuck, he informed Spungen that he would not skate. 'You have to,' he was told. 'We're counting on you.' Minutes later, having started the routine, Curry fell over and refused to get up. 'He'd taken a dive and faked this injury,' insists Spungen. 'Next thing I'm in an ambulance with him, and after that he was on his way back to New York.'

Behind him in Copenhagen were 16 skaters, a conductor, an ice engineer and a freelance symphony orchestra. Now that he had deserted, even the loyalty of Curry's fiercest disciples began to crack. Although Spungen offered a convenient scapegoat, Curry's absenteeism defied comprehension. 'We all knew we were in really big trouble without him,' says Starbuck. 'It was totally crippling for the company. Very selfish. Very inconsiderate ... people who'd been prepared to obey him and follow him were left there with no money. It was unprofessional and heartless. He cared nothing for us at that moment.'

For Starbuck, at least, there was an out. 'I was able to yank out my credit card and go home.' For the rest, there was merely confusion. All the remaining concerts in Copenhagen had been immediately cancelled, as had a string of dates in Gothenburg. No one dared ask how much they'd lost. Unable to fly so many people back – and hopeful that Curry might yet return – Spungen battled to manage cash flow carnage while damping down a growing rebellion.

> I'm saying, 'Hang in there ... we've got friends out there ... it's all going to cash in now' and they're saying, 'We know you have money ... we demand that you pay us'. I had maybe enough to give them some per diem money, maybe fifty bucks each. All the time I'm thinking, we're not getting paid because John has taken a dive and no one cares enough about you, oh great company ...

Meanwhile, at New York's JFK, Curry was trundling towards Clairmont 'in a wheelchair and smiling happily'. She, on the other hand, was quietly furious. After medical examination revealed no serious injury, Curry apparently pleaded with her not to be returned to Scandinavia; a request which, understandably, given what was at stake, left her unmoved. A few days later he was back on a flight to Bergen, promising to remain calm and rest his knee ready for the final sold-out performances of the tour.

Not everyone in the company was glad to see him back. During their ten days spent marooned in Denmark and Norway, confusion had given way to anger. No one was getting paid. Musicians were having to busk in the streets. Cookies were substituting for proper meals. 'Things were building and boiling over,' remembers Kossi. 'People were meeting and talking.' Those who didn't blame Curry, blamed Spungen. 'It might have helped if we didn't have a 56-piece orchestra,' observes Bill Fauver.

Less than six months after New York had worshipped at its feet, the troupe was ripping apart at the seams. 'That fall in Scandinavia was him saying, "I can't take any more. I'm done",' thinks Lea-Ann Miller. 'None of us believed he was hurt. Only his heart was hurting. It was a collapse. No more. Everyone has a limit. I think he simply cracked.'

With Starbuck back from the States, Bergen had been a triumph. In one of Europe's most beautiful cities, Curry had shown no signs of his disputed frailty. Alone on the ice, his performance of *Moon Skate* seemed saturated with tragic portent. Everyone, privately, knew an ending was near. No one more than JoJo. There had even been an omen. For years she'd performed *Tango Tango* in the same seductive purple silk. During Curry's absence, it had been ruined in a wash. 'Something had happened,' says Starbuck. 'The dress had been killed and although Gayle [Palmieri] had done a great job making a new one, it just wasn't the same.'

It felt for me then the jig was up. We didn't know where we were going next. Everyone was going home. There were no bookings in the foreseeable future. I needed to get on with my life. You just sort of know. On that last night in Bergen, everyone knew it was our last *Tango*. Everyone came out from their dressing rooms to watch from the wings. John didn't say anything, but he knew it was the last time too. He gave me a special squeeze before he went out for the solo start. It was very emotional when we did our last bow with all its drama. I remember just running off, crying. There was a rose on my dressing room table when I got back with a note from John.

Starbuck would never tango with Curry again. As a keepsake, the remnants of her purple dress were made into a heart-shaped pillow. Few women had ever stirred Curry quite like she had. Or ever would again. 'We all felt there was a love affair going on,' muses Spungen. 'And that it was a very conflicting thing for both of them. Certainly, they very much loved one another, but whatever was going on there, John had not come to grips with it.'

'Sometimes we had a closeness off the ice, but it was hard to get to know him,' admits Starbuck. 'In retrospect, I wish I'd known then what I know now. I think I could have been a better friend to him. Not that he was ever willing to let people into his life.'

By December she had gone, and Curry's bedraggled survivors were back home. Despite Starbuck's departure, Bergen had restored a veneer of optimistic belief. Not everyone was giving up yet.

Eleven

'Silently the senses'

Few things confer mystery on an artist quite like an unfinished masterpiece. From Mozart, a piecemeal Requiem mass. From Antoni Gaudí, the bones of a Catalonian cathedral. And from John Curry – out of the smoking wreckage of Scandinavia – would come the *Firebird*. Unfinished, unseen; no trace of it remains; no performance was ever given. Its only witnesses were in Vail, where it briefly flew, before the long-crumbling edifice beneath it finally brought Curry, his company and his abandoned last creation crashing horribly to the ground.

It had only ever been the most slender of lifelines. From a wealthy Manhattan entrepreneur had come an offer no one had felt able to refuse. Sander Jacobs had made his fortune in real estate, fashion and cosmetics, but it was Broadway and the arts which brought him pleasure. During a conversation with Curry the previous July, Jacobs had made an extraordinary offer. In return for a $150,000 loan, Curry would deliver him a 'full-length ice dance ballet of between 45 and 50 minutes' based on Stravinsky's *The Firebird*. The completion date was to be March 1985 and the money could not 'be used to pay existing debts'. Clearly someone on Jacobs's team had been doing their homework.

By 8 January – after spending Christmas in England – Curry had started work on the commission up in Vail. 'An air of joviality prevails,' wrote Cathy Foulkes in her diary. 'There is a good deal of hugging and kissing going on.' No one was fooling themselves, however. The shine was tarnished. Even the faces were different. JoJo had not returned, and, after criticising the Scandinavian debacle, neither had Bill Fauver. 'Not required,' he'd been told. 'I was straight out to the tune of $5,000 wages and expenses.' Shortly afterwards – with Lea-Ann Miller – Fauver headed for Australia with Torvill and Dean.

It was like he'd always said. 'You never knew which John you were going to get.' After Bergen, Fauver had got the unforgiving one. Lori Nichol, on the other hand, had just been reacquainted with the sweet one. After a chance meeting with Curry at Denver airport, she'd been welcomed back – six pounds lighter – alongside Gabriela Galambos, a strikingly beautiful 18-year-old from Switzerland. 'After three days in Vail, John put his arm round me and said, "Gabriela, Would you mind losing a bit of weight?" I said, not a problem at all.'

John hadn't changed. If anything – for reasons which would shortly become apparent – his moods were worse, and his absences from the rink were growing longer. As temperatures outside sank to -40°C Curry's remaining skaters wrestled with Stravinsky's perplexing score, hidden beneath layers of clothing.

'John has just mentioned that with leg warmers pulled over my skates I look like a Shetland pony,' noted Foulkes, wryly.

> His tone implies hatred for the breed [and] after removing the offending articles I rejoin the rehearsal ... Within the confines of John's dictatorship, I am a pawn. Contrarily in 'real' life I am not easily manipulated ... Others in the company join me in living this contradiction. I don't think any of us know how to alter it.

In tantalising fragments, Curry's vision for *Firebird* was unfolding. To Nathan Birch it felt like 'the best work he ever did'. On one day they might work on the climactic high-speed 'Infernal Dance'. On another, the girls would toss golden apples to one another in the 'dance of the maidens'. Nothing about it was easy. During the long days – often starting before dawn – rehearsals would sometimes disintegrate in chaos. 'Panic is not very far away,' recorded Foulkes, adding: 'There is some consolation in knowing that I have plenty of confused company, John included.'

During the evenings, there would be hot baths and, on rare occasions, a few hours reading Jane Austen aloud with Curry and Rob McBrien. Even after seven years, Foulkes remained apprehensive in her leader's company. 'I still have a difficult time with small talk and idle chatter around John. I am reticent about verbalising trivial considerations, superfluous ideas – general clutter.' Curry, on the other hand was happy with his cup of Earl Grey, with three sugars and copious milk. 'Just occasionally with John,' recalls Fauver, 'you'd get a glimpse of the sun through the thunderclouds.'

Returning from a New York trip, on Valentine's Day 1985, he'd bought hearts and cupids for the female skaters. A special card had been printed, bearing a photograph of his smiling 14-strong troupe. That evening in his apartment 'the family' (as Foulkes called them) dined on gourmet food brought up from Denver by their friends Charles and Ann Cossey. For dessert, a cake had been produced bearing two candles for the company's birthday. 'Now we are two,' mused Foulkes. 'Just like Christopher Robin and equally unlikely.'

> John does the honours and then settles back against the kitchen wall cradling one of the children in attendance. Matthew [the Cosseys' son], under normal circumstances, is an uncontrollable bundle of youthful energy. Tonight, in John's arms, he is completely calm. John looks meditative. I've never seen this side of him and it is enough to make me swallow hard. How very human.

It was no longer a quality that Elva Clairmont ever saw. During a February trip to Vail she'd found him 'snappy and sarcastic and … irritated by my presence'. Around the same time, Lori Nichol had torn a hamstring during warm-up and been flown home to Canada at Curry's expense. On every level it was a tragedy. For the first time, she'd felt trusted and admired. As Curry pondered who to cast as his Firebird, Nichol's name had repeatedly topped the list.

Ultimately, no one would ever be the Firebird. Nor would his vision run in theatres, night after night, as skating's first serious challenge to works like *Swan Lake*, a full-length ice ballet imbued with everything he'd ever learned from Solihull to the snowy wastes of Colorado. On 8 March, work on his Stravinsky adaptation was ended. Whatever it might have been was lost. Curry's company was in terminal meltdown. 'Overdue bills must be settled before we can perform,' accepted Foulkes. 'This comes as very harsh news when all one wants to do is skate.'

In the locker room of the Dobson Ice Arena, the skaters said their farewells. 'John is there taking off his skates. This is always the worst goodbye. He gives me a hug and a kiss. I will miss him the most.' There was pain ahead for Curry, too. Finally, he knew everything.

––––––

Splitting with Parnes and Singer had been easy. This time it was bloody, frightening and horribly complicated. Since the previous year – against Elva's instincts – Columbia Artists Management (CAMI) had been acting as Curry's exclusive booking agent without any conspicuous results. 'After six months they had done absolutely nothing,' she claims. Fully confident that Curry wanted to break with them (notwithstanding the complication of their $250,000 loan), Clairmont had quietly identified a potential new agent who already felt bullish about '$2 million worth of guaranteed bookings'.

When news of this proposed switch reached the Met – where Curry was due to perform that summer – Jane Hermann was displeased. As the venue's fixer, she could not afford to flirt with disaster again. One lost night had been one too many and a trusted big-hitter like Columbia Artists had been proffered as part of the solution, not another problem. 'By the end I thought they [Clairmont and Spungen] were incompetent,' she says 'CAMI was a big agency … If John had a future he needed the right people around him.' Events now moved with horrible swiftness.

For some time, Curry had been playing a double game. To Clairmont, he'd appeared eager to dispense with CAMI's services. In separate conversations with Hermann, however, he'd been more circumspect. By mid-February, he was ready to jump. According to his later testimony, the skater accused Clairmont of firing CAMI on 13 February without consulting either himself or their 'adviser' Jane Hermann. Curry's hollow indignation was disingenuous, but it no longer mattered. His backing for Clairmont had been withdrawn. In the power struggle between two women, Elva had lost.

'I knew John had had it with Elva,' insists Hermann.

> I'm sure I'd have said this company has now got to be managed like a proper business, with a company manager on the road, a

fiscal officer, an agent to book you ... professionals ... you can't
have some little ditz running around ... John didn't need to
sense this. I said it. I'm extremely candid. No one ever has any
difficulty in knowing where they stand with me.

On the weekend of 16 February – two days after the company's
birthday cake – 'Hermann advised Curry of CAMI's termination
along with *several other facts* of which she had only just become
aware'. The 'facts' would eventually amount to a very sobering
list.

In total, the John Curry Skating Company was over $1 million
in debt. Among the big figures were the $250,000 CAMI advance;
$105,000 owing to Sander Jacobs for the aborted 'Firebird' project;
$224,000 to West Nally; $49,376 in back taxes; $48,547 to the
Musicians' Union; and $64,590 owed to Curry directly for monies
borrowed from his company, Frozen Assets. In addition, the failure
to pay the Chicago musicians had led to a local blacklisting followed
by the threat of a national boycott of all future Curry productions.

Among the smaller debts were telling sums of $4,100 to Kevin
Kossi; $9,000 to JoJo Starbuck; $1,749 to Patricia Dodd and
$4,000 unpaid legal fees following the sacking of Keith Davis.
Choreographers, car hire firms and costume supervisors were all
waiting for money. Even the estate of George Gershwin was hanging
on for $1,500 in unpaid royalties.

Given this turmoil, it was hardly surprising if the *Firebird* was
refusing to fly. Or that rehearsals had been abandoned. Most of the
skaters were missing pay and, as the details spewed out, Curry's co-
directors were left dangerously isolated. 'Jane Hermann was the
worst thing that happened to us,' says Clairmont today. But the
tragic numbers were hardly Hermann's fault.

As the news sank in, the troupe co-signed a letter to Clairmont
and Spungen citing 'financial delinquencies' and 'a spirit of
recrimination'. While thanking the pair for their 'tremendous
achievement', the skaters urged both to consider their positions. 'If
anyone clings to the status quo,' the letter added, 'the company will
dissolve.' It was brutal, but it was merely a prelude. At, or around
the same time, Clairmont took a telephone call from Curry in her
New York office. A few minutes later, when she passed the phone
to Spungen, they had both effectively been sacked.

I asked if he would speak to me directly and he acquiesced. So I went over to Nancy Streeter's. Jane Hermann is there. His agent is there. It was like an interrogation. John would say, 'I heard a, b and c' and I would explain what 'a, b and c' were all about. Every question posed I had an answer. Maybe not one he wanted to hear but totally above board. In the end he just said: 'This is simple. I can't work with you any more' … Some of the most powerful people in the industry were saying, 'John, we can make this continue for ever for you. Come with us and be our friend. Or stay with Elva and David and see what happens' …

Neither would ever see Curry again. The trio would be bound together for months, however, by a complex chain of legal aftershocks. Since Curry couldn't actually fire his former partners, he had formally resigned his directorship on 22 March. Amidst the revelations it now seemed that Curry's truncated three-year contract with West Nally – the investors behind *Symphony on Ice* and Tokyo – had never been formally assigned to the John Curry Skating Company. Away from this bewildering carnage, only one thing seemed absolutely clear. Curry's pre-emptive resignation had left his former partners exposed to massive debt. Far less certain was whether their former friend could ever skate again, even if he wanted to.

———

Curry had always lived his life in distinctly separate orbits. Boxing off his world made sense to him; helped him cope. This way, nobody knew everything. This way, he could stay detached. Yes he had sensed impending meltdown. But by shutting it out he'd been able to continue, wrestling with Stravinsky in the mountains, one pure world untainted by one much less so. If it had been foolish to ignore the warning signs, that was who he was. He had believed. So too, surely, could the suits. Somewhere there would always be another saviour. That's what he did. He made people fall in love with him.

Recent events had unstitched all that. Neat compartmentalisation was no longer possible. Orbits were colliding. Legal threats were in the air. There were sworn statements to give, attorneys to hire and creditors to appease. To Curry it was like an icicle had been plunged into his artistic soul. Scared and homeless, he turned to Nancy Streeter for guidance. Nancy had never wavered, even when he had. Quietly she had been drip-feeding donations into his ailing company. Now she would provide both a shoulder, and a list of influential New York contacts, to help put her 'son' straight.

Throughout March – as so often before – Curry laid low in her apartment. By mid-April, he'd retreated to his mother's home in Warwickshire, from where he penned thanks to his steadfast Manhattan landlady. 'At the age of 35 I find my life is anything but "together",' he wrote. 'I must and will do something about that. Being at home in England makes me feel better – the countryside is bursting into new life and the air is fresh and sweet. I'm almost afraid to say it but it looks as if my problems are moving towards settlement. I'll keep you posted.'

Curry's caution was well-merited. If anything, his tribulations were getting worse. According to Clairmont and Spungen's rose-tinted projections, Curry's company had been on course to gross $3.4 million in 1985, and $3.6 million the year after. All that was now dust. Uncertain of his contractual status, the Met had cancelled its two-week summer booking. At the same time, a US producer planning to televise *Firebird* had pulled out citing the 'strong element of uncertainty'.

Unperturbed by the background rumblings, however, the Kennedy Center in Washington was still holding two weeks free for him from 8 August. After two months in England, Curry leapt in. Performing as the John Curry Skaters – not as the John Curry Skating Company – he would return to the ice. But this, too, would be bloody.

Behind the scenes, the lawyers had been inching towards an amicable and legally binding resolution; 'some sort of nominal fee for turning the company over to him, or whoever he had behind him,' explains Spungen. By accepting this, however, Curry and any subsequent backer would have assumed responsibility for over $1 million worth of debt. Unsurprisingly, someone on his team had seen a better way. Under a new company name, Curry could waltz free of his liabilities, taking with him, to Clairmont's horror, the same skaters, costumes and choreography that her own creditors had paid for.

Midway through his Washington comeback, her legal team struck back. Under the gaze of District Court Judge Thomas F. Hogan, a motion was filed for injunctive relief claiming breach of contract, intentional injury to business and trademark infringement. Curry, it was claimed, had absconded with a fully formed product someone else had bankrolled. By incorporating his own name in the title of his new company, he had also violated the prior trade name of the John Curry Skating Company. In effect, Curry's use of his own moniker as a skating 'brand' was under frontal attack.

Judge Hogan was buying none of it. Curry's 'right to use his name will not be lightly wrested from him', he ruled. At two separate hearings – in August and October – the complaint was dismissed and Curry's shows in Washington had been allowed to proceed. Once again, he'd escaped. Once again, others would mop up the mess. He was free. But he would never run a company again. And the financial cost had been ruinous.

High in the mountains, the joy was bleeding away. On the surface, rehearsals for the Kennedy Center had gone well. Curry's rich vein of creativity had continued. But beneath it everyone knew the end was coming. Foulkes had found him 'preoccupied and distant'. Although the sun still streamed into the Dobson Ice Arena, the old spark was missing. 'Like Fleetwood Mac without the original players,' thought David Santee. 'The show wasn't what it had been. I don't think I even went to rehearsals. My recollection is that it was over at that point. John had taken so much and that was it.'

With his ownership of earlier work under scrutiny, Curry had worked demonically on new material. Some of it was among his best. And no one could ever say that it had been stolen. When the Washington run opened, there were five 'world premiere' pieces, and at the heart of their best was Patricia Dodd – balletic and beautiful and finally elevated to a sumptuous duet with Curry himself. 'A closely danced pas de deux that depicts a farewell suffused with erotic memories,' said one review. Tellingly, their dance was called *Remember Me*. To the very end, Curry would always be a master of the oblique.

Inevitably, this was a coda awash with anti-climax. The skaters had been given barely five weeks to prepare. Previously, they'd have had ten. Opening night had been plagued by soft ice, burst pipes and blue-spouting fountains. Falls and stumbles had peppered the evening. 'Ragged and under-rehearsed' was the verdict of one critic. Others could find no fault in any of it. 'Undimmed in its glory,' said the *Washington Post*. 'It was, if that's possible, more spectacular, more artistically rewarding and more elegantly performed than the show Curry brought us last summer.'

Hidden among the audience for one performance had been Tim Murphy. Curiosity – and respect – had brought him back. 'I pretty much cried all the way through,' he admits. 'Not because I regretted my decision – I didn't – but because it was so beautiful. I always knew we'd had a tiger by the tail, but I'd never actually seen it. You can't see a dance that you're in, and now I was seeing it and it was like wow. This is unbelievable.'

Washington clearly agreed. Every night the Kennedy Center was rocked by standing ovations. Like a decade before, *L'après-midi d'un Faune* was at the heart of their triumph. 'It was in the first show and it was in the last show and every one in between,' says Foulkes. 'But I knew it was for the last time in Washington.' On 24 August 1985, Curry, his 13 skaters and Charles Barker's full orchestra took their final bow. They would not be coming back. Virtually none of Curry's sublime work would ever be seen again. It was a tragedy, but the model was broken. In just three weeks their final run had lost a catastrophic $400,000.

If Clairmont and Spungen allowed themselves a bitter smile of *schadenfreude*, it was understandable. Their much-derided alliance with Curry had seen him fêted in London and New York. Without them, his new backers – whoever they were – had withdrawn in weeks. 'I'm sure a lot of people hate Elva, or blame her, but the main thing is: it happened,' says Kevin Kossi. 'And there's only one way this could have happened. You take a bunch of crazy risk-takers and a bunch of artists and put them together. Real business people would have said it doesn't make money. Therefore it ain't happening.'

None of which seemed to have been grasped by Curry's fickle skaters. As the sulphurous mud flew, barely one of them reached out to their former paymasters, and Spungen especially – who'd laboured from Kalamazoo to Copenhagen – found that collective slight almost unbearable:

> There wasn't a deep enough hole for me to crawl into. All of that time, all we'd been through, and no one bothered to pick up the

phone and call me an asshole. I'd have loved 12 people to yell at me for everything wrong they thought I'd done. Instead, it was a dome of silence. There were also accusations of stealing money. We were with them when they were with us. Where did we put it? Where did it come from? From the 2,000 people in an 18,000-seat arena? Is that where we got it from? The worst thing was that total closure. It was as if we never existed.

Time has mellowed that antipathy. Today most of Curry's survivors speak with fondness for Spungen and respect for Clairmont. 'It was she who spearheaded this fearlessness,' admits Starbuck. 'Maybe she screwed up. Maybe she just kept saying yes to John and it eventually caught up with her, but the ride was really great while it lasted.'

It would be horribly costly for them both. Clairmont had lost $124,000 and 'suffered humiliation, ignominy and financial ruin'. 'I was an outcast in the world I loved,' she says. With his own losses spiralling towards $150,000, Spungen was forced to file for personal bankruptcy. Shunned by the world of skating – 'through inference and innuendo' – he grew a thick beard and took the dusk to dawn shift driving Yellow Cabs around weekend Manhattan. 'Elva and I never did it for ourselves,' he says finally. 'There's no evidence otherwise. And, yes, I loved the guy ... but I pitied him as well.'

———

That autumn, no one seemed too sure where Curry had gone. Almost all of his old hiding places were fading away. AIDS had poisoned the well of Fire Island, and he never went back. In October, the Mineshaft club had called time on its Dionysian entertainments. Within a year, the Anvil would follow, closing its doors on jockstrap contests and 'uncut night events' deemed too risky by the health inspectors sweeping through New York's blighted gay haunts. A scene that had once entranced him was now in its death throes.

Failure had hurt him badly and he possessed neither the desire – nor the energy – to start again. Between spells at Nancy Streeter's apartment, there were trips to London for meetings with his agent, Jean Diamond. If she could find him any acting, he would take it. There was a simplicity to theatrical work, which he craved. Slowly he resumed the coaching lessons he'd let go. In one he was asked how he might be reincarnated. As a magnificent jewel on a velvet cushion, he'd replied. At others, he still struggled with the weakness of a voice confined by a lifetime's introversion. 'I think if I'd spent a quarter of the time on myself that I spent on skating, I'd be a little more comfortable,' he'd once said.

Simpler diversions now yielded pleasure. Returning to Manhattan from England, he would include boxes of Weetabix in his luggage. When the ponds froze on Central Park, he might quietly glide between the reeds and the mystified ducks; mostly alone, but once – to her delighted surprise – with Patricia Dodd. As his days passed, so too did the legal impediments that prevented his return. But he had no intention of going back. In his mind, he'd been the victim of monstrous fraud and injustice. The names of his former partners were rarely ever mentioned again. There were new friends now; new escape tunnels to wriggle through.

Patricia Crown had first met Curry through Nancy. A New York lawyer, she'd been instrumental in steering the skater through his recent 'divorce', a process that had seen them grow close. 'Very, very close,' she says. 'Physically, he was one of the most beautiful people I've ever laid eyes on.' It helped that Crown was single at the time. It helped more that she was also bright, sympathetic and had a country house out at Amagansett on Long Island, just two blocks from the growl of Atlantic surf. For Curry, it was the ideal place to recharge. After the mountains, the healing sea and the circling gulls.

'In the past I'd shut it down in the winter, but with John we kept it open and went for weekends,' recalls Crown.

> It was desolate, and desolation appealed to him. We'd light a fire. He'd taken his records out there and we'd listen to music. We'd walk on the beach and collect wood for the fire. He'd cook. He was the most wonderful, inventive cook. You could put him in front of any fridge and he'd make the most fantastic meals. He could never take people out. It was not within his means.

A state of calm was descending. Curry's mania had either gone into remission or back into its box. Now that he was no longer obligated by self-imposed demands, the smile had returned and to Crown he appeared the quintessence of English charm.

I don't know how anyone could not have fallen in love with him. There was a beauty about the way he moved and spoke and an enormous sensitivity in everything he did. He wrote beautifully and was a very, very funny person and brought that quarter-turn perspective to everything which allowed him to see things differently.

Between trips out to Amagansett – once in a February snowstorm – Curry and Crown's friendship deepened. In New York they were the Thanksgiving guests of Mia Farrow and Woody Allen. As a gift, he bought a foot-high pine cone for his host. 'He was rather enamoured of Mia,' says Crown. 'And although his means were limited his eye and imagination were not.'

During the fall, to enjoy the purpling leaves, the skater and his lawyer travelled to a former Shaker colony in Massachusetts where procreation and sexual contact had been forbidden. 'I could have been a Shaker in another life,' he told her. His affair with Shaun McGill was now clearly over. 'John knew he was not successful with intimate relationships,' she says. 'There were no partners that I knew of in New York.'

Around Christmas, 1985 – according to an interview given 18 months later – Curry 'hung up his skating boots', he thought for good. At the Broadmoor Arena in Colorado Springs, with the 'Sunset' movement booming out from Grofe's Grand Canyon Suite, Curry skated alone and then stepped from the rink. 'I had done it for 30 years. I had accomplished everything I set out to accomplish. I was happy to stop.'

Four months later, he was back in England, hungry for work. Living out of a suitcase, he flitted from friend to friend – Alan Bates included – often disappearing and returning days later without explanation. After years as his companion, the ex-dancer Gillian Lynne was surprised by nothing. Curry had been her flyaway guest in the South of France, New York, London and Gloucestershire. 'You'd think, "Oh dear, off we go then" and off he went.'

When she could, Lynne – and others – would help him prepare for auditions. By May 1986, none of them had led to a job. In a letter to Cathy Foulkes, congratulating her on passing her legal exams, he told her he would be appearing as Zach in *A Chorus Line* at a small theatre at Matunuck on Rhode Island. 'I shall sing and dance. Cross your fingers for me.' Puzzlingly, it was never mentioned again. To stave off boredom, he retreated to his mother's bungalow in Binton, decorating her living room and tending the roses.

Gradually, too, he was rediscovering his pen. In tireless redrafts of self-penned limericks, Curry found an unexpected outlet for his love of the absurd:

> Charlie Stoke was a hell of a bloke
> He always ate kippers for tea.
> He rode on his horse, as a matter of course
> From eleven till quarter to three.

Running his skating company had obsessed him. Without it, there was proper time for Nancy again. Perhaps he already knew how much he would soon need her. From Warwickshire, he wrote remembering 'the 4ths of July that I have spent with you'. 'Best of all was 76 watching the fireworks from Brooklyn Heights and feeling part of it all … my love of America and my feelings for you and your family are all so closely woven together – thank you dear Nancy'. Gainful employment, he told her, was imminent. 'Lots in the wind,' he said. The money would be useful. By his own estimation his legal costs now stood at $120,000.

Travelling light helped. Living for free helped even more. In London, he had a new shelter when required. Peter Farmer was a 50-year-old artist and theatre designer, with a sharp sense of humour and a fine collection of records and books. Although he no longer recalls how or where they met, Curry had become a welcome guest at his flat off Kensington High Street. 'Peter Farmer was a bit of a charmer,' ran one of Curry's verses.

No rent would ever be asked or expected (Curry's room was tiny) and their friendship flourished along its own eccentric lines. 'I never knew when he'd come or for how long,' says Farmer. 'He was quite a lost soul. If John was there, John was there. He never formally moved in or out. Sometimes he slept with me. Sometimes he slept on the sofa. We both slept on the floor sometimes.'

Although the two were lovers, neither man exerted claim over the other.

We were not possessive. There was not the drama of high romance or breaking up. He'd meet other partners. He was not frustrated in that way. He'd meet someone and they'd be *the* person, and we'd have to put up with that for several weeks and there'd be a declining again. He was really only interested in working. He was such a workaholic and from that your life suffers. He also knew he couldn't act terribly well, although whether he acknowledged that, I don't know.

Curry was living in perpetual motion. In London he had Peter Farmer and others. In New York, he'd briefly taken an apartment on West 76th Street. Instead of the ice, he now slid between people and landscapes, with no discernible dip in his mood. The pressures were gone. If there were frustrations, he was not unhappy. 'Floating around', as Farmer put it, seemed to suit him. 'There was a danger of taking his moods too seriously,' he adds. 'Sometimes he just wanted his own way. He was very straightforward. He liked cooking. He liked gardening. He liked an ordinary life and he had a uniquely wonderful sense of humour.'

He was also fastidiously precise. Gillian Lynne had noticed his 'meticulous cleanliness'. He and Farmer had even enjoyed mild spats about washing the glasses correctly. To Curry, stains and smears were unacceptable. 'It had to be perfect. Things had to be neat and I think that reflected the exactitude of skating. He was also very secretive; very private; a bit of a mystery person really. He always liked reading a quiet book. Didn't like loud parties. We just liked each other and if he trusted you, then he trusted you a lot.'

By the late summer, despite the optimism of his letters to Nancy, Curry hadn't worked for a year. In a cheery letter to Foulkes ('greetings from jolly old England') Curry bemoaned his failure to land a part. 'These months in London flew by – unfortunately that is all they did.' From American public broadcasting had come a proposal for an ice skating show which he had declined. 'Majic [sic] on a shoestring budget again I'm afraid. And I really don't want anything else to do with skating.'

As Christmas approached, he was desperate. Finally, however, there was an offer on the table. That year, the pantomime at the Liverpool Playhouse was to be *Cinderella*. If he wanted it, the part of Buttons was his; paid employment until 31 January. By mid-

November, he was stepping out of Lime Street railway station into a raw wind blowing straight off the Irish Sea. Few English cities can be as bleakly damp as Liverpool in winter. Few parts seemed more ill suited than Buttons. To his own surprise, he adapted happily to both. 'Rather a handsome city,' he told Nancy, adding that 'his four songs and dancing' seemed to be going rather well.

It was a long way from the New York Met. Instead of Manhattan's elite, Curry stepped out every night in a bell-hop's suit to entertain 600 raucous children guzzling popcorn. As the unrequited lover of Cinderella, Curry's role required him both to galvanise the audience and make them laugh. Neither task came naturally, but neither was he a dud. 'He wouldn't have done it for eight weeks if he hadn't enjoyed it,' notes Andrew Curry, who, with Rita, and his partner Celia, had travelled north to see the infant hordes yelling 'behind you' at their illustrious family member.

Backstage – with John facing a night alone at the city's Edwardian hotel, the Adelphi – Curry's fellow cast saw a more familiar side to the skater. 'There was a sadness about him,' recalls Clovissa Newcombe. 'Not quite a regret but a deep sensitivity. Very shy. Very private. He told me he'd never belonged to a group of friends as a young man, and this was clearly not the most comfortable thing for him to do. But on stage he was very elegant, very classy. You could see the skater in him.'

It was more difficult for Curry than anyone could ever know. As Christmas and New Year passed, January dragged a chill off the River Mersey, which ate into his bones. When the house lights came up and the cleaners mopped away the debris, Curry's stage smile was swept away with it. Peter Farmer was right. He was secretive. Now he had the biggest secret of all. Seeing his family in Liverpool had been lovely, but he couldn't tell them. Heinz Wirz was different. When his friend arrived from Switzerland, Heinz would know what to say.

It had been years, and Wirz brought treats. Two boxes of rich Swiss chocolates for Curry's incorrigibly sweet tooth. A joint of marijuana for when Wirz had gone. Curry's gift to his former lover was much harder to swallow. On the darkened steps of the Adelphi Hotel, the skater heaved off his burden. Finally the tests had let him down. He was HIV positive.

It is impossible to be certain when – or where – Curry was diagnosed. Since he never, or rarely, discussed his sexuality he was unlikely to do the same with his condition. Although Wirz was quite probably the first person he'd told, the revelation was not an invitation for open discussion. Two days later, when Heinz received a letter from Liverpool, it made no mention of their conversation. The shutters had been slammed down. 'You made me feel so happy and I thank you for that,' Curry wrote.

Unless absolutely necessary, few others would be told, and – even with those who knew – all discussion of his illness would be off limits, unless broached by Curry himself which was unlikely. There had already been one strangely coded telephone conversation with his mother, which arose directly out of Wirz's trip to Merseyside. That, too, had been dripping with the unspoken.

> We had the best talk we have ever had and I think it will be a great help in the rest of my life – and hers. While we spoke I cryed [sic] very deeply – the first time for years – and I told her many things that have been causing me distress, Mother spoke very calmly and with great compassion. I felt very much lighter and quite drained at the end of it all – I even spoke about my fear of 'aids' – so you can tell it was a much more personal conversation than we have ever had before. All this could only have taken place after your visit.

It would be four years before mother and son spoke like that again. Thankfully, Curry was keeping busy. The work – albeit un-glamorous and badly paid – was beginning to flow. From Liverpool he travelled directly to Belfast, where the Lyric Theatre was staging an adaptation of *Hard Times*. For years, Curry had methodically been working his way through the novels of Charles Dickens. It would be a joy, he told Wirz, 'to speak some of the great man's words'. Nothing else about Belfast was quite so pleasant.

Outside the theatre was a sectarian war zone. 'This week alone six men [dead]. Last week eight,' he wrote. A few yards from his digs in Adelaide Park, a restaurant was blown up. Shortly before he arrived, a blast had shattered windows at his lodgings. Inside the Lyric, the four-strong cast had taken four parts each and Curry floundered with the gravelly northern inflections of fictional 'Coketown' and its merciless headmaster, Thomas Gradgrind. There was also a huge amount to learn. But neither the 'armoured cars that look like grey rats' nor the workload seemed to bother him. If a jobbing actor's life was what he wanted, he had found it. 'Great fun,' he told Nancy. 'My favourite theatre experience so far.'

It was exactly 21 years since Curry had won his first medals. As hard as he tried, he couldn't quite rip skating from his blood. Alone in his room, Curry watched the World Championships on television and bitched mercilessly about the skaters in his letters. 'Isn't the Canadian girl terrible? – Miss Piggy,' he griped to Wirz. 'All in all there was little of great beauty ... PS If you can, please put a "special" cigarette in [your] letter.' From London, he heard news that Shaun McGill was in England for a televised version of *Sleeping Beauty* on ice along with Foulkes, Dodd and Nathan Birch. 'It might turn out nicely,' he noted. 'I hope so.' But it was not for him. None of it was. Vail was another life, and in Northern Ireland he'd found another man.

Like Curry, David Delve was in his late thirties. Unlike Curry, Delve was an actor who knew his trade. In the 1970s he'd featured in the BBC's *Poldark*. In the 1980s he'd turned up in *Blackadder* and Agatha Christie whodunnits, adding to a string of theatre credits which included *Guys and Dolls* and the Royal Shakespeare Company's triumphant 1985 reinvention of *Nicholas Nickleby*, a production that had taken him from Stratford to Broadway, and which Curry had almost certainly seen. Delve was a priest's son, thoughtful, calm and kind, and in Belfast – where the actor had been visiting a friend – the two had struck up a rapport, which soon deepened.

'I think it's fair to say we fell in love but how far John goes into love, I don't know,' admits Delve.

> He said he was, but was he? It certainly started quite quickly. We had a night on the Isle of Man just talking. He liked to talk. But in his life at this time he was a bit of a fish out of water. He didn't know where to live. A lot of his contemporaries had died and he didn't want to go back to the States any more. He was trying to find what he could and couldn't do. You provided what he might require for that particular moment.

With *Hard Times* finished in Belfast, Curry returned to England where Delve's 'minute' flat in Kilburn gradually became his home. Everywhere he landed, he seemed to have less in his bags. What few possessions Curry had ever owned (apart from his motorbike) were carelessly scattered between London, Warwickshire and New York. These days, even his physical presence seemed fragmented. That May, for two weeks, he sang Irving Berlin classics in *Let's Face the Music* at The Mill at Sonning Theatre, a restored eighteenth-century flour mill on the River Thames near Reading. The following month, *Hard Times* enjoyed a fringe revival at the King's Head in Islington.

It was good to be occupied. Without work there was too much time to think. In the early summer, there'd been more bad news from America. The lover of his old friend Billy Whitener had been diagnosed with AIDS. So, too, had another New York companion. 'Bill is alright [but] what a terrible time, Nancy,' he wrote, adding sadly that he was too broke to help with either man's medical costs. In London he vaguely harboured hopes of buying his own place, telling Delve that Nancy would stump up his deposit. Nothing now remained in the US account of his company, Frozen Assets. The only thing left was 'the wretched ice machine', for which he could no longer afford the storage.

During a live BBC radio interview, broadcast on 28 June, Curry sounded weary and disenchanted. 'I came back from the USA with empty pockets ... I lost everything I made ... I made the mistake of trusting some people who I really shouldn't have trusted,' he said, adding that he really was finished with skating. 'If I went on the ice I'd be terribly rusty and I wouldn't like people to see me in that condition.' Acting and singing were the future now.

When asked to select his favourite songs, Curry's choices seemed uncharacteristically bland. Only with hindsight could the clues be discerned. 'All the men come in these places and the men are afraid,' sang Tina Turner in 'Private Dancer'. And from *Phantom of the Opera* the line 'Silently the senses abandon their defences'. It seemed unlikely Curry had not chosen his lyrics with care. Or that a message was not there for those who truly listened. 'He was really just a little boy lost,' thinks Delve.

Meanwhile, if Curry still yearned for stardom he hid it well. In a letter to Nancy, his complaints about lousy Equity pay were tempered by genuine optimism. 'I feel that [money] will come and that I am laying very good foundations for my career.' Undeterred by the empty seats in Islington, he still auditioned furiously and by the autumn he was touring as Orsino in *Twelfth Night* and the hapless young Marlowe in *She Stoops to Conquer*. The reviews, as they had been in Belfast, were warm; no more. Light comedy, it seemed, might be the way forward. 'The silly ass in *Just William* would have suited him,' thinks Delve. Even Penny Malec – previously unconvinced by his Shakespearean forays – was moved to tell Nancy that 'John was an excellent fop ... I think character acting will probably be his forte.'

Sadly, no amount of minor success could staunch the gush of bad tidings. In early November, news reached Curry that Roger Roberts had joined the list of the dying. In New York, he'd fallen from his bicycle and the wound hadn't healed. That had been the start. Among Curry's jumble of photographs was a snap of his tousle-haired Welsh friend, gloriously bronzed and squinting against the Fire Island sun. It was terrible news. The man had appeared indestructible. But then so had Liberace and America's 4,135 other AIDS victims that year. So had John Curry.

In Britain there were fewer dead, but the mood of public disgust still bordered on terrifying. 'People were being thrown out of their homes because their parents didn't want to know them,' recalls Delve. A senior policeman had accused gay men of 'swirling about in a human cesspit of their own making'. Tolerance was unwinding. Secrecy and shame were taking its place. If asked, Curry would say Roberts had liver cancer. With homophobia on the rise, it would be foolish to expect compassion. And yet, despite the risks, many gay men were still indifferent to precaution. 'We thought we were immortal,' rues Peter Farmer.

At Delve's Kilburn flat, the disease was casting its own shadow. Before they'd even met, the actor had been aware of Curry's reputation. During his stint in New York with the RSC, Delve had spoken to one crew member who'd had casual sex with Curry, adding that 'he was always down at the Anvil'. Nor was Delve unaware of the skater's masochistic urges. Since falling in love with Curry, however, Delve had remained faithful. With AIDS off the leash, it made sense to be monogamous. Delve, too, was losing his dearest companions.

In the flat upstairs, the actor's closest school friend lay dying of AIDS. Curry fumed at the time Delve spent ministering to him. 'There was this thing that you were his somehow,' he explains. 'He did not like the attention I would pay to my own friends.' It was hypocrisy of the highest order. After a year together, Curry had still not told Delve that they were sharing both a bed, and – in all probability – a virus. When he finally mustered the courage to inform him, the actor was stunned.

> We had a long, heated discussion into the night. It was almost like him saying, 'Oh, by the way, I have AIDS', so I was shocked, but I don't lose my temper. My father was a priest and people would come to me with their problems, so I tried to reason it out but anything unpleasant he wanted to dismiss; he wanted to blow it away. We continued in the full knowledge that he was HIV. It's like suddenly your partner has cancer. So you deal with it.

Delve was lucky. For whatever reason, he had not been infected, but by the spring of 1988 his relationship with Curry was over. In a letter to Nancy, the skater said he'd been thrown out. 'All very unexpected and strange.' But Delve remembers it differently. 'He just didn't come back one time,' he says. 'I honestly don't think he had a clue where he wanted to get to any more.' Once again, the acting work had dried up. Television dramas didn't want him, and while picking up a sock his recalcitrant back had clicked and laid him low for a month. It was the least of his worries.

Gradually, Curry's letters back to Nancy Streeter were getting longer, and more frequent. In New York, cutting edge medical research was underway which might benefit him. None of it would come cheap, but Nancy would help, and Curry well knew how to touch her generosity.

In a carefully planted line in March 1988, he'd mentioned seeing a Manhattan specialist if, or when, he could afford the flight. Four weeks later, he was heading back from a New York consultation penning thanks back to her for the ticket. Throughout his competitive years, she had been his rock until the day – as with David Delve – he'd drifted away. Now, in unspeakable circumstances, the skater's 58-year-old benefactor was firmly back on his team, with both her love and her money at his disposal.

In New York and London, Curry was discreetly canvassing medical opinion. Recent trials of a new drug called azidothymidine (AZT) had suggested that replication of the HIV virus could be slowed, leading to a delay in the onset of full-blown AIDS. In the United States, it had just become the first government-approved inhibitor. No one knew precisely what its side effects might be. No one was seriously touting it as a cure but any hope was better than none. In London, Curry had been told he could have it on the NHS, but not if he travelled abroad. Uncertain how to proceed, he talked to Nancy Streeter.

> [My doctor] said that I was in the top health range of those people who are HIV positive. He thought my blood was in good condition and that I was perfectly fit. He said, 'If you were to do nothing you would probably live for five more years without any illness and perhaps much longer. Perhaps you would never become ill' … he thinks I should go to some kind of counselling and he wants me to find a lover! All in all I was quite surprised.

Once again, Curry's address had changed. On the sunny terrace of a rented flat in West Kensington, carnations flourished and the evening fragrance of honeysuckle filled his rooms at dusk. Time to 'dream and scheme' he told a friend. Very quietly – and despite everything he'd said – Curry had returned to the ice. The previous December he'd skated on New Year's Eve at Garmisch-Partenkirchen in Bavaria. Earlier in the year, David Delve had watched him giving a private lesson at dawn down at Richmond rink. Since then, the National Skating Association had persuaded him to run a series of classes for pre-teen children in London and Solihull. They were oversubscribed and noisy, and Curry had loved it.

By mid-May, he was back in Manhattan preparing for a low-key comeback. As a guest of the Ice Theatre of New York – an organisation built in his image – he performed two solos at the Sky Rink of such stunning intensity reviewers were left gasping for words. 'Mr Curry remains his incandescent self,' noted Anna Kisselgoff, in the New York Times. Although Curry alone knew what propelled him, one prescient observer had detected a 'ghost of melancholy' in his movement to Verdi's Attila.

'Watching him,' wrote Mindy Aloff, in the *Nation*, 'one marvelled again at how intimate and immediate and how much of an art, ice skating can be … his ten minutes swept by like ten seconds.' John Curry, she concluded, had the tragic demeanour of a clown, 'dramatic, infinitely expressive and quite alone'.

The following month – to mark the opening of a new skating facility – the Ice Theatre performed the same show in Andorra. 'A pretty part of the world, but nothing sensational,' Curry wrote on a postcard. He wasn't there for the mountain views. Since their split before the 1976 Olympics, his former coach Alison Smith had stayed out in Spain, and Curry's trip facilitated a reunion up in the Pyrenees.

Two years before, she'd proudly watched him at the New York Met. During the curtain call, he'd raised his hand towards her box and made her take a bow. In every way, it was she who had 'set the bird free'. But still he could not tell her of his illness. That news would have to come later. 'When I did hear, it just killed me,' she says. 'He was one of those people, like Heinz, I really thought we were going to grow old together.' After Andorra, the two great friends never saw each other again.

For the next few months, Curry trod water. There was still no work and, as yet, he was undecided about the merits of AZT. According to some reports, high doses caused damage to bone marrow and muscle tissue. He also had growing concerns about his illness leaking to the press. For over two years, stories had been written speculating on the health of rock singer Freddie Mercury. High-profile AIDS victims sold newspapers, and one talkative health worker might easily unstitch his cover. Curry had tasted public humiliation in Britain before. He would not be exposed to that again.

There was another, more pressing, reason for silence. The previous year, the United States had implemented a travel ban preventing HIV-positive foreigners from obtaining permanent immigration status or entering the United States without special waivers. It wouldn't directly affect Curry – he'd held a green card since the late 1970s – but it was a horrible sign of the times and it would remain in force until 2009. By mid-November, he was already on his way back there anyway. Moving targets were the hardest ones. Killed or cured, he would keep this secret for as long as he could.

Brian Grant was dead. Now, so was Roger Roberts. Faced with a double leg amputation and a slightly extended lifespan, or a swift morphine-comforted exit, Roberts had chosen death. It was all too close, all too soon. 'John was furious with Roger for getting AIDS,' says Penny Malec. 'He was also terribly angry with him for dying.' Years before, the Fire Island three – Whitener, Curry and Roberts – had talked about retiring together into the Californian sunset. Never had Curry's aversion to sentimentality been so tested. Or his need for distraction so pronounced.

That Christmas he'd surrendered to a boisterous Streeter holiday. Three days later – 'refreshed and happy' – Curry flew to Baltimore for a 'Happy New Year USA' television special. In the two years since his company broke up, Tim Murphy and Nathan Birch had set up on their own. It was young and fragile but The Next Ice Age was devoted to perpetuating Curry's vision. JoJo Starbuck would be there. Likewise his old flame, Shaun McGill. Each of them had reasons to be apprehensive but during rehearsals at the Inner Harbour Ice Rink, Curry's composure never wavered.

It was a relief, he told a watching journalist, to have someone else calling the shots. 'I don't have to worry every morning about what I'm going to tell everyone to do.' Nor, as yet, were there any glaring signs of physical diminishment. If symptoms had surfaced, only Curry and his doctors knew what they were. Everyone declared HIV positive was alert for them and the watchfulness alone was exhausting.

Liquid bowels, falling weight, swollen glands, forgetfulness, sores around the mouth, anus and genitals, blotches on the skin. It was the devil's own checklist and every clear day was a blessing; just as unexplained tiredness and night sweats were a curse. Very shortly, Shaun McGill would be watching for them, too. Around 1989, at the age of just 27, the virus was already replicating itself in the blood of Curry's Canadian ex-lover.

Once it was there, death was almost a certainty. The only questions left were when, and how. Typically, in the days immediately after infection, there would be a few non-specific symptoms. Unusual muscle aches, perhaps. Or an unexplained rash. Often these early signals went unnoticed, and after a week they would disappear. Sufferers then became asymptomatic, their bodies giving no outward clues to the presence of a predator that was slowly dissolving their immune system.

Inside the host's blood, the white 'helper' cells which had kept them healthy were being ambushed and destroyed. Dispiriting regular checks measured the speed of this annihilation. When sufficient damage had been done – and that could take anything from one to 15 years – the body was defenceless. Tuberculosis, pneumonia, cancer and chronic organ failure were among the horrors that might then follow. In Britain, Curry had already been warned that his 'helper' cell count was low, possibly following a bout of shingles. In New York, Patricia Crown – one of the very few who 'knew' – pleaded with him to try AZT.

> I asked him if I could speak directly to the doctor about it, and John gave me that permission. The doctor then gave me very generously of his time, during which I asked him whether he would give his own child AZT in similar circumstances. He said that he would and I urged John emphatically to change his mind which he did. For a while.

Nancy's peerless Manhattan contacts had paid off again. With her husband Frank on the board of trustees at the New York Hospital on the Upper East Side, she'd identified a young medic who could help. Thirty-three-year-old Jonathan Jacobs wasn't promising a cure, but his fury at the hostile marginalisation of the city's gay men – and his radical pastoral programme to alleviate their stress – had struck a chord with Nancy. At her urging, Curry had joined his list of patients.

'There was a sweetness about him,' says Jacobs. 'He was always very deferential; very polite and dignified. Appreciative, accepting and courageous. His closeness to Nancy was very special.' Every month, Curry slipped into the unit on 68th Street for a blood test. Eventually, like almost every other victim, he experimented with AZT, taking five pills a day and hoping that anaemia, headaches and muscle problems wouldn't be a consequence. 'For years we thought it actually worked,' admits Jacobs. 'It was difficult to separate signs of advancing disease from side effects, and on those huge doses it was not unusual to have side effects ... but we had nothing else, so we encouraged people to take it.'

Curry's reluctance to take AZT was forgivable. For a man in denial, medication of any sort was an unwelcome and expensive unknown – initially $7,000 for a year's supply. And if the rumoured side effects proved correct, his ability to perform might be impaired, thereby increasing his dependency on others.

As it was, his financial reliance on Crown, Streeter – and also, periodically, Gillian Lynne – was rising. Throughout May, he had kicked his heels at the Streeter apartment. Every sniff of work was pursued. Following a short break in France, he'd returned to campaign fiercely for a part in the Peter Nichols farce *Privates on Parade*. After three auditions, he was in.

Between July and September, Curry was back under the nightly spotlight at the off-Broadway Roundabout Theater. As Lance Corporal Charles Bishop – alongside the *Carry On* star Jim Dale – Curry played the conscience-stricken member of an army 'song and dance' unit entertaining British troops stationed in post-war Malaya. As one half of a homosexual couple, it was perfect casting. It was also uncharacteristically revealing. Every night he was required to appear naked in a communal men-only shower scene.

Built around female impersonation, crude jokes and lashings of gay innuendo, the play lampooned a fading Empire through the camp antics of the troupe's misfit showmen and their cross-dressing 'Jungle Jamboree'. From day one, its director Larry Carpenter had found Curry to be 'a hard worker, accessible and funny'. There had been no inkling of diva, and the skater's HIV status – which Carpenter had become aware of – had stirred no anxieties. 'I suspected that John was "playing" very hard at night after the shows, but it never affected his work.'

According to one review it was 'a gloriously funny evening of caustic social and political commentary'. Although Curry's performance passed largely unnoticed (Nancy Streeter thought him 'not so good'), the revival had still picked up the 1990 Drama Critics Circle Award for Best Foreign Play. On 30 September, however, after 94 performances, the run quietly ended. Again, Curry wasn't to blame. New York simply wasn't ready to laugh about homosexuality, and the skater – wearing white linen, Reebok trainers and exuding good health in the publicity pictures – was out of work again. He was also 40 years old.

If it was any consolation, AIDS, and the baffled search for a cure, had become a worldwide obsession. Around the time *Privates on Parade* folded, an estimated ten million people in 145 countries had been infected. Erroneously, a dead French-Canadian flight attendant had even been pinpointed as 'patient zero', and at the opening of Britain's first hospital ward for HIV sufferers, two years earlier, Princess Diana had offered her bare hand to be shaken by a dying AIDS victim. Both stories made international headlines.

Although American police officers still donned long-sleeved rubber gloves for gay demonstrations, the princess's gesture was symptomatic. In the West, fear was moderating. Toilet seats were no longer deemed a health risk. Women and even children were dying now. So, too, were heterosexual men, haemophiliacs and careless needles users. By the late 1980s, 87 million Americans had received a copy of the government-sponsored booklet 'Understanding AIDS'. New, and cheaper, drugs were being hastily trialled and rushed on to the market and the first ever World Aids Day had been staged just before Christmas 1987, backed by the World Health Organisation.

The notion of 'safe sex' came too late for Roger Roberts, Shaun McGill and John Curry, but by minuscule increments the stigma was lifting. Support groups were forming. Funds were being raised. Big public events were tearing away the veil. In November, Curry himself had taken part in one – 'Skating For Life' – turning out on a makeshift rink off Lexington Avenue in New York alongside Robin Cousins and his former rival Toller Cranston.

'He did not look at all well,' thought Cranston. 'Our one and only conversation took place in the men's dressing room, where our close proximity forced him to say hello. After his terse greeting I responded, "Well, hello John. Speaking to me this decade, are you?" That was all either of us said.'

Cranston was from another age; another box. Curry could handle the rumours and the snide comments. Three years had passed since his diagnosis, and – to his eyes, if not other people's – there had been no physical change. Once again he chose to spend Christmas with the Streeters, seeing out the 1980s behind their curtains in traditional festive style. 'Another year has passed and we made it,' he wrote in his card to Nancy. 'Thank you for all your love and help and for being you.' Apart from the continuing defiance of his immune system, Curry had few reasons to be cheerful about what lay ahead.

Between January and May, he was out of work. Desperate for privacy, he'd found an 'adorable' apartment in the Chelsea district on

West 23rd Street. 'He was not a taker,' says Patricia Crown. 'But people were very generous to him; people like me and Nancy were happy to make his life a little easier.' Gradually, it seemed, Curry was withdrawing. Although the acting classes – and the medication – continued, the auditions had dried up. Curry's name was no longer hot. Added to this, there 'was also a sense of fatalism among all gay men at this time,' thinks Crown. 'I remember going with John to buy new white shirts because he was attending yet another funeral.'

In the early spring, a lifeline landed from Baltimore. The company founded by Tim Murphy and Nathan Birch – The Next Ice Age – wanted him to choreograph for a concert at the city's rundown Northwest Ice Rink. For three weeks, Curry moved into their 'dump of an apartment', happy to engage in trivial banter, no longer insistent upon luxury accommodation. 'I liked him at the end,' remembers Murphy. 'All of a sudden he thought my jokes were funny. We had a deck out the back, which he called the best room in the house. I liked being in his company. He liked being in mine. This was a different, kinder John.'

Down at the rink, months of stifled longing were bursting free. To the lush strains of Johann Strauss's 'Blue Danube', Curry fashioned a piece for just four men: himself, Birch, Murphy and Shaun McGill. 'I really want this piece to be about friendship,' he told them. This time, there would be no bullying, and no sulks. By opening night, he had fashioned what Murphy branded a 'masterwork'; a piece of such elaborate beauty that their audience, crammed on to hard wooden bleachers, had risen to their feet. 'It was four men skating together,' says Birch, 'so in its own odd way it was shocking for some people to see. But it was not sexual at all. It was pure perfect movement.' It was also a poem fuelled by Curry's unuttered sense of loss, something the *Baltimore Sun* had unwittingly captured in its review:

> As the music starts, the quartet drifts on to the ice holding hands and arranged in a sculptural mass. The feeling is like seeing a sleigh pass before your eyes. As the music builds … the dancers entwine and interlace themselves in mind-boggling configurations … Mr Curry's work is full of brilliant nuance.

Just how nuanced only Curry himself knew. The 'dashing coda' in which his 'rakishly flung figure is supported by his trio of cohorts' had an ominously funereal ring, but the skater's physical condition had rung no alarm bells. To Birch it seemed as if 'he had aged a little bit', but the *Washington Post* had noticed nothing. Curry's solo work was 'outstanding', they said under the headline: 'Brilliance in the rink'.

If it was to be his last headline for skating, and his last piece of original choreography, Curry had left his public with a dignified flourish. 'I skate now because it's fun,' he'd recently told a reporter. 'I've discovered a freedom and happiness in it which I thought had disappeared.' Not everyone had been embraced by his spirit of friendship, however. During the Baltimore show, Patricia Dodd had performed two solos, without comment from her former mentor. 'He wasn't talking to me and there was an anger. I saw he was slimmer, but I didn't put it together. He knew that he was dying, and I didn't.'

Back in New York, nothing had changed apart from the weather. Unable to find work, Curry pulled even deeper into himself. 'He'd walk around the city, go to acting classes,' says Crown. 'I don't think he socialised intensively at this time. He had this loner streak and he could be prickly. He could decide he didn't want to talk that day, or see people.'

When lured to Manhattan social functions – especially around beautiful women – he could still be 'vibrant and energetic', still a fountainhead of charm. 'Every time you took him some place it burnished your status as well as his own,' thinks Crown. 'He was very successful at having people want to take care of him ... Yes. I fell in love with him. But I also thought Elva had been in love with him. He liked beautiful women ... He liked beauty.'

By September, Curry's funds, as well as the lease on his Chelsea apartment, had run out. At Crown's invitation, he moved in with her on West 13th Street while building work at her new place uptown was completed. 'It was a pretty tense period for both of us,' she admits. 'He was so screwed up. There was such mental complexity. I loved him unreservedly, but he found it very hard to accept this. I'm sure people with such low self-image do not think themselves worthy of love.' Alongside his course of AZT, Curry had unenthusiastically agreed to weekly sessions with both a psychiatrist and a cognitive therapist. While one probed his past, the other urged him to 'live for the moment'. For almost the first time, he was revisiting deep-buried memories from behind the doors of 946 Warwick Road.

'He had talked about his family before, but rarely,' says Crown.

> He didn't like his father. His father humiliated him. He'd say: 'Here's Michael, he's my oldest. Here's Andrew, the middle son. Here's John, we were hoping he'd be a girl.' There were terrible stories of humiliation. After his father's death he told me that everyone was delighted. 'We were all so happy. We were free of him.' Nothing I ever heard about his father was positive.

Almost every day, Curry still drew comfort from his skating. Up at the Sky Rink, he glided alone or gave lessons to both bumbling beginners and aspiring competitors. 'We paid him, but not very much,' recalls Moira North, founder of the Ice Theatre of New York. 'This was not a stellar thing, but he was always professional and correct. Not a diva at all.' Alizah Allen had been one of his students. Between the ages of ten and 12, she'd surrendered herself to his guidance. From the mandatory straight back, and the controlled arms, very little had changed since 1976.

'He told me that if you skate beautifully to the point of distraction, all the tiny imperfections will be ignored. He was very invested in making me put emotion in, whether it was a story or a feeling I was expressing. He helped my body become an instrument moving to the music.' Being only a child, Alizah saw little evidence of physical decline. Others could now see it all too clearly.

'I remember the terrible day in New York,' says Gillian Lynne. 'It was winter weather'.

> We'd all agreed to meet for brunch at Mortimer's on Madison Avenue, and Peter [Lynne's husband] and I were early and having a coffee when the door opened and in came John. He had a woolly hat on and I saw him look around the room and – from his expression – I saw him gear himself up to say it. I can see that hat and the big black coat he loved. John didn't cry, but Peter cried; burst straight into tears. I felt like it but hung on. John just sat there looking desperate and I decided there and then that the minute he needed it, we would help.

Nancy Streeter's help was already flowing freely. In late February, Curry had secured the part of a vicar in an obscure Tennessee Williams play (*You Touched Me*) at the Drury Theater in Cleveland. As rehearsals got underway he'd told her: 'Lots of hanging about. Still, I am working. Here enclosed are some more hospital bills … Oh well!' Like *Privates on Parade*, however, the play stalled and had closed by early April. And like Patricia Dodd in Baltimore, one reviewer had innocently noticed a change in John Curry. 'He is superb … but so wan and sedentary that one could never imagine [he] is a champion figure skater.' Finally, it was becoming impossible to hide.

As Curry's weight fell, the skin on his face was beginning to tighten around his skull. Around Greenwich Village, he'd known dozens of men with the same spectral look: the dark-hollowed cheeks; the receding eye sockets; the oddly prominent teeth. Curry knew exactly what it meant. On his arm at about this time he had found 'a small brown patch'. It was the moment he'd known would come. Nothing was more symptomatic of full-blown AIDS than Kaposi's sarcoma, the cancerous lesions that blossomed on the skin and gums. Almost five years after diagnosis, the virus had won. 'It was a horrible shock,' he said later. 'I started to prepare myself to come home.'

Since Christmas he'd been living alone, and rent-free, in Patricia Crown's old apartment. When it came to it, there wouldn't be much to pack. After Cleveland, the phone had stopped ringing. 'He had very few artistic outlets,' says Crown. 'He had less energy and was starting to need a higher degree of care.' Fleetingly, in mid-May, there had been an unexpected validation; a happy opportunity to savour what had been – and what might have been – when he was handed the prestigious Capezio Dance Award at a glossy ceremony in Manhattan.

Finally he was recognised as the dancer his father had forbidden him to be. Scanning the list of previous winners, Curry saw the names of Fred Astaire, Bob Fosse, Jerome Robbins and Nureyev. Now his name was there, too. After a tearful speech and celebratory dinner party at the Streeter apartment, he honoured his hosts, Nancy and Frank, for all they had done. 'Without your love and help over the YEARS!! I would not have been in a position to even be considered. Thank you both for being such a happy part of life.'

Six weeks later Curry was gone, leaving his dance award in Nancy's care. He would never be back. 'The AZT is some that I have left over,' he added, before flying out to London on 1 July 1991, taking no more luggage than he'd arrived with 20 years before. Back then he'd been coming to New York to live. Now he was returning to England to die. As the plane banked, he could see an unbroken line of surf stretching north to Fire Island. Behind him was the last performance he ever committed to tape. Knowing how glorious he had been, it is still almost impossible to watch.

For an obscure television special – in front of hugely grotesque letters spelling HOLLYWOOD – Curry skates for three minutes to Mozart's Concerto for Flute and Harp. Wearing an austere black outfit, he gives a performance of exquisite grace and heart-breaking simplicity. Tape degradation, however, has drained all colour from the image and what survives is starkly monochrome and hissing with distortion.

As the music ends, he smiles broadly in silhouette, raises his arms and flutters his fingers. At that moment – with its echo of a night in Innsbruck – the focus sharpens, and Curry's ravaged face can clearly be seen. 'Ladies and gentlemen, John Curry,' booms the voice of the announcer. Cheering bursts out. There is a brief shot of an audience clapping. And then it is over.

Twelve

'The kiss of the sun'

On a warm summer's morning, the hourly train from London squealed gently into Coventry railway station. As the carriage doors slammed open, Rita Curry scanned the passengers for her youngest son. Over two decades, she'd become habituated to a diminished role on the fringe of his life, gleaning what she could from the stream of newspaper cuttings and greetings cards. She knew – and probably cared to know – nothing of his love life. And unlike Nancy, she had been shielded from his illness for five years. By Rita's own admission, his time in America had been 'something of a mystery'. Now he was coming home, and she didn't really know why.

Alongside her was John's brother Andrew, and together they scanned the passing faces for one they recognised. But her son was not making it easy. On the train, he'd been anxious not to be identified. 'Someone got off the train with a cap on,' Rita remembers. 'He had a load of books under his arm, his coat belt was trailing on the floor and just one case.' It was John, but it was scarcely the John they had been expecting. Over lunch, back at her bungalow in Binton, he wasted no time in telling her why.

> He said, 'I suppose I'd better tell you I am ill. You'll have to look after me.' I was very angry, I know that. I did explode. I told him I didn't have to look after him but I would. I was so angry that I didn't know. I also realised I hadn't been told for a very long time. But knowing him, that was just his way of talking. Maybe it's mine as well because I can be pretty blunt when I want to be. After that everything ran smoothly.

For the next three years – between Curry and his mother – AIDS would be the illness without a name. Little further discussion was ever sought, or invited. Without qualification or judgement, Curry's mother would stand by him to the end. 'They will find something,' she had whispered to him on his first day back. And, like everyone, he had to hope they would. But that was not why he'd returned. While they looked for a cure, his mother's incurious hard-headedness was precisely what he needed. Inside her bungalow, they could manage this together. 'New York, when you are ill, is no place to be,' Curry confided. 'I wanted to be here around people who I knew and loved when things got really bad.'

It could not have been more different from Manhattan. Tucked into a woody pleat of Warwickshire farmland, the village of Binton seems content with its bucolic anonymity. Just a short drive away from Stratford-upon-Avon, with its coach trips and half-timbered coffee shops, Binton has no pub, no shop and no post office. From its sleepy centre, older thatched properties give way to a handful of modern bungalows on its outskirts. Each one backs on to open fields. Centuries-old oak trees pepper the gardens. Hedgerows bustle with colour and life, and the seasons are the only things that ever really change.

For the dying Curry it could not have been better. From the kitchen, his mother indulged his schoolboy weakness for puddings. From his tiny bedroom – scarcely big enough for a bed and a wardrobe – he dispatched letters and cards to the world he'd forsaken. When they were sealed – especially later when he was too weak – Rita would walk down the lane to the post box for him. She didn't know who he was writing to and she never asked. 'He never said he was upset. He never cried. I never heard him say he was scared,' she says. 'And yet it was a long time to have that knowledge stuck in your head.'

It helped that Curry had returned at the height of summer. Corn was ripening in the rolling fields. Bees browsed the sweet lavender and feathered flocks gorged on Rita's bird table. Slowly, but with growing enthusiasm, Curry discovered the joys of gardening. All his life he had pulled patterns and shapes from his imagination. Now, in a garden, he could do the same. With sometimes misplaced gusto, he attacked overgrown trees and grass choked by moss. 'He once told me he wished he'd been able – when he was still well – to sit around and do nothing,' recalls Heinz Wirz. 'He loved this time he had on his own.' When he became tired, he read or watched television. For days on end, he would see no one but his mother.

'I have enjoyed a lovely summer here in Warwickshire,' he wrote to Cathy Foulkes.

> I've been working very hard on the garden … and in a few years time it should look rather good … I am going to remain here in England for the foreseeable future. NYC was really getting me down on just about all levels … I am quite enjoying middle age – so much less worrying – less fraught. Give my love to your mother. Tell her I'm on my last unread Dickens novel 'Our Mutual Friend' – going very slowly – not sure if that's because I despise the characters or because I shall not know what to read next. Keep safe.

Far away in Boston, Foulkes remained ignorant of her friend's illness. Like many men with AIDS, Curry still felt emotionally hamstrung by profound feelings of shame. In New York, his medical team had laboured to help him, and hundreds of others, regard it merely as a disease and not a biblical curse. Homosexuals, they argued, should not be on trial, any more than the man with tuberculosis in his sneeze. It was a virus. No more, no less. 'No one tried to get this illness. It was not caused by being gay,' explains his American physician, Jonathan Jacobs. 'These men were berating themselves, and we tried to lift that burden from them.'

Curry's ferocious need for privacy, however, transcended any such wisdom. In September, when Penny Malec had asked him directly about AIDS, Curry flatly denied it. 'We had a very awkward evening in which he talked about suicide and then he didn't get in touch with me,' she says. When Patricia Crown was in Britain around the same time, he refused even to see her. Other sufferers were no different. On 22 November, Freddie Mercury had finally told the world he had AIDS. Twenty-four hours later he was dead. In Binton, for as long as humanly possible, Curry would prune the roses and dodge the questions. Intrusion was unwelcome. Even from those who loved him the most.

As yet, Curry's strength was holding up. Shortly before Christmas 1991, he'd felt well enough to visit Heinz Wirz in Bern and from there the pair had travelled by plane and train to Garmisch-Partenkirchen. On an open-air rink, under icy blue skies, Curry had quickly worked up two short routines for a public concert. Skating on the same bill was Toller Cranston.

> I suspect that John had not been practising much and his routine contained one solitary single jump. When John finished, he came backstage, breathless and close to fainting from exhaustion. Had I known that he was ill from AIDS I would not have made the remark that I did ... With John gasping for air I said, 'That was a lovely single axel you did.' It was a cruel way of damning him with faint praise [and] today I regret having made that comment.

The two would not meet again. Nor would John ever be seen again on skates. Back in Binton, he waited impatiently for the days to lengthen. 'The spring is bursting forth,' he told Nancy Streeter in late February. 'It was so pleasant yesterday I spent the day in the garden. Everything is peaceful and calm. I am very content.' Only Curry's regular London hospital visits now intruded upon his rustic confinement.

Every few weeks, usually after he had been driven there at breakneck speed by his mother, Curry's condition was checked at St Mary's Hospital in Paddington. Nearby was the hotel in which his father's own sadness had played itself out 26 years before. Now it was his son's turn. Inside the clinic, Curry's diminishing army of 'helper' cells were counted; the lower his 'score', the higher the chance that his immune system had been infiltrated. Weakness, weight loss and lesions were already evident. Blood transfusions were sometimes required to tackle anaemia. Behavioural changes caused by the destruction of his brain cells had also been noted. 'He was going slightly bonkers,' thinks Malec. Having finally told her he had AIDS, Curry was refusing to see her and blanking all calls. For Nancy Streeter, he reserved even greater indignities.

In New York, John's illness had galvanised her like nothing before. As parents disowned their dying sons; as insurance companies refused HIV-related medical expenses; and as hospitals turned away HIV patients, she had become the New York Hospital's first volunteer co-ordinator, helping stitch together chaplains, nurses, social workers, psychiatrists and carers into an extraordinary network of solace. Behind it all was her love for John. Since his departure from her side, she'd felt bereft and his letters – however warm – told her nothing of his failing health. In early May, she pleaded with him for more information, to which Curry lashed back:

> I am fine and enjoying life here very much. If you want details of how many pills I take [and] what my 'counts' are and all that, please put your mind at rest and know I shall not be sharing those details with you. As for you saying you understand the disease … no one does. If only they did! Why is it you cannot accept the information I do feel I want to share with you and leave it at that? Not everyone wishes to talk about everything.

A few days later, Curry's hostility deepened. Hearing that Nancy was planning to visit him in June, he told her: 'I do not want any visitors. It always leaves me exhausted and disturbed. I know you may be disappointed by this and I do not mean to be unkind. I just do not wish to have visitors or see people.' Curry's turmoil was understandable. Every week, he was slipping further down. His once taut muscles had evaporated. There were lines on his forehead, and his fast-thinning hair was swept back from a face lost in bone and shadow.

In the spring, news had reached him that Shaun McGill had succumbed. 'Hard to believe that one so full of energy and spark should be dead,' he wrote. For Nancy – for any of them – he couldn't be what he'd once been. At least with Rita there was no pressure to perform.

To distract him, and as his garden greened, Curry had acquired a lesser sulphur-crested cockatoo which he'd christened Lily, and to which he'd become deeply attached. 'You would love her,' he told Foulkes. 'She is friendly, affectionate, BEAUTIFUL and very much fun and I love her to bits.' When the sun shone, Curry would read under a tree with Lily on his shoulder. When it rained, the two came inside where she squawked and unhooked the curtains, while Curry tried to teach her the rudiments of language.

Not since childhood had Curry owned a pet. Not since Ricky, the boxer dog that had once eaten his birthday cake. Back then, Ricky would have died for John, and at night in Binton the white-feathered Lily stood ghostly watch over Curry from her cage inside his bedroom. It was to be a disheartening vigil. By early September 1992 – around his forty-third birthday – her master's health went into a steep decline. With his weight down to 8st 12lb, he was rushed into St Mary's feeling 'weak as a kitten'. 'I thought this is it,' he later admitted. 'I'm fading.'

Few things are more deadly to AIDS patients than tuberculosis. Although treatable, the disease still kills one in three of those who become infected. Curry was lucky that his medical team had caught his symptoms early, but the scare had badly rocked him. 'I got away with it [but] I find myself praying and saying to myself: "You are such a hypocrite. You shouldn't be doing this. You haven't believed since you were a little boy." But I do pray. Over the last year I have been thinking more and more about spiritual – rather than religious – things and wondering what it is like to be dead.'

In the throes of his panic, Curry's hard-line reclusiveness shifted dramatically. If he was dying, what was there to hide? Companionship reasserted its potency. Linda Davis had visited. So had Nathan Birch, his young American acolyte, supplying chocolate biscuits and foot massages for his former leader. From New York, Nancy Streeter had responded swiftly to Curry's request for bedside company. So, too, had Patricia Crown, flying in for a September weekend fully expecting her friend to die. On her way into his room at St Mary's, she bumped into Alan Bates coming out. Curry's true friends were showing their colours.

'Bates was wonderful,' reveals Andrew Curry. 'He didn't care what other people thought of his friendship with John, whereas some other well-known people suddenly distanced themselves. Genuine people stick around you when things aren't great, and he was one of them. A really, really lovely man.'

After their earlier spat, Curry and Penny Malec – the girl whose sofa he'd hidden behind in 1976 – patched up their quarrel. 'It seems that not having to guard his terrible secret any longer has relieved John of an awful burden,' Penny told Nancy. 'Except for being ill and weak he was more internally relaxed and like his old self than for years. He can't talk much but is glad to see people and a bit bored at being in hospital – a good sign, I guess.' In a brief but deeply moving letter, Cathy Foulkes had also, finally, been told.

I have something to tell you which you have probably heard already. I have AIDS. Presently, I'm fine and mostly I have been – there have been a few sticky patches. Still, I am OK now and who knows!! I am not traumitized [sic] – I think – and 'inside' I am peaceful. I love being at home again and not having to teach and skate is a welcome relief to this old body. I would like you to come and visit me when you are over – my energy is very much come and go – so I hope you will be understanding.

This is not a very uplifting letter, but dear Cathy, do not worry or be sad – I have had an extraordinary life – by any standards – I've met with great success and happiness – and at times the reverse. So keep your pecker up. Lots of love. John.

Sadly, there would be no last embrace between the faune and his nymph. During a trip to Britain, Foulkes telephoned Binton but was advised that Curry was 'too tired for visitors'. 'We were going to try for another day but the window closed and I went back to the US,' says Cathy. 'I will live with that lingering regret until my days are done.'

Inevitably, as knowledge of Curry's ailing health spread, media interest was beginning to bubble. In August, possibly tipped off by nursing staff, the *Daily Mirror* had run the headline 'Let John die in peace' over a report which claimed his death was now 'only a matter of time'. At the London flat of Peter Farmer, where Curry still sometimes stayed, photographers on stepladders had been spotted at the windows. By the late summer, the intrusion had even reached Binton where Curry, flicking a wet tea-towel, had driven one reporter from their door.

For once, however, he could see a positive in the ghoulish curiosity. Since returning home, Curry had earned virtually nothing. If the papers wanted his story, they could have it; but only at a price; and only if he was pulling the strings. According to his London agent Jean Diamond, Curry's motives were purely altruistic. 'Not financial at all,' she says. But given his revulsion for disclosure, that seems unlikely. For years he'd supported his mother. Even if it required a deal with the devil, he would help her again.

Earlier that summer, he'd received a letter from a *Mail on Sunday* writer, Fiona Barton, requesting an interview. A few weeks later she'd been formally approved at an interview with Curry's London agent. 'I was effectively auditioned by her,' recalls Barton. 'There was a negotiation which I wasn't part of and we definitely paid some money. I don't know how much but he'd fallen on hard times and wanted to leave his mum OK.' For Curry, this would be a humiliating act of supreme self-sacrifice. At their first meeting in St Mary's, the stunned Barton had seen him 'scooped off the floor by a nurse' after collapsing during a blood transfusion. Unable to continue, they'd met again a few weeks later in Binton.

'He appeared much better,' recalls the writer.

> He was very open. Very perky. Not a tragic figure. He knew that he didn't have too long, and it was as if it was all there waiting to pour out. He'd thought long and hard about it, and I certainly didn't have to ask too many questions. I remember particularly his phrase: 'I wasn't a saint, but I wasn't a whore either.' He seemed calm. Not angry. He knew it was all over.

When her article was written, Barton called Curry and read it to him over the phone. He was happy. On Sunday 4 October – spread across two full pages – it was published under a sub-editor's brutal headline: 'All my friends died of AIDS. Now it's my turn'. Within hours, the story was circulating the globe. If the news was shocking, the pictures were even worse. To millions of people, John Curry was still frozen in 1976; still the same smiling, curly topped young genius. What they saw now was a stick-thin middle-aged man wearing an awkward grimace and a cardigan over his hospital pyjamas.

What they read, however, was a miracle of life-affirming positivity. Every line of it was shot through with Curry's extraordinary courage. There was no blame; no self-pity; and not one scintilla of fear. 'One has to make the best of it. You could be lost in a fog of despondency every day but I'm not,' he claimed. 'I have tried to see what is good around me and to think back on my … unusually exciting life, so I think that is better than a grey existence that goes on and on … I had everything and loved every moment of it.'

After the Olympics, Curry had defied convention and declared himself to be a homosexual sportsman. On the cusp of his own death he had done it again. No other AIDS-stricken public figure had confronted their fate quite like this. All around him, others were clutching feebly to their badly kept secrets. Within a month, Rudolf Nureyev would enter the Paris hospital in which he would die the following January. Not until the dancer's death would his AIDS diagnosis finally emerge. In the manner of their passing at least, Curry had utterly outclassed the man who had so inspired him in life. 'I am talking about this because I think the more open people are, the easier it gets for everybody else because it demystifies it,' he said. 'I don't want other sufferers to be frightened like I was ... After all, no one is immune.'

It was a gold medal performance, and, overnight, virtually all media interest had gone. Curry's searing honesty had killed the story, leaving nothing to chase. For Curry himself, the weary realities of his daily survival swiftly returned. To raise more money he'd sent his Andy Warhol – a personal gift from the artist – for auction at Sotheby's in London. Five thousand pounds would buy more than sentiment, and life, or what remained of it, had to be paid for.

When required, he still hared down to St Mary's in Rita's car. 'Hurry up, Mother,' he would say. Not that she needed any encouragement. Sometimes, she would wait and then rush him back. On others, he would stay in hospital overnight or drift into London to see friends. 'He never seemed to belong anywhere,' thinks Richard Digby Day. 'Even when he was at home it was as if he was a visitor.' For regular companionship, there was now only his mother and the daily visits of his steadfast brother Andrew. Regrettably, Lily's incessant squawking had necessitated her return to the pet shop.

'Even when he was ill, AIDS was never mentioned when he came to stay with me,' remembers Peter Farmer. 'He didn't want to be a special case. He just wanted to go on as we always did. I saw him coming backwards and forwards from hospital. Everyone knew where it was going, but he didn't know the word "self-pity". He just took it all and got on with life.'

By early 1993, though he had put on a little weight over Christmas, Curry's Spartan-like fortitude was wilting. Throughout the winter, his beloved garden had been blanketed in leaves and frost. But, as the earth stirred, the skater's energy levels did not. And with so little left to say, even his letter-writing had ground to a standstill. In their place, Curry pursued a belated new outlet for his obsession with creative perfection. In his long, lonely hours, caressed by the smell of home baking, Curry had turned to needlepoint, creating work of flawless beauty.

Rendered in subtle colours and intricate detail, each one framed its central image in geometric borders of delicate complexity. If he made a mistake, he simply started again, however many hours that might require. No two pieces were the same, and each was gifted to his closest friends. To Alan Bates, a portrait of the actor's Derbyshire home. To Penny Malec, a richly detailed visualisation of Curry's own country garden, complete with ripe strawberries, fruit-laden trees, a lone bee on a blossom and six geese winging homewards. In the corner is the minute silhouette of a figure with his back to a tree and a cockatoo on his arm. Above that are the initials J.A.C. along with four lines of verse: 'The kiss of the sun for pardon; the song of the birds for mirth; one is nearer to paradise in a garden than anywhere else on earth'.

By substituting the original words 'God's heart' for 'to paradise', Curry had ruined the poetic metre and shown his agnostic hand. In every other respect, however, his work had fused the grace of a Japanese print with the pattern-making of his lifetime on ice. Like his long-ago school figures, Curry's samplers were the product of the same tortured ambition to eliminate human error from art. 'If you truly want to understand John,' Penny Malec insists, 'just look at his needlework.'

As 1993 ticked by, apart from goodbyes there were very few other pulls on his time. During a day trip to Stratford, he'd bumped into his former lover David Delve. The two hadn't met since the split. It was good to be reconciled. During another rare burst of energy, Curry had travelled to watch Millicent Martin in a play at Brighton's Theatre Royal. She'd already seen him in hospital and given him a kiss. 'Are you sure you want to do that?' he'd asked. 'Absolutely,' she'd replied.

In Brighton, he'd arrived for the matinée and Martin had installed him in the royal box. 'It had a little anteroom with sofa and chairs if he felt unwell,' she says. 'He was very thin and he could only manage a few minutes and that was it. I asked him, "Why didn't you tell us? Did you think we'd walk away?" I gave him a hug and his body was so frail. I told him, "I wish you had told us". And he smiled and thanked me for that. Then I saw him at the stage door afterwards and that was the last time.'

Back home he still received occasional letters from old friends. Almost all of them went unanswered. JoJo Starbuck had written – so had Dorothy Hamill – but heard nothing back in reply. 'I knew he was dying and wouldn't see him again. I wanted to share with him how much he'd done for me. I wanted him to know there's a loving god who cares about him. Maybe I sent it to the wrong place. I just don't know.' Even Nancy Streeter was again struggling for his attention.

'He wrote me a couple of times and said he really didn't want to see Nancy,' recalls Ellen Streeter. 'This was probably in 1993. They were horrible letters about my mother. I thought it was pretty harsh but he was tough about it. I'm sure she was rebuffed and I'm sure that was painful.' In February, Ellen saw for herself just why her old friend was proving elusive. At a Cotswolds hotel, Curry had agreed to meet her for lunch. 'He was really sick and frail and looked like an old man and we both knew it would be the last time.'

Two decades before, they'd all crammed into the Streeter station wagon and headed for the coast. Ellen remembered sitting in the back with John, a summer breeze blowing and the radio playing a song whose lyrics she couldn't understand: if you can't be with the one you love, love the one you're with. 'I said I wasn't sure I really got that, but John said, "I do. It makes perfect sense."' Maybe now it made more sense, with Nancy an ocean away and Curry clinging on to his fragile dignity. 'It was about holding on to the memory of the last time,' says Ellen. 'He must have felt really alone. Not even 50 and dying.'

Thankfully, there would be one last trip to the sea. Leaning on a stick, and supported by Alan Bates, Curry had travelled down to Cornwall. The two men had stayed openly together in a hotel overlooking the wave-swept sands. 'I'm not ill,' Curry told the reception staff. 'I have AIDS.' Much later – when Curry was dead – Bates would remember that moment. 'He admired it because he'd never, ever have done it himself,' says Penny Malec. To the end, Curry's nerve was holding, even if his strength – now weakened by an immune system in total free fall – was not.

By Christmas 1993, an awful feeling of imminence was closing in. On a last visit to Binton, Heinz Wirz – his unwavering friend

– had been shocked by Curry's condition. The two had talked wistfully about old times. Curry had lain on his bed and fretted over his needlework. 'We held hands and he was lovely, and I remember asking him to see if there were any old pictures I could have, and he said yeah, yeah I'll do that, I'll tell Mummy. But obviously it never happened.'

In his last Christmas card to Nancy he wished her 'peace, health and joy' for 1994. Just a few days later, in the last letter she ever received from him, he thanked her for the silk shirt she'd sent. 'A very nice holiday,' he told her in strong, flowing hand. 'No snow or anything like that, but all in all it was great.' Desperate for enlivenment, he'd spent the Christmas break with Gillian Lynne and her husband Peter Land in the Gloucestershire countryside. 'He was poorly, very poorly,' says Lynne. 'And funnily enough I had also picked up some horrible thing and I was in bed and knew I couldn't go anywhere near John, so he just came and sat in the bedroom doorway. We laughed about it. He said, "Well, this is not really us, is it?" But then there's nothing to do but laugh in the end, is there?'

As winter dragged into 1994, Curry's decline accelerated. The once prodigious appetite was failing, and his emaciated frame, weakened by a parasitic bowel infection, was growing rapidly weaker. Around St Mary's, it was rumoured that Elizabeth Taylor had sat by his bedside, holding his hand. Three years before, the actress had established her own fund-raising AIDS Foundation. 'You are never alone,' she was said to have told him. But no one seemed really sure if she'd been. And Curry was in no condition to confirm or deny. What he could do, however, was help his mother for one last time.

The Warhol was gone. Now only his three medals remained – the European, Olympic and World Championship golds – won in Geneva, Innsbruck and Gothenburg during the golden days of 1976. According to Sotheby's they would fetch £15,000, and nothing and nobody – not even Rita – could dissuade him from selling them. For years, he'd never even looked at them. There was no point in arguing. The sale date was set for 5 July. It was a date he would never see.

By the middle of April, Curry's optimism was no longer enough. Sensing that the end was close, Rita warned close friends that time was running out. Every time Penny saw him now, she said her goodbyes. On the 14th, Alan Bates slipped into Binton and said his own farewell. A few hours later, Gillian Lynne and her husband arrived to do the same.

> It was so sad. His face was all eyes. All the muscles round his cheeks had gone, but he was still beautiful. After we'd been there an hour, Rita asked if we'd like some coffee and we said, 'Yes we'd love some' and this bony finger went up 'Mum, I'd like one too'. She brought a beautiful cup and a saucer – silly woman – and it was rattling and rattling, and it took him ages, because of his muscles, to manage a sip. And then because he was so fastidious, Peter quickly understood and got tissues and gently wiped his mouth. John said he was thinking of choosing a lamp for his room and we had a catalogue on the bed and we all chose these lamps together and then we left.

Around eight hours later, sometime in the night. Rita found that her son had fallen out of bed. The doctor was called, along with his brother Andrew, but there was nothing anyone could do. After seven years of disease, John Curry's heart had simply stopped.

Only the year before – with his childhood memories stirring in Cornwall – he'd told Alan Bates that he'd never actually wanted to be old; and never wanted a long life.

'I just hope I have done something with it,' he'd added.

He was 44. He was all but penniless. But he had done something with it.

Acknowledgements

No one deserves more gratitude than John's mother Rita and brother Andrew. No questions were off limits, and the skater's jumbled boxes of papers were entrusted to me without condition or qualification. Even in her late nineties, Rita has a memory that burns brightly. Many things in this book, however, will have shocked and saddened her. It is to Rita's eternal credit – and Andrew's – that they placed no caveats on my work. 'As long as it is honest' was their watchword, and I can assure them both (along with Andrew's charming wife Celia) that it is that.

A handful of others deserve particular mention. In every sense, Heinz Wirz has been a boon. Without his precious letters from Curry, covering the formative first years in London, this book would have been a shadow of what it is. No email ever went unanswered. No subject was taboo. Alongside him, Meg Streeter also has my special gratitude. Following the sad death of Nancy – during the writing of this book – she and her sister Ellen allowed me to read every one of the letters Curry had sent to her mother over 15 years. To say this was a treasure trove would be an understatement. Once again, this required courage, and I thank the Streeter family for it.

Alongside them, special thanks must go to Penny Malec, Cathy Foulkes, Lorna Brown and William 'Billy' Whitener, four of John's closest friends. Each was subjected to long interviews, telephone calls and emails over a sustained period of time. Cathy, especially, supplied encyclopaedic details which run through almost every page; from skater's personal contracts to intimate, and deeply moving, letters. Tears were not unusual during many of these protracted conversations. Mine included.

In no particular order, I am also hugely indebted to the following. Dorothy Hamill; Haig Oundjian; Jane Eenhorn; Dr Baruch

Fishman; Alison Smith; Toller Cranston; Elva Clairmont; Robin Cousins; Bobby Thompson; Courtney Jones; Nancy Streeter (who I was able to speak to shortly before she died); David Singer; Christa Fassi; Shelley Winters; Patricia Dodd; Stanley Taub; Felice Picano; Jocelyn Cassia; Gayle Palmieri; JoJo Starbuck; Nathan Birch; Twyla Tharp; Jirina Ribbens; Tim Murphy; Sander Jacobs; David Santee; Kevin Kossi; Adam Lieb; Eliot Feld; Mark Hominuke; Lar Lubovitch; Jean-Pierre Bonnefoux; Gabriela Galambos; Lori Nichol; Dita Dotson; Moira North; Larry Carpenter; Peter Dunfield; Sally-Anne Stapleford; Gillian Lynne and Peter Land; Richard Digby Day; Peter Farmer; Janet Lynn; Charles Cossey; Jean Diamond; Brian Gazzard; Charles Barker; Bill Fauver; Lee-Ann Miller; Patricia Crown; Joe Lorden; Amy Danis; Tom Fowler; Jane Hermann; Dick Button; Stanley Plesent; Julian Pettifer; Clovissa Newcombe; Millicent Martin; Mark Alexander; Malcolm Sinclair; Paul Heath; Fiona Barton; Donald Pelmear; Maggie Mille; David Spungen; Jacqui Harbord; Linda Davies; David Delve; David Barker; Dr Jonathan Jacobs, Alizah Allen, Keith Money, Susan Holmes, and Sarah Murch, who first planted the seed of this endeavour.

Help was also forthcoming from the Terence Higgins Trust, from Solihull School (who still had John's form positions) and NISA, the National Ice Skating Association. None of which would have mattered but for the industry of firstly my agent Mark 'Stan' Stanton to start with, and, secondly, my delightful Bloomsbury editor Charlotte Ayteo.

Few books cover this period, but four proved particularly useful. The long-deleted 'coffee-table' book Curry co-authored with Keith Money (called *John Curry*) gave useful insights into his movements up to 1978. Dorothy Hamill's *A Skating Life* reflected her own experiences in a very similar world. Toller Cranston's shamelessly eccentric memoir *Zero Tollerance* pulls no punches, although it, too, is out of print. Finally, *Black Ice*, the hugely divisive book written by Elva Clairmont (under her married name of Oglanby) soon after Curry's death.

Although *Black Ice* purports to tell the whole of Curry's story, its key focus is the period during which Elva Clairmont, David Spungen and Curry worked together. Soon after publication, under immense pressure from various quarters, the book was withdrawn from sale with only a small number sold. During my researches, I discovered that – curiously – very few of those who campaigned against it, ever took the trouble to read it to the end. Those who did found a work which was journalistically suspect but nevertheless laced with startling truths. According to Elva, it was largely based on extensive tape-recorded interviews with Curry which were subsequently lost. Many of the quotes which are directly attributed to Curry, therefore, cannot be authenticated. For that reason, I have used very few of them.

Finally, I must thank my wife, Kay. For over two years she has lived in a peculiar *ménage à trois* in which the third party was a dead homosexual ice skater. Far too often I was with him when I should have been with her. Without her calming patience and her shrewd insights this story might well have consumed me. Hopefully we can now lose our gooseberry and return to a twosome. Much as I revere John Curry, he has been at times a gloomy bedfellow for both of us.

Last of all. Although Curry is gone, his work is not. On the internet – on YouTube – you will find almost every one of the glorious performances mentioned in this book. Find them. Watch them. And then read this book all over again. He really was that good.

Index

DATE			